IRISH REPUBLICAN WOMEN IN AMERIC

IRISH REPUBLICAN WOMEN IN AMERICA

Lecture Tours 1916–1925

JOANNE MOONEY EICHACKER

IRISH ACADEMIC PRESS
DUBLIN • PORTLAND, OR

First published in 2003 by
IRISH ACADEMIC PRESS
44 Northumberland Road, Dublin 4, Ireland

and in the United States of America by
IRISH ACADEMIC PRESS
c/o ISBS, 5824 NE Hassalo Street, Portland,
Oregon 97213-3644

Website: www.iap.ie

British Library Cataloguing in Publication Data

Mooney Eichacker, Joanne
Irish Republican women in America: lecture tours, 1916–1925
1. Women in politics – Ireland – History – 20th century
2. Ireland – Politics and government – 1910–1921 3. Ireland – Politics and government – 1922–1949 4. United States – Politics and government – 1919–1933
I. Title
941.5′0821′082

ISBN 0-7165-2688-3 (hardback)
0-7165-2719-7 (paperback)

Library of Congress Cataloging-in-Publication Data

Mooney Eichacker, Joanne 1934–
Irish republican women in America: lecture tours, 1916–1925 / Joanne Mooney Eichacker.
p. cm.
Includes bibliographical references and index.
ISBN 0-7165-2688-3 – ISBN 0-7165-2719-7 pbk.
1. Ireland–Relations–United States. 2. Ireland–Foreign public opinion, American–History–20th century. 3. Lectures and lecturing–United States–History–20th century. 4. Public opinion–United States–History–20th century. 5. Irish Americans–Attitudes–History–20th century. 6. Republicanism–Ireland–History–20th century. 7. Irish–United States–20th century. 8. Ireland–Politics and government–1910–1921. 9. Ireland–Politics and government–1922–1949. 10. Women–Ireland–History–20th century. 11. United States–Relations–Ireland. I. Title

DA964.U6 M66 2002
941.5082′1–dc21

2002190200

Typeset in 11pt on 13pt Sabon
by FiSH Books, London.
Printed by MPG Books Ltd., Bodmin, Cornwall

To my grandchildren, Joshua Lohse and Elizabeth Lohse

and in loving memory of my dear brother, Doug Rose

Contents

List of Illustrations

Foreword

It has sometimes been difficult to have such a famous grandmother as Hanna Sheehy Skeffington. How could I follow her tremendous legacy? Yet, as a child I did not know she was famous, as she never appeared in the history books and the suffrage movement was not taught as a topic. However, my father used to tell me about her, for example how she was left-handed like me and (recounted with some pride) how she was imprisoned for breaking windows (with her left hand) in Dublin Castle. I also sensed that I had inherited some of the family stubbornness that she had in good measure. Of course I also knew about my grandfather, Francis, and how he had been shot in Portobello Barracks. My grandfather's name did feature, briefly, in the history books.

I never knew Hanna (she died before I was born), but I do just remember Muriel MacSwiney. She used to live in Paris in the 1960s and I remember her visiting my father (for it seemed to be he whom she sought out) when we were staying in my French grandparents' house in Amiens (north of Paris) and having a long intense conversation with him. I do not know how I gathered what I did about her (I must have been about seven or eight), but she seemed rather formidable, dressed in dark clothes, spoke good French as well as Irish and had strong republican views. I think she also talked politics with my grandparents, who were communist in outlook – and I read in this book that Muriel had joined the Communist Party. She seemed to take particular interest in me and I still have two French children's books, beautifully illustrated, that she sent me for Christmas and signed using the Irish version of her name. She may have been seeking my father's help concerning relations with her own daughter and thus gave me, his only daughter, more attention. Her husband, Terence, of course, was in the history books, but again I had no idea of who Muriel was in her own right.

Now women are beginning to become known and it is on reading Margaret Ward's biography of Hanna that I began to see *her* true place in Irish history. I knew Hanna had been in the United States with her son, Owen (my father), and there were various memorabilia from that time around the house, such as a series of pictorial guides to the birds and flora of the western United States, with Owen's name on them in gold lettering. There was a copper spoon engraved 'BUTTEMONT' that I assumed for a long time was from a place like Buttevant in Co. Cork. These were from Hanna's first tour of the United States, directly after her husband's murder during Easter Week 1916. But I did not know much more than that, though in later years I remember my mother showing me the passport photo of Hanna with a priests' signature on the back swearing it was Mrs Mary Gribben – the name Hanna used to escape to the United States. But the detail, extent and success of this tour have really only come back to light with Joanne's meticulous work. And now those household items have a much greater significance for me. In fact, since last year, places like Butte, Montana have a very strong resonance for me personally, as my story is now linked with Hanna's.

I have lately been trying to honour not only Hanna and Frank, but both my parents, Owen and Andrée Sheehy Skeffington, with a project I am attempting with the family home in Dublin. I was reading the family history and sorting through yet more of the family papers and I became fascinated with Hanna's American tour. So with the project in mind and the idea of adventure, I embarked on trying to follow Hanna across the United States, to find some of her venues and see if could I pick up on any collective memory of her visit. It was then that Margaret suggested I contact Joanne, of whom I then knew very little. I emailed her, wondering would she reply or have any information for me, and to my delight I received an immediate reply. She was thrilled at my idea and promised to dig out Hanna's itinerary, as she had compiled it. It was only when I received this that I realised how important Joanne's work would be to me. I now had a whole list of the venues where Hanna spoke, the exact date and often the names of those who presided or spoke alongside her. Joanne, with her immediate generosity, was the key person in making my tour happen. With the help of a map of the United States I was able to plot out Hanna's tremendous voyage.

I then searched the web and emailed likely Irish interest groups and soon had the bones of a tour of my own planned. Joanne and I have since met several times and become firm friends. We did a double act, talking on Hanna and on the other women's tours, at the annual American Conference for Irish Studies in New York last June – and our session was packed to the walls! I was able to put more pieces into the jigsaw of my United States tour and I finally embarked on a two-month journey last October.

I started in Seattle and was taken to the Moore Theatre where Hanna spoke. I went on to San Francisco and found the Knights of the Red Branch Hall where she spoke a few times – and where she was arrested one time. But sadly I found the 6,000 seat Dreamland Auditorium which Hanna 'filled to suffocation' was gone, as was the sense of the Irish community that once gave her such a tumultuous welcome. This was not surprising as San Francisco, like New York, Boston or Chicago still has a large Irish population, but so large it would be hard to track down individuals with family or other memories of her visit.

Not so in Butte, Montana, where I went after California. I was given a terrifically warm reception, if smaller-scale than Hanna's. 'Your grandmother really turned us around on her visit', I was told and clearly they intended turning *me* around. Hanna was there on June 3 1917 and a banquet was held in her honour by the Ladies' Auxiliary of the Ancient Order of Hibernians at the Finlen Hotel. The modern-day version of that Auxiliary hosted a brunch in my honour the morning of my public talk. Hanna was taken down a mine in Anaconda and I was taken to view the now closed open-cast Berkeley Pit. This is where the copper spoon came from.

I had heard, too, of a man called 'Skeffington' Sheehy – and it was he who introduced me before my public talk. He explained that he was given the name 'Skeffington' on first attending the Butte Christian Brothers in the 1930s by a Brother O'Dwyer, recently arrived from Ireland. It was in honour of my grandfather, Frank, whom Brother O'Dwyer had admired very much. 'Skeff' knew all about Frank and we talked like long-lost cousins! Another surprise was to find Hanna's signature in the Sullivan family missal. When I called to visit Verne and her brother Fr. Sarsfield Sullivan, they produced the page and Hanna's name was there – with Caitlín Ní Beoláin (Kathleen Boland) and Linda Uí Chearin (Linda Kearns), who date the visit as February 19 1923. There is also Constance de Markievicz's name (1922) and Éamon de Valera (1919), among others, but clearly Hanna's first visit in 1917 pre-dated all the other campaigners of that era. Those signatures show how important Butte, with its then population of *c.* 80,000, was to Irish activists.

I therefore owe the success of my tour to Joanne. And when I arrived at a city where Hanna spoke (among the other key cities I visited were Los Angeles, Chicago, Boston, and New York), I searched the local press archives and gleaned what information I could on Hanna's visit(s) and talk(s). That took a lot of work, but it was infinitely easier in that I had a precise series of dates from Joanne and could directly find the relevant microfiche. I had some small idea then, how much work it was for Joanne to conduct this continent-wide search for documentation tracing not only Hanna's tour, but that of all the other Irish women campaigners.

This puts the women's role of the time into context. They aimed to promote the cause of Ireland and generated not only support, but funds for Ireland. They toured the United States at least as much as the men did and Hanna alone of all of them, was received by President Woodrow Wilson, in Washington in January 1918. Yet when they returned to Ireland and the Free State came into being, women were gradually pushed out of the limelight and public office. This was firstly indirect as the men of the Sinn Féin Executive – on which Hanna was one of four women in 1919 – decided which election seats the women would contest: only Constance Markievicz was allocated a winnable place. But in the new Free State, each successive government passed laws specifically to exclude women from jury service, from senior civil servant jobs and, as married women, they were eventually barred entirely from the civil service.

This book is therefore a very important reminder that women did a lot more for the Irish cause than take up guns in 1916, such as Constance Markievicz did, or help ferry messages and tend the wounded. They played a full and equal role in the shaping of Ireland, at least as strongly abroad as in Ireland itself, in the years leading up to and following the Treaty. The book is so important in redressing some of that imbalance, so that when we think of the leaders of Ireland of the time, we think of all the strong women as well as the men. And that is normal.

MICHELINE SHEEHY SKEFFINGTON
Hazelbrook Cottage, Dublin
June 2002

Acknowledgements

THE JOURNEY TO study the tours of these courageous, tenacious, and politically astute Irish Republican women began with Dr Louis Bisceglia, my teacher at San Jose State University, San Jose, California. I honour his memory. Along the way I had tremendous support and help from Dr Billie Jensen and Dr James P. Walsh, also my teachers at San Jose State University.

Thank you to the staff of: the Archdiocese of San Francisco, Chancery Archives; American Irish History Society, New York City, New York; Harvard University, Houghton Library, Cambridge, Massachusetts; Oregon State University Library, Corvallis, Oregon; San Francisco Irish Cultural Centre, San Francisco, California; San Jose State University Library, Special Collections, San Jose, California; Stanford University, Hoover Institution Library and Archiveså, Stanford, California; University of California, Berkeley, Bancroft Library, Berkeley, California; University of Iowa Library, Iowa City, Iowa; University of Nebraska, Love Memorial Library, Lincoln, Nebraska; University of San Francisco, Richard A. Gleeson Library, Donohue Rare Book Room, San Francisco, California; and the University of Wisconsin-Madison Library, Madison, Wisconsin.

The State Historical Societies of Illinois, Iowa, Nebraska, Kansas, Minnesota, Indiana, Ohio, Pennsylvania, Tennessee, and New Jersey, provided the state newspapers on microfilm so crucial to this research. The Public Libraries of Seattle, St Louis, Omaha, New Orleans and Boston also provided newspapers on microfilm.

Thank you also to the staff of the National Archives in Washington D.C. and College Park, Maryland; Mr T. Desmond, National Library of Ireland, Dublin; Seamus Helferty, University College Dublin Archives; the staff of the National Archives, Dublin; the Pearse Museum, Rathfarnham, Ireland; and Peter Young, Military Archives, Rathmines, Ireland. A special thank you to Jill Messerli and Mary Goldsmith of the Cedar Rapids Iowa Public Library, Cedar Rapids, Iowa, Inter-Library Department, for their caring and perseverance over time.

Editor, Linda Longmore, believed in this project and was a source of encouragement. Dr Maria Luddy graciously gave of her intellect, patience and time to make this by far a better book.

Thank you to my wonderful family: Steven and Debbie Lohse; David Lohse; Michael, Mary, Joshua and Elizabeth Lohse; Sandra and Robert Russell; and Doug and Shirley Rose. My husband, R.C., not only gave me his support and caring, but also shared this journey with me. Thank you for your patience and understanding.

JOANNE MOONEY EICHACKER
Amana, Iowa
June 2002

Abbreviations

AARIR	American Association for the Recognition of the Irish Republic
ACCI	American Commission on Conditions in Ireland
ACII	American Commission on Irish Independence
AOH	Ancient Order of Hibernians
Clan	Clan na Gael
Cumann	Cumann na mBan
Dáil	Dáil Éireann
Fianna	Fianna na hÉireann
FOIF	Friends of Irish Freedom
GPO	General Post Office
INAVDF	Irish National Aid and Volunteer Dependants' Fund
Inghinidhe	Inghinidhe na hÉireann
IRA	Irish Republican Army
IRF	Irish Relief Fund
IVDF	Irish Volunteers' Dependants' Fund
IWFL	Irish Women's Franchise League
IWW	Industrial Workers of the World
IWWU	Irish Women's Workers' Union
IRB	Irish Republican Brotherhood
KRB	Knights of the Red Branch
NAVDF	National Aid and Volunteers' Dependants' Fund
RIC	Royal Irish Constabulary
TD	Teachta Dala (Deputy)
UIS	United Irish Societies
WIEL	Women's Irish Education League
WPDL	Women's Prisoners' Defence League

Chronology

	1916
April 18	US Secret Service raids office of the German Consul General in New York City.
April 23	Easter Rising.
April 29	Rebel surrender and arrest, including Countess Markievicz.
	1917
January 6	Hanna Sheehy Skeffington's first mass meeting at Carnegie Hall, New York City.
April 6	United States enters World War I.
June 15	San Francisco Centre of the California Civil League cancels Hanna Sheehy Skeffington's meeting.
	1918
January 11	Hanna Sheehy Skeffington visits President Woodrow Wilson to present him with the Cumann na mBan petition for Ireland's right to self-determination.
January 22	US Post Office suspends mailing privileges of the *Irish World, The Gaelic American* and the *New York Freeman's Journal.*
February 16	Hanna Sheehy Skeffington tells of British attempt to kidnap her.
February 22–23	Third Irish Race Convention held in Philadelphia.
April 22	Sacramento County Council of Defense denies Hanna Sheehy Skeffington opportunity to speak at meeting.
April 24	Hanna Sheehy Skeffington arrested in San Francisco.

April 25	Hanna Sheehy Skeffington appears before US Commissioner in San Francisco — case dismissed.
June 27	Hanna and Owen Sheehy Skeffington return to Ireland.
November 11	World War I Armistice.

1919

January 21	Beginning of Irish War of Independence.
May 3	American Commission for Irish Independence arrives in Dublin.
June 23	Eamon de Valera arrives in New York City.
June 28	World War I Peace Treaty signed at Versailles.
September 28	First Irish Bond-Certificate Drive begins in the United States.

1920

August 12	Terence MacSwiney arrested at Cork City Hall.
October 25	Terence MacSwiney dies of hunger strike.
October 20	American Association for the Recognition of the Irish Republic (AARIR) founded.
November 18	Hearings by the American Commission on Conditions in Ireland begin in Washington D.C.
December 4	Mary and Muriel MacSwiney arrive in New York City.
December 8	Mary MacSwiney testifies before the American Commission on Conditions in Ireland in Washington D.C.
December 9	Muriel MacSwiney testifies before the American Commission on Conditions in Ireland in Washington D.C.
December 18–25	Mary and Muriel MacSwiney hold meetings in New England.
December 31	Muriel MacSwiney presented the Freedom of the City Award at New York City Hall by Mayor John Hyland.

December 9	Eamon de Valera returns to Ireland.

1921

January 1	Muriel MacSwiney returns to Ireland.
January 7	Mary MacSwiney begins her US lecture tour at a mass meeting at Madison Square Garden, New York City.
January 21	Hearings by American Commission on Conditions in Ireland end.
January 24	Professor Edward P. Turner holds rebuttal meeting to Mary MacSwiney's January 23 meeting at the B.F. Keith's Theatre in Cleveland, Ohio.
February 8	Mary MacSwiney speaks to the legislature and state officials in the state capitol in Madison, Wisconsin.
February 11	The Texas House of Representatives refuses to adopt a Senate concurrent resolution to invite Mary MacSwiney to speak to both the House of Representatives and the Senate.
February 14	Nebraska state legislature votes against an invitation to Mary MacSwiney to speak before them.
February 16	Mary MacSwiney speaks to both Houses of the Kansas legislature in the House of Representatives.
February 17	Mary MacSwiney speaks to the joint assembly of the Oklahoma legislature in the House of Representatives.
March 8	Mary MacSwiney addresses the California state legislature in the Senate Chamber.
March 31	Mary MacSwiney speaks before a joint session of the Illinois legislature.
April 18	Mary MacSwiney attends first annual AARIR Convention in Chicago, Illinois.
August 12	Mary MacSwiney returns to Ireland.

December 6	Anglo-Irish Treaty signed.

1922

April 7	Countess Constance Markievicz and Kathleen Barry arrive in New York City.
April 9	Countess Markievicz speaks at a mass meeting at Laurel Gardens in New York City.
May 8	Countess Markievicz and Kathleen Barry recalled to Ireland to take part in the 'Pact' election of June 24.
May 31	Countess Markievicz and Kathleen Barry return to Ireland.
June 28	Irish Civil War begins.
September 17	The Irish Republican Soldiers' and Prisoners' Dependants' Fund formally launched in New York City.
September 22	US lecture tour of Muriel MacSwiney and Linda Kearns for the Irish Republican Soldiers' and Prisoners' Dependants' Fund begins at the Lexington Theatre, New York City.
October 22	Meetings held in honour of the second anniversary of the death of Terence MacSwiney at the Earl Carroll Theatre in New York City and the Academy of Music in Brooklyn.
October 22	Hanna Sheehy Skeffington arrives in New York to attend meetings held in honour of the second anniversary of Terence MacSwiney's death as head of the Irish Women's Mission, along with Kathleen Boland.
October 22	Hanna Sheehy Skeffington, Kathleen Boland and Linda Kearns complete Muriel MacSwiney's lecture tour of the Western section of the United States as the Irish Women's Mission.
November 12	Muriel MacSwiney arrested in Washington D.C. for picketing the British Embassy.

November 15	The case against Muriel MacSwiney for picketing the British Embassy in Washington D.C. dismissed.
November	Muriel MacSwiney recalled to Ireland by Eamon de Valera.
July 7	Muriel MacSwiney returns to Ireland.
	1923
April 10	End of Irish Civil War.
May 15	Farewell reception held in Washington D.C. for Hanna Sheehy Skeffington's departure to Ireland.
	1924
May 18	Mrs Margaret Pearse begins a lecture tour of the US in support of St Enda's School at the Brooklyn Academy of Music in Brooklyn.
October 11	Mrs Margaret Pearse returns to Ireland.
	1925
January	Mary MacSwiney arrives in the United States to begin a lecture tour in support of the Irish Republic and to assist in the revitalization of Irish-American organizations.
February 8	Mary MacSwiney begins her lecture tour at a mass meeting at the Earl Carroll Theatre in New York City.
April 25	Turmoil over whether or not Mary MacSwiney entered the United States without a passport begins.
November	Mary MacSwiney returns to Ireland.

Preface

IRELAND, HELD IN bondage as an English colony for seven and a half centuries, initiated its struggle for independence in the Easter Rising of 1916 in Dublin. Led by a handful of men and women and not supported by a majority of the Irish, it set in motion a chain of events that would lead down a painful path to eventual independence from England. The price was high: loss of lives, a War of Independence, a Civil War and a divided country. However, the dedication of those men and women who believed in an Irish Republic was complete and without reservation.

These Irish women, Hanna Sheehy Skeffington, Mary MacSwiney, Mrs Muriel MacSwiney, Countess Constance Markievicz and Mrs Margaret Pearse were all directly or indirectly involved in the Easter Rising, they all shared a deep love and commitment to Ireland, and above all, they held in common their devotion to the Irish Republic. They came at different times to conduct lectures in towns and cities across the United States. Although each lecture tour involved fund-raising, money did not overshadow their individual primary goals and, in particular, their commitment to the freedom of Ireland. They conducted tours throughout the United States in the years between 1916 and 1925, although they were not the only women Irish republicans to visit the United States during this period.

These women did not hold in common a class, religion, educational or political background. The Easter Rising of 1916 changed all their lives in some way. Hanna Sheehy Skeffington and Mary MacSwiney held advanced university degrees. Hanna, a suffragist and pacifist, wife and mother, became a widow when her pacifist husband, Francis Sheehy Skeffington, was shot by a firing squad. She set her work as a suffragist aside to devote her time to telling the true story of Francis' murder and to fight for an Irish Republic.

Mary MacSwiney was a teacher and was content to organize food preparation and housing for volunteers in preparation for the Rising. Witnessing the hunger strike and death of her brother, Lord

Mayor Terence MacSwiney of Cork, solidified her unyielding support and loyalty to a Republic of Ireland.

Mrs Muriel MacSwiney, the wife of Terence, became a young widow and mother, and a new Irish republican in her early twenties. Although the trauma of Terence's death influenced her health for the rest of her life, she became an active republican rebel during the Civil War, with an increased political astuteness.

Countess Constance Markievicz was an accomplished horsewoman and artist before she became second-in-command of the Irish Citizen Army. She took an active combat role in both the Rising and the Civil War. Many imprisonments affected her physical health but not her spirit. Politically, she became a Cabinet member in the Republic of Ireland Dáil Éireann.

Mrs Margaret Pearse had quietly raised a family of four children. With the death of her two sons, Patrick and William, after the Rising, she took up their work in support of the Irish Republic and of their school, St Enda's in Dublin. She became a businesswoman and politician as she neared seventy years of age.

The Irish were supported tactically and financially by Irish-Americans. Visits by Irish republicans to the United States to raise funds were necessary for the Irish and welcomed by the Irish-Americans, who supported them in many ways. The tours of all the women coincided with a political climate in the United States that was uneasy because of World War I and the political differences and animosity between Irish-American leaders and President Wilson and his administration. Eamon de Valera's tour of the United States to conduct a bond-certificate campaign for the Republic of Ireland further aggravated a division that was already occurring in the Irish-American organizations, Clan na Gael and the Friends of Irish Freedom. De Valera thought it necessary to found a new Irish-American organization before he returned to Ireland, the American Association for Recognition of the Irish Republic, which became a strong force in the Western section of the United States. The signing of the Anglo-Irish Treaty in 1921 and the Civil War that followed confused and permanently divided Irish-Americans.

Each woman came into this overwhelming environment, while friends and family remained in a war-torn Irish homeland. They each maintained extremely hectic schedules with meetings, interviews, receptions, publicity, organization and travel. They received praise wherever they visited, but they also coped with rejection and criticism. These women were all complimented by the American press for their eloquence, their dignity and their intellect.

Each, in her own way, displayed irrefutable courage, tenacity, leadership and a political astuteness unlike most of the women of the world at that time.

CHAPTER 1

The Making of Irish Republican Women: The Rising; War of Independence 1919–21; Civil War 1922–23

THE WOMEN DIRECTLY or indirectly involved in the 1916 Easter Rising, the War of Independence and the Irish Civil War shared a deep love of and commitment to Ireland and above all, when it was over, held in common their devotion to the Irish Republic. Each in her own way displayed irrefutable courage and tenacity by stepping outside the norm of femininity that was expected of women at that time. Although some women had participated in the Inghinidhe na hÉireann, Cumann na mBan and Irish Women's Franchise League, the 1916 Easter Rising gave rise to a new level of political participation. It also led to the lecture tours of Hanna Sheehy Skeffington, Mary MacSwiney, Countess Constance Markievicz, Muriel MacSwiney and Margaret Pearse, conducted in the United States between 1916 and 1925 in support of a Republic of Ireland.

The Military Council of the Irish Republican Brotherhood (IRB) in Ireland, in consultation with Clan na Gael (Clan), the militant Irish-American organization, set the date for revolution as Easter Sunday, April 23 1916. The Clan provided the funds and secured Germany's promise to furnish guns and ammunition. On Easter Monday morning, while most Dubliners enjoyed the holiday, 1,528 men and women, under the command of Patrick Pearse (IRB Director of Organization) and his deputy, James Connolly (organizer of the Irish Citizen Army), marched from Liberty Hall, just north of the Liffey River in central Dublin, to the General Post Office (GPO) and other strategic buildings. The republican tricolour flag of green, white and orange was hoisted to the top of the GPO and Patrick Pearse read the Proclamation of the Irish Republic that declared independence from England and established an Irish Republic.[1] (See Appendix 1.)

The Irish Volunteers and the Irish Citizen Army fought the Royal Irish Constabulary (RIC), the Dublin Metropolitan Police and the British Army for six days before they surrendered on April 29. Historians who have examined the event have stressed that the press and government initially accredited the Rising to Sinn Féin, but they played no role.[2] Although the organization of Sinn Féin, at the time of the Rising, was outmoded, the growth of republicanism as a request of the Rising revitalized it. The name 'Sinn Féin' became the identification of the republican movement. The establishment of a Republic, by physical force if necessary, and removal of British authority from Ireland became its first goals.[3]

British soldiers rounded up the rebels and marched them through the streets of Dublin to Richmond Barracks and Kilmainham Jail. With thousands of Irish men fighting in the British Army in World War I, many onlookers cursed, jeered and spat at the 'Sinn Féiners'. British civil authorities decided not to imprison the insurgents and turned them over to military courts for trial.[4]

Over a ten-day period, firing squads executed fifteen Irish nationalists, including the seven signatories of the Republican Proclamation. Patrick Pearse's brother, William, was executed, although he held no position of leadership in the Volunteers. Thomas Ashe and Eamon de Valera escaped the firing squad because of a delay in being brought to trial. Countess Constance Markievicz, sentenced to death, was granted 'mercy' because of her sex.[5]

By July 1 1916, over 3,075 women had been arrested and taken to Richmond Barracks; over 1,800 were held without trial. British soldiers assaulted citizens in the streets of Dublin. Francis Sheehy Skeffington, respected pacifist, feminist and editor of the *Irish Citizen*, was arrested and shot without a trial.[6] This English brutality, the executions of the fifteen Irish nationalists, the extensive press coverage of Grace Plunkett for her marriage to Joseph Plunkett in Kilmainham jail hours before his execution and of Countess Markievicz, the 'eccentric aristocrat', triggered a re-evaluation of Easter Week by the Irish public and the rebels became martyred heroes.[7]

BACKGROUND

The typical historical overview of the Easter Rising of 1916 includes the role of Countess Markievicz. Her activist role in the nationalist and labour movements and her leadership during the Rising justify her place in Irish history. However, other women played important and sometimes dangerous roles prior to, during and after Easter Week 1916. These women of varied backgrounds and social classes took separate paths to the Irish republican nationalism, which corresponded to the overall political events in Ireland.

The Countess wrote in the *Irish Citizen* in December 1914 that three great movements were taking place in Ireland: 'the national movement, the women's movement and the industrial one', yet as 'each converged on 1916 they moved at their own pace'.[8] Irish middle-class women not only supported these movements, but also formed their own separate organizations in order to have an independent political voice.

The alliance of Irish republican women can be traced back to the formation of Inghinidhe na hÉireann in 1900, the Irish Women's Franchise League (IWFL) in 1908, the Fianna na hÉireann in 1909, the Irish Citizen Army in 1913 and the Cumann na mBan in 1913. After Easter 1916, many of these women gained fame and recognition for their political activism in support of the Irish Republic.

During the early development of the Irish independence movement, Maud Gonne MacBride and Helena Molony, dedicated nationalists, founded the Inghinidhe na hÉireann (the Daughters of Erin) in October 1900 'to work for the complete independence of Ireland',[9] and 'with a commitment to the physical force tradition of Irish republicanism'.[10] According to Countess Markievicz, Inghinidhe was 'always in favour of the most extreme action possible'.[11] It developed as an early feminist and Irish nationalist organization. Although known as 'working girls', its early members were not of the working class.[12]

In *Unmanageable Revolutionaries*, Margaret Ward comments on the importance of Inghinidhe:

> Had not Inghinidhe existed, a whole generation of women would never have developed the self-confidence which eventually enabled them to hold their own in organizations composed of both sexes. No matter what reservations might be expressed concerning some of their

> policies, their importance is that they rebelled against their exclusion and by their very existence opened up a whole world of new possibilities for women.[13]

Alongside, but not aligned with Inghinidhe, the Irish Women's Franchise League, organized by Hanna Sheehy Skeffington and Margaret Cousins, feminists and pacifists, held its first meeting on November 4 1908. From its inception, women involved in the nationalist movement were antagonistic toward the IWFL.[14] Conversely, IWFL members, who came from a cross-section of all classes, political parties and religions, were also involved in Irish nationalism. Although many had strong links to the labour movement, their primary goal remained the achievement of women's suffrage. Hanna criticized the Inghinidhe's position on the suffrage movement on the basis that Irish women could not rely on Irish men to provide them the vote even after independence.[15] The feminists saw women as an oppressed group and the franchise as the major symbol of citizenship, no matter what political implications were involved. The nationalistic women argued that 'the national issue was of such overwhelming importance that it could not be divorced from short-term political ends'.[16]

Fianna na hÉireann (Fianna), sometimes referred to as the Irish Boy Scouts, is considered Countess Markievicz's greatest contribution to Irish nationalism and the Easter Rising. Along with Bulmer Hobson, a member of the IRB, she organized the Fianna in August 1909 'to train boys in the old tradition of the Gaels' to take arms against England in the cause of Irish independence.[17] The Countess purchased rifles and trained the boys in the use of them on the land surrounding her cottage near the mountains.[18] The IRB later used her Fianna handbook as a training manual, particularly for drill and rifle exercises. The Fianna's original members formed the nucleus of ready-trained officers of the IRB.[19] Speaking of the importance of the Fianna, Patrick Pearse remarked that the boys were trained to work for an Ireland 'not free merely, but Gaelic as well, not Gaelic merely, but free as well',[20] and that 'if the Fianna had not been founded in 1909, there would have been no Volunteers in 1913. The Easter Rising of 1916 would have been impossible'.[21]

The third movement in Ireland, labour, converging on Easter 1916, organized the Irish Citizen Army as a self-defence force during the Great Walkout Strike in Dublin in 1913. The Citizen Army, headed by James Connolly, socialist and labour leader, was praised by some for its sexual equality—far more, they claimed, than the Irish Volunteers.[22] The Citizen Army constitution states 'the Citizen Army shall be open to all who accept the principle of equal rights and opportunities for the Irish people'.[23]

Countess Markievicz and Dr Kathleen Lynn became commissioned officers, men and women drilled together, and first-aid classes were co-educational.[24] The Countess drew all the maps for the Rising and prepared plans for the takeover of strategic points. The Military Council appointed her as Connolly's deputy — to take over his responsibilities in case he was captured or injured.[25] However, Connolly did not plan that the women of Cumann na mBan or of the Citizen Army should do any actual fighting. They were to serve as cooks, medical auxiliaries and couriers.[26] Nonetheless, the women did carry arms.[27]

Nora Connolly (daughter of James Connolly) and Margaret Skinnider (a young teacher living in Glasgow), both members of the Citizen Army and Cumann na mBan, individually took on dangerous missions prior to the Rising illustrating their commitment to Irish nationalism.

Nora, a member of the Belfast Cumann na mBan, was asked by her father to make a secret trip to the United States since it was too dangerous to communicate in writing. If caught, she risked death for treason for herself, her father, Countess Markievicz, Tom Clarke and Sean MacDermott (members of the IRB).[28] The purpose of the mission remains unknown. Historians suggest that it may have been to make contact with Germany from the United States through Irish-American connections there or it may have pertained to British anti-submarine operations.[29]

Upon her arrival in New York, Nora stayed with Padraic Colum (Irish poet) and his wife, Mary, for several weeks until it was deemed safe for her to return to Ireland.[30] At the request of John Devoy, leader of Clan na Gael, she brought back money and letters for Roger Casement, a member of the Volunteers. Casement had been in Germany in an attempt to obtain arms and ammunition for Ireland and to raise an illegal Irish Brigade from the Irish prisoners of World War I in German camps. Devoy paid Nora's return passage to Ireland on the *Lusitania*.[31]

Margaret Skinnider (a member of the Glasgow Cumann na mBan) became a member of the Citizen Army through her friendship with Countess Markievicz. She learned to shoot at a Glasgow rifle club and smuggled in military equipment on her frequent trips to

Ireland.[32] During Christmas 1915, she brought detonators over on the Glasgow boat and delivered them to the Countess in Dublin.[33] They both gained experience in using explosives by testing dynamite in the hills around Dublin.[34]

Corresponding to the changing political situation in Ireland in 1913, nationalist women organized the Cumann na mBan as a counterpart to the Irish Volunteers and merged it with the Inghinidhe. At its first public meeting in April 1914 in Dublin, a circular was distributed stating its objectives:

1. To advance the cause of Irish liberty.
2. To organize Irish women in the furtherance of this object.
3. To assist in arming and equipping a body of Irishmen for defence of Ireland.
4. To form a fund for these purposes to be called the 'Defence of Ireland Fund'.[35]

Taking a traditional approach in her inaugural keynote speech, Agnes O'Farrelly ruled out the probability of women taking a direct part 'in the defence of Ireland', except as a last resort, and dismissed the possibility of the discussion of politics. However, she believed nationalist women should:

> extend their domestic concerns to the public sphere: 'Each rifle we put in their hands will represent to us a bolt fastened behind the door of some Irish home to keep out the hostile stranger. Each cartridge will be a watchdog to fight for the sanctity of the hearth'.[36]

Cumann na mBan initially appealed to those women whose husbands, fathers or brothers were involved with the Volunteers. Like the Inghinidhe and the IWFL, its first members were independent women who had the time to devote to its organization. In August 1914, there were forty branches, some with one hundred members; by October there were sixty-three branches. Many women were also active members of the suffrage movement who, when the outbreak of World War I aggravated the tensions between the two movements, gave their full commitment to Cumann na mBan.[37]

Countess Markievicz, a member of the executive committee of Cumann na mBan, complained they were 'an animated collecting box for a male organization'[38] and that:

> today the women attached to national movements are there chiefly to

> collect funds for the men to spend. These Ladies' Auxiliaries demoralize women, set them up in separate camps, and deprive them of all initiative and independence. Women are left to rely on sex, charm, or intrigue and backstairs influence.[39]

By the end of 1915, Cumann na mBan adopted a militaristic attitude and, in October 1915, it designed its own uniform. The insignia showed the words 'Cumann na mBan' written in Celtic script encircling a rifle. Members were specifically selected to accompany the Volunteers on their marches, manoeuvres, and combat training missions.[40]

By acquiring suffragist speakers like Hanna Sheehy Skeffington to appear on their platforms, Cumann na mBan was able to identify the nationalist cause with that of women.[41] Louise Gavan Duffy, in her recollections, writes:

> There were women on the Cumann na mBan committee who were suffragists; others of different opinions, but so urgent, so important was the work of the Volunteers, that we could not afford to divide. Everything was put aside and we were ready to do what we were told: carry messages, give first aid, make meals, in short any work.[42]

THE RISING

Approximately ninety Irish women took part in the 1916 Easter Rising; sixty were Cumann na mBan members, the remainder belonged to the Citizen Army. They were 'predominately religious, sober in habits and drcss, hard working and conventional'—teachers, students, factory workers and trade unionists.[43] With few exceptions, they served as nurses, cooks and couriers; however, these jobs were not without danger. They not only carried messages to and from headquarters in the GPO, but also crossed British lines to bring in food and ammunition, sometimes hidden in their clothing. Some women held up food trucks for their contents. Women in the Citizen Army served in the Ambulance Corps and also took an active part in the fighting.[44]

The representation of republican women by the Irish press changed over time through the Easter Rising, the War of Independence and the Irish Civil War. Nationwide news coverage ignored the women who participated in the Rising.[45]

Women, whether members of the Citizen Army or Cumann na mBan, were not welcomed by all Irish insurgents during the Rising. Eamon de Valera, in command of Boland's Mill, told the women who came to the mill that he did not want them:

> 'I said we have anxieties of a certain kind here and I do not want to add to them at the moment by getting untrained women, women who were clearly untrained for soldiering—I did not want them as soldiers in any case'.[46]

He later admitted he should have used their help instead of utilizing his men as cooks when they should have been fighting. He also commented that women in the Rising were 'at once the boldest and most unmanageable revolutionaries'.[47]

Countess Markievicz, active in the nationalist, suffrage and labour movements, took the most militant, dramatic and publicized role of the women who participated in the Rising. At the time the leaders of the Citizen Army were informed that the Rising would take place and were given their assignments, she was accepted by Tom Clarke and the members of the Provisional Government as one of Connolly's 'ghosts'.[48] She later wrote:

> 'Ghosts' was the name we gave to those who stood secretly behind the leaders and were entrusted with enough of the plans of the Rising to enable them to carry on that Leader's work should anything happen to himself.... Connolly had appointed two staff officers—Commandant Mallin and myself. I held a commission, giving me the rank of Staff Lieutenant.[49] (See Appendix 2.)

With a dramatic flair, the Countess arrived at Liberty Hall dressed in a dark green woollen blouse and tweed knee breeches, black stockings, a black hat trimmed with a spray of feathers and armed with a small automatic pistol and a Mauser rifle-pistol.[50] She was also described as carrying a rifle with a fixed bayonet.[51] As second-in-command to Commandant Michael Mallin of the Citizen Army, she was placed in charge of digging trenches and barricading gates at St Stephen's Green. She found the work exciting once the fighting began and took care of 'any sniper who was particularly objectionable'.[52]

When Mallin decided that St Stephen's Green was indefensible, he sent the Countess, along with two other women and four men, to secure the Royal College of Surgeons on the west side of the Green.[53] Although accounts of her entry into the College vary, it seems the Countess rang the bell at the front door. When no one answered, she 'blew the lock with her pistol and entered', ordered the caretaker and his wife to be locked in their rooms and the building searched. There she discovered sixty-seven rifles, fifteen thousand rounds of ammunition and other supplies. The College of Surgeons then became republican headquarters for the area.[54]

The Countess is reported to have been a capable combatant during the fighting. For instance, as she and William Partridge, a member of the Citizen Army, observed British soldiers marching down Harcourt Street, she fired into the group. Margaret Skinnider, in her position as a sniper, saw two officers drop to the ground. The Countess took aim again and the soldiers retreated the way they came.[55] The Countess had no qualms about shooting an enemy. When Constable Michael Lahiff tried to enter the Green and refused to retreat, she shot him with her Mauser rifle. She is reported to have repeatedly shouted, 'I shot him'.[56]

The Countess ended Easter Week with the same dramatic flair with which she started. As she and the others at the College of Surgeons surrendered on Sunday, April 30 to British Captain de Courcy Wheeler, she took off her pistol and kissed it 'reverently' before handing it over. When Captain Wheeler offered to drive her to Dublin Castle, she refused saying she would march at the head of her men as she was second-in-command and would share their fate.[57]

At her trial, on May 4 1916, she pleaded guilty to participating in the Rising, not guilty to assisting the enemy and guilty to causing disaffection. She stated: 'I went out to fight for Ireland's freedom, and it doesn't matter what happens to me. I did what I thought was right and I stand by it'. She was found guilty and sentenced to death 'by being shot'. However, the Court recommended mercy because of her sex and commuted her sentence to 'Penal Servitude for Life'.[58]

The only female casualty during the Rising, Margaret Skinnider, craved more action than her role as courier provided. Mallin agreed to use her as a sniper and sent her out with a party on Wednesday evening to set fire to houses behind the Russell Hotel. British soldiers fired on them, killing one man and seriously wounding Margaret. She was carried back under fire to the College of Surgeons and a few days later taken to Vincent's Hospital to recover.[59]

Dr Kathleen Lynn, Captain and medical officer of the Citizen Army, set up and headed a medical station in the City Hall. At the time of surrender, she was the only officer present and tenaciously insisted on following the proper military procedure in conceding to the surrender herself. The British military were at first unsure whether their code of conduct would allow them to accept surrender from a woman.[60] After her arrest, she was sent to Mountjoy Prison.[61]

Other women of the Cumann na mBan and Citizen Army held out through Easter Week until the final surrender on Sunday, April 30. Nora Connolly, Brigid Foley, Marie Perolz, Nora Daly, Eily O'Hanrahan and Miss Wyse Power were couriers. Helena Molony assisted Madeleine ffrench-Mullen, who was in charge of the Red Cross and the commissary at St Stephen's Green. Louise Gavan Duffy set up a kitchen in the GPO. Lily Kempson and Mary Hyland seized supplies at gunpoint. Áine and Lily Ceannt were with Eamonn Ceannt in the South Dublin Union. Rose MacNamara and sixteen Cumann na mBan women who joined Ceannt at Marrowbone Lane Distillery insisted on surrendering with the men.[62]

At the time of the rebel surrender, Nurse Elizabeth O'Farrell was selected to act as emissary between the British authorities and the insurgents. At 12:45 p.m., she walked out from the GPO into the street holding a Red Cross flag. She told the nearest British troops she was sent by Pearse and wanted to deliberate. She was sent back by the British to inform Pearse that he must surrender 'unconditionally'. She then carried Pearse's surrender to the other rebel command posts.[63]

Hanna Sheehy Skeffington could not know at the start of the Easter Rising that her own feminist path would 'converge' so dramatically with nationalism and republicanism. Neither she nor her husband, Francis Sheehy Skeffington, both feminists and pacifists, took an active part in the Rising.[64] However, because neither of them could stand by when others needed support, Francis worked to organize a citizens' militia to prevent widespread looting in Dublin.[65] Hanna had been named as a member of a five-member Civil Provisional Government to be put into effect if the Rising proved successful. During the early part of the week of the Rising she brought food to the General Post Office and offered to deliver messages to the various encampments.[66] With the arrest, without charges, and execution of Francis during the Rising, the course of Hanna's life, and that of their seven-year-old son, Owen, changed forever.

Although Maud Gonne MacBride had been exiled from Ireland for twelve years after her divorce from Major John MacBride, she maintained her political connections in Ireland from France. She had remained active in Inghinidhe with the help of Helena Molony and was elected honorary president of Cumann na mBan in 1914.[67] While in Normandy for the 1916 Easter holidays, she received incomplete and garbled accounts of the fighting during Easter Week. She believed Connolly had been killed, the Countess arrested and Pearse wounded, and immediately decided to return to Ireland.[68] When she was refused permission, she outwitted the British officials by travelling in disguise.[69]

Outside of Dublin, Mary MacSwiney, president of the Cork Cumann na mBan, kept busy at home preparing food and arranging for accommodations for Volunteers. She also assumed responsibility for the care of dependants of Volunteers. Although she did not completely support the Rising initially as she felt the rebels were not prepared, she would become one of the most ardent supporters of the Republic once it was proclaimed.[70]

AFTER THE RISING

Seventy-seven republican women were arrested after the Rising. Most were released in May; however, six women were deported to English jails: Helena Moloney, Winifred Carney, Brigid Foley, Marie Perolz, Nell Ryan and Constance Markievicz.[71]

Commenting on the aftermath of the Easter Rising, Brian Farrell, in 'Markievicz and the Women of the Revolution', states:

> It was immediately after Easter Week that the women came into their own. Proving, if the proof were needed, that this was no romantic affair of a couple of headstrong and flamboyant personalities but a full-fledged and broadly based movement. Within a couple of days of the rising Mrs Tom Clarke was again picking up the threads of the IRB conspiracy.[72]

On the Tuesday following the execution of her husband, Tom, Kathleen Clarke set up the Irish Volunteers' Dependants' Fund (IVDF) to distribute the IRB fund of £3,100 he had left with her. The most immediate task was to organize aid for the dependants of Volunteers who had been killed or imprisoned. Kathleen selected only female relatives of the executed men of the Rising to serve on the committee. All the women were Cumann na mBan members, except Mrs Margaret Pearse. Kathleen became president; Áine Ceannt, vice president.[73]

John Reynolds placed his office at 1 College Street, in Dublin, at the disposal of the IVDF. Cumann na mBan collected and distributed the fund in Dublin and across the country. Kathleen's sister, Madge Daly, and members of Cumann na mBan organized a branch in Limerick; Mary MacSwiney organized one in Cork.[74]

Kathleen, Sorcha MacMahon (a member of the Central Branch of Cumann na mBan), and John R. Reynolds, drew up a petition to set up the fund, which was then published in the newspapers. It was required that the petition be reviewed by the Government Censor prior to publication. He disallowed the first name that was submitted—Irish Republican Prisoners' Dependants' Fund. It then took eleven days to resubmit the name, Irish Volunteers' Dependants' Fund, and by that time another group had set up a fund for the same purpose. Kathleen believed it to be controlled by the Irish Parliamentary Party and knew she would have to fight it.[75]

Irish public officials had founded the second fund, the Irish National Aid Fund, with no direct connection to the Easter Rising. Kathleen had been urged to negotiate a merger with them, but refused. When Clan na Gael learned of the two funds, they sent John Archdeacon Murphy from the United States to convince Kathleen to agree to a merger. She resisted because of the deep connection of the Irish Volunteers' Dependants' Fund to the Easter Rising, but finally agreed. The IVDF accounts were audited and its paperwork and money handed over to a joint board. The two funds became the National Aid and Volunteer Dependants' Fund (NAVDF). Kathleen worked for the NAVDF until 1929.[76]

Joseph McGrath, who had been at Jacob's Factory during the Rising but escaped arrest, had been the Irish National Aid Fund's first secretary. When men who had been in the Rising were released from prison, he resigned. In February 1917, Michael Collins, an IRB member who had been stationed in the GPO during the Rising, became the paid secretary of the NAVDF. At the same time, he became the chief organizer of the IRB. By April 1917, £107,069 had been raised by the NAVDF.[77]

Republican women worked in many different capacities after the Rising. In general, they put their own plans and projects on hold and went where they were most needed by the Irish Republic. Nora Connolly, Margaret Skinnider and Nellie Gifford toured the United States in the first months after the Rising to lecture for support of the dependants of the martyrs and to enlighten the American public on the events of the Rising.[78]

By the end of 1916, Hanna Sheehy Skeffington began the first of her four lecture tours in the United States to explain the circumstances of her husband's death to the American public and to see that justice was done, to gain recognition of the new Irish Republic and to raise funds for Sinn Féin. Mary MacSwiney, Terence MacSwiney's sister, and Muriel, his widow, travelled to the United States in December 1920 to testify before the American Commission on Conditions in Ireland in Washington D.C.[79] Muriel returned to Ireland in January 1921. At the request of Eamon de Valera, President of the Irish Republic, Mary remained in the US to tour in support of the Irish Republic. Countess Markievicz arrived in New York in April 1922 in support of de Valera and the Republic of Ireland. Mrs Muriel MacSwiney returned to the United States in September 1922 to aid the Irish Republican Soldiers' and Prisoners' Dependants' Fund. Hannah Sheehy Skeffington conducted the second tour in 1922–23 as head of the Irish Women's Mission. Mrs Margaret Pearse, mother of Patrick and Willie, began her tour of the United States in May 1924 in support of Eamon de Valera, the Irish Republic and to solicit funds for Patrick Pearse's school, St Enda's. Mary MacSwiney returned to the United States in January 1925 to raise funds for the Irish Republic and to attempt a reorganization and unification of Irish-American organizations. Kathleen Clarke also toured the United States in 1923–24 and Maud Gonne MacBride in 1927.

Five of the six women who took their seats in the first Dáil Éireann (Assembly of Ireland) in January 1919 were relatives of men who had been executed or involved in the Rising: Mrs Margaret Pearse, Mrs Kathleen Clarke, Mary MacSwiney, Mrs Kate O'Callaghan, and Dr Ada English.[80]

The importance of the role women played in the Easter Rising in 1916 was summed up in 1917, when the Cumann na mBan claimed [the women of Easter Week]

> have regained for the women of Ireland the rights that belonged to them under the old Gaelic civilization where sex was no bar to citizenship and where women were free to devote to the service of their country every talent and capacity with which they were endowed.[81]

Helena Molony, member of the Citizen Army, described the role of women in the Rising:

> I feel they might as well ask me what did the tall fair-haired men do in the wars and what did small dark men do. My answer in both cases is the same: they did what came to their hands to do—day to day, and whatever they were capable of by aptitude or training.[82]

Countess Markievicz wrote in *Cumann na mBan* in 1926:

> The memory of Easter Week with its heroic dead is sacred to us who survived. Many of us could almost wish we had died in the moment of ecstasy when, the Tricolour over our heads we went out and proclaimed the Irish Republic and with guns in our hands tried to establish it. We failed, but not until we had seen regiment after regiment run from our few guns. Our effort will inspire the people who come after us and will give them hope and courage. If we failed to win, so did the English. They slaughtered and imprisoned, only to rouse the nation to a passion of love and loyalty—loyalty to Ireland and hatred of foreign rule.[83]

The 1916 Easter Rising forced changes within the Cumann na mBan, the IWFL, and the trade union movement. The Cumann na mBan grew in numbers, became more active, less subordinate and more feminist. Large numbers of younger women joined the Cumann na mBan. Many members of the IWFL became more supportive of nationalism. Those supportive of nationalism became more involved in the trade union movement.[84] Nationwide, the majority of Irish workers, male and female, were members of Sinn Féin, the Volunteers or Cumann na mBan. The undivided objective of all three groups was the freedom of Ireland and the working class.[85]

On July 4 1918, Dublin Castle labelled Cumann na mBan, Sinn Féin, and the Volunteers as 'dangerous associations' and declared their meetings illegal.[86]

WAR OF INDEPENDENCE

Throughout 1918 Ireland drifted into acts of terrorism and war. By 1919 a full-scale guerrilla war (Irish War of Independence) developed between British forces and the Irish Republican Army in spite of the fact that the original Sinn Féin philosophy did not include the use of armed force in order to gain independence.

There was no beginning date of hostilities—acts of violence had occurred sporadically. On the very day that newly elected Sinn Féin representatives declared Ireland independent and established Dáil Éireann in Dublin, January 21 1919, an event occurred in Soloheadbeg, County Tipperary, which escalated the fighting and is considered to be the beginning of the war. Irish Volunteers Seamus Robinson, Sean Treacy, Dan Breen, Sean Hogan and five others killed two RIC members and captured the gelignite they were transporting.[87]

The Volunteers were independent of Dáil Éireann and tended to act on their own. There was a general lack of agreement in the Dáil and within the Volunteer headquarters as to what their responsibilities should be. The fact that some Volunteers were members of the secret IRB added to the confusion of their mission and responsibilities.[88] In August 1919, the Volunteers took an oath of allegiance to Dáil Éireann and became the Irish Republican Army (IRA). Although Sinn Féin and the IRA had many of the same members, and Sinn Féin was more politically oriented and the IRA more militant, they remained independent from one another.[89]

Raids by the Volunteers for arms and ammunition increased in the first months of 1920. British raids and arrests were countered with Volunteer attacks on RIC barracks, which held arms and ammunition. The British solution to the increasing guerrilla warfare waged by the IRA was to send in 7,000 Black and Tans (named for their khaki jackets and black pants and hats), unemployed ex-soldiers, and 6,000 Auxiliaries, ex-Army officers. The Black and Tans were paid ten shillings a day; the Auxiliaries one pound a day—paid mercenaries.[90]

The Black and Tans began arriving in Ireland in March 1920, the Auxiliaries in August 1920, and what has been called 'A Reign of Terror' began. The war then took place not on the battlefield, but in towns where women and children were killed, family homes and businesses destroyed, jobs lost and the food supply endangered. The terror had less to do with the number of troops than the destruction and horror they caused. J. J. Lee has written that 'the new recruits were too few to impose a real reign of terror, but numerous enough to commit sufficient atrocities to provoke nationalist opinion in Ireland and America, and to outrage British liberal opinion'.[91]

Women became involved in hiding on-the-run IRA soldiers and small groups of IRA Volunteers in 'safe houses' in the countryside and isolated villages where their homes were vulnerable to attack and prone to night raids by the British troops. Threats of physical violence and sexual assault were reported.[92] Other women worked as nurses, couriers, scouts, intelligence agents, fund-raisers, and they buried the dead. They also knitted, washed and cooked. Some women dangerously undertook smuggling subversive documents in their underclothing. Kathleen Clarke travelled from Limerick to Dublin with £2,000 for Michael Collins strapped to her body.[93]

At the end of 1919, leaders of the women's organizations came together to demand the formation of an international committee to investigate the imprisonment of Irish 'political prisoners'. Because the women remained successfully undercover during the war, it is estimated that less than fifty were imprisoned. Most of them received short sentences.[94]

To meet the requirements of war, the Cumann na mBan reorganized into divisions to place it on a military footing to correspond to the structure of the IRA so that every IRA Company had a branch of the Cumann na mBan attached to it. To coordinate this partnership, members of the Cumann na mBan executive toured the countryside, which was under martial law and subject to surveillance and searches, gathering statistics on branches and district councils. The majority of these women were in their early twenties and had joined Cumann na mBan after the Rising. Training camps were set up with six-hour-a-day classes in first aid, nursing, drill signalling, map reading, care of arms and lectures on the organization of the Cumann na mBan. By 1921, Cumann na mBan had 800 branches.[95]

Following the American Commission on Conditions in Ireland hearings in Washington D.C., the American Committee for Relief in Ireland was set up to collect and ship food and clothing to Ireland. In Ireland, the White Cross Fund was established at the end of 1920 to coordinate and distribute the donations. Additionally, they raised funds throughout the United States. By August 1922, over £1,500,000 had been raised. The committee of the White Cross Fund was composed of many women of the Easter Rising: Áine Ceannt, Hanna Sheehy Skeffington, Nancy O'Rahilly, Kathleen Clarke, Maud Gonne and Erskine Childers' wife, Molly.[96]

IRISH CIVIL WAR

After the truce ending the war was signed, Cumann na mBan was the first national organization to reject the Treaty. All six women in the Dáil (Kathleen Clarke, Countess Markievicz, Mary MacSwiney, Margaret Pearse, Dr Ada English and Kate O'Callaghan) rejected the Treaty. The Dáil voted in favour of a resolution proposed by Countess Markievicz: 'This executive of Cumann na mBan reaffirms their allegiance to the Irish Republic and therefore cannot support the Articles of Treaty signed in London'. Cumann na mBan members demonstrated outside the Mansion House when the first meeting of the Provisional Government took place.[97]

When the fighting broke out at the Four Courts at the start of the Irish Civil War, Cumann na mBan members set up first aid stations, transported arms and equipment, issued news reports, and worked as couriers. When the fighting moved out of Dublin into the countryside, once again the women responded by sheltering wounded men and working as couriers and secretaries. Beyond that, little could be done when the fighting became concentrated in the mountain regions.[98]

Cumann na mBan members were actively involved in the Civil War and became vulnerable to arrest. Free State authorities were able to quickly identify and arrest them. Over 800 women were held in Kilmainham prison, others in Mountjoy, North Dublin Union, Cork jail and small local prisons. It has been estimated that up to 2,000 members were held during 1922–23.[99]

As the number of republicans taken prisoners and placed in crowded jails and camps increased, the Women's Prisoners' Defence League (WPDL) was formed. The League publicized the conditions of prisoners, traced missing relatives, mounted vigils outside jails and publicly protested executions.[100]

Growing involvement of Republic women in the war brought criticism against them by the Free State Government, the Catholic Church and the press. The Free State Government complained in a report issued January 1 1923 that:

> Neurotic girls are amongst the most active adherents to the irregular [Republican] cause, because hitherto it has been safe to be so. They disfigure the walls of Dublin with lying propaganda, and they are active carriers of documents, arms and ammunition. Many of them have been known to accompany men on expeditions of murder, concealing arms in their clothes until required, and taking them back when used, relying for safety on the chivalry of those whose deaths they were out to encompass.[101]

The Catholic Church, which supported the Cumann na nGaedheal Party and the Free State Government, excommunicated all republicans in October 1922. The press, under strict censorship, was ordered by the Army Publicity Department to call Republicans 'irregulars' and to refer to them as 'troops' rather than an 'army'. They supported the government's stand against the republicans and carried regular reports of the arrests of republican women. Reports of armed women threatening violence were common, as well as headlines such as 'Armed woman holds up Dublin policeman' and 'Women Carrying Rifles'.[102]

After the Civil War, many republican women were unable to get jobs, suffered financial hardships and were persecuted by the Free State authorities, which 'represented them as threats to public order and national stability'.[103]

CONCLUSION

Although the women of the Rising, the War of Independence and the Civil War did not represent all Irish women, they stepped out of the traditional role of the 'cult of true womanhood and domesticity' to fight for their own political beliefs, or for those of their husbands, sons or brothers—an act of courage in and of itself. They stepped out to support the Irish Republic in non-traditional and traditional roles—wherever they were needed. It was their dedication to a free, Republican Ireland that led Hanna Sheehy Skeffington, Mary MacSwiney, Countess Constance Markievicz, Muriel MacSwiney and Margaret Pearse to exhaustively tour the United States to raise both funds and support. At the same time, they contributed to the political involvement of women of Ireland to become the most politically astute women in the world at that time.

CHAPTER 2

Irish-American Republican Nationalism: National Organizations and Leadership

FROM THE TIME of the mass migration from Ireland to the United States during the famine, Irish-American nationalism developed and manifested itself in organizations such as the Young Irelanders, Fenians, Land League, Clan na Gael, Ancient Order of Hibernians and Friends of Irish Freedom in the major cities of the United States. Lawrence J. McCaffrey states in *The Irish Diaspora in America*:

> Irish nationalism jelled and flourished in the ghettos of urban America as a search for identity, an expression of vengeance, and a quest for respectability.... The development of an Irish identity among American immigrants speeded the progress of Irish nationalism on both sides of the Atlantic.[1]

The Irish in America maintained a strong financial and political connection to the Irish in Ireland so that for every action in Ireland, there was a reaction in the United States. Many of the leaders of Irish-American organizations had been exiled to the United States after arrests in Ireland for their political activities and subsequent imprisonment in England. Alan J. Ward states in *Easter Rising*:

> They [Irish-Americans] were the ones who financed and sustained Irish Nationalism in the years before the Rising, and they were the ones who kept alive the dream of an independent Ireland when most at home would have settled for less.... They supported the revolutionary movement in Ireland that led to Easter Week 1916.[2]

The Irish-American link to Ireland can be traced back to the mid-1850s when one out of two families in Ireland communicated with a friend or relative in the United States. It is estimated that between 1848 and 1887, money from North America to the United Kingdom exceeded $170 million, with approximately nine-tenths sent by Irish-Americans to Ireland.[3]

The 1916 Easter Rising triggered a need for political activism in the Irish-American organizations. World War I, the pressure of British propaganda in the United States and the pro-German attitude of several Irish-American organizations led to accusations of disloyalty from fellow Americans. Once the war began however, Irish-Americans not only fought in the war in Europe, but their organizations sponsored Liberty Bond rallies and fervently declared their loyalty to America.

Irish-Americans appeared unified until Eamon de Valera's arrival in 1919. His personality clash with the Irish-American leader, Daniel Cohalan, resulted in a split within the organization of the Friends of Irish Freedom (FOIF). While some of the older leaders on the East Coast continued the work of the FOIF, the West Coast, particularly California, shifted their total allegiance to de Valera and his new organization, the American Association for the Recognition of the Irish Republic (AARIR). With the signing of the 1921 Anglo-Irish Treaty, the beginning of the Irish Civil War and the creation of the Irish Free State, the division in loyalties, East and West, in the United States became more pronounced. The AARIR in the conservative Midwest, with the exception of Illinois where they had considerable strength and numbers, remained for the most part small in numbers and support.

THE EAST

The first important Irish-American organization, the American Fenians, founded in 1858 by John O'Mahony, paralleled the Irish Fenians. The American Fenian organization grew dramatically during the American Civil War, but with the failure of their raids into Canada in 1867 and 1870, the movement faded.[4]

The rise of Irish-American nationalism began in America in 1867 with the growth of Clan na Gael out of the Fenian Brotherhood. John Devoy, born in County Kildare, headed the Clan after his release from prison in England and arrival in the United States in

1871. More secretive, militant and disciplined than the Irish Republican Brotherhood (IRB) in Ireland, the Clan financially supported the IRB and favoured revolution. In 1900, Devoy and the son of Cork immigrants, Daniel F. Cohalan, then a New York attorney, reorganized the Clan. They collected and distributed money through a front, the Irish National and Industrial League of the United States.[5] When Devoy founded *The Gaelic American* in 1903 in New York, it became the Clan's 'mouthpiece'.[6] Joseph McGarrity immigrated to the United States from Tyrone at the age of sixteen to settle in Philadelphia. He was elected to the Executive Council at the 1912 Clan Convention and became a member of the Revolutionary Directory. He remained a member of the Clan until his death in August 1940.[7] Clan member Tom Clarke, who was from County Tyrone and a close friend of Devoy, served fifteen years in a British prison and immigrated to the United States in 1899 upon his release. After his return to Ireland from the United States in 1907 to reorganize the IRB, he became the communications link between the IRB and the Clan.[8]

In 1916, the Clan formed a new Irish-American organization, the Friends of Irish Freedom. This was headed by Cohalan who was by then a New York State Supreme Court Justice. Fifteen of the seventeen members of the FOIF Executive Committee were also members of the Clan.[9] The FOIF constitution had as its prime objective to 'encourage and assist any movement that will tend to bring about the National Independence of Ireland'.[10] Its membership grew to approximately 257,000 in 1919.[11]

Concerned about possible United States intervention in World War I, the FOIF, which viewed World War I as a conflict between militaristic empires, prepared a message on February 10 1917 to President Woodrow Wilson. It set forth reasons why America should not become involved in foreign wars and protested the proposed legislation aimed at suppressing 'so-called revolutionary conspiracies against friendly foreign Governments'.[12] The FOIF feared that American troops would be sent to Ireland to prevent further rebellions if the United States became involved in the war and that Irish-American actions against England could be interpreted as treason to the United States.[13]

Once the United States entered the war in April 1917, most Irish-Americans placed their loyalty to the United States ahead of their commitment to Ireland.[14] Following the armistice of World War I on November 11 1918, Irish-Americans again contributed money and guns to Sinn Féin in Ireland and pressured the United States Government to recognize the Irish Republic.[15]

The Irish Progressive League was founded on October 25 1917 as the Irish-American reaction to the entry of the United States into World War I. Their primary purpose was to ensure that Ireland would be represented at the peace conference after the war. The League was 'more aggressive in its actions, more critical of Wilson and the US government, and more overtly left-of-centre than most Irish American Organization's. The League attempted in early 1918 to aid Irish resistance to conscription. Peter Golden, General Secretary of the League, petitioned President Wilson on behalf of the Irish people to save them from forced conscription by the British Government. The FIOF replaced the League in prominence at the end of World War I. The League supported Eamon de Valera's mission in the United States in 1919. When de Valera created the AARIR in November 1920, the League closed its doors and gave its full support to it.[16]

On November 12 1918, the Irish Progressive League held a mass meeting in New York to demand recognition of Ireland as an independent nation. The FOIF sent a memorandum to President Wilson requesting the Republic of Ireland be given a place at the peace talks in Versailles, and the Foreign Affairs Committee of the House held hearings on 'the question of Irish independence'. At the same time, the political scene in Ireland changed with the December 1918 post-Armistice election. Sinn Féin won 73 of 105 Irish seats in the Parliament. However, the Sinn Féin candidates, including Countess Constance Markievicz, refused to take their seats at Westminster and met instead in Dublin as Dáil Éireann to govern Ireland in the name of the Irish Republic. The Dáil elected Eamon de Valera President.[18] When Sinn Féin proclaimed a Declaration of Independence on January 2 1919 and established Dáil Éireann, Irish-Americans endorsed it. The FOIF began a new campaign for the recognition of the Irish Republic by the United States.[19]

Michael Collins, a dominant member of the Irish Republican Brotherhood, reorganized the Volunteers into the Irish Republican Army (IRA). By 1919, an all-out war between the IRA and the Royal Irish Constabulary was under way. The British fought a disorganized campaign in the beginning. In March 1920, ex-servicemen recruited in England and labelled the Black and Tans, a brutal and undisciplined group, were sent to Ireland where they committed many atrocities over the next year. A truce was arranged in July

1921 when the fighting between the IRA and the Black and Tans stalemated and public pressure mounted.[20]

Eamon de Valera's 1919 visit to the United States to raise funds for the cause of Ireland, to obtain President Wilson's support for the Irish Republic and to gain the support of both American political parties, triggered a split in the Irish-American leadership.[21] A number of Clan leaders considered him 'too tepid in his hostility to Britain'.[22] Devoy and Cohalan broke with de Valera, while Joseph McGarrity, editor of the *Irish Press* in Philadelphia, continued to support him.[23] Several issues, such as the Bond Certificate Drive launched by de Valera, his comments regarding a 'British Monroe Doctrine' and his appearance at the US political conventions in 1920 erupted during his stay in the United States. However, it is important to understand that fractures in the Irish-American political structure happened prior to his arrival.

Tensions arose between Cohalan, Devoy and McGarrity at the Irish Race Convention, February 22–3 1919, in Philadelphia over the formation of an Irish Victory Fund established to 'educate public opinion'. The goal of the campaign was set at $1,000,000. When the drive ended on August 31 1919, a total of $1,005,080.83 had been raised. Questions then arose over disbursement of the Irish Victory Fund.[24]

John Devoy presented a resolution at the National Council of the FOIF on June 11, that twenty-five per cent of the fund be sent to Ireland to 'carry out the necessary work of sustaining the Irish Cause and defending it against English attacks'. In addition, the National Council would send an additional $50,000 to be added to the initial $10,000 as soon as it determined the fund balance would permit the transfer. The Irish Victory Fund financed the enormous FOIF campaign against Wilson's proposed League of Nations. It was also agreed that the transfer would not be made public.[25]

Shortly after his arrival in New York City on June 23 1919, de Valera and Cohalan developed a 'mutual antipathy'. Cohalan 'insisted that Irish-Americans should work to oppose British foreign policy interest in general and Anglo-American cooperation in part'. Conversely, de Valera was 'interested only in Ireland and had no quarrel with Anglo-American harmony'. He wanted 'Irish-Americans to fight for Ireland, not against Britain'.[26] John Devoy's biographer, Terry Golway, has stated in *Irish Rebel* that:

> It's clear from the public record and from private correspondence that

> Eamon de Valera came to the land of his birth [the United States] believing that as president of the Irish Republic he was the spokesman and leader of the Irish at home and abroad.[27]

Controversy between Eamon de Valera and the Irish-American leaders escalated over de Valera's proposal to float a loan of $5,000,000 by the issue of bond certificates to be used for Irish national purposes. An internal loan of £250,000 was offered to the public in Ireland and an external loan of £325,000 was sold in the United States in bonds.[28] On September 20 1919, de Valera informed the National Trustees of the FOIF of his preliminary arrangements to place the bond certificate subscription before the American public. Judge Cohalan and attorneys Michael J. Ryan, Richard F. Dalton and Judge Goff believed any attempt to sell the bonds of the Irish Republic without their official recognition in the United States would be regarded as a violation of the American 'Blue Sky' laws.[29] Joseph McGarrity supported de Valera; however, a committee of Cohalan, Thomas Hughes Kelly, Bourke Cockran, Richard F. Dalton and John D. Moore recommended raising funds through the sale of bond certificates instead. In the end, de Valera followed the advice of the Cohalan committee.[30]

On September 28, de Valera notified Frank P. Walsh, Chairman of the American Commission on Irish Independence (ACII), that Dáil Éireann had authorized the issue of $10,000,000 bond certificates of the Republic of Ireland for sale in the United States. The bond certificates were to be issued from December 1 1919, in denominations of $10, $25, $50, $100, $250, $500, $1,000, $5,000 and $10,000.[31] On September 29, the trustees of the FOIF recommended a loan to the American Commission of Irish Independence, through de Valera, of funds not to exceed $100,000.[32] The National Council of the FOIF approved the loan and furnished the names of the 70,000 members of the FOIF to de Valera.[33]

The complexity of the transfer of funds controlled by the FOIF from the Irish Victory Fund led to the later confusion and misunderstandings between the Irish-Americans and the Irish. Mistrust became an integral part of the issue of whether the $100,000 was a loan or a donation due, in part, to the fact that the FOIF had not published official figures of the Irish Victory Fund. They believed the fund to be their own asset to be controlled only by themselves.[34] Joseph McGarrity remained critical of the FOIF and believed the money was collected for Ireland and that it be given to Ireland—not just a portion of it.[35]

In a letter, on March 7 1921, Michael Collins informed James O'Mara, who had headed the bond drive in the United States, that the Dáil cabinet had decided the $100,000 was a donation and asked that a transfer of funds be made to the Self Determination Fund. That amount was transferred on April 29 1921. Once the transfer was made, the question then was whether to issue bond certificates to the FOIF.

After the Anglo-Irish Treaty was signed, Harry Boland, special envoy of the Irish Republic to the United States, issued the following statement on the status of bond certificates under the Provisional Government: 'The Irish Republican Bond Certificates will be exchanged for 5 per cent bonds as soon as the government of the Irish Free State is organized and operating. No change will be made as a result of the agreement entered into between the British Government and the Irish plenipotentiaries'.[37]

The status of bond certificates remained in question for many years. When de Valera left the United States on December 9 1920, $2,500,000 of the more than $5,800,000 that had been raised in bond certificates remained in the Guaranty State Deposit Company and other banks in New York. De Valera, James O'Mara and Bishop Fogarty had been appointed trustees. After the Anglo-Irish Treaty was signed, de Valera and Collins agreed this money would not be used for Republican Party purposes. In August 1922, the Irish Free State Government secured an injunction to prevent the banks from issuing the money to de Valera or to James O'Mara. Because Dr Fogarty supported the Provisional Government, he was not named. The Free State Government then applied to the New York Supreme Court to be named the legitimate successor of the funds raised in the United States for the Republic of Ireland. De Valera contested. On May 11 1927, the New York Supreme Court ruled that neither the Republican Party nor the Irish Free State Government was entitled to the money and ordered it to be returned to subscribers.[38]

The next round of friction between de Valera and the Irish-American leadership received a great deal of criticism on both sides of the Atlantic concerning his Cuban analogy in which he asked: 'Why doesn't Britain do with Ireland as the United States did with Cuba? Why doesn't Britain declare a Monroe Doctrine for the two neighbouring islands?'[39] De Valera had used the condensation of a speech he had prepared to deliver in Worcester, Massachusetts, as the basis of an interview he gave to the *Westminster Gazette* on February 5. The article was reprinted in the *New York Globe* under a 'misleading headline'. *The Gaelic American* then published the reprinted article.[40]

In an attempt to clear up the matter, de Valera issued a correction to the summary of the *Westminster Gazette* article by adding to his 'Why doesn't' question:

> But there are even other ways in which Britain could safeguard itself if this plea were really an honest plea. An international instrument could easily be framed—as in the case of Belgium—an instrument that meant more for the safety of France, as the last war proved, than the actual possession of Belgian territory especially if such possession were against the will and despite the protests of the Belgian people.... In a genuine League of Nations the contracting parties could easily, by mutual compact, bind themselves to respect and defend the integrity and national independence of each other, and guarantee it by the strength of the whole. But England preferred—and prefers a League of Empires—an unholy alliance to crush liberty, not a sacred covenant to maintain liberty.[41]

John Devoy conceded the above statement to be exactly as he received it from de Valera's headquarters, but contended that it differed from the *Westminster Gazette* and *New York Globe* articles. He also admitted the corrected statement was stronger in its indictment of England; however, he still took exception to de Valera's 'suggestion of Ireland of something similar to the American Protectorate over Cuba and his reference to an English Monroe Doctrine for "the two neighbouring Islands".' Devoy felt his previous objections still held because de Valera's reference to the Platt Amendment should not be made 'without bringing in the whole text of it, which gives the United States rights in Cuba which it would be suicidal to give to England in Ireland'.

In an exchange of letters, de Valera asked Cohalan to condemn Devoy's attacks against him in *The Gaelic American.* Devoy had written: 'President DeValera's proposal comes to the Irish in America like a bolt from the blue.... [he] would be well advised to let his proposition remain in its present stage and allow it to be threshed out in the newspapers on its merits'.[44] Continuing the argument, de Valera wrote to Cohalan on February 20 1920 that 'I am answerable to the Irish people for the proper execution of the trust with which I have been charged. I am definitely responsible to them and I alone am responsible'.[45] In rebuttal, Cohalan replied to de Valera on February 22: 'I know no reason why you take the trouble to tell me that you can share your responsibility to the Irish people with no one. I would not let you share it with me if you sought to do so. That is a matter between them and you'.[46]

After the turmoil the Cuban analogy had created settled down, another set of issues arose to further divide de Valera from Cohalan and Devoy: the 1920 US political conventions. The National Council of the FOIF set up a committee to 'wait on the Republican and Democratic Conventions' to petition for a plank in the party platforms favouring recognition of the Republic of Ireland. When de Valera showed no interest in supporting the committee, Cohalan met with him in Washington on May 22 to discuss the Chicago Republican convention. Cohalan rejected a proposal submitted by John E. Milholland that the FOIF advance $50,000 to launch a publicity campaign at the convention. In spite of Cohalan's position, de Valera sent Milholland to Chicago to begin the campaign. Frank P. Walsh, Bourke Cockran and other Irish-American leaders urged de Valera not to attend the convention, but he proceeded against their advice.[47]

Patrick McCartan, a representative of the Irish Republic in the United States, described the situation in Chicago:

> So there we were—President de Valera, Mellows, Nunan and I—all four of us, members of foreign mission, trespassing on American hospitality. And our trespassing did not end with our presence.
>
> We opened offices, with huge circus posters outside on Michigan Boulevard; headquarters at the Blackstone hotel—at the Convention centre.... There was no chance of offending America that we did not take.[48]

From his headquarters de Valera sent out press releases, pamphlets and a daily newspaper. He turned down a suggestion by Irish-American leaders that he withdraw from the convention to allow Cohalan to present Ireland's position. Cohalan and Devoy submitted a plank to the convention committing the Republican Party to support the right of the people of Ireland to elect their own government. De Valera submitted a competing resolution to commit the Republicans to recognize 'the elected Government of the Republic of Ireland' and demanded that the convention drop the

Cohalan-Devoy resolution. De Valera's plan was defeated by a vote of eleven to one by the Subcommittee on Resolutions. The subcommittee approved the Cohalan plank by a vote of seven to six; however, when de Valera announced his opposition to its inclusion in the tentative draft of the Republican platform, it was withdrawn. As a result, the final platform did not include a plank addressing the Irish question.[49]

In order not to repeat their Chicago experience, the FOIF leaders decided not to participate in the Democratic convention held in San Francisco. De Valera should have been aware that he faced an uphill battle and recognized that members of the Democratic Resolution Committee were aware that President Wilson did not want a plank dealing with the recognition of the Republic of Ireland. In spite of these unfavourable conditions, de Valera and Frank P. Walsh appeared before the Resolution Committee on June 29 to argue for recognition of the Irish Republic in the Democratic plank. The committee voted against de Valera's plank by a vote of thirty-one to seventeen. An amended plank was also voted down by a vote of 665 to 402. On his own, de Valera could not gain the support he sought for the official recognition of the Republic of Ireland to be included in the election campaign.[50]

The final blow to the FOIF and to the unity of Irish Americans occurred, on October 20 1920, when de Valera called a conference in Washington D.C. of Irish-American leaders to announce the formation of a new organization, the American Association for the Recognition of the Irish Republic (AARIR), and to launch a bond-certificate drive with a goal of $10,000,000.[51] There existed then three divisions of Irish-American power in the United States: the FOIF with Cohalan and Devoy, Clan na Gael with McGarrity and the tremendous growth of the AARIR with Father Peter Yorke on the West Coast. According to Sean Cronin, the AARIR 'supplanted' the FOIF, 'proving that de Valera was a more important name to the American Irish than Devoy and a better political tactician than Cohalan'.[52]

Three thousand supporters of de Valera met in secret session at the Central Opera House in New York to draw up the constitution of the AARIR. Hundreds were turned away when they failed to give the Celtic password. The purpose of the meeting had been announced to be the discussion of the welcome of Mrs Muriel MacSwiney, widow of Terence, the late Lord Mayor of Cork who died in a hunger strike, and Mary MacSwiney, his sister.[53] Muriel and Mary were in the United States to appear before the Commission on

Conditions in Ireland in Washington D.C. The formation of the AARIR shattered Irish-American unity and dealt a blow to the FOIF that they never recovered from. By the end of 1921, AARIR membership numbered 700,000 and FOIF membership had decreased to 20,000.

THE WEST

From the time of its heavy influx of immigrants during the Gold Rush in California, Irish nationalist movements developed concurrently with national organization commitments, including support for the Young Irelanders, the Fenians, the Land League and the Gaelic League. In 1890, the Gaelic League sponsored a statewide movement under the leadership of Father Peter C. Yorke of San Francisco and the attorney Joseph Scott of Los Angeles. In 1902, Yorke, known as the 'labour priest'[54] founded and edited *The Leader*, the only Irish-American newspaper in California.[55] After the 1916 Easter Rising, California Irish-Americans determined that militant measures were necessary to free Ireland. The formation of the FOIF in California by Yorke and Scott carried forward a 'new dominant militant republicanism'. Yorke was the principal spokesman for the Irish Republic in California until his death in 1925.[56]

Because of their previous pro-German position, the FOIF in San Francisco conducted four Liberty Loan campaigns to demonstrate their loyalty to America once the United States entered World War I.[57] Prior to the war, in a front page article in *The Leader*, Yorke charged President Wilson with 'conspiring to ally the United States with England . . . to stir the people of this country to a feeling of great resentment against Germany'.[58] However, to verify Irish-American nationalism and loyalty, at the same time he pledged loyalty to the United States once war was declared:

> Though we must bow our heads to their decision, as we are bound to do by our oath of allegiance, not for fear or by compulsion, but for conscience sake and love of country, and though we shall loyally do our full duty to the State in whatsoever manner the constituted powers demand, still before the blow has fallen let us go on record concerning our stand.[59]

After the war, the FOIF launched a national political campaign for self-determination for small nations—including an independent Irish nation.[60]

Before de Valera's return to Ireland, Yorke founded the California AARIR at a state convention of the FOIF held in Fresno in November 1920. The California FOIF merged completely with the AARIR, unlike the New York FOIF, which completely divorced itself from de Valera. The convention delegates pledged to dedicate themselves to the recognition of the Irish Republic, to the financial support of de Valera, to condemn all British military action in Ireland, and to support the national AARIR.[61]

By January 1921, eighty-five branches of the AARIR, under the direction of Yorke, had been formed with more than 5,000 members. California became the fourth largest AARIR in the United States, behind Massachusetts, New York and Illinois. The California headquarters of the AARIR was established in San Francisco in the Grant Building, Seventh and Market Streets. Membership rallies were open to the public, all American citizens were eligible for membership and required a commitment to work for recognition of the Irish Republic by the United States Government.[62] Although the AARIR became the most active Irish-American organization in California, it was supported by other established Irish-American organizations, such as the Ancient Order of Hibernians and the Ladies' Auxiliary, the Knights of the Red Branch and the Cumann na mBan.

California women organized in support of the Irish Republic. The Women's Irish Education League (WIEL) was founded in 1920 to educate the American public on the Irish cause and to raise funds on its behalf. Other less permanent organizations were founded to conduct special campaigns as the need arose, such as the American Commission on Irish Independence (1920) and the Irish Relief Fund (1923). The Ancient Order of the Hibernians (AOH) was founded in Ireland to protect the Catholic religion. Its motto was 'Friendship, Unity and Christian Charity'. The AOH was first introduced in the United States about 1836 as a secret benevolent organization and was organized in San Francisco in March 1869.[63] By 1880, there were ten divisions who met in the Hibernian Hall once a week.[64]

De Valera attended the Fifty-Third Annual Convention of the AOH and Ladies' Auxiliary, in July 1919, held in San Francisco at the Exposition Auditorium. Mrs Mary McWhorter, president of the Ladies' Auxiliary, announced a goal of five million individual investors in Irish Republic bond certificates. The women of the Auxiliary worked nationally for the Irish cause in support of de Valera.[65]

San Francisco Fenianism continued on in the Knights of the Red Branch (KRB) as a branch of the Irish Confederation. Founded in 1869, they were dedicated to 'principle, honour and virtue'.[66] The KRB rented a hall on Market Street, opposite what is now Grant Avenue, and furnished it with a library, billiard tables, gymnasium and established the first Gaelic School in the United States. They later assisted Yorke when he organized the California Gaelic League.[67] Many mass meetings and fund-raising events were held in their new hall at 1133 Mission Street. Records of the KRB, a secret organization, have not survived.

The Cumann na Ban held meetings, with a focus on teaching the Irish language and history, in the KRB Hall on the second and fourth Thursdays of each month. They urged that 'all women of Irish blood should as far as they are able, assist our Volunteers at home and abroad to carry on the good work'.[68]

During his visit to San Francisco in November 1919, de Valera set up a state branch of the American Commission on Irish Independence. In February 1920, Archbishop Edward J. Hanna was appointed as Honorary Chair of the San Francisco Executive Committee of the ACII in charge of the sale of the bond certificates, ranging from $10 to $10,000. The AOH and the Ladies' Auxiliary, the United Irish Societies (UIS), the FOIF and clergy supported the ACII.[69] The ACII California bond-certificate drive surpassed its quota of $1,500,000 by March 1920 and set a new goal of $2,000,000. Although the drive officially concluded on March 17, the canvass continued in most of the state.[70]

The San Francisco Women's State Executive Committee of the ACII established their headquarters on the main floor of the Palace Hotel. They held their first meeting in the Knights of Columbus Auditorium, 150 Golden Gate Avenue, on February 26 1920, to promote the sale of bond certificates. The Honorable Andrew J. Gallagher stated that five hundred ladies had volunteered to canvass the city on behalf of the drive.[71] Father Yorke, principal speaker of the evening, commented to the hall, which was packed to capacity, that 'the Irish women of California . . . must be prepared to put forth their best efforts in the coming bond certificate drive, for the task was the most important thing they had ever been asked to aid'. He explained that the Irish people for the 'first time were being asked to help finance an Irish nation'.[72]

The Women's Irish Education League (WIEL) was organized in

May 1919 to provide on-going education on the Irish cause. By 1922, the WIEL had a membership of over 2,000 Americans and Irish-Americans, men and women. The WIEL promoted political activism, such as anti-British picketing, boycotting English goods and media protests. The League sponsored the labour publication *The Rank and File*, first published on May Day, 1920.[73] They sponsored not only mass meetings, but also fund-raising events such as 'Old-Fashioned Irish Nights' with dancing, food and Irish entertainment, whist and dancing, and 'parlour meetings' in the homes of members.[74] The meeting speakers and their subjects focused on educating 'Americans on the Irish question and its people'. These included Kathleen O'Brennan and Minnie McCarthy on 'Women in the Irish Republic'; author Horace A. Wade on 'The Spirit of '76'; Rev Stanislaus Dempsey on 'The Irish Character Analyzed'; Professor B. H. Lehman, University of California, on 'Writers of the Irish Revolution'.[75]

Charlotte Anita Whitney[76] and Minnie McCarthy presided at a meeting of 1,500 women of the WIEL, on May 22 1919, in the Native Sons' Hall to support the cause of Irish freedom. In accordance with a vote, telegrams were sent to Senator James D. Phelan, Senator Hiram Johnson, the President of the Senate, and the Speaker of the House asking that no peace treaty be ratified that did not include recognition of the Irish Republic. Kathleen O'Brennan, sister-in-law of Eamonn Ceannt and a Dublin newspaper woman, spoke on 'Women in the Irish Republic'.[77]

More than 500 women of the WIEL met at the St Francis Hotel, on June 9, to elect permanent officers and formulate plans for a statewide campaign to inform the public of Ireland's demands for independence and to spread the truth about Ireland. Their headquarters was set up in the Phelan Building, Room 1068.[78] The *San Francisco Chronicle* reported that 'their work was national in scope and international in character'. They pledged political, moral and financial support to aid Ireland to gain full independence as well as recognition of the Irish Republic.[79]

Kathleen O'Brennan left San Francisco, on June 14 1919, to tour Nevada and enlist new members to increase the strength and effectiveness of the WIEL. On her return to San Francisco, the WIEL held a meeting at the St Francis Hotel on July 14. Kathleen reported the founding of several branches of the WIEL in Nevada. She asked that help from the United States to Ireland not be given as a gift, but in payment for the freedom the Irish helped America win in 1776.[80]

The WIEL invited the general public to a mass meeting at the Dreamland Rink, on Steiner Street, between Sutter and Post, on September 12 1919, to present arguments on the League of Nations question. The purpose was not to plead the Irish cause, but to give the women of the city an understanding of the pro and con issues connected with the League. Mrs Ida Finney Mackrille, San Francisco suffragist, opened the discussion with arguments favouring the League. Mrs Fred H. Colburn, lecturer and author, and Annie Laurie of the *Examiner* presented the opposition.[81]

To protest the incarceration of Terence MacSwiney, Lord Mayor of Cork, by the British, sixteen members of the WIEL prevented the loading of the British steamer *Muncaster Castle* on September 8 1920. They convinced thirty longshoremen to walk off the job and appealed to them to boycott all British vessels. They pointed out that longshoremen in New York and Boston had taken similar actions. The banners carried by the pickets read: 'You Are Not Dependent Upon England—Let Her Do Her Own Dirty Work', and 'Every Pound Handled For an English Vessel Has Blood on It—the Blood of Brother Irish Workers'. The pamphlets they distributed warned:

> Workers of San Francisco, every pound you put aboard or take off an English vessel has blood on it, the blood of brother workers in Ireland. Don't get blood on your hands. Don't help a government that starves men to death. Terence MacSwiney is starving to death that others may live as free men.[82]

The WIEL published and distributed a pamphlet calling for the boycott of English goods, 'To Stop Atrocities in Ireland, Discrimination Against American Shipping, and the Opium Trade'. They asked that Shell Oil products, Colgate products, Scotch Shortbread, Eton's Highland Linen Stationery, Colman's Mustard, Lea & Perrins Sauce, Dundee Marmalade, Cheddar cheese and other British products not be used. They contended that traditionally, 'trade follows the flag', but more correctly 'the flag follows trade' so 'show that the Stars and Stripes are good enough for you—'.[83]

Marie C. Dillon, Executive Secretary of the WIEL, forwarded to *The Monitor* a letter sent to E. D. Coblentz, managing editor of *The San Francisco Examiner*, in protest of the 'very anti-Irish attitude' in which the proceedings of the Dáil were reported by Hayden Talbot and other *Examiner* correspondents in Dublin. The WIEL claimed that the reports indicated the 'enormous significance of what English controlled cables would mean to Ireland'.[84]

The women of San Francisco responded to the needs of the Republic of Ireland by organizing several different groups to actively work at all levels from door-to-door canvassing to organizing meetings and fund-raising events. Newspaper coverage of their activities, however, diminished after de Valera returned to Ireland.

THE MIDWEST

Learning of the Black and Tan attack and the burning of the city of Cork on December 10 1920, the American Red Cross offer of help to the people of Cork and the subsequent British Red Cross refusal, the Celtic Cross Association was formed in Chicago. It was incorporated under the state laws of Illinois and set up a yearly membership fee of $1.00. All preliminary administrative costs were paid out of a 'Founders' fund furnished by contributors. In effect, this freed up all other contributed money to relief work. The officers were Mary F. McWhorter, president; Mrs McGivney, secretary; and Mrs Annie Johnson, treasurer. The Bishop of Killaloe, Dr Fogerty, distributed the fund in Ireland.[85]

DE VALERA RETURNS TO IRELAND

John A. Murphy, in *Ireland in the Twentieth Century*, states that de Valera's eighteen-month American tour was an enormous financial and personal success and at the same time a failure because of dissensions in Irish-American leadership, the failure to secure official American recognition of the Irish Republic and the failure to secure a voice at the Peace Conference.[86]

De Valera was smuggled aboard the S.S. *Celtic* and left the United States in December 1920 to return to Ireland. At the time of his departure to Ireland, although the eastern Irish American leadership suffered, the AARIR in the west rapidly grew in support and unity under the leadership of Joseph Scott and Father Peter Yorke.

The legacy of the division between de Valera and the Irish-American community continued long after his return to Ireland. The elimination of the FOIF on the West Coast and its reduction of power and membership on the East Coast, would affect the lecture tours of the Irish Republican women who began their tours after his departure: Mary MacSwiney, Mrs Muriel MacSwiney, Hanna Sheehy Skeffington's second tour, Countess Markievicz, Margaret Pearse and Mary MacSwiney's second tour. Their press coverage, the size of the audiences attending the lectures and the funds raised all suffered.

THE ANGLO-IRISH TREATY AND THE IRISH-AMERICAN SPLIT

On December 6 1921, the British and Irish Republic representatives signed the 'Articles of Agreement for a Treaty between Great Britain and Ireland'. Dáil Éireann split on the issue of the Treaty immediately. The Anglo-Irish Treaty (London Treaty) was accepted, on January 7 1922, by a vote of sixty-four to fifty-seven and the Irish Free State Government was established. The six women Dáil Éireann deputies unanimously opposed the Treaty.[87] De Valera and his cabinet resigned.

Anti-Treatyites supported de Valera's alternative to the Treaty, Document No. Two, which promoted his idea of external association (Ireland within the states of an English Commonwealth), omitting the oath and the provision for a governor-general, and mention of the King only as head of the 'association'. Pro-Treatyites accepted Dominion status and a post-Treaty Boundary Commission that would redefine the border of Northern Ireland.[88] Although de Valera claimed the majority of people were opposed to the Treaty, the initial first reaction of most people was favourable and there was relief that a settlement had been reached and a feeling that independence would come.[89] January to June 1922 became a period of confusion and conflict between the 'Treatyites' and 'anti-Treatyites'.

Armed clashes between the opposing groups eventually broke into Civil War on June 28 1922, lasting until April 10 1923, when the republicans laid down their arms. With no amnesty granted them, the republicans went 'on the run to avoid arrest'. During the years of the Irish Free State Government, 1923–1932, William T. Cosgrave, a participant in the 1916 Easter Rising, headed the pro-Treatyite Cumann na nGaedheal conservative government.[90]

The events of 1921–23 profoundly affected the Irish-American republican nationalist campaigns of the FOIF and the AARIR, and further split Irish-American leadership. The FOIF and Devoy and Cohalan strongly supported the Irish Free State Government. The

Clan and Joseph McGarrity remained loyal to de Valera and the Irish Republic. The AARIR, particularly in California, continued to support de Valera and the Irish Republic. Father Yorke maintained that the AARIR had to remain active for the Irish Republic.

During a general convention of Clan na Gael in Boston, July 13–14, the League of Nations and the World Court were denounced. The Free State Government was accepted with the reservation that it 'would not be regarded as a final settlement and that work for the establishment of an Irish Republic and the unity of the Free State and the North of Ireland must continue. DeValera and his associates were strongly denounced'.[91]

The AOH had supported the FIOF and the Easter Rising. They collected money in support of the dependants of those who had died during the Rising or were in prison. During the War of Independence, they supported Dáil Éireann and the Irish Republican Army. First de Valera's split with the FIOF and the subsequent formation of the AARIR and then the Anglo-Irish Treaty caused a split within the organization.[92] The AOH supported Cosgrave and the Free State Government, while the Ladies' Auxiliary of the AOH supported de Valera and the Irish Republic.

During the AOH National Convention in Montreal on July 16, Eamon de Valera and 'his followers' were denounced. The Irish Free State was 'approved of, with the reservation that the new condition [the Treaty and creation of the Free State Government] was accepted only as a step towards complete independence'.[93]

In a letter in 1923 to Judge Daniel Cohalan, P. T. O'Sullivan, Chairman of the AOH of Illinois, spoke of de Valera and Mrs McWhorter, National President of the Ladies' Auxiliary of the AOH:

> Well, things don't seem to grow much better in Ireland. Is it not amazing that so many of the Irish people can be found to be misled and fooled by such a demon as DeValera. John Devoy was correct in saying that he is the worst influence that ever appeared on the state of Irish politics. You certainly measured him up properly before he was many days in this country. There is still a small element of radical Bolshevists here in Chicago, shouting for him. They are led by Mrs McWhorter. She, I believe, is entirely selfish in the matter as, for some years past, she has made well on Irish affairs and she is now desperately fighting to hold her place.[94]

The Ladies' Auxiliary of the AOH conversely adopted a resolution at their national meeting held in Washington D.C. on January 27:

> Resolved. That we send our congratulations to the newly organized International Irish League of the World organized in Paris, France, and pledge it and its president, Eamon de Valera, the support and assistance to bring about the ultimate realization of the hopes and aspirations of the Irish people, a free and absolutely independent Ireland.[95]

In a public statement they pronounced their support of the Irish Republic and 'in full sympathy with their Irish sisters in Ireland, who are equally outspoken for the full, unqualified and absolute independence of their native land'. The Cumann na mBan's proclamation of support of the Irish Republic during their convention in Dublin on February 5 was viewed as 'a bugle call to the women of Ireland to manifest that zeal and spirit of self-sacrifice which they have always displayed in every good cause worthy of their support'.[96]

At the close of the Irish Civil War, a second bond certificate drive was launched, but financial and political support no longer existed. At the Second Annual Convention of the AARIR in San Francisco, on February 22 1922, Yorke resigned because of his inability to cope with the confusing conditions in Ireland and its effect on the California AARIR. The AARIR never regained the strength in California that it had before the 1921 Anglo-Irish Treaty.[97]

With de Valera's loss of the Irish Civil War, many Irish republican families became destitute when family members suffered imprisonment. During July 1923, branches of the AARIR, along with organizations of the United Irish Societies, were revitalized to aid in a campaign to provide relief for the families of more than 16,000 Irish republicans held in Free State prisons. Campaign headquarters for the California Irish Relief Fund (IRF) were opened in Room 202 of the Grant Building in San Francisco. On October 1 1923, Father Yorke launched the San Francisco IRF campaign at a mass meeting at the Hibernian Hall.[98]

The 1921 Treaty, the establishment of the Irish Free State Government and the Irish Civil War affected Irish republicanism nationwide. According to Alan J. Ward, in *Ireland and Anglo-American Relations*, many Americans who supported Ireland did not understand the 'distinctions between limited autonomy, that is home rule, Dominion status, or complete republican independence'. In addition:

> The record shows that the American press lost interest in Ireland in 1922, that there was a great diminution in the amount of political material flowing into the State Department from its agents in Ireland, although atrocities in Ireland were well documented, and that in 1922 the American government exchanged agents with the Irish Free State without significant opposition in the United States.[99]

Reaction to the Treaty and the Civil War differed strongly between the Eastern and the Western sections of the United States—shown by the formation of new supportive organizations to aid the Republic of Ireland in the West. Support grew in conservative Middle America, but not to the extent of either the East or the West.

These conditions had a direct effect, particularly on the second lecture tours of Mary MacSwiney and of Hanna Sheehy Skeffington with Kathleen Boland and Linda Kearns. Countess Markievicz and Mrs Margaret Pearse were able to draw large crowds to their lectures in spite of the existing conditions, because the American press enhanced their romantic images.

Eventually, De Valera's defeat in the Irish Civil War brought changes to the AARIR, but did not cause its collapse. According to Timothy J. Sarbaugh, 'By 1925, the AARIR, the last vestige of Irish republicanism in California, lost all of its political activism and became de Valera's personal collective society'.[100] The AARIR and its cause survived into the 1930s, although Yorke died in 1925.[101]

CHAPTER 3

The Wilson Administration vs Irish-American Leaders, 1916–19

THE POLITICAL PROBLEMS faced by Irish-American leaders and Hanna Sheehy Skeffington, Mary MacSwiney, Mrs Muriel MacSwiney, Countess Markievicz and Mrs Margaret Pearse during their lecture tours in the United States relate not only to the tensions during the years 1916–1920, but go back to the 1880s. The early conflicts between President Woodrow Wilson and Judge Daniel Cohalan and John Devoy escalated and spread throughout the Irish-American organizations and the Wilson Administration during World War I, throughout the time of the treaty negotiations at the Peace Conference in Paris, culminating in the rejection of the Versailles Peace Treaty and the League of Nations by the United States Senate. Discord continued after the war with the administration's indifference to extensive American press reports of atrocities committed by the British Army, in particular the Black and Tans and the Auxiliaries, in Ireland during the Irish War of Independence.

Underlying issues combined to greatly affect American public reaction, both Irish-Americans and those of other ancestry, to the lecture tours. The continuing struggle of labour unions versus big business and government, combined with the growing fear of socialism and communism, all supported a general unrest. The planned and well-publicized eradication of the International Workers of the World (IWW) became part of the tension. Hanna Sheehy Skeffington's friendship with politically active women during her first tour caused her negative public reaction and criticism at times. American newspapers nationwide, particularly during Hanna's first tour, featured large headlines pertaining to both the IWW and to the

Tom Mooney trial. A carry-over of the same problems had an adverse effect at times on Mary MacSwiney's tour in 1920. Confusion over the Anglo-Irish Treaty and the Irish Civil War and a split in Irish-American leadership influenced Muriel MacSwiney's tour in the United States and brought her criticism and little press coverage. Countess Markievicz's tour lasted only two months before Eamon de Valera recalled her to Ireland due to worsening wartime conditions. The American press praised her elegance and mystique and her positive romantic public image survived. When Mrs Margaret Pearse came to the United States to raise funds for Patrick's school, St Enda's in Dublin, she was praised as a true picture of motherhood.

England's active propaganda in the United States influenced Americans in all walks of life. England zealously courted the United States as an ally during World War I. This propaganda continued in intensity during the Peace Conference after the war, during the signing of the Anglo-Irish Treaty and during the Civil War in support of the Irish Free State Government.

The fear of socialism and unionization of labour had begun during the rise of capitalism in the United States before the turn of the century. The unrest caused by miners' strikes, such as the Molly Maguires in the 1880s, and of the threatened invasion of Canada by the Fenians in the 1860s and 1870s were not that distant. The Russian Revolution against imperialism deeply troubled England. They already had trouble in Ireland—would India be next? That same fear of communism plagued the United States for many years to come.

PRESIDENTIAL CAMPAIGN—1916

New York Supreme Court Justice Daniel F. Cohalan, a member of Clan na Gael, had participated in American politics as an adviser to Charles F. Murphy, leader of Tammany Hall (the Democratic Party machine in New York City with a reputation for corrupt business practices). Murphy opposed Woodrow Wilson's nomination for President at the Democratic convention in Baltimore, Maryland in 1912. Four years later, during the Presidential campaign of 1916, Cohalan supported Wilson's Republican opponent, Charles Evans Hughes and the Wilson-Cohalan/Devoy feud began.[1]

Before the United States entered World War I and was officially neutral, both FIOF leaders, Daniel Cohalan and John Devoy, editor of *The Gaelic American*, opposed President Wilson's foreign policy.

After America entered the war in April 1917, the animosity between the Wilson administration and Irish American leaders escalated. The FIOF worked to keep the United States out of war up to April 1917. After the US entered the war, Cohalan warned Irish-Americans to give their country full support. However, President Wilson denounced Cohalan and Devoy as 'hyphenates' who had been disloyal to the United States.[2] Charles Tansill in *America and the Fight for Irish Freedom* alleges:

> In dealing with the actions of the Wilson Administration, it should be kept clearly in mind that the President was usually quite willing to use his vast powers to prevent any possibility of the erection of an Irish Republic. Home Rule, upon conditions prescribed by the British Government, was as far as he was inclined to go. With regard to outstanding Irish-Americans, we have seen that he permitted Secretary [Robert] Lansing [State Department] to forge very dubious evidence in an attempt to encompass their ruin. Forgery soon became an accepted practice in certain branches of the government.
>
> In this regard, the agents of the United States Secret Service earned a questionable reputation. They were unceasing in their attempts to furnish evidence that would seriously compromise Irish-Americans and certain Irish patriots who kept alive their dream of an Irish Republic.[3]

US Secret Service agents raided the office of the German Consul General in New York City on April 18 1916. They allegedly captured correspondence of Daniel Cohalan and John Devoy to Berlin revealing the date of the Easter Rising. The US State Department turned it over to the British Embassy. Although Cohalan denied it, a message, allegedly sent at Cohalan's request from the Germany Embassy in New York to Berlin outlining Easter Rising strategy, was among the seized documents.[4]

SIR ROGER CASEMENT

The case of Sir Roger Casement further accelerated Irish-American discord with Wilson and his administration. Casement retired from the British Foreign Service in August 1913 and returned to Ireland to work in the nationalist movement. Because of his dislike for Americans, he believed Germany was best suited to help Ireland's cause. Casement had played an important role in the gun running at Howth, Ireland, on July 26 1914, by persuading his friends to furnish half the funds needed to purchase guns and ammunition in Germany.

In order to raise funds for the Irish Volunteers, Casement travelled to the United States to enlist Clan na Gael support. He went on to Germany in October 1914 in an attempt to persuade the German Government to provide armament to Ireland. He also hoped to raise an Irish Brigade from Irish prisoners in German camps who would return to Ireland to fight for Irish freedom. This plan failed.

Casement did not support the Easter Rising and believed the only way he could save Ireland was to stop the Rising. He requested that the German Government furnish a submarine to facilitate his return to Ireland. He and two companions landed along the coast in County Kerry on April 21. After his landing craft was discovered and reported to the police, he was arrested, taken to Dublin, imprisoned in the Tower of London, tried for treason and sentenced to death.[5]

In an attempt to save Casement, eight US Congressmen petitioned Wilson to intervene with the British Government. In addition, the United States Senate adopted a resolution requesting that President Wilson convey their request for clemency for Casement to the British Government. Delivery of the resolution to the White House, then to the State Department and also to the American Embassy in London was delayed to the extent that it reached the British Foreign Office at the very time of the execution of Casement.[6] John Devoy reacted to this tragic delay by launching an attack on President Wilson in his newspaper, *The Gaelic American*:

> That President Wilson hates the Irish with the implacable hatred of the Ulster Orangeman—the stock he comes of—has been shown so many times since he became President that there can be no successful denial.[7]

THE IWW, SOCIALISM, TOM MOONEY AND THE RED SCARE

The 'Red Scare' in America, the on-going efforts of big business to suppress and/or eradicate labour unions, and fear, particularly of the Industrial Workers of the World (IWW), contributed to political tensions during the tours of Hanna Sheehy Skeffington and Mary MacSwiney. The front pages of the newspapers across the United States during this period carried bold headlines of IWW tactics and prosecutions. A large number of the members of the IWW were Irish loggers and mine workers. The IWW, known as Wobblies and defenders of the syndicalist doctrine, was organized in 1905 as a society of workers using a policy of direct action: strikes, boycotts, propaganda. The union endorsed Karl Marx's theory of class struggle between workers and capitalists. The IWW later utilized collective bargaining, but continued the use of strikes.

Tom Mooney, arrested in San Francisco in 1916, for setting off a bomb that killed ten people and injured forty, was convicted and sentenced to hang. The trials of Mooney, his wife, Rena, and Warren Billings, his associate, captured front-page headlines and coverage across the United States for several years. Mooney, Irish, a socialist, pacifist, and labour organizer, along with Rena and Billings, was attempting to unionize a division of the United Railroads in San Francisco. In spite of indisputable evidence contradicting his guilt, Mooney fought for twenty-two years against the elaborate frame-up that held him in the San Quentin Prison. California Governor Culbert Olson granted Mooney a pardon just after taking office in January 1939.

With a watchful eye to Russia and the Russian Revolution, the fear of Bolshevists and Socialists ran rampant in 1919–20 in America. Communism began to spread among liberal Americans, particularly those foreign-born. However, at their peak there were only about 60,000 Socialists in the United States in 1919.[8]

Hanna Sheehy Skeffington and Mary MacSwiney came under Secret Service surveillance of their activities, particularly their lectures. Their movements were followed and stenographic notes taken of their lectures. The records of their surveillance are contained in the Department of Justice files under the heading of 'Bolsheviks and Socialists'. No evidence of subversive activities or comments made by them was ever recorded.[9]

It must be noted that, while in the United States, Hanna Sheehy Skeffington established and maintained contact with labour activist Elizabeth Gurley Flynn and political activist Marie Equi, both members of the IWW. Hanna continued her close friendship with Alice Paul, a militant leader of the suffragist movement and founder of the National Women's Party. Other friends and acquaintances included Dr Gertrude Kelly and Katherine Lecky, of New York, Jane Addams, founder of Hull House in Chicago, and Emma Goldman, anarchist and organizer of the 'No Conscription League' during World War I.[10] She also held a meeting in San Francisco in support of Tom Mooney in 1918.

HANNA SHEEHY SKEFFINGTON AND PRESIDENT WILSON

Based on her visit with President Wilson in January 1918 to present him with a Cumann na mBan petition for Ireland's right to self-determination, Hanna Sheehy Skeffington was often asked to comment on President Wilson's personality. She would say that:

> It is an extremely complex one, and one that has been variously judged from every possible angle. I think the President's attitude towards progress may best be illustrated by his action upon a matter of internal American policy, namely: The Women's Suffrage Federal Amendment. It tends to show that while President Wilson is not of the type of the lone pioneer who would push ahead on a forlorn hope against any odds, he is guided usually by what one may call a policy of enlightened expedience, and there is no statesman in the world to-day who knows better the exact time to come in on the right side and to press a reform home to a successful issue, when the demand becomes imperative and insistent.[11]

Referring to President Wilson's stand on American support for self-determination for Ireland, Hanna believed:

> President Wilson is not the type that will lead, pioneer-like, a forlorn hope, or stake all on a desperate enterprise; but, on the other hand, he is one who by tradition (he has Irish blood in his veins) and by temperament, will see the need of self-determination for Ireland as well as for other nations. There will be sufficient pressure at home to keep the Irish question well in the forefront, and 'if only Ireland shows herself strongly for this solution', President Wilson cannot turn a deaf ear. As an American his view is naturally more sympathetic than even the most enlightened English view. Moreover, America is out, as he says, to see justice done all round, and it would be therefore a point of honour to see that such even-handed justice is meted out to all alike.[12]

Other than a few brief comments, Hanna never disclosed the subjects she discussed with the President during the meeting at the White House, nor any of his comments.

US POSTAL SERVICE SUSPENDS IRISH-AMERICAN MAILING PRIVILEGES

The Washington Post reported on January 22 1918 that, pending an investigation, US Post Office authorities in New York had refused mailing privileges to the *Irish World*, *The Gaelic American*, and the *New York Freeman's Journal*, 'three of the leading weekly publications in this country espousing the cause of Irish independence'. Robert E. Ford, editor of the *Irish World*, evidently believed the Cumann na mBan petition presented to President Wilson provided the excuse needed to quiet the Irish-American press when he stated: 'We were informed unofficially that the only reason for the Post Office Department's action was that all three publications published simultaneously a reproduction of a petition signed by the Irishwomen's council of Dublin, which was presented to President Wilson by Hanna Sheehy Skeffington on January 11 last'.[13] However, the Post Office Department attorney determined the three Irish-American newspapers to be in violation of the Espionage Act and approved the decision of the New York Postmaster to exclude their second-class mailing privileges.[14]

THE THIRD IRISH RACE CONVENTION, FEBRUARY 1918

The Third Irish Race Convention in Philadelphia, February 22–23 1918, drafted a resolution which called for the Paris Peace Conference to ' "apply to Ireland the great doctrine of national self-determination" and to recognize the right of the people of Ireland to select for themselves, without interference, the form of government under which they wished to live'.[15] A delegation made up of prominent Irish-American leaders was appointed to call on Joseph Tumulty, President Wilson's private secretary, to pressure him to arrange a meeting with the President. These were: Judge John J. Goff, Judge Daniel F. Cohalan, ex-governor Edward F. Dunne, Frank P. Walsh, Michael J. Ryan, Eugene F. Kinkead, Michael Francis Doyle, James K. McGuire and seventeen others.[16]

Tumulty had warned President Wilson not to ignore the Irish or the Irish-Americans. He warned that the Irish-American political strength, which had grown, posed a danger to the Democratic Party and to the President's own career. Tumulty felt that 'a refusal would play into the hands of the Sinn Féin element in America'.[17]

Illustrating the level to which the feud between Wilson and Cohalan had risen, the President agreed to meet the Irish-American delegation at the New York Metropolitan Opera House on March 3. However, at the last minute, he learned that Cohalan was in attendance and refused to appear. When the committee members learned of the situation, they unanimously declared that they would not permit Cohalan to leave the meeting alone. Before Cohalan left, he stated that 'the cause is bigger than any one man; the cause is bigger than I am. For its sake I will leave the room without question'.[18] The President then informed the delegation that he was unable to intervene in the domestic policy of other governments. Referring to the Irish question, he later told Ray Stannard Baker, a close friend, 'they [the Irish-American delegation] were so insistent . . . that I had hard work keeping my temper'. He later told David Hunter Miller, an American staff member of the Peace Conference delegation, that his first impulse had been to 'tell the Irish-Americans to go to hell'.[19]

On the other hand, when it became clear that Irish-Americans were suspicious of the League of Nations and unenthusiastic about the Treaty of Versailles, the President began to worry about their power in both the House and Senate. Prudently, he agreed to send an emissary, George Creel, formerly head of the War Information Bureau, to Ireland in February to investigate conditions. However, at the same time the President stated he was not prepared to quarrel with wartime allies over seating Ireland at the Peace Conference.[20]

Creel found during his meeting with Michael Collins and Harry Boland in Ireland that they were 'more reasonable in their demands than many Irish-Americans'. He reported to the President in March that the Sinn Féin victory in 1918 had been complete and felt that:

> The old Irish Party and Home Rule were thoroughly repudiated, although the leaders of Sinn Féin were not at that time completely serious in their demands for an Irish republic. If the British government would institute dominion status with county options for Ulster, it would be 'accepted as a satisfactory adjustment of the situation. However, if it is not done within the next two months, sentiment in Ireland and America will harden in favour of an Irish republic'.[21]

Creel also believed that an Irish settlement was crucial to the President in view of the power of the Irish-American lobby.[22]

AMERICAN COMMISSION ON IRISH INDEPENDENCE AND THE PARIS PEACE CONFERENCE: 1919

Irish-Americans believed that when World War I ended, President Wilson would live up to his promise of self-determination for all small nations, including Ireland. Disappointingly, when Senators James Phelan, of California, and Thomas J. Walsh, of Montana, petitioned the President for his support, they found his 'replies were polite but vague; he was aware of the problem, he would do what he could, but he must wait to see what opportunities presented themselves in Paris'. Consequently, the officers of the Irish Race Convention and a committee of twenty-five selected three distinguished Irish-Americans to serve on the American Commission on Irish Independence: Frank P. Walsh, New York attorney; Edward F. Dunne, former Governor of Illinois; and Michael J. Ryan, Public Service Commissioner in Philadelphia and former national president of the United Irish League of America. The committee, serving as the Irish-American delegation at the Paris Peace Conference, developed three objectives: to obtain safe conduct for Dáil Éireann members Eamon de Valera, Arthur Griffith and Count George Noble Plunkett, to Paris to plead the Irish cause at the Peace Conference; to plead the Irish cause themselves if safe conduct could not be obtained; and to work for the recognition of the Irish Republic.[23]

Michael J. Ryan attempted to unify Irish-Americans in a demand to the President that he insist the British issue passports to de Valera, Griffith and Count Plunkett to travel to Paris. He also insisted the President demand the Irish be allowed to sign the Peace Treaty separate from the British. In spite of all their efforts, the 'Irish problem' caused bitter feelings among some members of the American Peace Commission who felt it was a mistake to promote Irish recognition during the conference when it could be settled later by the League of Nations. Regrettably, meetings with the President on April 17 and again on June 11, the visit of the American Commission to Ireland during May, and the Senate resolution passed on June 6 supporting the admission of the Irish Republic representatives at the Peace Conference all produced no positive results.[24]

SUPPORT FROM THE US SENATE AND HOUSE OF REPRESENTATIVES

Irish-American legislators and their supporters attempted a series of resolutions in support of the American Commission on Irish Independence during the Paris Peace Conference. Thomas Gallagher of Illinois submitted Joint Resolution No. 357 in the House of Representatives (to be voted on in early March 1919) which requested members of the Peace Conference to 'favourably consider the claims of Ireland to the right of self-determination'. Senator James Phelan introduced a similar resolution in the Senate.[25]

The Phelan resolution remained in the Senate. However, House Concurrent Resolution No. 68 was substituted for House Joint Resolution No. 357:

> That it is the earnest hope of the Congress of the United States of America, that the Peace Conference now sitting at Paris and passing upon the rights of various peoples will favourably consider the claims of Ireland to self-determination.[26]

This new resolution was passed by 216 to 45 votes on March 4. However, it was passed too late to be voted on by the Senate.[27]

AMERICAN COMMISSION FOR IRISH INDEPENDENCE IN IRELAND

The members of the American Commission for Irish Independence were granted passports to travel to Ireland from Paris to meet with the leaders of the Irish Republic in order to later 'enlighten American opinion'.[28] They arrived in Dublin on May 3 1919 and travelled throughout Ireland. Generally they spoke on: 'Irish Independence from Britain, on an Irish republic, on the American model of republicanism, on the Allied war aims concerning small nations and self-determination, and on the powers of the Dáil Government derived from the 1918 election'.[29]

Their comments on these subjects produced strong adverse reactions from the British. The American Ambassador in London, John W. Davis, reported that Michael Ryan was:

> on all occasions [during the visit of the delegation to Ireland] violent and once or twice advocated action similar to that adopted in Easter Week in 1916. Messrs Walsh and Dunne, I understand, although they did not advocate armed rebellion, missed no opportunity of stating that they represented over 20,000,000 of American people, all ready to help to their utmost in assisting Ireland to achieve its objective—i.e. an Irish Republic.[30]

Wilson and his administration now had evidence to justify their refusal of support for Irish self-determination. And they once again succumbed to British pressure to stay closely allied to England's position that the problems with Ireland were internal ones.

When the Irish-American delegation persisted in their requests to meet with the President, Frank Walsh and Edward Dunne were granted an interview with him on June 11 during which he made the following 'fork-tongued' statement concerning Irish self-determination:

> You have touched on the great metaphysical tragedy of today. When I gave utterance to those words I said them without the knowledge that nationalities existed which are coming to us day after day. Of course, Ireland's case, from the point of view of population, from the point of view of the struggle it has made, from the point of interest it has excited in the world, and especially among our own people, whom I am anxious to serve, is the outstanding case of a small nationality. You do not know and cannot appreciate the anxieties I have experienced as the result of these many millions of people having their hopes raised by what I have said.[31]

On June 28 1919 the Peace Treaty with Germany was signed at Versailles. The Friends of Irish Freedom had appointed John A. Murphy of Buffalo as a supplementary member of the Commission; however, he arrived in Paris after the signing. On July 22, he requested an audience with Premier Clemenceau, but never received an answer. The work of the Irish delegation was complete.[32]

During the months the Irish-American delegates were in Paris, Colonel House tried over and over to secure a meeting of the delegates with Lloyd George to discuss safe conduct for the Dublin Dáil Éireann members in Paris to attend the conference. Each meeting was postponed until time ran out and the Irish-Americans returned to the United States.

AMERICAN COMMISSION ON CONDITIONS IN IRELAND, NOVEMBER 1920—JANUARY 1921

The American press began reporting in detail the atrocities committed in Ireland during the Anglo-Irish War, particularly after the arrival of the Black and Tans and the Auxiliaries. In reaction to the conditions in Ireland, pacifist Oswald Garrison Villard, editor of *The Nation*, created a Committee of One Hundred and Fifty. From the Committee, an American Commission on Conditions in Ireland was formed to hear testimony of witnesses who knew first-hand the conditions in Ireland. The Commission held hearings in Washington D.C. from November 18 1920 to January 21 1921.

Donal O'Callaghan, Lord Mayor of Cork, was called on by the Commission to testify to the destruction and murder in Cork by British troops and the Black and Tans. O'Callaghan became Lord Mayor of Cork after the death of Lord Mayor Terence MacSwiney.[33] Afraid of what he would report, British officials refused to grant him a passport. Daringly, he became a stowaway on board a ship, the *West Cannon*, headed for Newport News, Virginia.[34] His arrival caused turmoil within the Wilson administration and was reported daily on the front page of many newspapers across America.

After US Immigration officials discovered him, Secretary of Labor W. B. Wilson called in the State Department to investigate the circumstances surrounding his arrival. O'Callaghan was held in custody in Newport News until a decision could be made by one of the US departments.[35]

A tug of war for power and control began when the State Department refused to waive the passport requirement. Acting Secretary of State Norman H. Davis sidestepped any responsibility for dealing with O'Callaghan and passed the responsibility to Secretary of Labor Wilson:

> I beg to advise you that the Department does not feel that it is in a position to make in favour of Mr O'Callaghan an exception to the rule against allowing aliens to enter the United States without properly visaed passports. I, accordingly, respectfully request you to take the necessary steps in order to effect Mr O'Callaghan's deportation from the United States.
>
> Your Department is doubtless familiar with the President's Proclamation of August 8 1918, issued pursuant to the Act of Congress approved the 22nd May, 1918 and in connection with the case of Mr O'Callaghan, I beg to invite your attention to the following excerpt from that Proclamation: 'I hereby designate the Secretary of State as the official who shall grant, or in whose name shall be granted, permission to aliens to depart from or enter the United States.'[36]

Secretary Davis issued a written request for the deportation of O'Callaghan. The deportation was then referred to President Wilson to decide. The President referred it to his cabinet officers 'to iron out the inter-departmental difficulties'.[37]

Ignoring the State Department's order to deport O'Callaghan, Secretary Wilson granted him permission to land as a seaman. He would be 'permitted to land for the purpose of re-shipping on board any vessel bound for any foreign port or place, unless the Secretary of State directs that he be kept on his vessel'.[38] Secretary Wilson defended his actions in a letter to the State Department:

> There has never been any doubt in my mind about the authority of the Secretary of State to control the passport regulations wherever and whenever passports are required, but the Executive Order which accompanies the Proclamation specifically provides that seamen shall not be required to have passports and places their admission under the jurisdiction of the immigrant inspectors of the Department of Labour. Mr O'Callaghan is a seaman within the express meaning of the term as defined in the immigration laws...and the Executive Order accompanying the President's Proclamation....The identity and nationality of Mr O'Callaghan has been established to the satisfaction of the immigration officials, ...Taking all of the law and the facts into consideration, I can not concur in the judgment of the State Department that Mr O'Callaghan has improperly entered into the United States, or that the law has been violated in this case.[39]

The Lord Mayor was ordered to surrender himself to the Immigration Inspector at Norfolk, Virginia.[40] On January 19, Secretary Wilson issued a formal statement to the Chief of the Immigration Bureau recognizing the jurisdiction of the State Department. However, O'Callaghan's status of 'seaman' was not rescinded.[41]

Secretary Wilson then issued an order that O'Callaghan leave within twenty days, on February 11. Whether he left as a seaman or passenger did not concern the Department of Labor.[42] By February 11, O'Callaghan had already appeared before and given testimony to the American Commission on Conditions in Ireland in Washington D.C.[43]

CONCLUSION

The political tensions in the United States prior to, during, and after World War I impacted the first lecture tours of Hanna Sheehy Skeffington and Mary MacSwiney. Their activities were scrutinized by the Secret Service, who looked for any association with the

Industrial Workers of the World (IWW) or Socialists. At the time of their tours, front-page headlines of major newspapers across the nation featured large-scale efforts of the government to break up the IWW with arrests and convictions of its members. A number of scheduled meetings during their tours were cancelled because the owner(s) of the facility believed them to be Socialists. IWW literature was found on the floor of the hall Hanna spoke in the night she was arrested in San Francisco during her second tour in 1923.

Hanna was able to meet with President Wilson in the White House to present him with a Cumann Na mBan proclamation asking for recognition of the Irish Republic. Although Hanna could not discuss the contents of the meeting, it seems to have been an amicable one. However, within a very short time the mailing privileges of the Irish-American newspapers were suspended by the Post Office.

Beyond the war years themselves, the feud between President Wilson and Judge Daniel Cohalan and John Devoy caused the greatest strain for Irish-Americans during the Paris Peace Conference. Using delay tactics, the Wilson Administration kept 'Irish recognition' out of the Peace Conference. The House and Senate Resolutions were not passed in time to allow either Irish Republican or, in their place, Irish-American representation at the Peace Conference in Paris to argue for self-determination for Ireland. However, Irish-American Congressional leaders gained enough support in the House and Senate to reject the Paris Peace Treaty, including the League of Nations, which the President so strongly supported.

The arrival in the United States of Donal O'Callaghan, the Lord Mayor of Cork, as a stowaway diverted attention away from his purpose in coming to give testimony before the American Commission on Conditions in Ireland. The ensuing battle between the Department of Labor and the Department of State over the status of his arrival and the respective responsibilities of the two departments was covered on the front page of many American newspapers for several days. The confusion, however, did not prevent him from testifying before the Commission in Washington D.C. on the true conditions in Ireland.

In spite of the confusion over the Lord Mayor's passport, the arrival of Mary MacSwiney and Mrs Muriel MacSwiney in the United States to testify before the ACCI received very favourable front-page coverage in many newspapers. Mary's subsequent tour of the United States was given good news coverage in the many cities she visited across the nation.

CHAPTER 4

Hanna Sheehy Skeffington: The Militancy of a Pacifist, January 1917–June 1918

HANNA SHEEHY SKEFFINGTON, widow of Francis Sheehy Skeffington, and an Irish suffragist, was not the first Irish republican woman to visit the United States after the Easter Rising. Min Ryan, Margaret Skinnider, Nellie Gifford and Nora Connolly preceded her in the months immediately following the Rising.[1] However, Hanna, determined to carry on her husband's work as a 'militant pacifist',[2] set aside her work as an Irish suffragist to tour formally as the first successful Irish female nationalist lecturer in the United States.

Hanna's time in the United States was not without discord, prejudice and harassment. She was barred from meeting halls, prevented from speaking publicly, assailed for being a rebel, fanatic, and traitor. The San Francisco police arrested her. The British labelled her a dangerous person, attempted to kidnap and transport her to Canada,[3] refused her a passport to return to Ireland, and attempted to have her detained at the Angel Island immigration station in San Francisco Bay. The threat she posed for the British authorities is told in Hanna's own words:

> The British Agents in the United States are naturally very perturbed at the Irish propaganda on behalf of our small nation. They dislike particularly propaganda of such Irish exiles as myself who had come directly from Ireland, and could speak with first hand knowledge. As one of them observed: 'My objection to Mrs Sheehy Skeffington is that she has a lot of damaging facts.'[4]

The British also sent their own lecturers to the towns and cities she appeared in to speak against Sinn Féin and Ireland.[5]

On the other hand, masses of supporters and well wishers greeted her. The press described her as well educated, refined and a natural and eloquent speaker. She raised a large amount of money for Sinn Féin. Through her lectures, Irish-Americans united to organize additional Friends of Irish Freedom chapters in the United States.

The political climate in the United States at the time of her first visit in 1917–18 was tense and uneasy. The successful British propaganda machine rallied support to their own cause in World War I. Hanna initially spoke on the murder of her husband, Francis, and British militarism. America entered the war on April 6 1917, as an ally of England and the previous Irish-American pro-German position aroused suspicion. At the time of the United States' entry into World War I, Hanna added a new dimension to her lectures. She began to call for United States recognition of the Irish Republic so that Ireland would have a place at the Peace Conference at the end of the war. The advertising for her lectures and the resulting press reports reflected the new focus when the title of her lectures changed from 'British Militarism As I Have Known It' to 'What Does Ireland Want'?[6]

The Department of Justice began their surveillance of her activities in April 1917. Agents of the Bureau of Investigation infiltrated many of her lectures. In the end, they found that her lectures were 'extremely pro-Irish and anti-British but did not attack the United States'. The Military Intelligence Section of the War Department agents agreed on their assessment of Hanna's lectures: 'Her remarks could not be construed in any way as anti-American or anti-ally as she is quite well instructed as to her rights in speech from all appearances'.[7]

Hanna did not confine her lectures to only Irish-American organizations, but spoke to a number of other interest groups. She also made and renewed many lasting friendships during her time in America with other politically active and courageous women: Jane Addams, founder of Hull House in Chicago; Alice Park, suffragist; Elizabeth Gurley Flynn, socialist and IWW activist; Dr Marie Equi, suffragist and sympathizer of the IWW; Emma Goldman, anarchist and organizer of the 'No Conscription League; and Dr Gertrude Kelly and Katherine Lecky of New York.[8]

BACKGROUND

Hanna was no stranger to political activism. Both her father, David Sheehy, MP, and his brother, Father Eugene Sheehy (the 'Land League priest') spent six prison sentences in Tullamore, Mountjoy and Kilmainham jails for their involvement in the Land League and membership of the Irish Republican Brotherhood.[9]

Johanna (Hanna) Mary Sheehy was born on May 24 1877 in County Cork, Ireland. Growing up in a middle class family, Hanna received a Bachelor of Arts degree in modern languages from the Royal University in 1899 and a Master of Arts degree in 1902 by competing for and winning scholarships. She met Francis Skeffington while they both attended the university.[10]

When she married Francis Skeffington, on June 27 1903, they took each other's names to illustrate their commitment to the women's movement. Hanna Sheehy Skeffington helped organize and became active in the Irish Women's Franchise League (IWFL) in 1908. Francis Sheehy Skeffington supported the IWFL as an associate member. They both took an unpopular stand against World War I and Irish conscription.[11]

Both Hanna and Francis developed a militant stand as the suffrage movement in Ireland matured.[12] According to her biographers, Leah Levenson and Jerry Natterstad, 'To Hanna's mind . . . the women's movement would not become an important force without militancy being added to solidarity'. She supported the 'pillar box' attacks of suffragists in which small open bottles containing a black fluid were placed in mailboxes to damage their contents. Along with other members of the IWFL, she was arrested, on June 13 1912, and served a month's sentence in Mountjoy Prison for breaking windows in the General Post Office, the Customs House, the Land Commission Office and Dublin Castle.[13]

Hanna saw no contradiction in using militancy to protest war:

> War destroyed life in order to protect property she [Hanna] said; militants destroyed property in order to enhance the value of life. This being the case, she felt it was her duty as an Irish militant suffragist to make war upon war.[14]

As pacifists, neither Hanna nor Francis took an active part in the 1916 Easter Rising in Dublin. However, they held opposing views as to whether the Rising should have taken place. The rebels knew that success in a battle with the British was not possible. They hoped to take advantage of England's involvement in the war in Europe long enough to enable Ireland to put forth a claim that Ireland be included as a small nation during the peace negotiations at the end of the war. Hanna believed that James Connolly was correct to proceed with the Rising after Eoin MacNeill's countermand. Francis strongly opposed any bloodshed. He had hoped to organize an anti-taxation campaign in an effort to reduce the pressure of anti-government feeling.[15]

Francis found himself in the midst of the insurrection when he went into town on Easter Monday. To control the heavy looting, he formed a Citizens' Defence Force. The following day, he posted a few guards to prevent shops from being looted and hung posters advertising the first meeting of the Defence Force. On his way home that evening, he was apprehended and taken to Portobello Barracks. The following morning, under the orders of British Captain J. C. Bowen-Colthurst, he was shot by a firing squad without a hearing or trial.[16]

Hanna went into town the next day, Wednesday, to obtain information concerning her husband's whereabouts. She learned that he had been arrested, but could not ascertain where he was being held. She tried again on Thursday, but still learned nothing. On Friday, Margaret Culhane and Mary Kettle, Hanna's sisters, went to Portobello Barracks. They talked with Bowen-Colthurst, who denied any knowledge of Francis. The same afternoon she learned from a reliable source that her husband's body was in the mortuary of Portobello Barracks. When she asked the military chaplain of Portobello to reclaim her husband's body, he told her that Francis had already been buried. It would be many weeks before Hanna learned all the details of her husband's death.[17]

A court martial in Richmond Barracks, Dublin, in June 1916, found Bowen-Colthurst 'guilty but insane at the time of the murders' and confined him to an asylum.[18] Hanna, not satisfied with the verdict, travelled to London in July to storm the press with letters and besiege members of Parliament to convene a formal inquiry. Her tenacity yielded a full inquiry in August, but it proved unsatisfactorily narrow in its focus.[19]

AMERICAN TOUR

Still unsatisfied with the verdict in the court martial of Bowen-Colthurst and Prime Minister Asquith's offer of 'adequate and even generous compensation', Hanna decided to bring her story to

America and 'to tell the story of British militarism to every audience in the States that I could reach'.[20] In October 1916, John F. Byrne of New York City, a long-time friend, contacted Hanna to urge her to tour the United States without delay. The Friends of Irish Freedom (FOIF) in New York arranged and supported the majority of her tour.[21] John D. Moore, National Secretary of the FIOF, 26 Cortlandt Street, New York, managed her lecture schedule and the tour was arranged by zones so that needless railroad travel could be prevented.[22]

The initial major objectives of the lecture tour were to draw attention to British brutality against Irish opponents of conscription and the war, and to explain that Francis Sheehy Skeffington's death was not the result of the actions of an insane British officer, but 'deliberately planned by Dublin Castle'.[23] With few exceptions, the themes of her speeches did not vary: first on the evils of British militarism and later on Irish independence and inclusion in the peace conference after the war. She never refused an invitation to speak before any organization, 'from the most conservative and reactionary to the most advanced and democratic',[24] including suffrage, socialist and labour groups. She turned the funds she raised over to Michael Collins for Sinn Féin.[25] At times, cities appeared on her itinerary where the newspapers reported a suffrage meeting, but did not mention Hanna speaking at a formal mass meeting. She maintained a correspondence with suffragists, particularly Alice Park and Marie Equi, and an interest in the suffrage movement in the United States.

It is not clear how the day-to-day expenses of Hanna and the schools for Owen were handled. Fees for her lectures were collected for the FIOF, who then appear to have paid her expenses. In addition, Hanna also arranged for some of her own lectures. In a letter to the Editor of *The Leader*, she responded to an accusation of her lecturing in the United States to raise funds for her son's education and commented briefly on her finances: '. . . the proceeds of my lectures have gone partly to help to provide for his [Owen] future and partly to the Irish Relief Fund for the dependants of the imprisoned or executed Irish Volunteers'.[26] Hanna also arranged for the printing and sale of a pamphlet by Francis, *Democracy in Ireland Since 1913* and her *British Militarism as I Have Known It*.[27] The pamphlets were sold through the FOIF, but it is conceivable she had other avenues for marketing them.

The use of funds that Hanna raised for the Irish Republic seems in direct contradiction to the Sheehy Skeffington pacifism. Francis had argued that all violence was wrong, but as a nationalist he supported Ireland's right to self-determination.[28] Hanna had said that he would die for his cause, but not kill for it. For herself, Hanna held that a war for national freedom had to be evaluated differently:

> There are pacifists who hold with Tolstoi that resistance to all violence is wrong—I quite see the extreme logic of the position and if you hold to that view of course all war is equally hateful to you. But there are other pacifists (and I am one of them) who hold that while war must be ended if civilisation is to reign supreme, nevertheless there may still be times when armed aggression ought to be met with armed defence.[29]

Obstacles developed even before she left Ireland. The British denied her a passport when she refused to agree not to discuss Ireland or the war while in the United States, even in private conversations. Hanna and Owen, her seven-year-old son, departed from Scotland in order to circumvent the authorities and entered the United States in disguise and undetected as Mrs Gribben and Eugene Gribben:[30]

> I was determined, I say, to tell the American people the facts and also the real conditions in Ireland, and I used my experience as a suffragette and as one who has been in jail and knows the stupidity of the English policemen, to elude the spies and to come to New York City, which I have done.[31]

Between January 6 1917 and June 27 1918, Hanna spoke at over 250 meetings across the United States. From New York, she travelled through New England to Ohio, Illinois, Wisconsin, Missouri and on to the Pacific Northwest and California, and back again. She spoke to civic groups, university students, peace groups, socialists, suffragists, and Irish-American organizations. Enormous crowds attended these well-publicized mass meetings. Although some important American newspapers denounced her as a 'dangerous person who was endeavouring to stir up trouble for our British Ally',[32] most local newspapers across the nation liberally devoted space to coverage of her speeches and interviews, often giving her front-page coverage. She complained that she and Owen had been 'inundated in characteristic style by American newspapermen, photographs had been taken of us both (my boy and myself) . . . while many newspaper women insisted on making what are called "sob-stories" out of the case'.[33]

Hanna usually spoke on 'British Militarism As I Have Known It'. She wrote her own speeches and in her own words: 'was well primed as to documents, having managed to get various documents bearing on the case out before me. I confined myself entirely to facts without personal comment and allowed Americans to draw their own conclusions'. She spoke not only of her husband's murder, but also covered shootings, deportations, raids, and other 'horrors' taking place in Ireland under British military occupation. For special meetings, she also covered the problems with Ulster and the labour movement in Ireland. Her major speech, 'British Militarism As I Have Known It', was printed in pamphlet form for distribution in the United States, Canada, the Philippines and South America.[34]

'British Militarism As I Have Known It' covered the last days of her husband, Francis; his arrest and murder; the British refusal of an inquest; Hanna's search for Francis; the arrest of Hanna's sisters; the search of the Sheehy Skeffington home; the help of Major Sir Francis Vane in his search for justice and the arrest of Bowen-Colthurst; the second burial of Francis; the court-martial of Bowen-Colthurst; Hanna's interview with Mr Asquith; the Commission of Inquiry in England; public exposure of the Commission, other atrocities; the state of Ireland; the Volunteers; and the dream of Ireland. Secret Service agents who followed Hanna reported they could find nothing in her speeches that violated Federal laws. She was focused, eloquent and in control of her emotions. She displayed knowledge, not only of Irish and US politics, but also an understanding of world politics. Her quick sharp wit endeared her to most audiences.

THE TOUR BEGINS

Hanna first appeared before a crowd of 3,000 at Carnegie Hall, New York City, on January 6 1917. Journalists, Supreme Court Justices, clergy, labour leaders, leading suffragists and society women, filled the sixty-six boxes of the hall. Hanna commented that 'the meeting was attended by not only Irish. Pacifists, suffragists, Russians, newspapermen, judges and socialists were also represented'.[35] Owen sat beside her on the stage. Bainbridge Colby, an influential Irish-American politician, presided. The speaker's stand was covered with the green, white and orange flag of the Irish Republic.[36]

She referred to her husband's death as 'murder in cold blood' and stated that at least fifty other unarmed civilians had been 'murdered' by the British at the time of the 1916 Easter Rising.[37] She commented that the American press was hesitant to use the word 'murder' in reference to Francis' death, but stated that 'since a British tribunal and the House of Commons found Captain Bowen-Colthurst guilty of murder . . . she saw no reason why they should hesitate to use it'.[38]

Referring to her arrival in New York, Hanna said she learned after her arrival that the immigration authorities in New York had orders to detain her. The only reason they had not done it, she said, was because they did not recognize her.[39]

With her meetings in a different city almost every day, Hanna decided Owen needed stability and to be enrolled in school. During her New England tour, Owen stayed the winter with Irish-American leader Judge Daniel Cohalan and his family in Stamford, Connecticut.[40]

NEW ENGLAND AND THE EAST

During her whirl-wind tour of Massachusetts, Hanna addressed huge crowds in the New England states: Boston, New Haven, Springfield, Pittsfield, Westfield, Hartford, Bridgeport, Lawrence, Meriden, Torrington, Fitchburg, New Bedford, Salem, Lowell, Worcester, Malden, Holyoke and Waterbury. She also spoke at Columbia and Harvard Universities and at Wellesley women's college in New Haven, Connecticut.[41]

On January 14, over 2,000 people filled Fanueil Hall in Boston, with twice as many people unable to get inside, to hear Hanna speak. Mayor Curley chaired the meeting. *The Boston Globe* described her as 'a wonderful woman. Her self-restraint and self-control were remarkable. . . . The horrors of some parts of her narrative found echo in the sobs, the smothered indignation and the pallid faces of most of those present'.[42] Mayor Curley drew an interesting analogy: 'Fanueil Hall had always been an institution of protest. The wrongs perpetrated by many nations had from the beginning been protested against in the hall, but more protests had been held against England in the hall since it was built than against all other nations'.[43]

Hanna delivered a 'remarkable' address in Pittsfield, Massachusetts at the Union Square Theatre on January 21. Former Senator Thomas F. Cassidy presided. *The Pittsfield Daily News* reported that: 'Those present were simply amazed at the wonderful poise and self control of the speaker as she told stories perpetrated by the military authorities in Dublin that made the audience gasp with horror'.[44]

Hanna addressed a capacity crowd at Poli's Theatre in New Haven, Connecticut, on January 28 1917. She told the audience if she could convert one person to the cause of Irish freedom, she would have fulfilled the promise she made to her husband's memory:

> Skeffington has done more by his death for the cause of Irish freedom than he could if he had lived. Since the Irish rebellion there has not been a recruit to the English army from Ireland. We don't want reconciliation with England now. It is too late. We want absolute divorce, and will stand for nothing else.[45]

Speaking at the Alhambra Theatre in Torrington on February 3, Hanna told the audience that her baggage had been tampered with in New York—she thought by a 'representative of Great Britain' who had been ordered to follow her. She said that if the British officer was in the audience, she would be happy to allow him to search her bags at her hotel after the meeting.[46]

When Hanna arrived in Waterbury on February 4, she met Walter J. Farrell, 145 Washington Street, who had been one of the soldiers at Portobello Barracks at the time Francis was murdered. He wanted her to know that he had been so disgusted by the British killing of innocent people that he threw his uniform and rifle away and came to America. He was able to provide Hanna with new information about the execution of Francis.[47]

Hanna granted an interview to the *Waterbury Republican* during her stay at the Hotel Elton in which she discussed her pacifism and the Easter Rising:

> I am a pacifist, but of course I was in sympathy with the recent Republican Uprising in which my husband, although not a participant, met his death. The Rebels died for a noble cause, fighting for it in the way they believed that it would be won, and all true Irishmen were in sympathy with them.[48]

She spoke later to a capacity crowd at the Jacques Theatre. Attorney Francis P. Guilfoile presided.[49]

Hanna and Owen appeared together at Poli's Theatre in Meriden on February 11. She began her talk by reading the Irish Republican

Proclamation. She pointed out that the ideals contained in the Declaration were higher than those in the American Declaration of Independence because the Irish Proclamation asked for the equal franchise of men and women. She then related that when she told a high British official she was going to America to tell the truth about the Easter Rebellion, he told her, 'there was no such thing as truth in the present war'. To that she replied: 'It is the truth in the present crisis that Great Britain fears more than the biggest guns or any of the submarines'.[50]

Hanna lectured at the City Hall in Fitchburg, on February 12, under the auspices of the local FOIF. A reception was held in the common council chambers prior to the meeting. The press described her lecture as a 'lengthy one'.[51] She blamed John Redmond 'for the deaths of many misguided young Irishmen who went out and enlisted to fight for England, thinking she [England] had changed her position toward Ireland'.[52]

The following day, February 13, Hanna spoke at Columbia University to about 150 members of the Anti-Militarism League. She said that England had been 'swept up by Prussian militarism', which she described as a disease 'more malevolent than smallpox'. She continued: 'In time Great Britain will have to free my country, and will then learn that justice is better as an ally than fear and terrorism'.[53]

On February 14, Hanna spoke in Hartford, Connecticut at Parson's Theatre and then in New Bedford on February 15 in the High School Hall. Once again Hanna spoke on 'British Militarism As I Have Known It'. The meeting was held under the auspices of the FOIF. Toward the end of her speech Hanna spoke on the need for American support in the recognition of the Irish Republic:

> We want no half-way measures, but we want our freedom. It is not a domestic question, for England has never been a mother to Ireland. . . . The Irish look, therefore, to America to have her demand that Irish rights and grievances be brought up before the peace conference which will be the closing scene of the present war.[54]

Hanna appeared at Mechanics Hall in Worcester on February 16. John C. Mahoney presided. She told the audience that the English Government had been keeping a close watch on her since she began her lecture tour and she believed they had tried to kidnap her. She had received what seemed to be an invitation to speak in Toronto on women's suffrage, but felt it was instead issued for the purpose of having her cross over the United States border into Canada, so she had declined the invitation.[55]

Then while travelling to Buffalo, she was met near the Canadian border by a group of people wearing green badges who claimed to be a local committee sent out to meet and escort her. As she was about to board the train they had led her to, she looked down the railway platform to see another group of people desperately trying to get her attention. She stalled until the latter group joined her and learned they were the official committee sent to meet her. Hanna then learned that the train she had been about to board was bound for Canada, only a half-hour away. She never learned the identification of the first group, but assumed they had been sent by the British to lure her into Canada.[56]

On February 18 1917, Hanna spoke at Associate Hall in Lowell under the auspices of the FOIF. She was the guest of Mayor and Mrs James E. O'Donnell while in Lowell. The press reported that, 'there was nothing of the dramatic about her recital of the events that included the cruel and cowardly murder of her husband. It was a straightforward story'.[57]

Appearing on February 21 in Holyoke at the Knights of Columbus Hall, Hanna was applauded frequently and 'completely won her audience from the start'. Owen appeared on stage with his mother. She and Owen were the guests of Miss Mary Kennedy of Dwight Street while visiting Holyoke.[58]

A crowd of over 3,000 people turned out to hear her speak in Lawrence at the City Hall on February 22. Mayor J. J. Hurley presided. Attorney and Mrs J. P. S. Mahoney of Custer Street hosted Hanna during her stay.[59]

Not all of her lectures ran smoothly however. Hanna learned that prior to her lecture at Harvard University, pro-British President Lowell had forbidden the use of the scheduled hall when he realized Hanna would speak on Ireland. Angry students found a larger hall, over which Lowell had no control and a successful meeting took place.[60]

In Pittsburgh, Pennsylvania at the St Mary's Odeon, Forty-fifth Street, on February 23, Hanna spoke on conditions in Ireland: 'Whatever may be said of England, it is certainly true that the Irish never gave a mandate for war. Ireland because of her depopulation and impoverishment needs peace more than any other nation'.[61]

THE MIDWEST

Travelling on to the Midwest, Hanna spoke on February 25 at one of the largest and most successful meetings ever held in Chicago at the Orchestra Hall to over 3,000 people, including some of the most prominent people of Chicago. Rev Dr Thomas B. Shannon, pastor of St Thomas' Church and editor of the *New World*, chaired the meeting. It was reported that every mention of the independence of Ireland brought huge cheers.[62] However, during her lecture, a British gentleman shouted from the balcony, 'We came to hear the story of Ireland, and not your story of England'. The crowd yelled in response, 'put him out' while someone hit him over the head. Both men left the theatre immediately and Hanna remarked calmly with her quick humour: 'I would like to leave the story of England out of that of Ireland, but it can't be done'.[63]

Hanna described her meeting in Indianapolis, Indiana, on February 25, in Tomlinson Hall as her 'greatest meeting so far'. Over 5,300 people filled the hall and it was estimated that 2,000 people had to be turned away. Mr Maurice Connelly, a representative on the National Committee of FOIF, chaired the meeting. The American Military Band and the Juvenile Auxiliary Chorus of the FOIF presented a military programme.[64] In describing the desperate conditions in Ireland, Hanna informed the audience that the British in Ireland numbered 150,000 and asked for American help 'before the last pure remnant of the Irish race has been destroyed by famine on the one hand and conscription on the other'.[65]

RETURN TO THE EAST

Returning to New York, Hanna spoke to over 2,000 people at the Star Theatre in Buffalo, on March 4, to celebrate the 108th anniversary of the birth of Robert Emmet. Several hundred Irish Republican flags were distributed as souvenirs to the women in the audience and the programme contained a copy of the Irish Republic Proclamation. Father Henry A. Dolan, pastor of All Saints Church, presided. Hanna gave her opinion of German and English violations of international law and requested equal treatment of them by the United States:

> The great mass of our people see no difference in the principle which has allowed Great Britain for two and one-half years to starve

> Germany and the efforts that Germany is now making to apply the same methods of starvation to its enemy. The English blockade has hurt our commerce. The acts of Germany and Great Britain have equally violated international law. We ask then that any measure contemplated by the United States be directed impartially—as well against one country as the other.[66]

On March 24, Hanna spoke to a crowd in Portchester in St Mary's Hall. The audience was said to have 'listened with breathless attention'. A dance after the meeting to the music of McIntyre's orchestra of New York lasted until the early hours of the morning.[67]

In contrast to such a successful meeting, *The Rochester Democrat and Chronicle* reported that Hanna's next meeting in the Convention Hall in Rochester had been 'grossly mismanaged'. A notice in the newspapers the day before stated that the Irish Relief Fund Committee did not approve the meeting. The secretary of the committee, Rupert L. Maloney, had made arrangements for free use of Convention Hall for Hanna's lecture. The offer was later withdrawn and before the doors of the hall could be opened, Hanna had to use $75 of her own funds as a deposit. It was 9:00 p.m. when John A. Murphy finally introduced Hanna. An Irish flag was brought in and draped over the speaker's table while Hanna undauntedly began:

> There is enough Irish in me to make me doubly keen to speak when I realize that there is some intrigue going on to prevent me from doing so. This isn't the first time I have talked at a meeting where forces that were not in my interest were at work. I have frequently introduced myself at many meetings.[68]

John Moore, National Secretary of the FOIF, later wrote to Hanna concerning the Rochester meeting: 'Your letter from the Hotel Rochester reads like a detective story. You were courageous, ingenious and resourceful. It was a marvel to hold that meeting. . . . Their conduct towards you was incredibly contemptible'.[69]

Hanna then travelled to Providence, Rhode Island, to speak at the Providence Opera House on April 1. Thomas J. Cooney, presided. Hanna recalled that her uncle, Father Eugene Sheehy, had once spoken in Providence during a trip to the United States. She reminisced that: 'You will remember him as the Land League priest who was arrested with Charles Stewart Parnell, and my earliest recollection of my uncle was to visit him in prison as a child. The prisons play an important part in our education, the prison is our university and I have graduated'.[70]

According to the press reports of her speeches, Hanna seems to have very consistently made the same points over and over to her audiences. The United States entered World War I on April 6 1917. Once the war began, Hanna shifted the emphasis of her speeches from 'British Militarism' to self-determination for the Irish Republic and American support for Irish representation at the Paris Peace Conference after the war; the British Army of occupation in Ireland; food shortages; and anti-conscription in Ireland:

> We Irish exiles in the United States at America's entry into the war at first thought that all Irish Propaganda on behalf of self-determination for our Small Nation would have been made impossible, that our meetings would have been suppressed, and that we ourselves would be sent to prison or deported. To our great surprise nothing of the kind happened. Irish Propaganda went on, if possible, more strongly than ever.[71]

Once her tour began to move westward in the spring of 1917, Owen stayed behind with Lydia Coonley Ward at Hillside Farms, Wyoming, New York.[72] At times, he also stayed with the mother of Elizabeth Gurley Flynn, even though Judge Cohalan had warned Hanna against associating with her or Margaret Sanger, leader of the birth-control movement in the United States.[73]

RETURN TO THE MIDWEST

Hanna spoke in Cincinnati, Ohio on April 11 and at St John's Cathedral Auditorium in Milwaukee, Wisconsin, on April 12, under the auspices of the Milwaukee Branch of the Irish Relief Fund. A reception committee met her train and escorted her to the Plankinton Hotel. The Honorable Jeremiah Quin presided at the meeting and Mrs Marie Hickey Harrison sang 'The Last Rose of Summer'. Hanna spoke of the dream and the dreamers of the Irish Republic:

> Ireland is looking to the United States to assist in freeing Ireland from British tyranny at the close of the European War. I trust that the United States will see to it that Ireland is represented at the Peace Conference. I hope that we shall not see Ireland left under military

> rule, while Belgium, Finland and Poland are given their freedom. . . . Each uprising in Ireland marks a milestone on the road to Ireland's liberty. An Irish Republic may be a dream, but it is the dreamer who passes on the torch of liberty in each generation, and not the politician or statesman.[75]

Hanna's visit to St Louis, Missouri was described as the biggest Irish event of the year, if not in many years. She spoke to a capacity crowd at the Odeon Theatre on April 20. A white cross, with the American and Irish Republican flags on either side, decorated the stage. 'The Easter Martyrs' was printed on the cross and 'Who Fears to Speak of Easter Week' on the base. Nine easels, on either side of the cross, held the names of the martyrs of Easter Week. Once again, Hanna's primary appeal was for American intervention for the independence of Ireland at the Paris Peace Conference at the end of the war.[76]

During an interview with the *St Louis Star*, Hanna accused England of being 'the arch hypocrite of the world's history'. She related that her brother, Eugene, was fighting in France in the British Army and that her brother-in-law, Professor Kettle, had been killed in the war. She pointed out that: 'They put the Irish in the front ranks, the Scotsmen second, and the English last in the fighting line'.[77] Speaking on conditions in Ireland, she said there were no independent newspapers left in Ireland; the editors had either been executed or deported. At the time she left Ireland, people were facing starvation and trying to conserve their food supply. She accused the British authorities of taking food from the Irish and recounted that: 'As I am informed, one member of the House of Parliament said on the floor, when England began to export food from Ireland, "It is not likely that while the little dog has a bone, that the big dog will go without"'.[78]

THE WEST

After her meeting in St Louis, Hanna travelled to California where her first meeting was held, on April 29, in the Los Angeles Clune's Auditorium, which held 4,000 people. Joseph Scott presided.[79] She spoke of President Wilson's promise to small nations:

> We do not want America to stop short at Ireland in this splendid move in behalf of the democracies of the world. Now that America has taken a hand it should complete the work and give our beloved island the same rights as Belgium, Switzerland and Holland.[80]

At the close of her meeting, telegrams were sent to President Wilson and to the Speaker of the House, Champ Clark, with pledges of loyalty from the Irish-Americans of Los Angeles.[81]

Hanna then travelled to the Pacific Northwest to appear in Seattle, Washington. Dr and Mrs W. J. Griffin, 769 Thirty-Second Avenue, were her hosts. She spoke at a meeting at the Moore Theatre on May 27. Mr Frank J. Hannan presided. During her speech, she informed the audience that it was against British law for an Irish newspaper to mention her presence or her activities in the United States. The only American newspaper allowed in Ireland at that time was *The New York Times*.[82]

Hanna spoke two days later at a FOIF meeting at the Hibernia Hall in Portland, Oregon, on May 29 1917. She told the audience she felt America's entry into war would greatly aid the ultimate goal of Irish freedom.[83]

Hanna's arrival in Butte, Montana coincided with turmoil over the International Workers of the World and their anti-draft protests, and the on-going general labour unrest that had existed there since the 1890s. The Fenians had been active in Montana since 1866. Clan na Gael and the Ancient Order of Hibernians were also active organizations.

On June 1 1917, *The Butte Miner* reported that members of the IWW were flocking to Butte in great numbers for 'Draft Day', a nationwide draft registration, and they were planning to cause trouble. The Irish in Butte were upset by the draft order because they feared they might eventually have to bear arms against the Irish Republic.[84] Hanna also arrived in Butte the same day.

A delegation of prominent Butte citizens met Hanna's train and escorted her to the Finlen Hotel. She told the Ladies' Auxiliary of the AOH at a banquet held in her honour at the Finlen that 'personally I feel at home here. I almost think it is my country. At least I do not feel a stranger here'.[85]

On June 3, Ed Keenen and John McDowell were arrested for distributing anti-draft pamphlets, which called for a 'silent strike against the war'. The Pearse-Connolly Club took credit for the pamphlet. The next day, James Treanor and John Lennon, two of its officers, were arrested. Treanor was reported to be an IWW agitator from Los Angeles and San Francisco. Lennon was a miner at the Badger Mine in Butte and reported to be associated with the IWW.[86]

That same evening of June 3, 1,200 people filled the City

Auditorium in Butte to capacity to hear Hanna speak. She began her address by saying that people in the East had told her that 'she would not meet the real Irish until she came west, and that Butte was the greatest Irish town in the country'.[87] Hanna told the audience that: 'The common people of Ireland always have looked to the United States as the means through which they were to attain their independence'.[88] *The Butte Miner*, reported that Hanna was:

> particularly careful to avoid the impression that she was endeavouring to create sentiment against England, an ally of the United States in the present world war, but instead to arouse the people in America sufficiently to induce the Washington government to use its influence with the British government for the Irish people and their army.[89]

Disturbances continued on the streets of Butte. On June 5, the Pearse-Connolly Club led a large and unruly anti-draft protest march, ending in a 'small-scale riot' and more arrests. Thirty-two members of the Montana National Guard were called in to assist the federal, county and city police when the disturbance accelerated and more than 25,000 citizens congregated in the streets.[90] Twenty-three more men were arrested the following day. Three days later on June 8, a fire began at the Speculator Mine in Butte. It was said to be the 'worst catastrophe in the history of Butte mining' when 165 of the 410 workers in the mine died.[91]

It is not clear exactly clear why Hanna was in Butte at that time—it may have been coincidence. Butte had a large Irish population and all the tours of the women who followed her included Butte on their itinerary, along with Seattle and Portland. After her June 3 meeting, there was no further press coverage of her activities in the area. It is not clear when she left Butte to conduct a series of lectures in the San Francisco Bay Area. Hanna later wrote to John Devoy that her western tour was a great success. She described 'splendid meetings' in Los Angeles, Pasadena, Portland, Seattle and Butte. However, she also told of accusations by the press of being a 'traitor' and 'labour agitator':

> The result is that the bought press is getting uneasy. I was first rigidly boycotted by the local papers, but lately they have again emerged into the open against me, and I have been the object of anonymous attack and editorial vituperation: The *Los Angeles Times*, the Portland *Oregonian*, the *Butte Miner* and *Anaconda Standard* and today the *Helena Independent* have all denounced me as a 'traitor' spreading

> pernicious doctrine about 'our Ally' which, of course, is 'deplorable just now', and so on. I enclose a sample—I am made responsible for the recent riots in Butte![92]

No Secret Service agents ever found Hanna's speeches to contain subversive material, including those in Butte.

Hanna began to feel uneasy to be on the West Coast while Owen was in school on the East Coast. She may have planned to remain on the West Coast for some time as she had a circle of friends living in California and Oregon. Through friends, she found a Montessori school in Santa Barbara, Boyland, run by Prince Hopkins, a pacifist. Reports from the school and from Owen indicate he spent a happy and productive year there.[93] Owen's wife, Andrée Sheehy Skeffington, in later years wrote in *Skeff* that: 'the year he spent at this school [Boyland] was a form of paradise for Owen. All learning was made attractive'.[94]

Representatives of the FOIF welcomed Hanna when she arrived in San Francisco on June 12 1917. After setting up headquarters at the Palace Hotel, she began her lectures at the Knights of Columbus Hall on June 14, speaking on 'Military Autocracy and Conditions in Ireland'. The hall was filled to capacity, with every inch of standing room used, and hundreds were turned away. As she spoke, the crowd rose to their feet again and again to applaud her.[95] She reported for over an hour her version of her husband's death. She explained to the audience that she spoke without bitterness or vindictiveness and was not out for vengeance. Rather, she wanted 'to see the whole system of British government driven out of Ireland as St Patrick drove out the snakes. . . . It would be a poor tribute to my husband if grief were to break my spirit'.[96]

Far-sighted in her approach to world politics, Hanna stated she did not want democracy to 'stop short of the Irish Sea, but to begin there'. Contrary to England's claim, the question of Ireland was not a domestic matter but an international one. She claimed the cause of Ireland was identical to that of other small nations, such as Belgium and Serbia. She exhibited an understanding of international politics that was visionary and ahead of the times by proposing that: 'At the end of the war we hope to see a "United States of Europe" on the model of your own United States, where each state is free and independent, yet all are part of a great federation'. Ireland wanted to belong to a united Europe and did not 'want to be governed without consent as a British vassal'.[97]

During an interview at the Palace Hotel by *The San Francisco Examiner*, Hanna once again described food shortages in Ireland and the British 'army of occupation' there. She claimed that 150,000 trained men supplemented the British police force of about 1,200 in 'a semi-military organization in Ireland'. She predicted that the enforcement of conscription upon the Irish would produce 'another and bloodier uprising'. She made note of the fact that she had 'avenues of information' and knew what was going on in Ireland. News came to her in letters from Ireland that had not 'been passed by the censor'.[98]

Conflict and tension developed over Hanna's scheduled address to the members of the San Francisco Centre of the California Civic League on June 15. She had been met by a reception committee from the Centre upon her arrival and asked to speak at a luncheon at the St Francis Hotel. All arrangements were made and every table was reserved. After attending her lecture the previous evening at the Knights of Columbus Hall, the Directors of the Centre met and discussed Hanna's 'denunciation of British rule' and decided 'it would be impossible to have Mrs Skeffington speak before such a patriotic society as the San Francisco Centre'.[99] In their judgment, her remarks:

> although perfectly true, were painful. . . . As individuals we love to listen to her, but after her tremendous criticism of Great Britain . . . we felt we have not the right to present her now when we are allies of Great Britain.[100]

Miss Marion Delaney, President of the Centre, called on Hanna in person at 7:30 a.m. the next morning before Hanna was up. Miss Delaney told Hanna that the directors were sorry to cancel the luncheon; however, there had been a woman at the meeting who objected to Hanna's remark about England, 'and for that reason and because the United States was now in the war as England's ally the remarks... although perfectly true, were painful'. Hanna said later that she was astonished at having the meeting cancelled at the last minute 'because, as "Rugles of Red Gap" says, it isn't done at home'.[101]

After speaking at the Sacred Heart Hall, 40th and Grove Streets in Oakland, on June 16 1917,[102] Hanna returned to the Dreamland Rink in San Francisco on June 25. She lectured on the 'European Crisis and Conditions in Ireland' to a crowd of 8,000. More than 1,000 people had to be turned away.[103] Hanna began her speech by wittily thanking the women of the Civic Centre whose refusal to allow her to speak the previous week guaranteed the success of the present meeting.[104]

She spoke in Vallejo, California, on July 5 1917, and again in San Francisco at the Dreamland Rink on July 16 under the auspices of the Ulster-Celtic Benevolent Association on 'The Ulster Question'. For the first time during her tour, Hanna devoted the entire lecture to the Ulster question. She opposed Home Rule or a division of Ireland as a means of settling the Irish question. She insisted that the majority of Ulster's population, both Catholics and Protestants, with the exception of a handful of 'Carsonites and politicians', supported complete Irish freedom.[105]

In an interview in the *Chicago Examiner*, Hanna discussed Home Rule:

> During the first months of the war the Home Rule Act was placed on the Statute Book and received the ratification of King George's signature. Now Dictator George tears up England's 'scrap of paper', offering instead a mutilated measure of partial self-government to three-quarters of the nation. In September 1914, Premier Asquith came to Dublin to win Irish recruits for Great Britain's war. He asked the lives of Irishmen in return for Home Rule as 'the free gift of a free people'. Today thousands of Irishmen who responded to his appeal are fertilizing Flanders with their bodies, while his successor to the Premiership governs the 'free people' by a martial law enforced in the middle of a war for the 'small nationalities'.[106]

On another occasion, she 'dismissed' the Home Rule settlement that had been offered as a solution to the 'Irish question' before 1914:

> [Ireland] will continue to be but a pawn in the game, a land exploited for imperial ambitions, plunged into wars with which she has no interest or sympathy, a victim of secret diplomacy and entangling alliances, taxed for the upkeep of imperial armies and navies whose protection is problematical at best, an alien province misgoverned by absentees. This is the grim reality behind the glowing vision of colonial or other Home Rule.[107]

Hanna lectured at the Clunie Theatre in Sacramento, on July 19 and on July 22, at the Stockton Auditorium on 'An Account of Present Conditions in Ireland'.[108] She related to her Stockton audience that her husband, Francis, 'often said that he would die for his cause, but not kill for it'. She again described the 'cold blooded murder on the part of the British troops' during the Easter Rising.

'Young boys were shot down in the streets to instill into the Irish a proper respect for the British government'. She did not know what the Germans would do if they came to Ireland, but she did know what the English did. She proclaimed that:

> No Irish volunteer has enlisted in the British army since Easter 1916. There is no conscription in Ireland and there will be no conscription because the Irish have sworn to die at home fighting rather than to fight Great Britain's wars in Flanders and on the continent.[109]

It was reported by the press that the success of Hanna's lectures in the San Francisco Bar Area led to the organization of branches of the FOIF in Sacramento, Lodi and Stockton.[110]

At a farewell public banquet given in her honour, on August 2, at the St Francis Hotel in San Francisco, Hanna related to the audience that she had been under constant surveillance by two men during her stay in San Francisco. She expected them to follow her to Tacoma, Washington, where her next scheduled lecture on August 9 was due to take place at the Tacoma Theatre.[111]

Hanna reflected in her *Impressions of Sinn Féin in America* that the western section of the United States, especially:

> Butte, Montana and San Francisco, are more enthusiastically Irish, and now more enthusiastically Sinn Féin than any town in Ireland is. Moreover, in the west particularly the Irish blood holds the strings of government in their hands—judges, lawyers, policemen are usually Irish to a man. A large percentage of Irish among the soldiers and in the camps in California and in the State of Washington is a factory to be reckoned with.[112]

SOLICITATIONS FOR LECTURE DATES

It was not always easy for Hanna to arrange her own lectures. John Moore, National Secretary of the FIOF, managed the details of her speaking engagements, but she was always on the lookout for new ones. She had explored, evidently through the contacts she made in the various cities she spoke in, the possibility of expanding her tour into New Mexico, Nebraska, Missouri and Alaska, but to no avail.

Walter B. Dillon of Las Vegas, New Mexico, wrote to Hanna on August 13 1917 to advise her that he was unable to secure dates for speaking engagements for her—there were not many Irish in the state and he explained that his position as State Secretary of the Socialist Party made it difficult for him to do anything himself because he had been 'pinched' for his anti-war attitude. His advice to her was to pass up the state of New Mexico.[113]

In reply to Hanna's letter of September 9, William Moroney of Dallas, Texas suggested to her that if the political parts of her talks could be eliminated and the purpose of the meetings confined to assisting the Irish Relief Fund, he could consult his friends about a meeting.[114] In an attempt to smooth over his rejection, he and his family would be happy to see Hanna and Owen if they should decide to visit Dallas—an offer he later retracted.[115] The Ancient Order of Hibernians in San Antonio refused any association with her.[116] Hanna later held successful meetings at the Sacred Heart Church in Houston and in Galveston from October 17 to October 20 1917.[117]

Michael Hogan of Omaha, Nebraska advised Hanna that he could not arrange a meeting in Omaha because 'the majority of Irish who call themselves Nationalists here are rotten. . . . They are far different from the Irish of California, Montana or Colorado as chalk is from cheese. No spirit in them'.[118]

Redmond S. Brennan of Kansas City, Missouri also informed her that he could not arrange a meeting for her in Kansas City.[119] No reasons or excuses were given.

Catherine O'Gallagher of Tucson, Arizona wrote that Arizona people had no interest in Ireland and would have no interest in organizing anything that would hamper the war effort.[120]

Mrs Robert Griger arranged two lectures in Pueblo, Colorado, paid Hanna's rail fare and also provided her room and board. She guaranteed Hanna that a collection would be taken up and she would arrange for 'several private subscriptions' and halls for the meetings.[121]

On September 30 1917, Edgar Steinem of Cordova, Alaska answered Hanna's telegram from Tacoma advising her that finances for an Alaskan trip would be required in advance. He further advised her that, if she travelled north from Seattle, she would pass through British Columbia waters that might be patrolled by British warships. He suggested she travel incognito if she decided to make the trip.[122]

Joseph McGarrity requested a meeting with Hanna in New York on December 14. He invited her to spend a few days with both himself and his wife in Philadelphia before she left the States to meet with some people he considered important to her.[123]

1918

Irish-Americans founded the Irish Progressive League in the autumn of 1917 in reaction to US intervention in World War I to ensure that Ireland was represented at the peace conference at the end of the war. Hanna Sheehy Skeffington was one of the 'most prominent figures' in the League:[124]

> It was her [Hanna's] idea to establish an Irish National Bureau in Washington D.C., which would serve as a headquarters from which Irish propaganda could be distributed specifically in order to influence the US government. The league raised the money to finance this office, and even before it was in operation Mrs Sheehy Skeffington was polling congressmen and senators to find out where they stood on the Irish question with a view to drafting a 'blacklist' of those who were hostile or unsympathetic.[125]

This may have been the purpose of Hanna's visit to Washington D.C. during late 1917 and early 1918. She was also interested in the upcoming vote on the US women's suffrage amendment. 'The Woman's Party, led by Alice Paul and Lucy Burns (a militant break-away from the Suffrage Association) was the women's organization with which Hanna felt most in sympathy. Many of its members were Quaker and it took an anti-war position'.[126]

John Devoy, FIOF, appointed Seamus O'Sheel to introduce Hanna to important politicians.[127] She was joined in Washington D.C. by her friend, Alice Park, who worked for Congressman John Raker of California, Chairman of the House Committee on Women's Suffrage. Hanna and Alice Park were long-time friends who had, over the years, shared family happenings and political news. O'Sheel submitted to Devoy reports of the activities of Hanna and Alice Park. On January 6, he complained to Devoy that the hotel he thought Hanna would stay in 'refused her a room because they didn't want the patronage of Mrs Park, a pacifist, or her friends'. Accompanied by Alice, Hanna met prominent US suffragists.[128] Hanna was invited to lunch with Mrs Harvey Wiley. O'Sheel arranged for her to meet Alice Paul on January 11. Accompanied by Alice Park, Hanna met with Lucy Burns and other prominent suffrage leaders after the suffrage debate in the House gallery.[129] The suffrage amendment, the nineteenth amendment to the US constitution, was voted on and passed on January 10 1918, by 274 to 136 votes.

Congressman William E. Mason put his office in the House of Representatives' Office Building at Hanna's disposal as a 'headquarters for writing, dictating, resting or rendezvous'.[130] During this time Hanna met with Congressman John Raker, Senator Robert M. La Follette of Wisconsin and Congresswoman Jeannette Rankin of Montana, the first woman to be elected to Congress. When she learned that her friends, Nora Connolly and Margaret Skinnider, had visited Jeanette Rankin, she spent several days trying in vain to contact them.[131]

Early in January 1918, Hanna received a petition from the women of Cumann na mBan, along with a request that she deliver it personally to President Wilson. She believed it had been smuggled, although she did not know how. She knew that it had not 'passed by the Censor'.[132] With the help of Bainbridge Colby, President of the Shipping Department, and Joseph P. Tumulty, the President's private secretary, an appointment with the President was arranged.[133]

Accompanied by a delegation of thirty-eight, Hanna met with President Wilson on January 11 1918 for approximately an hour.[134] She presented him with a petition signed by all the members of the Cumann na mBan Council. According to Hanna, the petition 'put forth the claim of Ireland for self-determination and appealed to President Wilson to include Ireland among the small nations for whose freedom America was fighting'.[135] (See Appendix 3.) In her own words:

> Three days after President Wilson formulated his now famous 'Fourteen Points' and on the day after passing through Congress of the Federal Amendment for Women Suffrage throughout the States, I was accorded my interview—I was the first Irish exile and the first Sinn Féiner to enter the White House and the first to wear there the badge of the Irish Republic, which I took care to pin in my coat before I went. The President had been busy all the morning receiving American suffragists who came from all over the country to thank him in person for his advocacy of their cause.[136]

Although not at liberty to divulge the contents of their conversation, she could say she had discussed Ireland's rights, American support and his commitment to small nations.[137] Specifically, she asked that Ireland's cause be included in the war aims of the United States and urged America to 'attend to the matter of Ireland and Belgium and all of the small nations when the peace conference comes'.[138] She commented that when she reminded the President of his Irish ancestry, he bantered back 'Scotch-Irish, Madam'![139]

Hanna presented Champ Clark, Speaker of the House of Representatives, with a copy of the Cumann petition and met with Congresswoman Jeannette Rankin of Montana to thank her for the joint resolution proposing recognition of Irish independence by the United States Congress. She remained in Washington for several months interviewing senators and congressmen. She said: 'everywhere I was met with friendliness and sympathy, the atmosphere of Congress being more democratic and kindlier than the Tory clubroom of the British House of Commons'.[140]

On January 22 she spoke at a meeting at George Washington University in Washington D.C. From there she travelled to Springfield, Massachusetts where, on January 27, she spoke at a mass meeting of over 2,000 people at the Hibernian Hall. Two meetings had to be held because no one room was large enough to hold the crowd. She told the crowd: 'The Irish cannot be traitors to Great Britain because they have never sworn allegiance to her'.

Shortly after Hanna's meeting with President Wilson, US Postal mailing rights were denied, under the Alien and Sedition Act, to *The Gaelic American*, *The Irish World*, and *The Freeman's Journal*. She urged people to write to their congressmen and senators to 'adopt the Irish point of view about nationalism'.[141]

Hanna spoke at a Cumann na mBan meeting at Maenherchor Hall, Fifty-sixth Street and Third Avenue, New York, on February 7. Mrs Sarah McKelvey, President of Cumann na mBan, presided. Liam Mellows, Richard Dalton and John Devoy also appeared as speakers. Hanna was praised for her 'persistence and courage' in wearing down 'the efforts of English diplomacy to prevent her reaching the President'.[142] Hanna began her speech: 'I am very glad indeed to have the privilege of speaking before the Cumann na mBan because I recognize in them one of those valiant bodies that has in a true sense of the word "kept the world safe for democracy"'.[143]

Travelling once more back to the Midwest, Hanna spoke to approximately 300 people at a meeting in the Auditorium in Minneapolis, Minnesota on March 2 1918. Mayor Van Lear presided and introduced Hanna. She spoke on 'The Rights of Small Nationalities'. *The Minneapolis Tribune* did not comment on her speech, but did note that 'Socialists' rented the auditorium.[144]

Hanna gave a lecture, under the auspices of the Wisconsin

Forum, at the University of Wisconsin in Madison on March 4, on 'The Rights of Ireland and Other Small Nations'. She showed the audience a small flag-shaped pin she wore of green and orange, separated by a band of white—the insignia of the Sinn Féin movement. She said it symbolized the union of the north and south, with the white representing peace. She commented that it would be a 'police offence' to wear it in Ireland.[145]

In celebration of the second anniversary of the Proclamation of the Irish Republic, a delegation of members of the Irish Progressive League of New York visited Mount Vernon on April 6 to place a wreath on the tomb of George Washington. A card attached to the wreath read: 'To George Washington, Father of the American Republic, half of whose army was Irish, and whose ideals and principles were the inspiration of the men of Easter Week'. Members of the delegation included: Hanna Sheehy Skeffington, Nora Connolly, Eileen Gifford, Helen Merriam Golden, Peter Golden and Miss Daisy Lord. At a mass meeting in Washington D.C. commemorating the Proclamation the following day, Hanna exhibited her tremendous worldwide political insight that still holds true eighty years and another world war later when she told the audience:

> Ireland alone has lost half her population and more than half her commerce in a hundred years. Alsace-Lorraine and Bohemia have both got generous Home Rule Acts in the last ten years; they are fully entitled, both of them, to ask for full independence, but how much stronger is Ireland's claim?
>
> Even the most belligerent to-day—even Colonel Roosevelt himself—are agreed on two things: (1) that this war will be over sometime; and (2) that none of us want another. If you don't then you must remove the causes of future wars by setting all the nations upon a just and lasting basis and not one must be overlooked—or there will be trouble.[146]

Upon her return to San Francisco in April 1918, Hanna's first meeting was given in the support of a new trial for Tom Mooney. Thomas J. Mooney, a socialist, pacifist and labour activist, had been falsely accused, tried and sentenced to hang for dynamiting a 'Preparedness Day Parade' held in San Francisco on July 22 1916 in which ten people had been killed. President Wilson, New York Governor Jimmy Walker, author Upton Sinclair, unpaid lawyers and thousands of citizens supported Mooney in his fight for freedom. He remained in prison for twenty-two years before Governor Culbert Olson granted him a pardon.[147] A Mrs Mooney [Tom Mooney's mother], a 'white-haired old woman' had approached Hanna after one of her meetings in San Francisco in April 1917. Irish-born Mrs Mooney asked Hanna, 'Will you go to see Tom, my son'? Hanna said that was her first direct introduction to the 'world-famous Mooney case'. She visited Mooney a few days later in the city prison and attended the trial of Tom's wife, Rena, also being tried for her life.[148]

Prior to the meeting for Mooney, Declan Hurton of the AARIR in San Francisco sent Hanna a telegram warning her that he felt 'Ireland's case is greater than [the] Mooney case'. The people of San Francisco and the labour unions had opposing views of the case and he felt the majority of the Irish in San Francisco opposed her appearance at the meeting—that it would hurt their cause. Hurton evidently had second thoughts or was advised that he had been wrong because he sent a follow-up telegram the same day, April 18, telling Hanna to ignore his first wire.[149]

Hanna spoke at a meeting on April 16 at the Civic Centre Auditorium, organized by the Machinists' Union Lodge, endorsed by the San Francisco Labour Council and sponsored by the *Irish World* to petition support for a new trial for Tom Mooney.[150] After the Tom Mooney meeting, Hanna received a letter from E. D. Nolan, Secretary-Treasurer of the International Workers' Defence League, thanking her for speaking out for 'justice and fair play': 'The long weary miles you travelled . . . have now recorded themselves in the hearts of the toilers of the San Francisco Bay'.[151] However, a new trial for Tom Mooney was not granted.

Hanna then spoke on April 17 1918 at the Dreamland Rink on the 'Sinn Féin Movement'. A crowd of more than 6,000 people packed the hall. She made reference to a local newspaper article, which reported that she had refused to stand for the Star Spangled Banner in the Exposition Auditorium the previous week. To the charge she responded pointedly:

> Although I am not a musician myself, I know the difference between the American National Anthem and 'God Save the Queen'. I am always proud to stand up for the former, but never for the latter.[152]

She insisted that Ireland's case depended on being liberated at the end of the war and referred to President Wilson's remarks on 'the principle of . . . self-determination of nations upon which the modern world insists'. She said she had to believe the President; otherwise she would have to accuse him of the 'grossest hypocrisy'.[153]

Under conditions put forth by the Sacramento County Council of Defence, Hanna would not be permitted to address the audience at her meeting in Sacramento at the Native Sons' Hall on April 22 if she mentioned Sinn Féin or made an attack on England. Chief of Police, Ira Conron, and his force of policemen were to close the meeting if necessary. Lieutenant Swain of the United States Army also covered the meeting.[154]

Blanche Ribel, Chairman, presented Hanna with a bouquet of roses. When she thanked the crowd, Supervisor Robert E. Callahan mounted the speaker's platform in an attempt to stop her. With that, Hanna pluckily asked the crowd if they would like her to say a few words. In response to their shouts of 'go on', Hanna made a statement in support of free speech. When Miss Ribel stepped forward to persuade her to return to her seat, the crowd gave 'three cheers for Mrs Skeffington'.[155]

Her next meeting, protesting against Irish conscription, was scheduled in the Scottish Rite Auditorium in San Francisco on April 24; however, Hanna learned late that day that the hall would not be available. The hall had been denied her 'under orders from the Department of Justice, communicated to the superintendent of the building by Special Agent Don Rathbun.[156] Hanna then arranged to hold the meeting in the Knights of the Red Branch Hall, 1133 Mission Street. After she had spoken for almost an hour, Detective Jerry Ball of the Police Neutrality Squad, followed by seven federal agents, interrupted the meeting and informed Hanna she had to leave the platform and come with them. She demanded of them: 'Where is your warrant. Am I under arrest?'[157] The crowd remained in the hall to draft resolutions protesting the arrest of Hanna and William Short. A telegram to be sent to President Wilson was signed by the People's Council of America.[158]

She and William Short, a minister and a socialist, and chairman of the meeting, were taken to the Southern Police Station, where Special Agent Don S. Rathbun of the Department of Justice questioned her. She asked Rathbun to arrest her if she had violated the law. He told her she would not be arrested at that time. In a statement made outside his office, she said that if arrested, she would 'go on a hunger strike'.[159] Short was held without bail until the next morning for violating the Espionage Act.[160] *The Sacramento Bee* reported that: 'The police claim that in the hall where the meeting was being held IWW literature, distributed among those present, was found on the floor. It was said to be of a seditious nature'.[161]

Later at the Whitcomb Hotel, Hanna said she was bewildered at the actions of the authorities, saying that they treated her and Short roughly.[162] However, she said she 'intended to go after England rough-shod' and if attacking England was treason in this country, then she was guilty 'ten times over',[163] because she 'was not dealing with affairs in the United States [but] merely protesting against conscription in Ireland'.[164]

When Hanna appeared for arraignment before United States Commissioner Thomas E. Hayden on April 25, her case was dismissed. However, Short was accused of publishing a pamphlet entitled 'The Bulletin of the People's Council of America'. The United States District Attorney claimed it was 'intended to create disloyalty, mutiny and refusal of duty among persons belonging to the military and naval forces of the United States'.[165] He was later released on $10,000 bail while 'a case against him on charges of violating the Espionage Act was prepared for a grand jury hearing'.[166]

Hanna faced more trouble on April 28, when the management of the Dreamland Rink refused her admittance and refunded the deposit. Undaunted, she announced from the steps of the building that the meeting would move to the Knights of the Red Branch Hall. Hanna and her followers walked to Seventh and Mission Streets to begin the meeting.[167] She began her lecture with the bold statement: 'I have not the slightest intention to allow myself to be muzzled'. If stopped at any point during her address, she said she intended to refuse bail and to go on hunger strike. 'The last meal has passed my lips, as far as this country is concerned. . . . Dying for principle is in my family'.[168] She dared United States District Attorney John W. Preston to arrest or detain her.[169]

John Redmond, a San Francisco resident, was so impressed with Mrs Sheehy Skeffington's speech that he walked into the Bush Street Police Station the next day and tore up his draft registration card. According to Policeman Isaac Norris, he said: 'I heard Mrs Skeffington speak last night and they'll never get me now in their army'. He was jailed and transferred to the United States Federal Marshal.[170]

Hanna left San Francisco on April 29 1918 to return to Los Angeles, New York, New Jersey, Rhode Island and Washington D.C.

for speaking engagements before her return to Ireland.

Speaking in New York at a mass meeting under the auspices of the Irish Progressive League at Madison Square Garden, on May 4 1918, Hanna faced more criticism, negative press reports and editorials, and turmoil. *The New York Times* described the half-full Garden as 'a strange kind of gathering held at a time when Fifth Avenue was full of marching allied soldiers'. Liam Mellows and Patrick McCartan, both under indictment by the Federal Court, spoke. *The Times* reported that 'in parts [they] came very near crossing the line that divides sedition from loyalty', and John Devoy made 'very serious charges against the Federal Government'.[171]

The New York Life Insurance Company, as owner of the Garden, received a number of protests against permitting a meeting 'the avowed purpose of which was to attack one of the nations with which the United States was allied, and alongside of whose soldiers Americans were fighting'. That may have accounted for the half-full arena.[172]

During her speech, Hanna made note of her surveillance: 'I hope the Secret Service men are listening to me and have their pencils sharp'. At a point in her speech when she denounced England, two women became agitated and Dr Eleanor Keller of 55 East Seventy-Sixth Street, whose son was in the army in France, shouted: 'this is un-American. I protest against the words of this woman'. Several men in the audience started toward Mrs Keller. Mrs John Oakman, 3 West Sixteenth Street, who was with Mrs Keller, said she agreed with Mrs Keller. Mrs Oakman's son and brother were in France and her husband was stationed somewhere overseas. The police came to the rescue of the two women and escorted them out of the Garden through a side entrance.[173]

Hanna told the audience that the British authorities, with no reason given, had withdrawn her passport the previous week. In addition, she claimed Mr Preston, the Federal Attorney in San Francisco, had wanted to detain her in the Angel Island immigration station. It seemed to her that if it was treason to the United States to talk against conscription in Ireland, 'then I think the best place for any self-respecting man or woman is in prison'.[174] (See Appendix 4.)

Ironically, at the same time, British Ambassador Gerard requested she be sent home to Ireland as a 'dangerous agitator'. In a letter to the editor of *The New York Times*, Hanna reminded Ambassador Gerard that she was being detained by England and asked him to use his influence with the British Government to have her passport returned.[175]

A. G. Burleson, Postmaster General, US Post Office Department, may have helped Hanna with her passport dilemma when he complained to the Secretary of State about a letter to the editor by Hanna published in *The Irish World* on June 1 1918:

> I wish to state for your information that Mrs Skeffington has for many months made speeches and delivered lectures throughout this country on the Irish question of the most violent and incendiary character. Her utterances are carried in the Irish papers as news, have been given the widest publicity, and have done much harm.
>
> If it is possible for you to take this matter up with the British Embassy and arrange to have a passport given to Mrs Skeffington so that she may go back to Ireland, I am sure that this country will be relieved of one of the worse of the Irish agitators now here.[176]

The commotion that occurred during the Madison Square Garden May 4 meeting led to a series of letters from Dr Eleanor I. Keller, a consulting psychologist. She wrote to the Mayor of New York, but received no response. She later appeared before Mr O'Brien, at New York City Police Headquarters at the suggestion of Commissioner Enright. She then wrote to President Woodrow Wilson complaining that she and her friend, Mrs John Oakman, had been 'violently ejected' from Madison Square Gardens on May 4. She took 'issue with the treasonable statements made by Mrs Skeffington and others'.[177] The Chief of the Bureau of Investigation, Department of Justice, had already sent a memorandum to the Attorney General, on May 11, affirming that: 'None of the speeches fall within our statutes. It seems, therefore, that no further action should be taken'.[178]

A meeting held in the Central Opera House, Sixty-Seventh Street, New York, on May 19, came under the scrutiny of Federal officials. The official stenographic transcripts of the speeches of Liam Mellows, Patrick McCartan, Peter Golden and Hanna were forwarded to United States District Attorney Francis G. Caffey and Chief Charles W. DeWoody of the Department of Justice Secret Service. Liam Mellows was reported to have said that if President Wilson did not intervene in the Irish question, 'Ireland will be driven to seek help elsewhere'. Mrs Skeffington 'endorsed all that he had said'. Patrick McCartan hinted that England was going to try to obtain American aid to 'slaughter' the Irish. Peter Golden of New

York stated that in the event England 'massacres the Irish in Ireland the Government under which we live will have to massacre us'.[179]

During her speech Hanna wondered if the time would ever come when American boys would be drafted to fight in Ireland. She warned: 'You want to take speedy action to see that this does not happen'. She suggested that it was for the Irish-Americans to influence their government and one way of doing it was to transfer the Irish vote from the Democratic to the Republican Party. She said: 'All the Irish resolutions offered in congress had been offered by Republicans. You are to blame if you don't send men to Congress to represent you properly'.[180]

The speeches made during the mass meeting in Madison Square Garden were included in the investigation headed by Assistant United States District Attorney Earl A. Barnes. A statement made by Hanna at both the meeting at the Garden and at a meeting of the Socialist Conference of the People's Council, on May 26, came under scrutiny when she referred to 'President Wilson's failure to interfere in Irish matters and saying that unless he does interfere he will come to be known "as the greatest hypocrite in history"'. In addition, a comment she made at a San Francisco mass meeting which referred to her meeting with 'Hindu friends' was included in the investigation. The stenographic report noted that a large number of Hindus had been convicted in San Francisco for 'plotting on American soil to bring about revolution against British rule in India'.[181] The United States Attorney's Office, Department of Justice, responded to letters of complaint pertaining to the Madison Square Garden meeting stating that he knew of 'no provision of Federal Law which authorizes me to prevent meetings of this character'.[182] The Chief of the Bureau of Investigation, Department of Justice stated that 'none of the speeches clearly fall within our statutes. It seems, therefore, that no further action should be taken'.[183]

Finally, British authorities in New York City granted their passports, and Hanna and Owen left New York on June 27 1918. Owen was permitted to return to Ireland to attend school. Hanna was detained in Liverpool, England upon their arrival. In a letter to the editor of *The Gaelic American*, she wrote that it was not the intention of any 'returning exiles' to remain in England a moment longer than necessary. As soon as possible, she hoped to return to Ireland to take part in the fight against conscription.[184]

Avoiding the surveillance of the British police, Hanna returned to Dublin in August. British authorities took her into custody and sent her first to Bridewell Prison in Dublin and then to Holloway Prison in England. After refusing to eat, she was released and returned again to Dublin.[185] This was not her first time in jail, nor was it her first hunger strike. She had participated in hunger strikes in June 1912 and November 1913 during her imprisonment in Mountjoy Prison for suffragist activities.[186]

During an interview upon her return to Ireland, Hanna stated she intended to teach French and German in technical schools, to return to work as editor of the *Irish Citizen* and to return to her work as a suffragist in the IWFL. She intended to take the advice of George Bernard Shaw and petition for the right of women to sit as members of [the Irish Republican] Parliament.[187]

CONCLUSION

An examination of the enormous crowds she drew in the many cities she visited in the United States, the unifying effect she had on the Irish-American community and the strengthening of their Irish republicanism, prove her first tour of the United States a success. She came to the United States as a young widow, still in her period of bereavement, to tell the 'true' story of her husband's murder. In none of her speeches did she espouse anti-war activities by Irish-Americans. She spoke only of anti-conscription in Ireland and asked for United States recognition of the Irish Republic as an independent nation. Conversely, on instructions from Sinn Féin, she turned over the funds she raised, which she had been holding in an American bank, to Michael Collins, Director of Organization for the Volunteers.[188] American newspaper interviews and articles give no account of the amount of contributions and subscriptions.

The political scene in the United States during her tour was tense because of World War I, and the criticism of Hanna reflected the tension. She met each situation with courage, tenacity and a wit that endeared her to audiences. Irish-American nationalism was beginning to stir and the extensive newspaper coverage given to her addresses reflects this rustling. In praise of the success of Hanna's lecture tour, *The Gaelic American* reported:

> Mrs Skeffington has done more real good to the cause of Ireland during her short stay in America than all the Irish orators and writers who have undertaken to enlighten the American people for the past

twenty-five years. She has reached a class of American people who have never been reached before by a missionary from Ireland and has won them over. She has supplied our own people with unanswerable arguments that they can use with effect on their American neighbours.[189]

Father Peter Yorke, FOIF in San Francisco, wrote of Hanna's achievements in *The Leader* in 1918:

At the outset, her [Hanna] task looked like an impossible one. However, she had the fortitude and the courage of her convictions. She kept plodding along, spreading her propaganda in every section in the United States, and she was finally successful in convincing many millions of American people that Ireland is entitled to her independence.[190]

Hanna herself was happy with all she had accomplished during the nineteen months of her tour in the United States. She is quoted as saying: 'I am so glad that I undertook the tour. It looked impossible at first, but I must say that it was successful beyond my dreams'.[191]

Hanna's success on the other side of the Atlantic may be measured by the increased demand in speaking engagements after her return to Ireland. She spoke on a variety of subjects: the role of the United States in the fight for Irish freedom; conditions in Ireland; release of political prisoners; literary and historical subjects; and the socialist movement.[192]

Perhaps another measure of her success is evident by the fear she instilled in Dublin Castle. The British considered her a 'menace' and informed the police that 'no meeting addressed by Mrs Sheehy Skeffington can be permitted'.[193]

When the Anglo-Irish truce was arranged in July 1921, Hanna played a prominent role in the peace negotiations as an intermediary between Irish Republican President Eamon de Valera and Prime Minister Lloyd George.[194] At that time, she also held the position of Director of Organization for Sinn Féin.[195] Along with other republican women, she later opposed the Anglo-Irish Treaty and the Free State Government. She condemned the partition of Ireland and the oath of allegiance to the king.[196]

CHAPTER 5

Muriel and Mary MacSwiney: American Commission on Conditions in Ireland, December 1920–January 1921

During the time Eamon de Valera spent in the United States soliciting political and financial support for the Irish Republic in 1919 and 1920, Ireland drifted increasingly into acts of terrorism, guerrilla warfare and eventually into what was known as the 'Reign of Terror' with the arrival of 7,000 Black and Tans in March 1920 and 6,000 Auxiliaries in August. They killed women and children, burned family homes and businesses, resulting in the loss of jobs and an endangered food supply.

Donal O'Callaghan, Lord Mayor of Cork, gave a critical first-hand look at conditions in an article he wrote for a pamphlet published by the American Committee for Relief in Ireland, when he described the devastation of Cork 'like a human body from which the heart has been removed'. During a fire on December 10 1920 the total property loss amounted to over $15,000,000 [£51,750,000]. There had been thirty-three isolated fires during the previous three-month period amounting to damages of $5,000,000 [£17,250,000]. The fires created a housing shortage in Cork, loss of the commercial district and loss of jobs for 3,000 people.[1]

Oswald Garrison Villard and Dr William J. Maloney, a former British medical officer committed to Irish nationalism in the United States, formed an impartial committee, the Committee of One Hundred Fifty, to investigate charges of atrocities in Ireland. Committee members included five state governors, twenty-two

United States Senators, thirteen members of the House of Representatives, four Catholic bishops, four Methodist bishops and other public figures such as Jane Addams and Robert M. LaFollette.[2]

Frederic C. Howe, Chairman of the ACCI declared at the opening of the Commission's hearing on November 18: 'Only the direst necessity can justify a resort to arms for the adjustment of disputes in Ireland . . . and that conditions in Ireland "have created and are creating a widening rift in the friendly relations of English-speaking people, not only in America, but all over the world"'.[3] The Commission planned to send a mission to England and Ireland to investigate conditions and the economic situation in Ireland.[4]

Mary MacSwiney, Terence MacSwiney's sister, and Muriel, his wife, travelled to the United States in December 1920 to testify before the Commission.[5] Thousands of supporters greeted them in each city and town they visited on the East Coast before and after their appearances in Washington D.C. The press described them both as forceful and eloquent speakers. Mrs Muriel MacSwiney was praised for her youth, beauty and demeanour. Miss Mary MacSwiney was admired for her ability as a 'convincing' speaker with an absence of 'oratorical frills'.[6] *The St Louis Globe Democrat* described Miss MacSwiney:

> Of middle height, rounded figure, entirely feminine, a crown of rich brown hair very slightly greyed, dressed in deep mourning, the sister of the late Lord Mayor made an appealing figure. Colour high, chin long and firm, the upper lip very short, the nose retrousse and long, the forehead high and temperate, the Irish woman in many ways resembles a duodecimo figure of the famous contralto, Madame Schuman-Heinck. Her style of speech is that of the very newest American women, clear, cool, concise, direct, an appeal to reason rather than to the passions or to the emotions.[7]

After their appearances before the Commission, Mary and Muriel held meetings in New York, Massachusetts and New Hampshire before Muriel returned to Ireland on January 1 1921.

BACKGROUND

Terence MacSwiney became second-in-command of the Irish Volunteers in Cork in 1914, under the leadership of Tomás MacCurtain. With the confusion of orders and counter orders during the 1916 Easter Rising, Cork Volunteers did not participate. After the surrender and imprisonment of the Irish rebels in Dublin, British troops were sent to occupy Cork.[8] On May 3 1916, Terence was arrested and sent to prison in Frongach, North Wales. Upon his release in 1917, he married Muriel Murphy of Cork. Muriel's family, the Murphys, had not initially been sympathetic to the republican cause. Muriel became an Irish republican in 1915 when she met Terence MacSwiney at the home of a priest in Cork. Although she held no official position in any of the republican organizations, she claimed she took a part in the 1916 Easter Rising and 'in all other manifestations for Irish freedom'.[9]

On March 20 1920 Tomás MacCurtain, Lord Mayor of Cork, was shot dead in his Cork home. The Coroner's jury found that he had been 'wilfully murdered under circumstances of most callous brutality', by the RIC.[10] Terence MacSwiney succeeded MacCurtain as Lord Mayor of Cork. Terence was arrested during a meeting at Cork City Hall, on August 12 1920, for being 'in possession of documents, the publication of which would be likely to cause disaffection to His Majesty'. He and the ten men arrested with him went on hunger strike in protest against the arrests of public officials. On the third day, Terence was taken to Brixton Jail in England. He survived seventy-four days without food and died on October 25, 1920. His hunger strike received worldwide attention and further stimulated the rise of Irish nationalism.[12]

AMERICAN COMMISSION ON CONDITIONS IN IRELAND

In reaction to the atrocities committed by the Black and Tans in Ireland, the death of Lord Mayor Tomás MacCurtain, and the hunger strike and death of Terence MacSwiney, Dr William J. Maloney, a former British medical officer committed to Irish nationalism in the United States, conceived of the idea of an American Committee for Investigating Conditions in Ireland. With the help of Frank P. Walsh and the approval of Eamon de Valera, Oswald Garrison Villard, owner and editor of *The Nation*, supported the project and created the Committee of One Hundred Fifty.[13] From the committee, eight members were selected to form the American Commission on Conditions in Ireland (ACCI). Hearings were held in Washington D.C. from November 18 1920 to January 21 1921. Based on the final report of the ACCI, the American

Committee for Relief in Ireland was founded and raised $5,250,000 for Sinn Féin.[14] Sir Auckland Geddes, the British Ambassador, and Eamon de Valera were invited to provide the ACCI with a list of persons who could be called as witnesses.[15]

In Ireland, the Propaganda Department sent out requests to all cities and towns asking for information from their districts. Depositions needed to be detailed with the date, time, place, name and rank of the policeman, and name and regiment of the soldier. The depositions needed to be made before an attorney, the statements sworn to and signed and witnessed. Originals of threatening letters needed to be supplied. Atrocities were described and included: murders by the police and military, sacking of towns, burning of houses, assaults by the police or military on citizens, looting, raiding of homes (and the number of times raided) and destruction of property. Mr James O'Connor, solicitor, collected and reviewed the lists of atrocities and provided counsel to Dáil Éireann.[16]

MURIEL AND MARY MACSWINEY IN AMERICA

On December 4 1920, Mrs Muriel MacSwiney and Mary MacSwiney arrived in New York City aboard the *Celtic* to testify before the American Commission on Conditions in Ireland in Washington D.C.[17] Ten thousand supporters and a committee of over 300 people comprised of both Irish and sympathetic Italian organizations greeted them. Mrs Oswald Garrison Villard, along with Mrs Peter MacSwiney and Mrs Annie MacSwiney Dixon, cousins of Mary and Muriel, travelled out to the ship in the police patrol boat to welcome them. The wives of the Governor and Mayor also greeted them aboard. Jeannette Rankin, a congresswoman from Montana, headed a reception committee of 500 women. Harry Boland, secretary to Eamon de Valera, met them at Pier 60 at West Nineteenth Street. De Valera was unable to welcome them because of illness. Oswald Garrison Villard escorted them to a waiting automobile.[18]

Joseph F. Ryan, President of the Longshoremen's Union, spoke to Muriel as she emerged from the pier entrance. She replied: 'I am overwhelmed at this remarkable testimonial to my husband's sacrifice'.[19] The longshoremen of New York harbour, who had staged a protest strike against the imprisonment of Terence MacSwiney the previous summer, furnished a bodyguard for the two women.[20]

The procession made its way up Fifth Avenue to the St Regis Hotel. The crowd waved flags and sang American and Irish songs. With the exception of a short thank you for the warm reception, Muriel made no statement.[21] After resting a short time, Muriel gave out the following typewritten statement to the newspapers:

> I am deeply grateful for the wonderful reception given to me this morning and especially to the women of America for their generous tribute to my husband's memory. I have had many beautiful letters from America, even from American children, and I am happy to be in a country where so many, many people are thinking about the cause of Ireland.
>
> You will understand, of course, that I can say nothing about conditions there until I have appeared before the Nation's Commission on Ireland, which invited me here. My hearing is to be on Wednesday next I am told in Washington. But I should like to say that both my husband and I always expected that America would help us very greatly in winning our freedom.
>
> We feel in Ireland that America has a greater responsibility in the matter than any other land on account of her fine traditions and her war pledges, and because there are so many millions of our kin in this country.[22]

After a morning of shopping along Fifth Avenue, Muriel was the luncheon guest of the staff of *The Nation*, the newspaper published by Oswald Garrison Villard, at the Railway Club, 30 Church Street.[23]

Mary and Muriel attended High Mass on Sunday at St Patrick's Cathedral. In an interview after leaving the Cathedral, Muriel spoke of the conditions in Ireland:

> I was in Cork two nights before I started for America. . . . While there a terrible thing happened. A bomb was thrown by the Black and Tans at four men in the principal streets in Cork. One was a great friend of mine. Both his legs had to be taken off and he died next morning. But it has been still worse in some parts of Ireland, where they have prevented the people from going into food shops and shot up the towns. In several places the people have fled into the country in fear. . . . They go into the houses to shoot the people. The night before I left they went into houses in Cork and shot people straightway for no cause.[24]

Following mass, they met with Archbishop Hayes, and had lunch at the Hotel Wolcott with Mr and Mrs Frank P. Walsh. Mary spent the afternoon with Eamon de Valera at the Waldorf-Astoria.[25]

Mary and Muriel travelled from New York to Washington D.C. on December 6. They were met at Union Station by a committee headed by Mrs Champ Clark, wife of the former speaker of the House of Representatives, and Mrs James A. Reed, wife of the Senator from Missouri. After a reception in the presidential waiting room, they were taken by automobile to the home of Peter A. Drury, President of the Merchants' Bank, who hosted their stay in Washington D.C. Hundreds of people lined both sides of Pennsylvania Avenue during the procession.[26]

Muriel told the press at a reception held at the Peter Drury home that:

> the Irish people will be satisfied with nothing short of independence. . . . England has fooled us too often with promises to accept anything but independence now. The British argument that a free Ireland might be used as a base for her enemies is absurd. I know the English people and have many English friends whom I love, and there is every reason why a free Ireland should live in peace and harmony with their neighbour.[27]

HEARINGS OF THE COMMISSION ON CONDITIONS IN IRELAND

The following witnesses were called to testify at the hearings of the Commission: Denis Morgan, Chairman of the Urban Council of Thurles; John Derham, Town Commissioner of Balbriggan; the Lord Mayors of Belfast and Cork; the Chairman of the Urban Council of Mallow; Mrs Muriel MacSwiney; Miss Mary MacSwiney; Miss Irene E. Swanzy, sister of Police Inspector Swanzy of the Royal Irish Constabulary; the Rev James H. Cotter, Tronton, Ohio; Luke E. Hart, member of the Supreme Board of Directors of the Knights of Columbus; Francis Hacket, newspaperman, New York; Thomas C. Fogarty of New York, who had recently returned from a trip to Ireland; Captain E. L. MacNaghten, an Ulster Protestant; and Dudley Field Malone, former Customs Collector in New York. The British Embassy formally declined to attend because it 'could not approve the purposes of the inquiry', but stated that the British Government 'would not impede the attendance of witnesses'.[28]

Denis Morgan, college teacher and Chairman of the Town Council of Thurles, Ireland, was the first witness called to testify. He described the shooting up of Thurles by the RIC and told of a constable who was shot on January 20 1920. In retaliation, the constabulary made a midnight raid on ten homes and shops of townspeople known for their support of the Irish independence movement. He told how he and his family huddled on the floor all night to escape the bullets coming through the windows and doors. He described his arrest by a squad of eight members of the RIC when he left his home on January 30 to attend a meeting of the Town Council. When he asked what offence he was charged with, the answer was: 'No charge; just Government orders'. He was neither indicted nor tried. However, he was transferred from place to place, including the hold of a war ship in Cork Harbour, until he was taken to Wormwood Scrubbs Prison in London. When his five-year-old son died during his incarceration, he was not allowed to attend the funeral.[29]

TESTIMONY OF MARY MACSWINEY AND MRS MURIEL MACSWINEY

Mary and Muriel appeared at the second ACCI hearing held between December 8 and 19 1920. Mary spoke for one entire session and part of a second to give her views of Irish history and Ireland's struggle to preserve nationalism and Catholicism.[30] Muriel entered the hall between Oswald Garrison Villard and Jane Addams. She sat quietly during Mary's testimony, with only occasional whispered comments to her. Muriel took the stand the following day.[31]

The Commissioners questioned Mary on the following topics: the republican movement; the Rising of 1798; the Home Rule struggle; an explanation of Sinn Féin; family traditions; the early days of Terence MacSwiney; the Gaelic League; the Volunteers; Ireland as England's 'one bright spot' on the eve of World War I; the Cork Volunteers; Easter Week in Dublin; Easter Week in Cork; the first arrests; educators' views of republicanism in Ireland; the dawn of the Republic; Grattan's Parliament; the Act of Union; the taxation of Ireland; condition of Irish farmers; the Republican courts; the religious issue; and the truth about the police.[32]

Many of the statements contained in Mary's testimony to the Commission were included later in her lectures. She complained that 'England said she was fighting for the rights of small nations. We had absolutely as much right to our liberty as Belgium had'. She accused England of turning France against Ireland by persistently presenting Ireland as pro-German. 'Only my brother's death softened France'. She then asked how the American people had helped democracy by going to war. 'You people in America have not carried out the policies for which you went to war'. Referring to Ireland being in a state of war with England, she pointed out that officers captured during wartime should be given prisoner of war status and not treated as common criminals. She was convinced that if Terence had been given prisoner of war status, he would not have gone on hunger strike.[33]

Mary also discussed the situation in Ireland since the 1916 Easter Rising, the Sinn Féin Government, Dáil Éireann, and the breakdown of British civil control.[34] She described Sinn Féin as a policy not a noun, as she had seen it referred to in American newspapers. She described Terence's arrest and the uneasiness of the family for over a week when they could find no information on his whereabouts from the British authorities. Only after petitioning the English Governor, the Prime Minister and members of the House of Commons did she locate him.[35] She believed the British motive for letting Terence die was to force the Irish Volunteers into the open:

> And they [Lloyd George and the British] thought, since my brother had the confidence and affection of the Volunteers of Cork, that if they let him die, the Volunteers would lose their heads and come out into the open, and then they could shoot them down.[36]

She claimed there were three 'stumbling blocks' to American sympathy: the belief that the fight was religious, the Irish murdered policemen, and the difficulty of giving the British guarantees against Irish attack or use of the Irish coast for military aggression.[37] She said that outside of Ireland there was an impression that Catholics supported the Irish independence movement. After denying this, she asserted that Protestants and Catholics were equally represented.[38] (See Appendix 5.)

Seemingly in an attempt to downplay the importance of Mary's testimony, the New York correspondent of *The Irish Times* reported that:

> It is true that Miss Mary MacSwiney is not helping Sinn Féinism by the character of her evidence. Yesterday, for instance, she hotly defended the murder of fourteen officers in Dublin, declaring that each one of them was 'a proven spy', and invoking the example of America in shooting spies. The Dublin victims were only shot 'after

> fair trial and sentence'. The motive of Miss Mary MacSwiney's evidence was revealed when, obviously in obedience to those who are using her, she informed the Committee that America, far from making the world safe for democracy, made it safe only for England.[39]

Mrs Muriel MacSwiney testified on Thursday, December 9. *The American* described her as:

> Although twenty-eight years old, Mrs MacSwiney looks barely twenty. Her hair is worn in an old-fashioned tightly-wound knot on each side of the head. This and her small slight figure that seemed fairly swallowed up in the witness chair, added to the impression of youthfulness. She looks as if she had stepped from an old engraving.[40]

The topics the Commissioners queried Muriel on included: her first meeting with Terence; their marriage in jail; the birth of their daughter, Máire; the murder of Lord Mayor Tomás MacCurtain; the election of Terence as Lord Mayor of Cork; Terence's final arrest; his speech at his trial; his hunger strike; and the death of Terence.[41]

Muriel told of meeting Terence at Christmas time in 1915, their marriage in June 1917 in between two of his many times in prison, and their only real time together in Ballingeary, County Cork right after their wedding. Their daughter, Máire, was born while Terence was in prison in June 1918. She told of their house in Cork after he became Lord Mayor, and the fact that Terence could not stay with them even then for fear of being arrested. She and Máire talked to him on the phone during the day while he was in his office in the City Hall.[42] She related that Terence had been interested in independence movements since he was a boy. She felt that his charity and love of people were his best traits and he wrote beautiful poetry.[43]

When Senator David Walsh of Massachusetts asked her if 'the women of Ireland steeled themselves so much for their cause that weeping was unknown', she replied: 'Oh, I never cried'.[44] Muriel recounted her husband's arrest on August 12 1920 and the beginning of his hunger strike. She told that at first, the shock of it hit her hard, but she became resigned to it by the time of his trial and promised him she would not insist he take food. She became convinced at that time he would die unless the British Government released him. She stated: 'I know my husband was happy and I never, never would interfere with my husband in a matter of conscience.[45] It was his choice, it was the decision of his spirit'.[46] (See Appendix 6.)

Muriel and Terence's family were able to be with him in London during part of his seventy-four-day hunger strike. It took a tremendous toll on all of the family to endure his suffering. The worst of it came from knowing that the medical staff force-fed him during his unconscious times knowing how adamantly he was against it. Toward the end of his life, Muriel was told she would not be able to enter his room. A visit to the British Home Office to petition visitation rights was flatly denied. The next morning she collapsed and remained ill for some time. She was not allowed to be with Terence when he died and she became too ill to attend his funeral.[47]

At the conclusion of her testimony, Muriel visited the US Congress, on December 14. Many members recognized her as she entered the House gallery, left the floor to meet her, and invited her to the House Lobby. An informal reception was then held in the Senate Marble Room.[48]

The Irish Times Washington correspondent, negatively reported on December 11 that:

> The character of the evidence heard by the Committee and the tone of the 'disclosures' made by members of the MacSwiney family and others had too much the air of rhetorical exercise to create much effect elsewhere than among those already pledged to believe all evil of Great Britain.[49]

During their stay in Washington D.C., Mary read reports of a fire in Cork with estimated losses of $30,000,000. She feared the fire had been set as a reprisal for her testimony before the Commission. She reportedly stated that 'the opportunity given us by the American Commission to tell the truth about Ireland has not been palatable to England and it will not shock me to know that the unspeakable atrocity which followed was inspired by it. Civilized cruelty is worse than savage cruelty'.[50]

RETURN TO NEW YORK

At the conclusion of their testimonies before the Commission, Mary and Muriel returned briefly to New York City when Mary was called back to meet with Eamon de Valera. Because he would be returning to Ireland due to the escalation of the war there, he asked Mary to stay in the United States to complete the work he had begun. Because of her family obligations she would have preferred to return home to Ireland. She was co-guardian of Máire, as requested by Terence, and her sister, Annie, needed her support in the management of their school, St Ida's. She felt committed to carry on Terence's mission, and because of her own devotion to the republic, she could not refuse. Most importantly, de Valera had seen that 'she was shrewd, articulate and unintimidated by group or media attention' and convinced her to stay on.[51]

While in New York City, Muriel held an informal reception and spent twenty minutes in Mayor T. Collins' private office at city hall, on December 17. Harry Boland, Peter Brady and James O'Meara accompanied her. She commented during the visit with the Mayor that the warmth of her reception in the United States impressed her, but she was anxious to return home to Ireland to her child.[52]

CHRISTMAS AND MEETINGS IN NEW ENGLAND

Mary and Muriel travelled from New York City to Providence, Rhode Island. Mary appeared at the Providence Opera House on December 18. Hundreds of people had to be turned away an hour before the opening of the meeting. The overflow crowd then filled the Mayflower Theater, which held over 2,000 people. Hundreds who could not get inside the two large halls waited outside hoping to catch a glimpse of the two women. Former Congressman George F. O'Shaunessy presided over the Opera House meeting and Albert B. West presided over the Mayflower Theater meeting. Mary spoke to both audiences explaining the conditions in Ireland, relating the acts of British soldiers in Ireland and the destruction of British rule.[53] Muriel was not able to attend either meeting. Instead she met with Bishop Matthew Harkins and Bishop Coadjutor William A. Hickey and then went directly to the Narragansett Hotel to rest.[54]

The American press had lavishly praised Muriel's appearance and demeanour. However, she remained frail from the ordeal of witnessing the suffering and death of Terence. Muriel had testified to the American Commission on Conditions in Ireland that she supported Terence's hunger strike. However, a recent study questions whether, on the basis that she had not supported his first hunger strike, she did in fact support the latter.[55] Mary recognized the pressures Muriel had been subjected to by the retelling of the hunger strike during her appearance before the Commission. Muriel had previously suffered periods of acute depression and now required periods of rest due to complete exhaustion.[56]

Mr and Mrs John F. Harrigan of Worcester escorted Mary and Muriel from Providence to Boston, Massachusetts where they arrived at South Station on the afternoon of December 19 1920. More than 100,000 people lined the route and a parade of 8,000 accompanied them to the Copley-Plaza Hotel in Copley Square.[57]

Mary addressed a mass meeting at Mechanics' Hall that evening under the auspices of the American Association for the Recognition of the Irish Republic (AARIR).[58] Approximately 8,000 people filled the hall and at least 8,000 more could not gain admittance. Muriel was not able to attend. Before Mary spoke, the audience stood for a silent prayer in memory of Terence. It was reported that she:

> spoke slowly but clearly and used no rhetorical flourishes. Her language was simple, her indictment as carefully fortified with facts as an able lawyer's would be, and her logic forcible. She compares with such speakers as the late Mrs Julia Ward Howe, Miss Susan B. Anthony, or Mrs Carrie Chapman Catt.[59]

Mary began by explaining that she and Muriel 'are women in deep mourning' and she deeply appreciated the greeting of silent prayer given to her. She had come to America to explain what the Irish were fighting for:

> I believe with all my heart and soul that America meant what she said when she entered this great World's War . . . You said you entered the World War for the freedom of all peoples everywhere—all peoples everywhere—for liberty and self-determination and the undictated development of every Nation, great and small, to make the world safe for democracy . . . Do you know that Ireland is the only one of the white races in the world today that is not free? You were to make the world safe for democracy, and yet you have made us only safe for the British Empire.[60]

More than 5,000 men and women enrolled in the AARIR after the meeting. With several other mass meetings planned for the following week in the Greater Boston area, it was hoped that the drive would bring the AARIR membership to 250,000.[61]

Muriel was invited to speak to the Massachusetts Senate on December 20 1920. When she arrived at the State House at about 1:40 p.m., Joseph Noonan, watchman, Representatives James W.

Hayes and Patrick Melody, and Councilor Louis R. Sullivan escorted her through the building. The employees of the State House greeted her in the Hall of Flags. Speaker Joseph B. Warner received her in his office. She watched the Senate proceedings from the visitors' gallery before being invited into the Senate Chamber. She also visited the Executive offices; the Governor, Lieutenant Governor, secretary and other officials who would normally have been there were present to receive her.[62] Muriel sat on the Senate dais beside Edwin T. McKnight, president of the Senate. Although visibly ill, she expressed her gratitude to the senators:

> I never made a public speech, yet I want to tell you how grateful I am. I am sure my husband would be gratified also. We have always been friendly with America. We feel as you felt. You have got your freedom. We will get our freedom some day. As you have suffered, we are suffering now.[63]

At 4:30 p.m., a special parlour car arrived from Manchester, New Hampshire with a delegation to greet Muriel, Mary and Harry Boland, which formed only a portion of their escort when they left Boston's North Station for Manchester, New Hampshire. A delegation of 100 Boston schoolteachers had gathered to say goodbye, along with members of the Carrollton Branch of the AARIR.[64]

An escort of 500 men and women escorted Mary, Muriel and Harry from the train station in Manchester to their hotel. The American Legion Band played; Colonel M. J. Healy, as Chief Marshal, led the parade; and an honour guard composed of World War I and Spanish War veterans and members of the Knights of Columbus surrounded the carriage they rode in.[65] Because of continued fatigue, Muriel was unable to speak that evening; however, it was reported that thousands of people had to be turned away from the meeting when Mary and Harry spoke to an enthusiastic crowd.[66]

After their appearance in New Hampshire, Muriel and Mary spent Christmas with the family and guests of Senator Walsh in Clinton, Massachusetts. Muriel, Mary, Senator Walsh, Major Thomas L. Walsh, Miss May Walsh and Thomas E. Dwyer of Boston walked from the Walsh home on Water Street to attend High Mass at St John's Church on Christmas morning. After mass they returned home to a turkey dinner 'in the New England style'. Other guests at the Walsh home were from Boston, Worcester and New York.[67]

That evening, Christmas evening, Muriel addressed a Clinton audience at an informal reception held in her honour in the Clinton Town Hall. Senator Walsh, who told of the struggles of Ireland and how 4,000,000 people were fighting for freedom, introduced her. Muriel spoke only briefly, but asked the audience to 'work for Ireland, for honour and for right'.[68]

The largest meeting was held at the Worcester Theater where Muriel, Mary, and Harry spoke. Meetings were also held at the Alhambra Hall, Knights of Columbus Building and at the Casino.[69]

Continuing to suffer from complete exhaustion and needing to return to Ireland to care for her daughter, Muriel made the decision to return at the end of December. Muriel and Mary returned to New York City. On December 31, under a resolution adopted by the Board of Alderman, Mayor John F. Hyland presented Muriel with the Freedom of the City Award at the New York City Hall—the first time the honour was conferred on a woman.[70] Mrs Brandon Tynan paid tribute to Muriel when she presented her to Mayor Hyland:

> She stands as a saintly example of supreme self-denial, of patient suffering, or glorious fortitude of wifely devotion and of patriotic pride, because she willingly chose to lose her husband, the father of her child, rather than that he, by any act of hers, should depart from his high resolve . . . No greater love hath any woman than that, she sacrificed her love for the freedom of her people.[71]

MURIEL'S RETURN TO IRELAND

Muriel sailed the next day, January 1 1921 aboard the *Panhandle State* of the United States Mail Steamship Company's line. Before leaving the St Regis hotel, she expressed her gratitude to the American people:

> It is with a feeling of the greatest regret that I must take myself away from the shores of your great Republic . . . My last expressions are those of deepest gratitude, and my last request is that you may speedily relieve the devastation of Ireland and help it to stand by your side a free and independent nation.[72]

> When I came it was with a torn heart—its wounds, still fresh with the loss of a cherished husband—and having constantly before my eyes

> the sufferings of my beloved country, which has offended no nation, and yet is enduring martyrdom.[73]

Three thousand well wishers gathered at the entrance of the pier at West Thirty-Fourth Street. Cathleen O'Connell accompanied Muriel. Flowers and vases of American beauty roses filled their rooms.[74]

AFTERMATH OF THE AMERICAN COMMISSION ON CONDITIONS IN IRELAND

The American Commission on Conditions in Ireland: Interim Report published the following conclusions:

> We find that the Irish people are deprived of the protection of British law, to which they would be entitled as subjects of the British King. They are likewise deprived of the moral protection granted by international law, to which they would be entitled to as belligerents. They are at the mercy of Imperial British Forces which, acting contrary both to all law and to all standards of human conduct, have instituted in Ireland a 'terror' the evidence regarding which seems to prove that:
>
> 1. The Imperial British Government has created and introduced into Ireland a force of at least 78,000 men, many of them youthful and inexperienced, and some of them convicts; and has incited that force to unbridled violence.
> 2. The Imperial British forces in Ireland have indiscriminately killed innocent men, women and children; have indiscriminately assassinated persons suspected of being Republicans; have tortured and shot prisoners while in custody, adopting the subterfuges of 'refusal to halt' and 'attempting to escape', and attributed to alleged 'Sinn Féin Extremists' the British assassination of prominent Irish Republicans.
> 3. House-burning and wanton destruction of villages and cities by Imperial British forces under Imperial British officers have been countenanced and ordered by officials of the British Government; and elaborate provision by gasoline sprays and bombs has been made in a number of instances for systematic incendiarism as part of a plan of terrorism.
> 4. A campaign for the destruction of the means of existence of the Irish people has been conducted by the burning of factories, creameries, crops and farm implements and the shooting of farm animals. This campaign is carried on regardless of the political

views of their owners, and results in widespread and acute suffering among women and children.

5. Acting under a series of proclamations issued by the competent military authorities of the Imperial British forces, hostages are carried by forces exposed to the fire of the Republican army; fines are levied upon towns and villages as punishment for alleged offences of individuals; private property is destroyed in reprisals for acts with which the owners have no connection; and the civilian population is subjected to an inquisition upon the theory that individuals are in possession of information valuable to the military forces of Great Britain. These acts of the Imperial British forces of Great Britain are contrary to the laws of peace or war among modern civilised nations.
6. This 'terror' has failed to re-establish Imperial British civil government in Ireland. Throughout the greater part of Ireland British courts have ceased to function; local, county, and city governments refuse to recognise British authority; and British civil officials fulfill no function of service to the Irish people.
7. In spite of the British 'terror' the majority of the Irish people having sanctioned by ballot the Irish Republic; give their allegiance to it; pay taxes to it; and respect the decisions of its courts and of its civil officials.

CONCLUSION

Transcriptions of stenographic transcriptions taken during all of the proceedings formed a major portion of the Commission's final report. The proceedings were well covered by newspaper reporters who attended the public sessions. The *Nation* published most of the testimony weekly in serial form. The Benjamin Franklin Bureau, which published the *Interim Report*, gave away free copies. When the final report, *Evidence on Conditions in Ireland*, was published in July 1921, it was too late to sell well or to effectively shape public opinion since peace talks between Lloyd George and Eamon de Valera had begun.[76]

The results of the hearings of the Commission proved a disappointment to Oswald Garrison Villard, who viewed them as a failure. Villard's biographer, Michael Wreszin, believes the Commission produced a lengthy report; however, the press used Villard's German-American background and his pacifism against him. Despite its very distinguished members, the Commission was 'accused of being a propaganda agency created by pacifists and pro-Germans to discredit Great Britain and disrupt Anglo-American relations'.[77] Villard wrote to Jane Addams that at times he felt 'utterly sick' about the whole affair: 'I have often reproached myself for ever having asked you to join [the Commission]. Nothing I have ever done has focused such social pressure and intolerance on us as this'.[78]

It should be noted, however, that as a result of the findings of the American Commission on Conditions in Ireland, the Irish White Cross was formed in January 1921 to distribute relief to the estimated 100,000 who had been left destitute because of the war.[79]

Francis M. Carroll has written that 'perhaps the greatest success of the commission was simply in keeping the events in Ireland from November 1920 to January 1921 before both the American public and world opinion'.[80]

Also on the positive side, Muriel maintained a correspondence with Villard long after she returned home to Ireland. In a letter to him on October 27 1921, she expressed her gratitude to the American people: 'A great many more of our people would have perished of want of all kinds, only for the kindly help that came from your great hearted country; and material things are still in a critical state with us but the spirit of the people is wonderful'.[81]

CHAPTER 6

Mary MacSwiney: Uncompromising Irish Republican, January 1921–August 1921

MARY MACSWINEY INITIALLY travelled to the United States with her sister-in-law Mrs Muriel MacSwiney, to testify before the American Commission on Conditions in Ireland during December 1920. Newly widowed, Muriel returned to Ireland on January 1 1921 to care for her daughter, Máire. Mary remained in the United States at the request of President Eamon de Valera to tour in support of the Irish Republic. With few exceptions, she did not vary the theme of her speeches on British tyranny and the necessity of recognition of the Irish Republic. Between January and August 1921, she visited fifty-eight cities and spoke at more than 300 meetings.

The reception accorded her across the country varied. The *Chicago Herald-Examiner* described her welcome in Chicago as the 'greatest tribute ever paid a woman in this city', when 20,000 people attended her address.[1] The Massachusetts, Ohio, Wisconsin, Oklahoma, Kansas and California legislatures invited her to speak. Conversely, the Nebraska House of Representatives refused her permission to appear before them because her 'mission to the country [the United States] was not of importance to the people of Nebraska'.[2] The Texas House of Representatives also refused to allow her to speak because it was 'not the place of this country to meddle in the domestic affairs of foreign nations'.[3]

The *Akron Beacon Journal* commended her for winning so many friends in the face of hecklers in every large city in the United States. Her typical day was described as:

> Arise 5 o'clock to catch 6 o'clock train.
> Ride three hours, during which time she is dictating letters to her secretary.[4]

Change to interurban car line.

Ride another hour.

Reach destination. Met at depot by reception committee and taken to hotel for formal reception. She stands in line for two hours, shaking hands, briefly visiting, with each of the many who always seek an opportunity to know her personally.

Noon—speak at some civic club luncheon.

3 o'clock—speak before some gathering of associated women's clubs.

5 to 7—More hand shaking.

7 to 7:30—Dinner (sometimes).

7:30—Go to mass meeting, which lasts until 10 o'clock or after.[5]

BACKGROUND

Mary Margaret MacSwiney, born March 27 1872 as the eldest of seven children to two struggling teachers, John and Mary, was educated at the Ursuline Convent in Cork and graduated from the National University of Ireland. She taught in England and France for a short time until she entered Cambridge University. Supported with a loan from the Students' Aid Society in Ireland, she earned a teaching diploma as one of two Irish Catholic women in a class of 100, mostly men. After her parents' deaths, she returned to Cork to support the family as a teacher at St Angela's Convent School.[6]

Mary first became politically involved in the Munster Women's Franchise League in 1910.[7] In the beginning, she argued for the vote saying that without the right to vote, women 'were as irrelevant as the village omadawn or the children playing in the streets'.[8] She changed her views after joining the Cumann na mBan to a belief that 'if Ireland were free, women would get the vote' and that 'self-government for Ireland was the most important question'.[9] She also felt that the growing militancy of the suffragists was 'unsuitable to Ireland'.[10] Her growing Irish nationalism was greatly influenced by her younger brother, Terence. The MacSwiney home hosted many Sinn Féin discussion groups.[11] Mary felt her family had been republican for generations. They had come to County Cork from the North of Ireland in the fourteenth century.[12]

Mary MacSwiney founded the Cork branch of Cumann n mBan in May 1914. She later became one of the most uncompromising Cumann members,[13] and according to the remembrance of her activities by Monsignor Florence D. Cohalan, son of Daniel

Cohalan, 'the most radical follower of de Valera. There had to be a whole of Ireland and a Republic *now*.'[14] After leaving the suffrage movement the previous year amid controversy with the Irish Women's Franchise League (IWFL), she formally resigned from the Munster Women's Franchise League in November 1914 'owing to the fact that they (were) devoting their money and energy to war [World War I] propaganda, other than the purpose for which the society was founded'.[15]

On the morning of May 2, British soldiers arrested Mary MacSwiney in her classroom at St Angela's and held her until the same evening in Cork jail, along with other Cumann members.[16] Mary was dismissed from her teaching position on May 3 and told that 'not on any account' should she enter the school again. With a loan from a friend, she opened St Ita's Secondary School and Kindergarten in Cork.[17]

THE TOUR BEGINS

With the war worsening in Ireland, Eamon de Valera decided to return to Ireland in December 1920. Although Mary would rather have returned home, he convinced her to conduct an American tour to argue for recognition of the Republic of Ireland, promote membership in the newly organized American Association for the Recognition of the Irish Republic (AARIR), and to raise funds in support of the Irish Republic Government. At the time of de Valera's departure in December, there were $3 million of the more than $5 million he had collected in bond certificates still in American banks. Mary was then drawn into and left to defend de Valera's position in the bond controversy with the Irish-American organizations herself.[18]

The Irish Republic Government and her royalties from the publication of Terence MacSwiney's book, *The Principles of Freedom*, jointly subsidized Mary's tour. Mary donated royalties of $1,500 to the National Treasury, which were then applied to the purchase of her steamship ticket and other travel expenses. She was provided with a salary of $100 per week while in the United States for personal expenses, with $50 a week to pay for a companion-secretary.[19] Mary and her secretary, Catherine Flanagan, submitted reports to Harry Boland and James O'Mara on a regular basis detailing the attendance of meetings, their receptions, problem areas and successes or disappointments. Mary often relayed to them her opinions of what was needed in each area, and overall, to fully promote the Republic of Ireland. At times she chided them, at times she scolded them, but she always spoke directly and to the point. These reports were often written during over-night train rides between meetings after a full day of meetings, receptions and interviews.

Mary experienced criticism early in her tour after a meeting in Philadelphia. The editor of the *Philadelphia Public Ledger*, on January 7, challenged her integrity in an editorial under the title, 'Bad Irish Strategy':

> . . . What can be thought of an audience, presumably composed of intelligent and well-informed American men and women, who would sit passively and silent when a revolutionary missionary from Ireland—a woman—gave voice to such palpable misstatements as were uttered in this city this week by Miss MacSwiney. . . . It is charitable to suppose that Miss MacSwiney was the victim of malicious deceivers when she declared that 'the English are using borrowed gold from the United States * * * to devastate Ireland and to exterminate Irish liberty'.[20]

Proving she would not back down in the face of controversy or criticism and that she clearly understood world politics, Mary caustically replied from New York, on January 9:

> from the whole tenor of this editorial . . . it [is] palpably evident that the writer is English of the English even though he may be an American citizen. . . . The misstatements are not mine, I did not ask for the intervention of the United States on Ireland's behalf. Intervention means war, and I expressly said I did not expect America to go to war. . . . I said and I repeat that if America called home the loan as she is quite entitled to do, England would not be able to pay her army of occupation in Ireland; therefore America must accept a share of responsibility for the heinous crime against civilization, the perpetration of which would be impossible if England had not her $5,000,000,000 to use in the destruction of liberty.

She concluded by saying she had no fear 'of offending any real American. I am quite confident I shall prick many an Englishman, for to them the truth is always anathema'.[21]

Prior to Mary's first mass meeting in New York City on January 7 1921, she became embroiled in the 'Irish Bond' controversy between de Valera, Joseph McGarrity, Patrick McCartan and William J. Maloney, in conflict with Cohalan and John Devoy.[22] In defence of de Valera, she wrote to Devoy that she firmly believed the money raised in the United States for the Republic of Ireland was under the control and at the disposal of the Dáil Éireann Minister of Finance. As for the loan to the Republic:

> I feel sure that I need only point out to you that that money was a loan to our Government and that you are no more entitled to a voice in its disposal than you are to ask the British Government every detail of their expenditure of the ten thousand million dollars which you loaned them.[23]

John Devoy replied to Mary that because of her lack of accurate information of the causes of the differences between de Valera, the FOIF and the Clan, Mary did not understand the 'real situation'. He accused de Valera of waging war on the FOIF and the Clan, 'the only real friends of the Irish Republic in America with the object of destroying them and personally ruining their leaders'.[24]

The content of Mary's lectures varied little. Mary's biographer, Charlotte H. Fallon believes that even though her speeches seemed 'orchestrated, carefully charted, and planned, that was hardly the case. She sometimes had notes that had been jotted down but that was the extent of formal preparation'.[25] At times Mary provided drafts of her speeches and notes to John Devoy and Judge Cohalan in an attempt to encourage Irish-American and Irish unity.[26] Her years of teaching had trained her to speak extemporaneously, in addition to presenting a clear-cut focus and direction. She appeared never to be intimidated by hecklers or negative comments, and not afraid to express her opinions. She also demonstrated an extremely quick wit on many occasions.

Her speeches, as reported by the newspapers, stressed the need for US recognition of the Republic of Ireland; the atrocities being committed in Ireland by the Black and Tans and the Auxiliaries; recalling the US loan of $5,000,000,000 to England; France's recognition of the US Republic in 1776 and the need to recognize the conflict in Ireland as an all-out war with England (the war was not religious, rather economic and political). She did not expect Americans to go to war with England and she did not seek US military intervention. Over and over again she commented that she hoped her lectures would be attended by not only Irish-Americans, but also all other Americans, especially those who were anti-Irish or pro-British. In fact, she became adamant that non-Irish-Americans be invited to the meetings. Mary always reminded the audiences that the Government of the Republic of Ireland had been elected in 1918 and established in 1919 with the First Dáil Éireann. Mary's activities and lectures came under the surveillance of the US Secret Service. However, agents reported there was nothing 'of a radical nature' and 'nothing of an unusual nature in her talk, other than that which might be expected in an address of that character'.[27]

EASTERN AMERICA

Mary appeared at a mass meeting of 5,000 people in Madison Square Garden, New York City on January 7 1921. She reported that the bond drive promoted $10 bonds to be:

> reclaimed one month after the international recognition of the Republic of Ireland—at 5 per cent interest per annum from the first day of the 7th month after the freeing of the Republic of Ireland from British military control and said Bond to be redeemable at par within one year thereafter.[28]

Although she asked for relief for Ireland, her address centred on an appeal for recognition of the Irish Republic by the United States. She emphasized that 'she had not come to this country with a song of hate on her lips'.[29] A resolution was approved condemning the 'cruel policy' of the British Government in Ireland, along with a message of sympathy to the Irish people and $75,000 was raised for the American Committee for Relief in Ireland.[30]

Mary, accompanied by her secretary, Catherine Flanagan, began her cross-country tour in early January. Appearing in Albany, New York, on January 10, she spoke to women's organizations at the Ten Eyck and the Vincentian Institute. The press described her speech as 'one of the strongest and most sincere addresses ever delivered by a woman in this city'.[31] Speaking on the issue of whether the Irish people really wanted independence she said that when she left Ireland 'fully ninety-one per cent of the people were bent upon severing all relations with England'.[32] She referred frequently to her brother, Terence, claiming that he was 'murdered'. She also discussed and denied charges of Irish-German collusion during the World War.

She said that 'had it been true, the Irish would have been justified in being pro-German, as much as a person who, pinned down by a vicious burglar and rescued by a watchdog, would be justified in being pro-dog'.[33] Former Governor Martin Blynn introduced Mary to the audience at the Vincentian Institute as the 'Benjamin Franklin of Ireland'. The main point of her talk centred on the fact that the money loaned to England by the United States was being used to 'promote oppressive acts in Ireland'.[34]

Mary spoke next at the Schary's Krueger Auditorium in Newark, New Jersey on January 16. When thousands of people were unable to get into the auditorium, Frank P. Walsh, Major Eugene F. Kinkead and other speakers held an overflow meeting in front of the hall on Belmont Avenue.[35]

Her meetings in Buffalo, New York on January 19 were held in the auditoriums on the first and second floors of the Holy Angels School at Connecticut Street and West Avenue. A 'local loud band, a boy's choir and about forty priests' accompanied Mary to the platform.[36] Speaking under the auspices of the AARIR, Mary reminded the audience of the ideals proclaimed by the American people as they entered World War I:

> You said that you entered the war for the freedom of all peoples, everywhere, for the liberty and self-determination and the undictated development of every nation, great and small, to make the world safe for democracy. If you had carried out your ideals, Ireland would be free today.[37]

Resolutions were adopted protesting the Black and Tan atrocities and calling for recognition of the Irish Republic.[38]

The following morning she spoke at Canisius College. The students cheered for five minutes when she entered the hall. During her speech, she claimed that, 'if the United States recognized Ireland, in thirty days every other nation would do the same'. While in the Buffalo area Mary, along with local friends, took time off to visit Niagara Falls. She spoke later at D'Youville College and again at a dinner in her honour at the Lafayette Hotel.[39]

Mary arrived in Pittsburg, Pennsylvania, on January 21, where she attended a large reception and dance at the William Penn Hotel. The ballroom, which held 6,000 people, and the nearby auditorium of Kaufmann's store were filled. In addition, the tenth and eleventh floors of the hotel were crowded, as well as extra halls at Kaufmann's. Mary spoke four times to 18,000 people and also from the balcony of the hotel to 2,000 people in the lobby. She asked the audience to put pressure on their congressmen to recognize Ireland's rights.[40]

She spoke next in Cleveland, on January 23, at the B. F. Keith's Theatre to over 6,000 people on Ireland's fight for independence. In answer to the many questions that were asked, she told of the 'systematic process of strangulation being employed by England to crush the Irish nation'.[41] The meeting was paid for by 50-cent admissions. The following day, the *Cleveland Plain Dealer* devoted a full page to Mary's speech.[42]

At a meeting at the Satler Hotel of approximately 1,000 women, Mary's 'plea for justice' prompted Dr Edward R. Turner, a professor of European History at the University of Michigan, to hold his own rebuttal meeting in the Amasa Stone Chapel of the Western Reserve University on the evening of January 24. The *Cleveland News* reported that 'to his slender audience' Dr Turner had said that, 'recognition of the Irish Republic would do no good and would drift inevitably into such strained relations with England that war would follow'; that 'only recently had Ireland become civilized'; and that 'England had never tried to exterminate anyone'.[43]

Through the help of Mrs Adelia Christy, national director of the AARIR for Ohio, Mary met Professor Turner's attack head on by challenging him to an open debate. Mrs Christy offered to pay his expenses to and from the debate and the expenses of renting Keith's Hippodrome. She suggested the date of March 29, with the subject set at 'Great Britain's Government of Ireland Has Been Just and Should Continue'.[44] Before leaving Cleveland, Mary issued a statement that she did not expect the professor to accept the challenge.[45] She could not understand why he had not spoken out during the question and answer portion of her meeting held at the Satler Hotel. Professor Turner's editorials followed Mary across the country, yet he never met her challenge to debate with her in person.

Catherine Flanagan noted that 'a Mr Arnold', the editor of a Catholic newspaper, arranged to have Mary speak to the Ohio State Legislature and also the Kiwanis Club, where she was 'received splendidly'.[46] Mary spoke to the Chamber of Commerce on January 24,[47] and then returned to Cincinnati, to speak on self-determination for Ireland before a record-breaking crowd of over 5,000 at the Music Hall on January 27. Mrs William King of Ironton also spoke of the 'cruel injustices of which she was an eyewitness' when she visited Ireland the previous summer.[48]

More than 2,000 people listened to Mary speak the following day, January 28, at the Woodland Auditorium in Lexington, Kentucky. She also spoke at St Joseph's Hospital, St Catherine's Academy and at a public reception in the ballroom of the LaFayette Hotel. Mary described the AARIR committee in Lexington as 'mighty fine'. They had been organized only for two weeks and already had 300 members. Mary and Catherine travelled on to Louisville and then to Knoxville on January 31.[49]

Louisville had not been on the schedule; however, two last minute meetings were arranged. Mary spoke first at Ossoli Circle to 800 people and later at the Market Hall to 600 people. Most of those who packed the downstairs and gallery of the hall were reported to have been 'entirely sympathetic'; though 'a minority appeared to have come to listen only'. She urged those present to write to their congressmen to work for the recognition of the Irish Republic.[50]

The meeting in Nashville, Tennessee at the Ryman Auditorium, on February 1, was described as 'wonderful'. There were 3,500 in attendance, many of them legislators. Mary had been invited to speak before the legislature, but apologized for not being able to stay over in Nashville. In her address, she emphasized the United States position during World War I pertaining to the principles of self-determination for small nations. She said she did not 'come to stir up trouble between America and any other country, but to tell the American people what the Irish were fighting for and why they were fighting'.[51]

Appearing in Memphis, Tennessee at the auditorium of the Knights of Columbus Building on Jefferson Avenue, Mary spoke to an audience of 3,000. The press described her address as 'a pitiful story of oppression and . . . a passionate appeal to the United States for recognition of the Irish Republic'. She spoke of President Wilson's promises and failures:

> Had President Wilson's . . . promises to the world been kept by you, this world would have been a beautiful place to live in. . . . No man had a greater opportunity. . . . Your country has failed in its mission. You have failed to carry out your promises when you entered the war—you have failed, and your president has failed. Your country has been but the tool of England. . . .[52]

Approximately $2,000 in cash was raised for the Irish Relief Committee.[53]

Catherine Flanagan summarized Mary's time in Tennessee as 'creating the most favourable impression—and the enthusiasm is unbounded'. In spite of the Tennessee Irish-Americans having no formal organization in place, Mary had spoken to over 10,000 people.[54]

MIDDLE AMERICA

Mary met and confronted the regional conservatism of Middle America with political astuteness, patience and a composed demeanour. The press continued their praise for her eloquence. During the turmoil over her appearance before the Nebraska and Kansas Legislatures, she received word from home that her younger brother, John, had been arrested in Cork. All the while, she continued to write press releases, to encourage the leaders of the AARIR to step up their spending to promote the growth of the organization, and to attend back-to-back receptions, meetings, and interviews.

Mary spoke in St Louis, Missouri on February 3. While 500 found standing room in the corridor outside the doors of the meeting, others had to be turned away from the Odeon Theatre. During her address, she asked why the United States had 'recognized de jure or de facto governments', and had not recognized that of the Irish Republic. The following day, she spoke to the Catholic Women's League and the Queens' Daughters and held an official reception in the Elizabethan Room of the Congress Hotel.[55]

Mary appeared next in Chicago, on February 5, to speak to 250 nuns at the Knights of Columbus Hall on West Madison Street. She criticized the United States for their loan to England:

> financing the present reign of terror in Ireland. If America would demand payment of the five billion that England owes her she would not then be able to maintain an army of 200,000 cutthroats and jailbirds [Black and Tans and Auxiliaries] who now are busy exterminating the Irish race.[56]

Always dressed in mourning, Mary spoke of Terence often during her lectures. She paid tribute to him at a reception in the Congress Hotel by stating: 'Terence isn't dead. He lives on and his memory keeps men's hearts firm and the memory of his sacrifice is stronger than the cannon of the black and tans'.[57] She said that of the 200 wreaths sent from the United States for his funeral, sixty had come from Chicago.[58]

The following day she spoke in the Seventh Regiment Armory, 34th Street and Wentworth Avenue, to 16,000 cheering people. It took Congressman-Elect Stanley H. Kunz, Mayor William Hale Thompson and Mary ten minutes to quiet the crowd before she could speak. She reminded them that 'France's recognition of the colonial republic of 1776 made America a nation, which gave her the chance to become a great nation'. She asked why not 'become the noblest as well as the greatest? Why not give Ireland her just dues as you were glad yourself to receive them when you needed them?'[59] Following the meeting, $10,000 in cash and approximately $165,000 in pledges were collected for 'reconstruction work in Ireland'.[60]

Mary's final speech in Chicago, on February 7, was to 3,000 schoolteachers in the Olympic Theatre. Her speech focused on British propaganda in the United States. A total of $1,014.65 in donations was collected to pay expenses.[61]

Mary arrived in Madison, Wisconsin the following day, February 8, where she spoke to legislators and state officials in the capitol. The crowd was so large, the meeting was moved from the assembly chamber to the rotunda.[62]

A reception committee of 240 people welcomed Mary to Fort Wayne, Indiana. The local press described Mary as, 'a woman of great ability and education gifted with a logical mind, and possessing a comprehensive knowledge of the subject treated'. Her cousin Peter Golden, a prominent writer and lecturer, attended a state conference of the AARIR held simultaneously with her meeting at the Temple Theatre in Fort Wayne on February 10. Proceeds of the meeting were given to the Irish Devastation Fund.[63] The following day, *The Fort Wayne Journal Gazette* stated that the membership of the AARIR had been increasing in Fort Wayne and a significant number of new applicants to the local council were the result of the meeting.[64]

The Des Moines, Iowa Council for the AARIR sponsored Mary's visit in Iowa. A reception held at the Hotel Fort Des Moines on February 12 1921, was followed by visits to the larger public schools where she spoke to students about conditions in Ireland.[65] Dressed in heavy mourning, she spoke to over 3,000 people in the Des Moines Auditorium. Once again, she spoke of the courage of her brother, Terence: 'His martyrdom did much to bring America to a realization of the justice of the Irish cause. People knew the situation must be serious if a man would lay down his life for the cause he loved. It took a great deal of courage'.[66] During one of her afternoon receptions she was asked if England had any real reason for holding on to Ireland. She responded: 'Yes. . . . Just as much reason as the robber who stole my purse would have to keep it'.[67]

In a letter to Harry Boland, from the Hotel Fort Des Moines, Mary asked that the tour be run on a 'big scale for the next two months'. She knew there was plenty of money and she wanted half a million spent over the next two months, with two to four organizers assigned to every state. She felt recognition of the Irish Republic would come quickly if the message got out to the people. She had found local people to be poor on the whole—willing, but inefficient. She wanted 'good organisers, good speakers, plenty literature, *at once*'.[68] She chided her friend Harry:

> Write to me like a good boy and tell me you will be a brick and shell out generously. Don't spare money now. I know it will take a lot to do what I ask but it is only for two months. You can slow down again after that. If we do not succeed for recognition you will in that case only be throwing a sprat to catch a salmon as the result of all the organising would result at least in a bond drive of 20 million dols. Don't mind the possibility of malicious people talking of money used here instead of in Ireland. All we need care about is doing what helps Ireland most.
>
> Send me a wire on receipt of this and write me *at once*. Such a way to treat a lonely colleague. You ought to be properly ashamed of yourself. I am very angry with you and am not writing you now because I love you but because I want work done.[69]

With Dáil Éireann facing an escalating war and dwindling treasury, the funds she requested were never provided. Mary felt she was in the best position to know the political and economic climate of Irish-Americans and eventually resented and criticized de Valera for not honouring her grass-roots opinion.

Prior to Mary's arrival in Omaha, Nebraska, on February 13, A. J. Donohoe and Colonel John G. Maher sought permission for her to speak before the state legislature in Lincoln.[70] However, *The Omaha Bee* reported in a special edition, on February 10, that Representative J. Reid Green's resolution to invite Mary to speak before the House for fifteen minutes on Monday, February 14 was voted down.[71] The objections were stated as: 'The Nebraska legislature is here to transact American business for Americans . . . international problems should not be brought up here at this time . . . [and] the question of the Nebraska farmers is more paramount at this time than the Irish question to the people of Nebraska'.[72]

Further controversy arose over the scheduled introduction of Mary by Dr R. L. Wheeler, pastor of the Wheeler Memorial Presbyterian Church South Side, at her meeting in the Omaha Auditorium. The elders of the church voted at 11:00 a.m. the morning of the meeting that Dr Wheeler be 'forbidden' to introduce Mary. No reasons were given.[73]

Eight thousand people attended Mary's meeting at the Omaha Auditorium on February 13. She began her address by relating that she had just received news of 'new oppression' of her family by the English. Her youngest brother, John, had been arrested and imprisoned for possessing ammunition in Cork barracks. 'You don't know what that means. I know that recently two prisoners in those barracks have been murdered.'[74] Once again she reported during a speech that Professor Edward Turner had been submitting articles to newspaper editors again, this time in Nebraska. During the address she charged him as 'being an agent of Great Britain'. She complained that, 'Dr Turner seems to be following me about the country, refuting my statements, but when asked to meet me face to face and answer my objections, he has refused to do so'. She gave the audience specific examples of atrocities committed by England against the Irish people and explained that it was not a religious war; rather, it was political and economic. She asked that each of the 8,000 people in attendance send a letter each day of the week to their senator or congressman asking for recognition of the Irish Republic by the United States.[75] At the conclusion of the meeting, many people in the audience joined the AARIR.[76]

Mary spoke in Lincoln, Nebraska at the auditorium to a crowd of almost 4,000 on February 14. After Judge Edgar Howard of Columbus, Nebraska introduced her, Mary brought the Americans to task:

> [she] did not wish to talk only to the Irish-Americans, but to those who knew nothing about the conditions in Ireland. . . . Ireland, this winter is experiencing her Valley Forge, only it is not the men in this case who have to suffer, but the women and children. Thousands of women and children go hungry. All this has been brought on the people by the English government, who openly declares she intends to

> starve the people into surrender. England has refused to permit America to send relief to the Irish for this reason. How can a country like the United States stand for such atrocities as these.[77]

Mary arrived in Topeka, Kansas on February 16 to deliver three speeches. Speaking of the news of the arrest of her youngest brother, John, she commented: 'They write to me that he was arrested for having arms and ammunition . . . so it is very likely that they will kill my brother, if it is true that he had firearms. Perhaps they will hardly dare to do so, however, after what they have already done to our family'.[78]

During an interview, Mary was questioned on the part Irish women were taking in the politics of their country:

> Irish women have always received equal political rights with the men until England took control of the government. When we established our government there was no question about women's political stature. Hundreds of years ago Irish women sat in parliament in Ireland. Today they are standing shoulder to shoulder with the men of Ireland, working for Irish freedom.

She also commented that ninety per cent of Irish women attended school and received an education.[79]

Mary spoke to the Kansas legislature on February 16. After an informal reception in Governor Allen's office, she addressed both Houses in the House of Representatives.[80]

Speaking to a crowd of more than 5,000 at the Topeka Auditorium that evening, Mary said that American recognition of the Irish Republic would bring the recognition of other great nations of the world and it would gain a liberty for Ireland.[81] After the meeting, a state organization of the AARIR was formed with over 200 members, as well as a local organization of almost 500 members.[82]

Mary was invited to speak to the joint assembly of the Oklahoma legislature in the House of Representatives on February 17. Lieutenant Governor Trapp called the joint assembly to order and Senator Pete Coyne presided. The chamber and the galleries were packed for Mary's forty-five-minute speech. She began with: 'I have come to say a few words on behalf of a sister republic. I am asking that Ireland may obtain recognition as a republic, a welcome among the sister nations of the earth'.[83]

At a reception given by the AARIR at the Huckins Hotel, Mary warned the audience that: 'England has captured your oil and cotton fields, and is ruling them with her capital. But that is your business. ... You are in danger of having London for your capitol, instead of Washington. But that is your business. You can do so if you want to, but we are not satisfied to have London the capital of Ireland'.[84] She reminded the audience that 'ninety-one percent of the Irish people are for the republic.... Yet only forty per cent of your own Americans were in favour of the American Revolution'.[85]

Mary left Oklahoma City on Friday morning, February 18. A committee of over 100 welcomed her at a reception at the Hotel Tulsa in Tulsa that afternoon.[86] She spoke in the evening at the Tulsa Convention Hall where four Boy Scouts presented her with a large bouquet of roses. After Mayor T. D. Evans welcomed her, Mary told her audience that, 'England can't stifle the voice of freedom in our country'. Resolutions to the Secretary of State, the chairman of the Foreign Relations Committee, and to both the House of Representatives and the Congress were adopted at the end of the meeting.[87]

Mary returned to Oklahoma City on Saturday, February 19, to attend a state convention of the AARIR at the Huckins Hotel, where she spoke to approximately 100 delegates from all parts of the state. A membership campaign to recruit 15,000 members was developed. She later told her audience at the Central High School auditorium that: 'Whatever mistakes America may have made, everyone knows the real enemy of civilization is Germany's first cousin, England. I say again, and let there be no mistake about it, I am ashamed of every Irishman who was foolish enough to enlist in England's army'.[88]

THE SOUTH

On February 11, *The Dallas Morning News* reported that by a vote of fifty-four to sixty-one, the Texas House of Representatives refused to adopt a 'Senate concurrent resolution' inviting Mary to address both the House of Representatives and the Senate. An amendment by Mr Fugler was adopted which stated that 'it was not the place of this country to meddle in the domestic affairs of foreign nations'.[89]

However, Mary held successful, well-attended meetings in Fort Worth, Houston, and Galveston while in Texas. When she spoke at the First Baptist Church in Fort Worth on February 20, the *Fort Worth Record* reported:

> Miss MacSwiney had a wondrous story to tell, and as she gave forth fact after fact on the present condition of the people of Ireland, the audience swayed by the overpowering personality of the speaker, wept, and applauded by turns.[90]

A Committee of the AARIR met Mary and Catherine in Fort Worth to escort them to Dallas, where they were welcomed at the Adolphus Hotel. After a luncheon, Mary visited the Ursuline Convent.[91] She later spoke at the City Hall to almost 1,500 people.[92]

Mary spoke to a standing-room-only-crowd in the Houston Main Street Auditorium, on February 22, under the auspices of the AARIR. The *Houston Post* reported that: 'she denied that the Irish question was a domestic one. . . . that the Catholic Bishops or the Pope were concerned in the political question, and declared that the bitterest enemies of the Irish were the English Catholics'.[93]

The audience in Galveston, on February 23, was the largest to ever appear at the Opera House. Mary emphasized that: 'As America is to Americans, as England is to an Englishman, so Ireland is to Irishmen. Give me liberty or give me death is the attitude of Ireland today'.[94] She was the guest at a luncheon at the Hotel Galvez, visited several Catholic institutions in the afternoon, and later toured Galveston. She expressed regret at not being able to stay longer in Galveston, but said: 'I don't like your American sleeping cars and prefer to travel by day'.[95] The *Galveston News* praised Mary:

> Chatting with her in her parlour at the hotel one would not realize the terrible hardships which she has undergone, and which she is still undergoing. For Miss MacSwiney is the cultured, refined type of Irishwoman whose ability to master situations has given her the power to forget self in the ideal which she represents. She is thoroughly interesting as a conversationalist as well as on the lecture platform.[96]

Mary travelled next to New Orleans for a two-day visit. She spent her first morning sightseeing, with lunch at the Grunewald Hotel and she met informally in the afternoon with officers of the AARIR. At her main meeting at the Athanaeum, on February 25, Mary was escorted to the main auditorium by twelve Irish girls and introduced by Mayor McShane. She spoke on the regional differences within the United States by saying that:

> she found strong opposition to the Irish cause throughout the Southern states as the people of the South think that 'the question is a religious

> one and that the Catholics of Ireland would die persecuting the Protestants.' . . . She charged that the British have spent $130,000,000 in America to control public opinion and that the religious question was the most inimical to the Irish they had ever raised.[97]

From the Grunewald in New Orleans, Mary wrote to Mr James O'Mara, organizer of the AARIR headquarters office in New York, that the meeting had been 'magnificent—the biggest, they say, ever seen in this place'. It was estimated that approximately 9,000 people attended the meeting. Her continuing frustration with the lack of response to her many queries and requests to the AARIR was evident in her questions to Mr O'Mara when she asked him who was looking after the senators and congressmen in Washington and what lobbying was being done. She took him to task when she complained: 'Would you mind, for once instead of walking the streets at night, sitting down instead inside and walking your hands over some sheets of notepaper and answer my questions'.[98]

WESTERN AMERICA

Even though Joseph Scott and Father Peter Yorke, under the auspices of the AARIR, promoted Mary's visit to the West Coast, she still encountered resistance in Sacramento regarding a meeting with the California legislature, controversy over the rental of a hall and protests by the Sacramento Church Federation. However, her meetings in San Francisco, Portland and Seattle were great successes. The press continued to praise her quiet demeanour, her eloquence and her insight.

A special committee of representatives of local organizations welcomed Mary to Los Angeles. The Liberty Boys' Band provided music as cadets from the St John's Academy escorted her from the train to the Ambassador Hotel. Mary spoke, on March 4, at the Philharmonic Auditorium and at an informal reception at the Ambassador Hotel to teachers, nuns and other professional women. Once again, she urged American recognition of the Irish Republic.[99] When Mary left Los Angeles to travel to Sacramento, her Pullman car was filled with flowers, fruit and other gifts.[100]

Joseph Scott wrote to Peter Yorke that 'Miss MacSwiney swept LA as no other visitor from east or from Ireland has ever before. Her argument is most intellectual, convincing, and persuasive—poor woman is physically tired although wonderfully alert mentally'.[101]

Prior to her arrival, the California legislature adopted a resolution, on March 2, to invite Mary to speak at a joint session of the Senate and Assembly on March 8. Protests of the address by the Sacramento Church Federation began immediately.[102] The Federation denounced her address and claimed Sinn Féiners were trying to drive a wedge between America and the Allies. Sinn Féin purportedly prevented conscription during World War I in Ireland and Australia, and delayed it in Canada while our allies fought 'with their backs to the wall'. The petition, signed by Mrs L. C. Harbaugh, secretary of the Federation, requested the 'California Legislature not to invite anyone advocating the principles of Sinn Féin to address The People of the State of California through the Legislature'.[103]

Contention next arose concerning the location of the mass meeting to be held on March 8. P. C. Roddy and Dr J. W. O'Brien had rented the Masonic Hall, paid a deposit and stated the purpose of the meeting. When the members of the Masonic Lodge learned Mary MacSwiney would be the speaker, they refused to rent the hall. The meeting place then moved to the Stone Theatre.[104]

On March 8 1921, Mary arrived in Sacramento, under the auspices of the AARIR. Peter J. McCormick, president of the United Irish Societies, a San Francisco delegation; and a crowd of supporters greeted her.[105] Blanche Ribel, a member of the Sacramento AARIR committee, presented her with a bunch of California poppies and a statement of welcome:

> Dear Miss MacSwiney: We wish these first field flowers of spring, and especially the California poppies of this Golden State, to express to you, a visitor from afar, our cordial greeting from the Capital City, the heart of California.[106]

An AARIR committee escorted Mary to the Travellers' Hotel, where a delegation of Sacramento women greeted her and held an informal reception. She attended a luncheon held in her honour and later a social tea at the Convent of the Sisters of Mercy.[107]

Escorted to the Capitol by a brass band and parade, Mary addressed the State Legislature in the Senate Chamber on 'The Truth About Ireland'. She asked not to go on record; she only wished an opportunity to reiterate the conditions in Ireland.[108] Her reference to Ireland's intention to fight to the end brought applause. She maintained it was the duty of the United States, under its policy toward small nations, to recognize the Irish Republic, and asked that petitions be sent to Congress requesting recognition by the United States government.[109] She charged British troops with 'committing worse atrocities in Ireland than the Germans were ever charged with committing in Belgium during the World War'. With that, she displayed a proclamation of Cumann na mBan, which invited 'defiance' to England and pledged the women of Ireland to loyalty to the Irish cause.[110]

Every seat in the Stone Theatre was filled an hour before Mary arrived at the mass meeting. After an introduction by Dr James W. O'Brien, chairman of the meeting, she explained her only purpose in touring the United States was to obtain recognition for the Irish Republic. She stated she did not expect the American people to go to war with England, she did not seek military intervention, but she did seek recognition. To the allegation that she was here to stir up trouble between England and the United States, she simply said it was not true.[111]

Mary then spoke at the Hotel Statler to a joint meeting of women's clubs. Following a short address to the crowd gathered outside the theatre, Kathleen Byrne, of the AARIR, presented her with a bouquet of roses. Mary left Sacramento the following morning to travel to San Francisco.[112]

Joseph Scott and Father Peter Yorke met her at the Ferry Building in San Francisco. Exemplifying the apex of republican nationalism in California, she was escorted by a parade of approximately 50,000 people, headed by mounted police and a brass band from the Ferry Building up Market Street to her headquarters at the Fairmont Hotel. Father Yorke managed her California itinerary and a committee of 400 women arranged her stay and reception in San Francisco. Mayor James Rolph officially welcomed her to the city. The Board of Supervisors held a special session to hear her speak on the conditions in Ireland and the need for American recognition.[113]

Mrs Frederick H. Colburn hosted the AARIR reception and tea in the ballroom and Red Room of the Fairmont Hotel.[114] Mary impressed those gathered with her 'more than ordinary ability' as a speaker and her extensive knowledge of American and French history.[115] According to Florence Mullen, Women's Irish Education League, reservations were limited to 1,000. Alice Rose Power, a member of the Board of Education, chaired the reception committee. Mary read a statement from Cumann n mBan, asking her to 'emphasize the fact that the women of Ireland are not taking a pacifist attitude in the present [Anglo-Irish] war'.[116]

A crowd of over 15,000 people filled the Civic Auditorium on the evening of March 10. People sat on the floor around the speaker's platform, in the organ loft, on the steps of the galleries, and many were forced into the corridors and lobby. Her appearance brought applause and cheering that lasted several minutes.[117] Mary commented that she felt at home in San Francisco with so many supporters of the cause of the Irish Republic.[118] However, she explained:

> I have not come here to ask you to do or to think or to say any single thing, which would be subversive of or inconsistent with your duty as American citizens. . . . I want those of you who are of Irish blood to realize that it is not as Irish-Americans that you can best help Ireland today, but by being American citizens.[119]

Referring specifically to the Argentine Republic in 1819, Greece in 1821, Belgium in 1832, and more than a score of South American Republics between 1822 and 1852, she asked: 'why then could we [the United States] not recognize the Republic of Ireland?'[120] Mary claimed the most harmful distortion of the British propaganda programme was the assertion that the war in Ireland was religious. Ireland had carried on the struggle against England for 750 years. She asked pointedly: 'If this is a religious war today, what was it 400 years ago, before Martin Luther was born?'[121] Her most pointed remarks pertained to World War I and the peace treaty negotiations at Versailles:

> You went into the war—the World War—on behalf of the small nations of the earth. You laid down fourteen points, which were to be the basis of the world's freedom. We in Ireland analyzed all your statements, all your promises. You were fighting 'to make the world safe for democracy', to 'insure that no small nation would henceforth have to live under a sovereignty under which it did not wish to live'. You promised that as a result of your entry into the war, no great nation would henceforth be allowed to exploit a weaker nation for its own benefit. . . . and we in Ireland listened.[122]

> But—you have come out of the war, you have left 70,000 of your best and bravest dead on the field of France and Flanders, and you have left your beautiful ideals shatter on the diplomatic tables in Versailles.[123] (See Appendix 7.)

The California press bureau of the AARIR headquarters proclaimed the campaign to write letters to Washington D.C. a success. According to an AARIR member who had returned from Washington D.C., the legislatures were deluged with protests, some receiving 300 letters a day. He commented: 'so Miss Mary MacSwiney is evidently on the right track'.[124]

Mary travelled from San Francisco to Portland, Oregon on March 12.[125] She queried reporters during an interview at the Hotel Portland about the overall sentiment in Portland, in particular, and Oregon, in general, in order to prepare herself to answer questions pertaining to opposition to the Irish Republic and to address possible attacks during her address that evening. A committee of 160 representatives, headed by Mrs J. P. O'Brien, greeted her at an informal reception at the Portland Hotel.[126]

The Portland Auditorium that evening was packed with 4,200 people. Judge Kavanaugh introduced her. Mary asked for 'recognition of the Irish Republic without intervention'. She said the United States could free Ireland without firing a shot.[127] It was reported that the real success of the evening could be measured by the number of 'non-supporters' who listened to:

> Miss MacSwiney's splendid array of facts, which made them see the justice of Ireland's plea and has made them advocates for the recognition of the Irish Republic. The after effects of Miss MacSwiney's visit are more than usually successful, the press reports were favourable and the entire community has a grasp of Ireland's case that it never had before.[128]

Mary travelled from Portland to Spokane, Washington, on March 15, where she spoke eight times the following day. Keeping up a marathon-like pace, she began at Gonzaga University, followed by three talks at the Hippodrome Theatre, three at the Pantages Theatre and her main speech at the Knights of Columbus Hall during the evening. She predicted that the United States would recognize the Irish Republic by April 24, the fifth anniversary of the declaration of the Republic.[129] She announced she had been asked to visit Canada, but 'they will probably throw me in jail if I get there'. When asked if she would be afraid to travel there she answered: 'I would welcome it. What wonderful propaganda for us! It would be glorious. I have been thrown in prison before. Why? For nothing. Because I loved freedom and liberty'.[130]

From Spokane, Mary's next stop was Butte, Montana, where she spoke at the Broadway Theatre on St Patrick's Day, again under the auspices of the AARIR. It was noted in *The Butte Miner* that because of her deep mourning, no parties or celebrations were held. However, a reception was held at the high school auditorium in order for her to meet the women of Butte.[131] An American Legion honour guard escorted her from the railroad station through the main streets of town to the courthouse, where she gave a short talk. Anastasia and Molly O'Meara, 307 West Granite Street, hosted her during her stay in Butte.[132] President C. H. Clapp of the School of Mines introduced Mary at her evening meeting, where she pointedly asked for 'the freedom for which the world war was fought. Freedom was promised to all, they didn't say—except Ireland. You went to war to destroy militarism, then why does British militarism exist?'[133]

The high school auditorium was filled to capacity for Mary's next address to the women of Butte. For the most part, she reiterated her lecture of the previous evening. Following her address, she was presented with a copper plaque engraved in the words of her brother, Terence: 'It is not those who can inflict the most, but those who can suffer the most who will conquer[or]'.[134]

Speaking in Salt Lake City, Utah, on March 21, at the Salt Lake City Theatre, Mary commented that she had spoken at 240 meetings during a three-month period. She added that the receptions had been cordial and well received. Once again, she emphasized that she did not wish to speak to only Irish or Catholics, but to Americans in general, and particularly to those who were anti-Irish'.[135] She spoke the following day, March 22, to the Rotarians at a luncheon at the Hotel Utah.[136]

Mary travelled on to Denver, Colorado, on March 27, where she met with 500 Denver women at a reception in the Brown Palace Hotel. During an interview, she described the arrest of her brother, John, several weeks prior:

> It developed at the trial that John had been found with a revolver in his hand, but the farce court, which was employed, fearing to find against the family, which boasted a martyr, declared that another man had carried the revolver. Thus John with three others was sentenced to fifteen years penal servitude, and the other six were executed. . . . Young boys are sentenced to be shot after a summary hearing, and the life of any one who is suspected to be in sympathy with the Republican force leads a precarious existence.[137]

She complained of 'being constantly harassed even in this country'. She relayed that during the previous three weeks, four letters and several cablegrams from her sister, Annie, concerning the arrest of John had been intercepted and she had not received them. She also protested that 'nearly every communication which passes between us is tampered with before it reaches its destination'.[138]

Appearing on behalf of the AARIR, Lieutenant Governor Earl C. Cooley introduced her to a crowd of 10,000 people that evening at the municipal auditorium. She stood under a crepe-draped picture of Terence while the audience gave her an ovation. She wanted Americans to remember the recent report of Lord Northcliffe (in charge of English publicity in America) to parliament in which he boasted of spending approximately $150,000,000 in America in 'teaching Americans how to think'. She claimed a large portion of that amount was spent on the salaries of 10,000 British agents in America who did 'nothing but propagate the English viewpoint to receptive American minds . . . through English owned newspapers in this country and their name is legion'.[139] She was also the guest of honour at a reception at the Knights of Columbus Hall on Easter Sunday afternoon.[140]

RETURN TO MIDDLE AND EASTERN AMERICA

M. J. Manning, president of the Kansas FOIF, requested that all Irish in Kansas City, Missouri and also all residents, Irish or not, attend Mary's meeting at the Convention Hall, in Kansas City, on March 29, when she spoke for more than two hours on United States recognition of the Irish Republic.[141] In her talk to the members of the Patrick Henry Club at the Hotel Baltimore, she expressed her belief that 'a war, more horrible than the last is inevitable unless some basis for ruling the world is established. The freedom of Ireland is a necessary part of establishing this basis'.[142] Speaking of America's part in the future world order:

> You Americans cannot remain neutral. He who is not with us is against us. If you are so interested in England, then you are going with England against one small country. Insist on England paying her war debt and she cannot go on paying her Black and Tans and she will withdraw from Ireland her army of occupation.[143]

Among those attending the meeting was Lord Mayor Dempsey of Mallow, Co. Cork. Both he and Mary were presented with a book by J. O. O'Brien, *The Added Phase of American History*, which told of Irish participation in the American Revolution.[144]

After Mary's appearance in Kansas City, it was announced in *The Kansas City Kansan* that the goal of a new bond drive to be launched by the American Committee for Relief in Ireland would be $50,000. During the statewide drive, which began on April 4, local committees canvassed every county.[145]

Returning to Illinois, Mary spoke before a joint session of the Illinois legislature in Springfield, on March 31, and to the 'Mid-day Luncheon Club' at the Leland Hotel. She told the audience at the latter meeting comically: 'I do not want to give the impression . . . that our bishops and priests are against the Republic. Only a few of them are. And the reason is because they are old men'. After the laughter of the audience subsided, she sadly added:

> Old men are apt to be foolish and childish. They see the suffering and misery, which our people are undergoing, and they are apt to think that any government is better than to have those conditions continue in the cause of a new government. They are inclined to take the peace at any price view.[146]

The following day, April 1, Mary spoke to the Teachers' Federation at the high school auditorium. Her largest meeting was held later at the State Arsenal, during which she described the incredible events in her home the day before her brother, Terence, was arrested:

> On the twelfth day of last August a letter came to my home in Cork, addressed to the Lord Mayor Terence MacSwiney, or to Miss Mary MacSwiney. I opened it. The letter contained the information that a certain policeman was a spy, and held all the facts, which, according to the letter, should have warranted his arrest. It was anonymous. I knew that such letters were being sent to Irish patriots and that if they were found in their possession in the raid by English authorities which always followed their being sent, they were regarded as seditious literature and the person having them in possession was arrested. So I put the letter in the fire.
>
> That morning at half past ten my brother was arrested. They searched the city hall until 10 o'clock that night, and then came to my house at half past eleven and searched it, looking for that letter. Had that letter been found, this is what would have happened: that policeman would

> have been shot, and then my brother would have been arrested as an accomplice in his murder. But they never found the letter.[147]

She then precisely pointed out what she expected of President Harding:

> President Harding a few days ago wrote a note of sympathy with Irish wrongs to the association in America which is forming to attempt to right those Irish wrongs. That was very nice of President Harding. But what we want President Harding to do is to send to the Republic of Ireland official recognition of the United States of that Republic.[148]

The Illinois State Journal reported that: 'She never faltered in her ringing words of sincerity and conviction, and in her appeal for American sympathy with Irish wrongs, and American recognition of the Irish Republic'.

During an interview in the Northwestern Station upon her arrival in Milwaukee, Wisconsin, on April 2, Mary was reported to have shown 'resentment' when asked to comment on events in Ireland as 'riots and insurrection'. This was a point she stressed in all of her speeches and restated to the audience the need to clarify the situation in Ireland:

> We are not rioting, nor are we in insurrection. . . . We are at war fully as much as the American colonies were on the eve of French recognition of the American Republic. Was the battle of Lexington a riot? And the battle of Bunker Hill an insurrection?[149]

Mary attended a luncheon at the Hotel Astor and later spoke to a group of teachers at the Prister Hotel. She spoke at the Milwaukee Auditorium the following evening, where Mayor Hoan introduced her.[150]

She left Milwaukee to attend the first annual AARIR convention held in Chicago at the Medinah Temple, on April 18. The festivities began with a parade up Michigan Avenue of between 25,000 and 30,000 people. Banners carried by the marchers relayed messages such as: 'Thirty-six per cent of Washington's army was Irish'. Another read: 'One-fourth of the officers in General Jackson's army in the war of 1812 were Irish', and 'Burn everything British but its coal'. Mayor Thompson opened the convention with a welcome address; Attorney Frank P. Walsh gave the opening address. The cheering to welcome Lord Mayor O'Callaghan of Ireland lasted eight minutes. Mary followed the Lord Mayor onto the stage to speak on the responsibility of the United States to guarantee small nations the right of self-determination. The 5,000 delegates in attendance that evening pledged $2,500,000 'to wage Ireland's fight against England'. The pledge obligated 500,000 AARIR members to contribute $5 and was made after Harry Boland, as a representative of Eamon de Valera, stated in his speech that the struggle for Ireland's independence 'has resolved itself in a question of money'.[151]

Appearing at the Hotel Aster at a meeting of the Teachers' Council of the AARIR, Mary claimed that many American newspapers were sympathetic toward England and 'she did not doubt that the editorials of some of the metropolitan papers, including *The New York Times*, were written by hirelings of Lord Northcliffe'. She said that the only non-hyphenated people she met during her tour of this country were some of the Indians she saw on a reservation. She classified the pilgrims of the *Mayflower*, Washington, Clay, Webster, Jefferson and Lincoln as 'phynates'.[152]

Returning to Columbus, Ohio, on the evening of June 27, Mary 'expressed surprise that the United States has not recognized the Republic since this is the first time in history that it has refused such an action'. She said she believed that 'if it were left to the popular vote of the people, Ireland would be recognized tomorrow'.[153]

Mary spoke at the Armory in Akron, Ohio on July 3. She was escorted by a parade led by the Barberton Ladies' Band. During the evening meeting at the Colonial Theatre, she read from a London *Times* editorial, July 4 1919, by Lord Northcliffe in which 'he urged the spread of propaganda in America, and he boasted of having spent millions of dollars for it here before and during the American participation in the World War'. She once again warned the audience:

> Beware of British propaganda. . . . England built a paper wall of propaganda around Ireland. On the inside of the wall she wrote what she wanted Ireland to believe concerning the world outside, and on the outside of the wall she wrote what she wanted the world to believe concerning Ireland. But we have torn away the paper wall and have come out to tell the world our own story.[154]

Mary returned to Philadelphia on July 17, to appear at an Irish demonstration in Shibe Park where she spoke to at least 15,000 people. Three platforms had been erected so that addresses could be given simultaneously. Mary moved throughout the afternoon between the three platforms to accuse the United States of 'infidelity to Ireland' and to the American soldiers who had died in France because self-determination for small nations had not been achieved. She also claimed that:

> Ireland is the only nation in the whole wide world today that is not afraid of England. . . . The Irish love Ireland a hundred thousand times more than they hate England. Therefore they will be willing to forgive England if she clears out of Ireland bag and baggage and never comes back.

Cablegrams were drawn up and sent to Lloyd George, Eamon de Valera and President Harding urging the recognition of the Republic of Ireland.[155]

Mary wrote to Eamon de Valera from The Bellevue-Stratford Hotel in Philadelphia for further orders. She noted it had been almost eight months since she started her tour of the United States—'at his special request'. She had spoken to Harry Boland and James O'Mara and O'Mara suggested sending her on a Bond Drive. Harry thought that she had done 'her bit' and wanted to give her the option of returning to Ireland. She frankly told de Valera that:

> As for having 'done my bit', that plea is out of court, for none of us can be said to have done our part fully till Ireland is free or we are dead. If I leave here it will only be to do something else at home and the question is where I can be most use. I do not ask for any option in the matter being I hope as good a soldier as the next.[156]

After all the months she had been speaking in cities across the United States, she finally expressed her true feelings of a Bond Drive to de Valera:

> Frankly I hate the thought of the Bond Drive and doubt my effectiveness at it. I understand the Americans like to be flattered and I don't flatter them. On a few occasions when the question of money came up I pointed out that they had given England five thousand million and Ireland five million. I hate the meeting where they have those horrid collections with a man walking up and down the platform yelling himself hoarse trying to rouse the people to enthusiasm and generosity. It makes me quite sick. I am not much

> good as a beggar but I can always talk for recognition and let them infer the necessity for supplying the sinews of war.[157]

Mary supported and defended Eamon de Valera in his Bond Drive controversies, but there is no evidence in the records of her speeches that she actually solicited contributions for the bonds. However, she did strive to and succeeded in increasing the AARIR membership.

CONCLUSION

Mary concluded her tour to return to Ireland, on August 12 1921, to attend the Second Dáil as a deputy (Teachta Dála) from Cork, the area previously represented by Terence MacSwiney. Upon her departure from New York on the anniversary of the start of his hunger strike, she thanked the United States in his name for the welcome accorded her and for the work done to obtain recognition for Ireland.[158]

To evaluate the success of this first tour of Mary MacSwiney, the newspaper coverage should be examined. The American and Irish-American press favourably covered each event and reported her welcomes and addresses in great detail. The scheduled events were publicized well in advance and the events themselves usually received front-page coverage. Over and over again, Mary was praised for her eloquence, knowledge and demeanour.

She had arrived in the United States and began her tour at the height of controversy and division between Eamon de Valera and Irish-American leaders. In addition, tremendous tension between Irish-American leaders and the Wilson administration existed. She experienced moments of criticism, rejection and controversy. However, she remained composed, consistent and determined in her message—all the while displaying political astuteness, courage and a tremendous love of and commitment to the Republic of Ireland.

The Irish World reported Mary's tour as the most successful conducted by a United States visitor.[159] Her biographer, Charlotte Fallon, comments on her success:

> With the American tours of Eamon de Valera and Mary MacSwiney, the precedent had been established that Americans would give money without being in total command of the facts. . . . America contributed generously, asked few questions, and trusted that those responsible

would use the funds to obtain a suitable solution to Ireland's problems.[160]

Mary summarized the tour in her own words: 'It has been wonderful—this first big tour of mine'. However, she did not view the tour as an 'overwhelming success'.[161]

None of the Secret Service investigators who followed Mary to report on her activities and meetings found anything of a 'radical nature' in any of her speeches or 'of an unusual nature in her talk other than that which might be expected in an address of that character'.[162]

Through Mary's mass meetings, the AARIR grew financially and in numbers across the United States. The outpouring of support given to her not only demonstrated the willingness and ability of Irish-Americans to support the Irish Republic, but also her ability as an articulate and poised speaker to clearly define the conditions at the time and the urgent need, not only for American recognition of the Irish Republic, but also that of other nations of the world.

After her return to Ireland, she became one of the most ardent and outspoken republicans to oppose the Anglo-Irish Treaty. She spoke for two hours and thirty-two minutes at the Dáil session debating the Anglo-Irish Treaty where she denounced the Irish who opposed the rejection of the Treaty, all world governments (except the Irish Republican Government) and the American press, especially the Hearst newspapers.[163] On the evening of November 4 1922, Mary was arrested in Dublin, taken into custody, and imprisoned in Mountjoy Jail without charges under the Emergency Powers Act. She immediately declared she was on hunger strike as a protest against the illegality of her imprisonment. Cumann na mBan organized a campaign and a huge rally to support her release. The hunger strike received international attention and support, particularly in the United States Canada, and Australia.[164]

CHAPTER 7

Countess Constance Markievicz: Romantic Republican, April–May 1922

As a strong anti-Treatyite and Republican, Countess Constance Markievicz travelled to the United States in April 1922 to campaign for the support of Eamon de Valera and the Republic of Ireland. Factionalism and confusion over the 1921 Anglo-Irish Treaty reigned in Ireland and representatives of both the Irish Republic and the Irish Free State Government sought Irish-American support. At the time of her arrival in the United States, the beginning of the Irish Civil War, on June 28 1922, was still almost three months away.

Enormous crowds greeted Countess Markievicz and her delegation (Kathleen Barry, Austin Stack, J. J. O'Kelly, Father Michael O'Flanagan, Professor Stockley and Brian O'Higgins) during their tour across the United States. The peak of Irish-American republican nationalism and her 'romantic' reputation as Ireland's 'Joan of Arc' contributed to the publicity and fanfare given to her speaking engagements. The press emphasized her 'romantic' republican image as rebel, heroine and the 'glory of Irish womanhood'.[1]

BACKGROUND

Constance Georgina Gore-Booth was born February 4 1868 at No. 7 Buckingham Gate, London, to aristocrats Georgina and Henry Gore-Booth, members of the ascendancy in Ireland. Along with two sisters and two brothers, her early years were spent at Lissadell in

County Sligo. Constance Gore-Booth spent her young adult life as an artist educated in Paris, a poet and an expert horsewoman. She and her sister, Eva, founded the Sligo Women's Suffrage Society in 1896. In 1909, however, she abandoned the suffrage movement to become a militant nationalist. She appealed to the women of Ireland to 'take part in politics and in the national movement, not as women fighting for the franchise only, but for Ireland'.[2] She married Casimir Markievicz, a Polish Count and playwright and performed in many of his plays in the Abbey Theatre. Constance Markievicz became known in Dublin as 'the Countess' or 'Madame'. Biographer Jacqueline Van Voris describes her as:

> born into a charmed circle of privilege, wealth and power where she formed habits of leadership and service. In her middle years when she wished to extend privilege to others less fortunate, she rebelled against the class that nurtured her.[4]

Through her associations with labour leaders James Larkin and James Connolly, Countess Markievicz became active in the labour cause and became well known during the labour strikes in Dublin in 1913 when she set up a kitchen in the basement of Liberty Hall to prepare and distribute meals to the wives and families of the strikers. With the hope of forming 'women workers into an army of fighters', she became an active supporter of the Women Workers' Union.[5]

After her arrest and court-martial as one of the leaders of the 1916 Easter Rising, Countess Markievicz was sentenced to death and transferred to Mountjoy Jail and then to Aylesbury Prison in England. After her death sentence was commuted to life imprisonment, she was released in 1917 when Bonar Law, Leader of the House of Commons, released all participants in the Easter Rising.[6]

Countess Markievicz was rearrested in 1918 and imprisoned in Holloway Jail in London for a year. No charges were brought against her and she was never brought to trial. While in jail, she was elected the first woman member to the English House of Commons, but refused to take her seat. She returned to Ireland after her release to take her seat in Dáil Éireann as Minister of Labour—the first woman Cabinet minister in western Europe. Because of opposition to and suppression by the British Government, the Dáil went underground. Meeting in different houses and hiding places, they became known as the 'Dáil on the run'.[7]

Countess Markievicz was arrested again on September 26, 1920, imprisoned in Mountjoy and held for two months without a trial. She was then court-martialled on a charge of 'conspiracy' and of 'organizing the killing of soldiers' and sentenced to two years' hard labour.[8] Along with other imprisoned Dáil members, she was freed by the Truce of July 1921.

The second Dáil met in August to re-elect President de Valera and re-appoint Countess Markievicz as Minister of Labour. Along with the other women deputies, Countess Markievicz vehemently opposed the Anglo-Irish Treaty, which had been negotiated and signed by plenipotentiaries Arthur Griffith and Michael Collins. She saw the Treaty as a 'deliberate attempt to set up a privileged class'. In addition, she believed it to be 'dangerously vague'; that reference to 'the king' meant in fact the 'British Cabinet' and that the oath was a 'dishonourable oath . . . that can be twisted in every imaginable form'.[9] Dressed in a green Cumann na mBan uniform she spoke out during the Dáil debates to say: 'while Ireland is not free I remain a rebel, unconverted and inconvertible . . I have seen the stars and I am not going to follow a flickering will-o-the-wisp'.[10]

Eamon de Valera opposed the Treaty for many complex reasons. Based on the election of May 1921, he believed its terms to be in conflict with the wishes of the majority of the people. Article 17 of the Articles of Agreement contained no mention of Dáil Éireann and would allow the substitution of a Southern Parliament. He held that the representatives elected in the twenty-six counties had been elected to Dáil Éireann; the British maintained they had been returned to the Southern Parliament. De Valera vehemently opposed the partition of Ireland. The Agreement assumed the Partition Act of 1920 to be in force and supplemented it. He opposed as intensely the oath and negotiation with the British Government to 'reconcile Irish national aspirations with the association of nations forming the British Empire'. He also feared some of Ireland's ports might be permanently occupied by England.[11]

De Valera, in an effort to save the Irish Republic, re-drafted the portion of the Treaty dealing with External Association (Document No. 2) as an amendment to establish the basis of the Treaty as being 'entered into between sovereign States'.[12] He suggested Ireland could be 'associated' with the commonwealth without being a member of it.[13] He withdrew the document on January 4, prior to the vote on the Treaty. John Devoy and the Friends of Irish Freedom (FOIF) opposed the strategy of External Association and 'external as well as internal association of Ireland with the British Empire'.[14]

Dáil Deputies approved the Treaty by a vote of sixty-four to fifty-seven on January 6. Eamon de Valera resigned his presidency of the Republic of Ireland at the public session of the Dáil on January 9 1922. On January 10, Arthur Griffith was appointed President of Dáil Éireann. In compliance with the Treaty, a Provisional Government was elected on January 16. Countess Markievicz, Mary MacSwiney and Eamon de Valera attended the Irish Race Congress in Paris in February, along with Free State delegates. The Irish Republican and Free State delegates were already so divided they would not travel to Paris together.[15]

TOUR OF THE UNITED STATES

Countess Markievicz received the assignment from Eamon de Valera to tour the United States in April 1922, under the auspices of the American Association for the Recognition of the Irish Republic, to ensure continued support of the Irish Republic. De Valera had originally formally asked Father Michael O'Flanagan, TD, Professor Stockley, TD, and Countess Markievicz to form at least part of a delegation to the United States, based on their abilities to 'draw the crowds'.[16] On September 23, it was decided that the speakers would be sent to promote the flotation of a new bond issue. Countess Markievicz, Father O'Flanagan, Professor Stockley and Brian O'Higgins were designated as the 'Advance Guard'. The Minister of Foreign Affairs coordinated the arrangements for the tour with Harry Boland, representative of the Irish Republic in Washington D.C.[17]

At the same time, representatives of the Provisional Government, which would become the Irish Free State Government, also met with Irish-American groups throughout the United States to compete for support. Kathleen Barry, an active member of Cumann na mBan, a judge in the Irish Republic court and sister of Kevin Barry, accompanied Markievicz.[18] The other members of the delegation, Austin Stack, former Dáil Minister of Home Affairs, and J. J. Kelly, editor of the *Catholic Bulletin* and President of the Gaelic League, were already in the United States. They had established a headquarters at 8 East Forty-first Street in New York City. The two women left Southampton, on April 1, aboard the *Aquitania*.[19]

THE TOUR BEGINS

Arriving on a United States revenue cutter, fifty reporters and photographers boarded the *Aquitania* at the quarantine station in New York.[20] Reporter Marguerite Mooers-Marshall, of the *New York Evening World*, described Countess Markievicz:

> Despite her martial achievements she is not a martial looking person—frail, rather and almost deprecatory except when she is talking about the Irish Republic. Very tall and slender she has the stoop characteristic of so many women of her height. Her soft, waving ash-brown hair is done in the quaint psyche knot at the crown of her head, her eyes behind the eye-glasses are clear blue and there is a dash of pink in her thin cheeks. Her smile is charming. Back of everything she says one feels emotion like a flame.[21]

Countess Markievicz received flowery praises from the American press. They, perhaps because of her aristocratic background, perceived her as exotic and seemed enamoured of every aspect of her appearance and manner. Her clothes were described down to the colour of the trim of her dress and her stockings. Her lectures were well attended, the funds raised at the meetings were generous, although not as large as in the years before the Treaty. She always spoke against the Treaty, always restated her commitment to the Irish Republic and to Eamon de Valera and referred to the upcoming election scheduled for May 1922. She informed the American audiences that the Irish Republic needed support and aid and asked for their help. She always thanked Americans for their support. Her speeches were well received. Her tour, although initially set up by de Valera, was under the auspices of the AARIR. From the reports of major American newspapers, her speeches, even though she pulled in historical facts and delivered them with focus and direction, seemed spontaneous. Judging from the quotations from her addresses accredited to her by the press, Countess Markievicz was eloquent, knowledgeable and spoke with great ease.

Countess Markievicz and Kathleen Barry received an enormous welcome at the Cunard pier when they arrived in New York City, on April 7 1922, for a five-day visit. A large crowd, along with Austin Stack and J. J. O'Kelly greeted them.[22] Countess Markievicz told the press that the purpose of her visit was 'to put the truth before the friends of Ireland in the United States who so magnificently supported us in our fight'.[23] She said: 'the Free Staters have left us. [Michael] Collins and [Arthur] Griffith are traitors to the cause. I am willing to give up my life for the [republican] cause if it is necessary'.[24]

During her stay in New York, Countess Markievicz attended a secret Clan na Gael meeting; visited Irish labour leader James Larkin, jailed in Sing Sing Penitentiary for 'criminal syndicalism' for helping to organize the American Communist Party and spoke at mass meetings at Laurel Gardens in Newark.[25] *The Irish World* claimed that New Jersey had the distinction of being the 'stronghold of the Free Staters'.[26]

At a meeting of the AARIR New York District Councils at the Carmelite School Hall, on April 7, she thanked the more than 500 officers:

> I am glad to be here and to thank you and tell you how we all thought of you; how we appreciated your efforts; how we loved you and looked to you during all that time of terror, how the money you subscribed to the bonds helped to build up the Republic.[27]

As the principal speaker at a mass meeting at Laurel Gardens, on April 9, Countess Markievicz told the audience: 'make no mistake, the Republic you helped to build up still lives and is going to win out in the end'. She spoke of the two men [Arthur Griffith and Michael Collins] who signed the 'so-called Treaty' and said that it had been a 'great shock to Ireland. They proclaimed it as a great victory, but there was no rejoicing in Ireland'. She said she 'deplored' the articles of agreements requiring three separate pledges to the King of England. 'Anyone who has taken the Republic oath cannot take this oath and be loyal to Ireland'.[28]

THE EAST

After leaving New York, Countess Markievicz visited cities where Irish sympathy was strongest—Philadelphia; Detroit; Cleveland; St Paul; Minneapolis; Butte; Anaconda; Seattle; Portland; San Francisco; Los Angeles; Springfield, Massachusetts; Cincinnati; and Boston.

She arrived in Philadelphia on Good Friday, April 16. Joseph McGarrity greeted her at the railroad station. At a mass meeting on Easter Sunday at the Academy of Music,[29] she praised Eamon de

Valera and felt him 'worthy to be a comrade of George Washington'. At the mention of de Valera's name, the crowd rose to cheer. She gave thanks for 'all the money you have sent us in aid of the cause and I want to say those dollars gave us the courage to continue the fight'. *The Irish World* reported that the supporters contributed over $75,000 in cash and pledges.[30]

Just one week prior to Countess Markievicz's arrival in Akron, Ohio, the leaders of the Irish Free State held a conference in the same city on April 11 and 12. Piarais Beaslaí, Commandant General of the Irish Republican Army (then under the control of the Free State), headed the conference. John Forrestal, identified with Sinn Féin and James M. Sullivan, formerly a member of the US diplomatic service, accompanied him. He told a small group at the Portage Hotel that Ireland had no need of financial aid and that 'every cent of the millions subscribed to the Irish national loan would be repaid by the Government of the Irish Free State'. He stated the purpose of his mission to be 'to encourage friendly relations between the new Irish state and the government and people of America'. He spoke of the future of Ireland under the Free State Government: agriculture would be modernized, industry and harbours revived, national drama, music, art and athletics subsidized, reforestation begun, and replacement of the English poor laws with a humane legal system. Speaking against militarism, he stated that 'it was military despotism we fought in the war and it is no less ugly whether foreign or domestic and we will oppose it and beat it wherever it shows itself'. As reported by the local press, he made no mention of the tour of Countess Markievicz and the Republican delegation.[31]

Countess Markievicz, Kathleen Barry and J. J. O'Kelly appeared at a mass meeting at Detroit, Michigan on April 18. Austin Stack left the delegation to tour through the East with Father Michael O'Flannigan, Vice President of the Irish Republic, after the meeting. The Countess, Kathleen and O'Kelly attended a banquet in the Knights of Columbus Hall sponsored by the Kevin Barry Club and the Gaelic Club of Detroit.[32] From Detroit, the Countess and Kathleen travelled to Ohio.

Dressed in mourning, Countess Markievicz spoke at a meeting in the B. of L. E. Auditorium in Cleveland, Ohio on April 20. She began her address by shouting to the audience: 'I am a rebel and I hope there are many others here tonight'. She had previously said of herself that 'while Ireland is not free I remain a rebel, unconverted and unconvertible. There is no word strong enough for it'.[33] She claimed that Arthur Griffith and Michael Collins had broken their pledge to the Republican Cabinet and 'they will answer to God for their acts'. She blamed the border trouble on the Free State 'bunglers'. Between $10,000 and $15,000 was raised at the meeting.[34]

One week later, on April 22, Countess Markievicz spoke in South Akron, Ohio at Marian Hall, under the auspices of the AARIR. She told the audience that 'the Irish Republic still lives and will, in a very short time, blossom out into full life . . . and that the Free State will soon be a thing of short memory'. She accused Lloyd George of asking for the truce when British morale started to split. Kathleen Barry spoke of her brother's only regret that 'he had to die so soon in the cause and would have preferred to wait until Ireland was free, when he would gladly give up his life'.[35]

Countess Markievicz seemed to enjoy most aspects of the tour; perhaps after her time spent in prison what she enjoyed most was the freedom and being out of doors. She wrote often, with an almost child-like excitement, of the beautiful landscapes of the American countryside. She wrote to her sister, Eva Gore-Booth, that, 'everywhere we go we are fêted and get great receptions. Indeed, our only complaint is that we are much entertained for our entertainers take absolute possession of us'.[36] She enjoyed all the American cities and commented frequently on American homes:

> They [the houses] are so much nicer than the houses at home or in England and so much more comfortable and much cleaner and better divided-up. The bathrooms are a joy and even the small houses have them: walls and all of shining white tiles and cupboards built in to the walls, so convenient. Akron especially took my fancy. We drove out to the suburbs and even the poor houses stood alone among greenery.[37]

THE MIDWEST

Countess Markievicz, Kathleen Barry and J. J. O'Kelly arrived in St Paul, Minnesota on April 24. In a letter to her stepson, Staskou, Markievicz described St Paul as being 'on the Mississippi in the wilds of Minnesota'.[38] Speaking at a mass meeting at the People's Church, she stated that she firmly believed that the army would not swear allegiance to the Free State Government 'for its members know that the Treaty would not mean peace—it would not accomplish the things Irishmen have fought for more than 700 years'. She felt certain that the election scheduled for May would probably not be held. And, at the same time, accused the Free State people of making every effort to force the election. She told the audience that the republicans wanted to delay it until election machinery and registration lists could be organized. She believed there was no way a valid election could be held at that time.[39]

The delegation appeared at the Minneapolis Auditorium the following evening, where the Countess spoke on, why Ireland, at the coming ballot referendum, should vote to reject the proposed dominion status offered by England, as the alternative to war, under the title 'Free State'. *The Minneapolis Journal* described her as the 'firebrand of the Irish revolution'.[40] She told the audience of 1,000 that:

> Irishmen who swore allegiance to the Republic cannot acknowledge allegiance to the English king now, if they would meet in the next world the patriots who died for independence. If the Treaty held no other clause than that which designates the English king as head of the Irish army, it could not be accepted. . . . Ireland will fight to the bitter end to win the Republic.[41]

THE WEST

Perhaps her most enthusiastic crowds were in Butte, Montana. Butte had always had a very large population of Irish. Since the mid-1800s it had been the western mining centre, the centre of labour activity and unrest. The IWW had a stronghold in Butte; the Western Federation of Miners had once had their headquarters in Butte and still remained a strong force, as did socialism. Hanna Sheehy Skeffington, who had also felt at home in Butte, had an enthusiastic reception there in June 1917.

On April 27 1922, a committee of Butte men and women met the delegation's train at Three Forks to accompany them to Butte. The members of the Pearse-Connolly Club and their drum and fife corps met them at the train depot. The Countess wrote to Eva that, 'Butte was one of the places that stands out for its reception, for they met us with a band and an army. All Sligo seemed to be there!'[42] She said of Butte that, 'The scenery is beautiful, wild and rugged with patches of snow everywhere and real cowboys round up cattle in the fields'.[43] The Countess, Kathleen and O'Kelly were escorted to the Thornton

Hotel, where a crowd greeted them. *The Butte Miner* reported that, 'In spite of her long railroad ride and the lateness of the hour, Countess Markievicz showed no signs of fatigue, but talked to all who met her in a way that showed the indomitable energy which caused her to lead a battalion of republican troops in the famous uprising of Easter week six years ago'.[44]

During an interview, she said that she 'did not believe that the army [the IRA] would permit an election to be held on the question of ratifying the Treaty creating the Free State unless there should be a new registration and soldiers should be permitted to vote'. She felt that Ireland was in a stronger position at that time than when the Treaty was negotiated. Referring to the Black and Tans, she said they 'couldn't subdue Ireland although they practised cruelties, which outdid any of the atrocities in Belgium done by Germany during the war. If the Black and Tans couldn't break Ireland down the English army can't.' In response to the question of whether the people of Ireland wanted a renewal of war with England, she replied:

> 'I can't say, but people don't declare war. That isn't the case as we find it in history. There never would be a war if the people had to declare it. Not if the people had a chance to vote on it. The World War wouldn't have occurred if the people had had a voice'.[45]

The Butte Miner provided a complimentary, flowery and extremely detailed description of Countess Markievicz:

> Aristocratic in mien, in dress and in every gesture and tone, with an Oxford pronunciation, with the instincts and training of aristocracy yet bubbling over with the zest of her bottle for 'the people' of Ireland, Constance de Markievicz is more or less of a living paradox. She was born and reared in luxury—a countess in all that that implies to the European, yet a woman who was promoted to the second highest position in the Irish army for valor in action during the memorable Easter day turbulence in 1916, who served three years in jail after escaping the death sentence which was imposed on her by the British government and who 'just loves to talk to newspaper men', because, she said, 'that's what I'm here for to get my message before the American people' . . .
>
> The countess wore a very fetching hat, small and many coloured. Her feet were encased in small suede grey slippers. Trim grey silk stockings. A dress mostly black, but trimmed in red braid with a fancy

> design worked in red thread around the edges of sleeve and collar. The collar was rolled and lined with red silk, its cut was low and at the point of the 'V' two red American Beauty roses were pinned. She is rather sharp featured, clear yet some tanned of complexion and a person of much nervous energy.
>
> A pair of rimless eye glasses, somewhat accentuate the sharpness of her countenance and she talks abruptly and nervously.
>
> Her message she enunciated clearly and slowly, pausing at times to collect her thoughts and nervously twitching her fingers, or ran her fingers through her hair or 'pecked' excitedly with her forefinger.[46]

The press was equally impressed with the appearance and demeanour of Kathleen Barry when they reported her to be:

> A winsome Irish lassie, with dark blue eyes, the matchless skin of her soft climate, white teeth set behind a mobile mouth and a wealth of brown hair that the black sailor hat did not half conceal.[47]

The delegation spent two days in Anaconda, Montana and held a meeting at the A.O.H. Hall, on April 28, where Markievicz spoke once more on the Treaty as it pertained to the partition of Ireland and the British refusal to surrender Irish ports:

> This so-called Treaty—this home rule bill is dressed up as a treaty for the purpose of tricking the people of Ireland into giving a democratic sanction to the usurpation of the English king. It is worse than any home rule bill that was ever suggested, in that it also recognizes the partition of our country by England, which was a proposition that even the home rule party—the national party—refused to accept in a home rule bill.
>
> Four of our ports are held by the English, who can thus control our communications and our commerce.[48]

The following day, the delegation visited a copper mine. She referred to the mine as 'awful' and complained when the manager showed them the well-ventilated areas and newer machinery. Because friends who were in the IWW had encouraged her to ask 'awkward questions', she insisted on visiting the 'hot areas' where she saw men working with picks and drills. She said she 'saw a man drilling the copper ore without the water appliance to keep the dust down and breathing in copper dust eight mortal hours every day. . . . They told us few men live to be old in Butte, Montana'.[49]

Countess Markievicz, Kathleen Barry and J. J. O'Kelly held a meeting at the Butte High School Auditorium on April 30. W. W. McDowell, former Lieutenant Governor, presided. The Countess told the crowd that: 'We can give our lives and our money and are willing to do this if necessary, but we need help. We have come to you to ask that you remain with us until our purpose is accomplished'. Kathleen, in her plea for American support, told the audience that: 'We are getting near our goal and one great effort can reach it'. O'Kelly provided an insight into the fighting taking place in the area of Belfast in Northern Ireland.[50]

After leaving Butte, the delegation arrived in Seattle, Washington to speak at a mass meeting held in the Masonic Temple, Harvard Avenue and Pine Street, on May 3. *The Seattle Daily Times* stated that the object of her tour of the United States was to 'brush away the fog of misunderstanding disseminated throughout the United States regarding the Irish Free State'. She admitted to the audience that she was learning wherever she went that Americans were generally satisfied with the terms of the Anglo-Irish Treaty. She believed the situation was not thoroughly understood by most Americans. She congratulated the voters of Seattle on the election of two women to its council. She asserted that: 'When a woman is elected to public office, you may depend upon it, she'll be honest. She'll be braver than a man, fearless in her stand for the right and against rottenness in politics. She will take her office seriously and not use it for selfish purposes'.[51] Comparing the situation in Ireland to that in the America colonies in 1776, she pointedly reminded the audience that:

> America in 1776 would not have accepted from England what England offers Ireland today. The United States would not have consented to a governor-general with a power greater than a king. She would not have allowed England to have naval supervision of all her ports. Ireland wants her independence just as badly as did America in 1776.[52]

The following perplexing anti-Irish Republic editorial appeared in *The Seattle Daily Times* during the time the delegation held meetings in the city. It illustrates the confusion in the United States over the situation in Ireland:

> This time, it is the Dáil Éireann that takes the initiative in seeking peace by ordering both sides to cease their bickering and get together in discussion of a basis for unification. And, miracle of miracles, the contending leaders have heeded the command of the Dáil and ordered a suspension of hostilities.
>
> The situation bewilders the outsider. The fluctuations of Irish politics are too rapid, too involved for foreign observers. The killings are real enough and their number inspires both amazement and regret, but it is impossible to follow the fortunes of rival leaders or to estimate their authority or their following. One day, they are up; the next, they are down.[53]

Countess Markievicz, Kathleen Barry and J. J. O'Kelly arrived in Portland, Oregon from Seattle on May 4. They held two mass meetings, one at the Labour Temple, Fourth and Jefferson Streets and the other at the Pythian Temple. More than 1,600 people attended the meeting in the Labour Temple where Countess Markievicz proclaimed: 'The English Treaty is not acceptable to the Irish people because it is nothing but a trick to procure from the Irish people democratic sanction to the subjection of Ireland'.[54] Kathleen Barry made an appeal for funds. A resolution pledging continued moral and financial support to the Irish Republic was passed. The delegation left Portland the following day, May 5, to travel to San Francisco.[55]

On May 7 1922, Countess Markievicz, Kathleen Barry and J. J. O'Kelly arrived in San Francisco, under the auspices of the American-Irish Liberty League, 794 Mission Street. A committee of 100 civic and business leaders of San Francisco and Oakland greeted them at the Oakland pier. Representatives of the American-Irish Liberty League and other Irish societies, along with young girls dressed in Celtic clothing to represent Cumann na mBan and young boys dressed in the uniform of Fianna na hÉireann, met them at the San Francisco Ferry Building and escorted them to the Hotel Whitcomb.[56] During an informal reception at the hotel, Countess Markievicz told those assembled that in the 1916 Rising, as second-in-command of the Irish citizen army, she felt bullets fly past her like 'bees buzzing'. She said she saw a good deal of heavy fighting, but did not mind it. 'When your cause is just there is nothing you will not do.' She said she would gladly fight again when the time comes.[57]

Countess Markievicz appeared that evening at a mass meeting of more than 9,000 people in the Civic Auditorium. A colour guard bearing both the United States and Irish Republic flags and a squad of uniformed riflemen escorted her into the auditorium. The audience rose to its feet and cheered as she entered. Dr J. Franklin Smith presided as chairman. Miss Mary Crossan of the American-Irish Liberty League introduced her.[58] She recounted her experiences during the fighting in Ireland. She claimed that every [republican] woman in Ireland took an active part in the cause of Ireland. They fought side-by-side with the men, held political offices and became some of the most trusted spies and messengers in the Irish Republican Army.[59] In discussing the Treaty, Countess Markievicz declared the people who fought and bled for Ireland would not accept the terms of the Free State. She described the day the Treaty was signed as a 'day of mourning in Erin'. She accused Lloyd George of tricking the Irish representatives into betraying their country by accepting the Treaty and praised de Valera as one of the 'biggest men in the world'. She was convinced that when the people of Ireland realized the full meaning of the Treaty, they would unite with de Valera in opposition to it because 'Ireland is republican at heart and will assert itself again'. The press reported that she gave the appearance of being frail; however, when she spoke, her qualities of leadership became apparent.[60]

Speaking to an audience of mostly women in the Colonial Room of the St Francis Hotel on May 8, Countess Markievicz expressed her belief that Northern Ireland should not remain an 'outpost and seat of British authority. God made Ireland an island and the seas alone should be the boundary of the Republic'. She insisted that reports of dissension among the Irish people were highly exaggerated and were the propaganda of the British Government.[61]

RECALL TO IRELAND

Countess Markievicz and Kathleen Barry were recalled to Ireland while in San Francisco in order to take part in the 'Pact' election of June 24. The final attempt at peace was the 'Collins-de Valera pact of 20 May' agreed to by the Dáil and the Provisional Government. A national coalition of candidates from both sides [pro-Treaty and anti-Treaty] in Sinn Féin would be voted on by the Dáil.[62] O'Kelly immediately returned to Ireland from San Francisco.[63]

The Countess and Kathleen continued on to Los Angeles. A mass meeting held at the Trinity Auditorium on March 9, under the auspices of the AARIR, was noted in the *Los Angeles Times*. However, it gave no coverage of the meeting except to say that Countess Markievicz 'reviewed the history of the recent developments'. She had commented that there was no danger of Ireland becoming an ally of England's enemies once complete Irish independence was granted; that the quarrel was with the British Government and not with the English people.[64]

From Los Angeles, the Countess and Kathleen travelled on to and through Chicago. The *Chicago Tribune* commented only that they passed through Chicago, May 13, 1922 and that she had given her views on the Treaty: 'Establishment of the Irish Republic is the only way to assure lasting peace in Ireland. . . . The terms of the Treaty are worse than England offered to the American people at the time of the revolution'.[65]

THE EAST

Countess Markievicz and Kathleen returned to Cincinnati, Ohio, on May 16, for a day of rest and to visit friends, Mr and Mrs A.J. Castellini. Markievicz had met Mr Castellini, a long time friend of Ireland, at an Irish Race Congress in Paris.[66] They returned to New York to speak at a meeting before completing their tour in New England.

Speaking to over 2,000 people at the New National Hall, Driggs, Avenue and Eckford Street, in Brooklyn, New York, on May 22, Countess Markievicz promised: 'The Irish Republic will be continued until the last drop of Irish blood is shed for a cause which the people of Ireland believe is right and just'. She guaranteed the American audience that the Irish Republic was still 'standing and functioning'. She gave credit to the American people who helped build the Republic and asked them to help them [the Republicans] to maintain it. She declared: 'we are ready to war with England to show that we want nothing but a Republic'. Referring to dominion status within the Commonwealth of England, she stated: 'We don't want to be placed in the same category as Canada'.[67]

The Countess and Kathleen spent their last week in the United States in Massachusetts. *The Boston Telegraph* paid tribute to Markievicz prior to their arrival in Boston:

> Tomorrow a remarkable woman will visit Boston. While there has been unhappily, division of opinion as to the better method for Ireland

> to adopt in securing her freedom, no one has ever disputed the intellect or ability or vision or valour of Countess Georgina Constance Markievicz . . . Men may differ with her in opinion, but no one can deny that history will recognize her as one of the great women in the world's history. Rightly she has been termed Ireland's Joan of Arc.[68]

A reception and tea held at the Copley-Plaza Hotel in Boston preceded an evening meeting to address members of the Cumann na mBan. With the exception of a mass meeting scheduled in New York City, all of their other meetings scheduled after May 28 had been cancelled.[69]

The Countess and Kathleen appeared in New York City at a mass meeting on May 21 before a crowd of 5,000 people in Madison Square Garden. Every council of the AARIR and other Irish-American societies that supported de Valera and the Irish Republic attended. Tickets were advertised as being available from the headquarters of the AARIR at 8 East 41st Street, New York and from *The Irish World*, *The Irish Nation* and *The Monitor*. Proceeds from the ticket sales were pledged to the Irish Republic Fund.[70] The crowd cheered for six minutes when former Supreme Court Justice John W. Godd introduced Countess Markievicz. She announced that the Irish Republic was still functioning and would continue to do so, regardless of the Treaty. She claimed that Michael Collins and Arthur Griffith did not have the power to 'sign away the freedom of Ireland'. 'The Irish plenipotentiaries who negotiated the Treaty were to ascertain what and how much Ireland could get; not sign a treaty'. She said she did not understand:

> We had trusted those men as we had trusted ourselves. They had twice taken an oath of allegiance to the Irish Republic by our side and we could as little have believed that they could have signed that treaty as that we could have signed it ourselves. I do not intend to attack or condemn them.[71]

Before their departure to Ireland, the AARIR held a reception on May 29 at the Hotel Commodore. Countess Markievicz was reported to have commented that there would be no peace in Ireland until the British Government made peace with the Irish Republic. Both women later visited Mayor Hyland and stayed for almost an hour in his private office at the City Hall.[72]

Countess Markievicz issued a farewell statement to *The Irish World* in which she said: 'this flying visit of mine through your young Republic has given me great heart and encouragement. . . . Today we have Eamon de Valera and the Irish Republican Army to repeat Washington's words: "Nothing but independence will do".'[73]

On May 31, Countess Markievicz and Kathleen Barry returned to Ireland from New York aboard the *Berengaria*. During their time in the United States, anti-Treatyites had seized and occupied the Four Courts in Dublin. Countess Markievicz attended her last Dáil meeting on June 8 and made several election speeches. On June 28, 'Free Staters' opened fired on the Four Courts. The Irish Civil War had begun.[74]

CONCLUSION

Similar to the receptions given Mary MacSwiney in the United States, Countess Markievicz attracted large crowds and was received with enthusiasm and support. The news coverage of her tour was greatly reduced in the East due to the support of the Treaty by Judge Cohalan and John Devoy and the dwindling membership of the FOIF. Although she appeared frail, the dynamics of her personality and popularity contributed to the success of her tour in the United States. She seems to have received no negative criticisms from any of the newspapers that covered her speeches.

As the Minister of Labour of Dáil Éireann, the Countess was privy to political developments and dissentions within the government. Her dedication to Eamon de Valera and the Irish Republic was apparent in her speeches. However, her assessment of events and comments on the conditions in Ireland seemed exaggerated. She freely criticized Michael Collins, Arthur Griffith and the Free State Government. Her gratitude for the financial help given by the people of the United States was emphasized during many of her speeches.

With Countess Markievicz's departure and the beginning of the Civil War however, confusion among Irish Americans increased and there were never again such large crowds, news coverage, enthusiasm or support for the tours that followed.

Countess Markievicz evaluated her tour in a letter to Eva:

> We find great sympathy and support here and have got a lot of money. Subscriptions and pledges given at various meetings held, tot[al] up to over £20,000. Nobody likes the Freak State. They are trying to block

us by saying that we are making civil war in Ireland and I hear that they are organising stunts every night, firing off vast quantities of ammunition at nothing and pretending that we are attacking them.[75]

CHAPTER 8

Muriel MacSwiney with Linda Kearns: Irish Republican Soldiers' and Prisoners' Dependants' Fund, September–October 1922

THE CIVIL WAR was raging in Ireland. Muriel MacSwiney returned to the United States at the time of the second anniversary of the death of her husband, Terence, in September 1922. She arrived in New York with Linda Kearns, a Republican Army nurse, to tour the United States in support of the Republican Soldiers' and Prisoners' Dependants' Fund.

By the time Muriel returned to the United States, not as a widow in deep mourning weakened by illness and exhaustion, she had regained her strength, vitality and determination to fight for an Irish Republic. She had proved herself in battle in Dublin in the early days of the Irish Civil War and had become more outspoken in her commitment to republicanism. While in the United States, she faced hostility and criticism from the clergy and others with tenacity and courage. *The Irish World* once again praised her presence and demeanour:

> Two years ago this time the civilized world watched with unstinted admiration the brave little Irish girl (for she is as yet only twenty-five years of age) as she kept her lonely vigil for seventy-four days and nights at the bedside of her dying husband. Her sacrifice seems but to have increased her animation, intensified her enthusiasm and steeled her patriotism. Mrs MacSwiney has as much of the freshness of youth today as when, six years ago at the age of nineteen, she left an Irish convent.[1]

IRISH CIVIL WAR

When the Civil War broke out in Dublin, on June 28 1921, between Irish Republicans and Free Staters, Muriel took part in the initial fighting, along with other members of Cumann na mBan. Muriel, Linda Kearns and Kathleen Barry, stationed at the Hammam Hotel, were the only women who refused to leave when word was received that it would be shelled. When they eventually were forced to evacuate the Hammam, they crawled through a passageway, cut through its walls into the Gresham Hotel and escaped from there into an alley at the rear. However, they returned to the Hammam the following day to take up jobs as cooks. They knew the situation was hopeless, but they stalled for time in order to get the Republican defence organized outside of Dublin.[2]

Linda Kearns, a nurse who took part in the Easter Rising, had been arrested in 1920 for driving a car full of arms for the Irish Republican Army. She had been court-martialled and sentenced to ten years in prison. Her escape from the prison one year later became one of the most sensational incidents of the war. She also took part in the fighting in Dublin against the Free Staters. For several days she nursed the wounded during the attack on the Hammam Hotel.[3]

Muriel strongly opposed the Anglo-Irish Treaty and spoke out against it many times: 'This Treaty is the worst crime England has ever committed against Ireland in all the 750 years she had been endeavouring to conquer her in vain. It would never have been signed but for a threat of terrible and immediate war by England the warmaker'. It is difficult to evaluate Muriel's[4] speeches with so little press coverage. It appears that she prepared her own addresses and may have spoken from a prepared text or notes. Her focus on the Treaty and against Michael Collins and Arthur Griffith appear direct and organized. Her comments seem less formal than they would have if they had been presented from a professionally prepared speech.

THE TOUR BEGINS

The Irish Republican Soldiers' and Prisoners' Dependants' Fund was formally launched on Sunday, September 17 1922 in New York City with the formation of a national committee during a meeting held at the McAlpin Hotel. Sixty members made up the committee, with an executive committee of seven members. A subcommittee headed by Frank Walsh drafted an appeal to the American people to support the Republic of Ireland. Later that evening, a huge mass meeting was held in the Lexington Theatre, 51st Street and Lexington Avenue. Joseph McGarrity of Philadelphia called the meeting to order and Major Kelly presided. There were large delegations from Massachusetts, Rhode Island, New Jersey and other eastern states.[5]

The AARIR, Clan na Gael and other Irish-American societies sponsored the tour of Muriel MacSwiney and Linda Kearns in support of the Irish Republican Soldiers' and Prisoners' Dependants' Fund. Muriel's speeches focused on the Anglo-Irish Treaty; her belief that the British controlled Michael Collins and Arthur Griffith and the Irish press, her allegiance and loyalty to the Republic of Ireland and her gratitude to the generosity of Americans. This tour differed from those of Hanna Sheehy Skeffington, Mary MacSwiney and Countess Markievicz in which they appealed for American support of the Irish Republic and its complete freedom from England. Muriel and Linda focused on gaining financial support of imprisoned Irish Republican soldiers and their dependants and the promotion a boycott of English goods in both Ireland and the United States.

A reception was held, under the auspices of the AARIR and Irish Republican Soldiers' and Prisoners' Dependants' Committee, at the Lexington Theatre, on September 22, in honour of Muriel. Because many were unable to gain admittance to the theatre, overflow meetings were held outside. The crowd gave her a standing ovation as she rose to begin her speech in Gaelic and then finish in English. In part, she related that:

> Until the terrible disaster of the Treaty came we were the most united country in the world and if the negotiations in London had broken off, which was what all Irish people expected, England could have done nothing but gracefully retire. She would have been too afraid of you Americans to have restarted murdering all your relations in Ireland and we could have got rid of the British troops when they were forbidden to make war on us by refusing them food and lodging.
>
> But England knew this and fooled our delegates as she fooled President Wilson with her diabolical cunning. She has not beaten us yet, however. The Irish people have not and never will accept the Treaty. This is the truth. I have just come from Ireland and I know it.[6]

She also charged that: 'England furnished troops to fight at the Four Courts in Dublin and Lloyd George ordered Michael Collins to make the attack'.[7] Muriel paid tribute to Linda Kearns for the work she did during and after the Easter Rising of 1916. It was after midnight when Linda began her talk, but the audience stayed on. She declared the Republic of Ireland had been in existence since the Easter Rising in 1916 and the courts, police, local governments and the Parliament were still functioning. She stated that the Free State Government held money belonging to the Republic and that the British had given them possession of all the barracks in Ireland.[8]

The lack of newspaper coverage of the meeting was substantial. *The Irish World and American Industrial Liberator* reported that: 'The New York newspapers, as if by arrangement, ignored the meeting even though a city news representative supplied a report to every paper in the city'. *The New York Tribune* was the only morning paper that published a short article on the meeting.[9] Unlike the coverage they provided Hanna Sheehy Skeffington, Mary MacSwiney and Countess Markievicz during their tours, *The New York Times* did not cover Muriel and Linda's arrival in New York City or any of the meetings they held.[10] The division in the Irish-American organizations over the Anglo-Irish Treaty and their reaction to the Free State Government reduced overall support of this and future tours of Republican women. The loss of support of FIOF members Judge Daniel Cohalan and John Devoy and a large number of AARIR members directly affected the cohesiveness of their organizations and their willingness to publicize Republican efforts. Joseph McGarrity remained loyal to the Republican cause; however, he could not provide the resources to back this tour on the scale of the previous ones. Overall, *The Irish World and American Industrial Liberator* provided the most complete news coverage of the lectures.

CONFLICT IN WASHINGTON D.C.

Muriel and Linda's next lectures were held in Washington D.C., where Mr and Mrs Frank P. Walsh, 2319 Tracy Place, hosted them during their stay. On September 24, Muriel MacSwiney spoke at a meeting at the Coliseum, under the auspices of the AARIR, to raise funds for the Irish 'Irregulars' (republicans). About 500 people attended to hear her speak in support of de Valera and against the

Treaty.[11] The meeting had been plagued with conflict from the beginning, both in locating a hall and then in attendance by the clergy. The organizing committee had been denied the use of both the Knights of Columbus Hall and Gonzaga Hall. And, in spite of extensive advertising in local papers, plus the distribution of notices to all the Catholic churches on the morning of the meeting, Catholic clergy stayed away. There were no priests in the audience or on the platform.[12] It would appear they had been ordered to stay away by an official of the Catholic Church.

John F. Finerty, National President of the AARIR and Acting Chairman of the meeting, blamed Archbishop Curley of Baltimore for the loss of both the Knights of Columbus Hall and Gonzaga Hall and accused him of being 'a bad Catholic and a worse American'.[13] There were shouts of 'it is not true' from the audience and several people got up and left the hall.[14] During her address, Muriel referred to the Free State troops as 'English'. She told the audience that the Irish people had not accepted the Free State Government and never would, as it would mean swearing allegiance to the English king.[15]

The Washington Times, on September 25, printed a highly critical article in judgment of Muriel's address:

> Agnostic, foe of Catholicism, pacifist, though she mentions the deaths of Arthur Griffith and Michael Collins in the calm way one would speak of two pawns of an opposing chess-player swept from the boards and withal a devout believer in Irish autonomy at whatever cost—such is the Muriel MacSwiney of 1922.
>
> On her last visit to the United States, this fresh-faced young woman, who at present is a mainspring in the eccentric machine of which Eamon De Valera is governor, appeared as a testament to the self-martyrdom of her husband, Terence MacSwiney, Lord Mayor of Cork. Now she comes as a representative of the Irish intransigent . . . She wants funds for the relief of the dependants of Irregulars and for the hospitalization of wounded Nationalist fighters.[16]

The Washington Times also accused her of leaving her grief behind her, bobbing her hair and updating her view on 'things Irish'.[17]

Archbishop Curley was well known as an adversary of de Valera and the Irish Republic. He had been quoted in the *Dublin Independent*, on September 6, as saying that:

> He believed when the truce was accepted and Ireland's plenipotentiaries went to London, it was America's duty to not

> interfere in the settlement. Further that 'Americans never had and have no right to dictate to the people of Ireland what form of Government they should have . . . I am fully convinced that the men and women in American today who are raising money in aid of the present campaign little realize that they are assisting not in uplifting, but in the absolute destruction of the land they profess to love'.[18]

The Archbishop received better press coverage than Muriel's meetings. His remarks expressed the viewpoint of many Americans who supported the Anglo-Irish Treaty. And he placed the responsibility of the Irish Civil War squarely on de Valera's shoulders. Perhaps he spoke for many Irish-Americans who were tired of being asked once again to financially support a movement, which, from their distant viewpoint seemed to be losing credibility. *The World* printed a statement by the Archbishop in which he charged that, 'de Valera is the Villa[in] of Ireland', who would destroy Ireland economically. He believed that Americans who were sending money and arms to 'de Valera and his followers to be used against the Irish people are as guilty of murder as were the men who, under De Valera, shot Michael Collins'.[19]

During an interview on October 7, Muriel stated that she did not care what Archbishop Curley or other members of the clergy said about acceptance of the Treaty: 'The clergy has stood consistently against the movement for freedom. The young generation in Ireland is, I believe, being weaned away from the Catholic Church. It is thinking for itself'.[20] She believed the Treaty would be rejected if an honest election could be held and that Ireland's main hope for freedom remained the moral support of America and Europe. She recalled the beginning of the Civil War at the Four Courts, when, as a pacifist, she was really frightened. In fact, she said she wanted no more fighting. She had not come to the United States to solicit funds for prosecution of hostilities, rather for the relief of wounded men and their dependants. She believed the majority opinion could be influenced to support a total separation of Ireland from England, or 'absolute divorce'.[21]

NEW ENGLAND

Muriel MacSwiney and Linda Kearns began their tour through New England after leaving Washington D.C. Padraic F. O'Hegarty, of the

AARIR State Committee, arranged their tour in Massachusetts: three meetings in Boston; three in Lynn, Peabody, Salem on the same day; Somerville; New Bedford; Springfield and Holyoke on the same day; Lowell and Lawrence on the same day; Fall River; Worcester; Fitchburg; Pittsfield; Brookline; and Cambridge. Other meetings in New York, Connecticut and Rhode Island followed.

Muriel and Linda received a great reception at the Symphony Hall in Boston on October 1, under the auspices of the AARIR, with at least 4,000 people attending. Ex-servicemen escorted them up the main aisle of the auditorium. After they were seated, both of them were presented with a large bouquet of yellow chrysanthemums. Muriel said that she did not approve of fighting, killing, or helping anyone else to kill, but she would feel 'privileged to give my life for Ireland'.[22]

A few days later, on October 8, they spoke to a mass meeting in Lawrence at the City Hall, under the auspices of the AARIR. Peter MacSwiney, Muriel's brother-in-law, arrived unexpectedly at the meeting. When asked to speak, he claimed that the signing of the Treaty had been forced upon the Irish leaders. He said that at the time of the signing, 'every nation was against the cause of liberty, including America, even though she [America] herself had been through the same order of British tyranny'.[23] Linda was reported to be the 'most popular speaker of the day'. She accused Michael Collins of declaring war on his own authority and claimed that he had received his commission of General from the King of England—he was then as 'an Englishman born on the soil of Ireland'.[24] During her address, Muriel referred to the parts of the Treaty, which she asserted were offensive to the Irish people. She quoted Bernard Shaw's statement that: 'England would give anything to maintain Ireland as a base of operations in case of a possible war with the United States'. She claimed England was in full control of the Irish press and she appealed to all present to join a society for Irish freedom so that the truth might be known. She closed by speaking of the generosity of Americans and said that when Ireland won her freedom, she would repay the American people.[25]

Muriel and Linda arrived at the Fall River on October 12, to be met by a reception committee of the Major John McBride Council of the AARIR and several hundred others who came to pay tribute to the 'wife of the heroic Lord Mayor'. They spoke later at the Franklin Hall to a capacity audience. William McAuliffe, a former member of the American Expeditionary Forces, chaired the meeting.[26] Muriel was greeted with prolonged cheering when she rose to speak. She said help was needed then as never before in Ireland. She denied Ireland was in a Civil War: 'It is the same old enemy . . . the same old England, but in a new guise'. She said she came as a representative of her husband, 'to speak the words that he would speak were he in her place, to again ask the aid of the American people'. Several thousand dollars were pledged for the Irish Republican Soldiers' and Prisoners' Dependants' Fund during the meeting.[27]

The next meeting was held in the ballroom of the New Bedford Hotel, on October 12, under the auspices of the Ladies' Auxiliary, Clan na Gael and the AARIR. Muriel and Linda received a 'rousing reception' as they entered the hall. It was reported that Linda's speech 'was argumentative and forceful and she converted many Free Staters'. On the other hand, Muriel made 'a touching appeal on behalf of the Republicans' Dependants' Fund'.[28]

Muriel and Linda spoke at a meeting in Providence, Rhode Island at Fay's Theatre on October 15. Attorney Hughes of Boston, who delivered the opening address, referred to the statements of Archbishop Curley of Baltimore and ex-Governor Martin H. Glynn of New York and pointedly reminded the audience that:

> The people who are standing with De Valera are the mother of Patrick and William Pearse, the widow and sister of Terence MacSwiney, the sister of Kevin Barry, the two brothers of Joseph Plunkett, who was executed in 1916, the widow of Sheehy Skeffington and the fathers, mothers, sisters and brothers of others of the men who before the firing squad, on the gallows and in the field died for Ireland.[29]

In her address, Muriel stated that Michael Collins was killed in battle, not assassinated by the Republicans and that he met his death 'as any other "Englishman" would'. She reminded the audience that the Irish Republic was proclaimed in 1916, ratified in 1918 and 1921, but since the spring of 1921 the people had not been able to vote on it. She endorsed the boycott of English goods saying it would help America if they traded with Ireland and it would help Ireland gain her freedom. Linda spoke of the 18,000 republican men imprisoned by the Free State and the 40,000 republican wives and families who were suffering. At the end of the meeting, Mary O'Sullivan presented Muriel with a silver mesh bag, a gift of the city for her daughter, Máire, wrapped in the Irish colours of green, white and gold.[30]

Over 1,000 people gathered at Mechanics' Hall in Worcester on October 17. John F. Harrigan presided. Muriel opened her speech in

Gaelic, but continued in English to tell the audience that, 'Lloyd George had made a fool of everybody he had called into conference, including Arthur Griffith and even President Wilson. . . . The sacrifices for the Irish Republic in English jails seem to me the most wonderful work of all in our struggle for freedom'. In describing the treatment of Irish prisoners in English jails, Linda said that if she had a choice 'between a year's imprisonment and hanging, I'd take the latter and that is the usual sentiment among the Irish prisoners today'. When Linda spoke of the republicans in prison and of the suffering of their wives and families, she brought tears to the eyes of the women in the audience. A cash collection of $828.57 and pledges of $632, for a total of $1,450.57 was collected at the meeting.[31]

NEW YORK CITY

Muriel MacSwiney and Linda Kearns returned to New York City to attend two meetings held in honour of the second anniversary of Terence MacSwiney's death—October 22. One was at the Earl Carroll Theatre, 50th Street and Seventh Avenue in Manhattan and the other at the Academy of Music in Brooklyn. Muriel was the principal speaker at both meetings.[32]

The meeting at the Earl Carroll Theatre was held under the auspices of the AARIR, with Muriel, Linda, Hanna Sheehy Skeffington, Frank P. Walsh and Congressman Ryan as speakers. Hanna Sheehy Skeffington had just arrived in the United States to begin her cross-country tour for the Irish Republican Soldiers' and Prisoners' Dependants' Fund as head of the Irish Women's Mission. The speeches of Muriel, Hanna and Mr Walsh were described as 'especially brilliant'.[33] Muriel's speech was described as 'a masterpiece', during which she gave an analysis of the Anglo-Irish Treaty and the Free State Constitution and told of conditions in Ireland. She accused England of being 'afraid to do in her own name what she was doing in the name of the Free State'.[34] Frank P. Walsh paid tribute to Terence MacSwiney and added that, 'Ireland could never be free until the British Empire is destroyed. . . . I glory in the removal of Lloyd George. He is the vilest traitor to democracy that ever lived'.[35] Hanna Sheehy Skeffington received a warm welcome. Her speech quoted Archbishop Croke in words she had heard as a child: '"I am unchanged and unchangeable". That is the position of Irish people today'.[36] Almost $1,000 was collected for the Irish Republican Soldiers' and Prisoners' Dependants' Fund. In addition, Mr Hartnett, the State Treasurer of the Massachusetts Relief Drive, presented over $6,500 in pledges from the New England meetings.[37]

Later that day, Muriel, Linda, Hanna and Rev J. E. Sheehy spoke at the memorial meeting at the Academy of Music in Brooklyn. Muriel described her husband's death and suffering. She told of conditions in Ireland and blamed England for the 'internal strife' there. During her address, Linda claimed that 'Michael Collins was not assassinated . . . but killed in a battle between IRA men and Free State troops, the IRA being unaware of his death for some time'.[38] Over $1,300 was collected at the meeting and pledges of $12,000 were received from the Brooklyn Councils of the AARIR.

ARREST IN WASHINGTON D.C.

It is not clear when Muriel returned to Washington D.C. or if she held any mass meetings there. *The Irish World* described her arrest for picketing the British Embassy, along with other women, demanding the release of Mary MacSwiney who was on hunger strike in a Dublin prison.

The Irish World printed a photograph, with the caption, 'Mrs Muriel MacSwiney and Her Companions Picketing the British Embassy at Washington'. Muriel is shown carrying a huge placard, which reads: 'England Murdered My Husband TERENCE MacSWINEY. Will Americans Permit the English Free State to Murder His Sister, Mary MacSwiney?[39] Muriel and eight other women, members of the AARIR, were arrested for picketing the British Embassy. The placards that were seized by the police carried messages such as: 'English Efficiency Killed Terence MacSwiney in 74 Days. How Long Will it Take to Kill Mary MacSwiney'? 'The Free State is England's Smoke-Screen'. 'Will America Permit England to Murder Another MacSwiney?' 'Germany Shot Edith Cavell; England Tortured Mary MacSwiney. Which Would You Choose?'[40]

The case against Muriel and the other women was based upon the argument that the statute under which they were charged was intended to prevent 'the shaming and insulting of a foreign representative's home, office, or servants' as analogous to the 'shaming or insulting of the representative in person'. The banners the women carried, it was claimed, were insulting to Sir Auckland Geddes, the English

Ambassador, even though he was not in the embassy at the time.[41] The defence, represented by John F. Finerty, president of the AARIR, proved that the British Ambassador was not in the embassy at the time of the picketing. On November 15, the cases against Muriel and the other women were dismissed after a short hearing because the evidence 'did not measure up to the intent of the law'.

Upon release from custody, Muriel said she 'expected nothing else'.[42] Her only worry was for the safety of Mary MacSwiney, who was in her twelfth day of hunger strike and for her four-year-old daughter, Máire, who was being cared for in a home in Ireland that had been attacked by the Free State troops and she had heard no word for several days. Muriel may have had a reoccurrence of her previous medical problem because she then announced that, because of a recent illness, she would rest for a short time in Virginia before she continued her tour speaking for the Irish Republic.[43]

RETURN TO NEW YORK CITY AND RECALL TO IRELAND

Muriel MacSwiney returned to New York City within a week to speak at a meeting, under the auspices of the AARIR, in the Carmelite School Hall, East 29th Street in New York City, on November 26. The meeting was reported to be a success, with a total of $1,150 collected for the Dependants' Fund and $1,100 for the Defence Fund.[44]

When Eamon de Valera recalled Muriel to Ireland, he requested that Hanna Sheehy Skeffington and Kathleen Boland, sister of Harry J. Boland and a member of Cumann na mBan, complete the tour of the Western section of the United States for her. Linda Kearns continued on the tour with Hanna and Kathleen.[45] Muriel MacSwiney sailed to France from New York City on July 7 on the SS *Rochambeau*. According to the British Consulate-General in New York, the reason for 'her hurried departure is that her child is ill in Europe but, on the other hand, it is stated in Irish circles that she has crossed in order to have consultations with friends of the so-called Irish Republic on the Continent'.[46] Newspaper reports give a confused account of her activities. It was reported that Muriel attended a public meeting in Dublin, on July 27 1923, where she proclaimed that the 'supporters of the Irish Free State have no influence in the United States and are able to obtain hearings in only one or two places'. She was later reported to be living in Paris.[47]

BLOCKADE OF THE IRISH CONSULAR OFFICE

The Irish World later reported that Muriel joined in a republican campaign in Dublin at the end of 1923, when she and other members of the Irishwomen's Republican Mission blockaded the Irish Consular Offices at 119 Nassau Street. Although the offices had been opened and furnished with Irish Republican funds, Lindsay Crawford, who had been appointed Consul of the Irish Free State, refused to turn the offices over to Laurence Ginnell, the newly appointed Ambassador of the Irish Republic. The women continued their blockade until Crawford sued for a truce on December 30. Crawford drew up and had the managers of the building sign an agreement to keep all persons out of the locked-up offices until January 2. Muriel and the women defiantly announced then that they would return to their blockade duty on January 2.[48]

CONCLUSION

Muriel MacSwiney's tour was poorly covered by the American press. They carried neither advance notices nor coverage of the meetings. Only Joseph McGarrity's, *The Irish World*, gave accounts of the meetings. McGarrity continued his support of the Irish Republic while Daniel Cohalan and John Devoy and his newspaper, *The Gaelic American*, supported the Treaty and the Free State Government. Judge Cohalan also agreed with and supported Archbishop Curley, who spoke out so strongly against Muriel's addresses. With the Irish Civil War raging, the uncertainty over the future role of Irish-Americans in the internal affairs of Ireland and the increasing split in the Irish-American leadership became more pronounced. The membership of the FOIF at this time was approximately 20,000.

In spite of the lack of publicity, Muriel MacSwiney and Linda Kearns were generally greeted with welcome and praise. Their meetings were well attended—often with an overflow crowd. What was missing was the massive, oftentimes front-page press coverage and the general organization of the previous tours of Hanna Sheehy Skeffington, Mary MacSwiney and Countess Markievicz.

CHAPTER 9

Hanna Sheehy Skeffington: Irish Women's Mission with Kathleen Boland and Linda Kearns, October 1922–May 1923

When the Anglo-Irish truce was arranged in July 1921, Hanna Sheehy Skeffington played a prominent role in the peace negotiations as an intermediary between the Irish Republican President Eamon de Valera and British Prime Minister Lloyd George.[1] At that time, she also held the position of Director of Organization for Sinn Féin. Along with other republican women, she later opposed the Anglo-Irish Treaty and the Free State Government, the partition of Ireland and the oath of allegiance to the King.[2] She also served on the executive committee of the Irish White Cross, which was set up in 1920 to distribute the funds raised by the American Committee for Relief in Ireland. The funds were distributed to victims of the war not otherwise entitled to compensation.[3]

Hanna Sheehy Skeffington concentrated and continued her support of republicanism and nationalism during the War of Independence and Irish Civil War. She returned to the United States in 1922 during the height of the Irish Civil War to tour, at the request of Eamon de Valera, as head of the Irish Women's Mission, with Kathleen Boland and Linda Kearns. When Muriel MacSwiney, on tour of the United States for the Irish Republican Soldiers' and Prisoners' Dependants' Fund, was recalled home to Ireland, Hanna, Kathleen and Linda completed her tour of the western section of the

United States, under the sponsorship of the American Committee of Irish Republican Soldiers' and Prisoners' Dependants' Fund. More than 40,000 Irish Republicans, relatives of the 18,000 men in jail, were cared for largely by this fund. Kathleen Boland, sister of Harry J. Boland, the first Irish Republican envoy to the United States, was a member of Cumann na mBan and Linda Kearns had been on tour with Muriel MacSwiney (see Chapter 8).[4]

Shortly after Hanna's arrival in New York City from Dublin in October 1922, she requested the editor of *The Irish World* to publish an appeal on behalf of the Irish Republican Dependants' Committee to collect funds for the families of 6,000 prisoners who had not been brought to trial. She stated that unless funds were received, women and children would starve during the winter while the men were imprisoned or deported. Widows and sisters of the martyrs of 1916 volunteered their time to the organization, which spent nearly $5,000 a week in aid. Some families had eight to eleven children or aged parents to care for.[5]

The *New York Call* reported that during an interview Hanna Sheehy Skeffington charged the Free State Government with 'ill treatment of prisoners'. She was said to have stated 'that her party intended to "wear down the Free State Government as they wore down British rule by making it impossible through active and passive resistance"'.[6]

Each woman spoke during their addresses of their own losses in the struggle for freedom from the Easter Rising, the War of Independence and the Civil War. The topic of the Treaty and the horrors of the Civil War took precedence as the focus of all the addresses. Kathleen and Linda were adamant in their belief that Michael Collins and Arthur Griffith had betrayed their people and sold out to England. Hanna was careful to avoid speaking of Collins or Griffith. Her knowledge of world politics was clearly in evidence over and over again as she suggested solutions to the current problems in Ireland. She spoke often of the external association clause of the Treaty and her belief that what was good for Canada, was not good for Ireland.

THE TOUR BEGINS

As previously mentioned Hanna Sheehy Skeffington joined Muriel MacSwiney and Linda Kearns at two of the meetings held in honour of the second anniversary of Terence MacSwiney's death on October 22. One of these was at the Earl Carroll Theatre and the other at the Academy of Music in Brooklyn. Muriel, Hanna, Linda and Revd J. E. Sheehy addressed the meeting at the Brooklyn Academy of Music. Over $1,300 was collected in cash and $12,000 in pledges received.[7]

Hanna visited James Larkin, the Irish labour leader, in Sing Sing Prison. She reported he was in good health and good spirits and that he was very well informed on Irish affairs—more than most of the people she had met in America.[8] She also travelled to Pittsfield, Massachusetts to address a meeting on November 5, held in memory of the death of Terence MacSwiney.[9]

THE EAST

Kathryn Heaney, 32 Blackville Street, Dorchester, Massachusetts, described in a letter to her cousin, George Staunton, in Ireland, a reception for Muriel and a meeting held by Hanna. She complained that the 'hyphenated class of Irish we have mixed up with us in the club' [Irish-American club], had attended a reception for Muriel MacSwiney. She added that Hanna Sheehy Skeffington had been in Dorchester the previous week collecting funds for the Republic of Ireland in another part of the club building. When an invitation was extended to Hanna to join the others after the meeting, 'you may be sure Mrs Skeffington came right in and took up a collection, too, and she did not go away without telling them just what she thought about them'. Hanna had said she would speak to any group any time. Kathryn Heaney related that Hanna 'told them that she would never apologize to any Irish organization for asking for a few dollars to help out the Republic'. Kathryn added that the club had meetings and collections for that purpose 'all the time'.[10]

Linda Kearns wrote to her friend, Annie Smithson in Ireland, on November 6 1922, that: 'Mrs Sheehy Skeffington, Mrs MacSwiney, Kathleen Boland (Harry's sister) are doing a tour of the US, but Mrs Sheehy Skeffington must be back in Ireland for Christmas—She is a very clever woman and it will be hard to find a substitute'. Linda also reported that: 'America is a very wonderful country and I love it and the American people are with us heart and soul. They do not resent our wrongs and they sympathize with us in our sufferings and they also approve of this stand we are making for freedom and independence'.[11]

$..............................   Date..............................

REPUBLIC OF IRELAND

First Loan Subscription of the Elected Government of the Republic of Ireland

To EAMON DE VALERA, PRESIDENT OF THE REPUBLIC OF IRELAND

I..............................hereby tender to the Government of the Republic of Ireland the sum of $..............................This sum is voluntarily subscribed by me. Neither the President of the said Republic of Ireland nor the Government of the said Republic nor its agents are under any obligation to repay this sum, or to pay interest on said sum to me or to my heirs until the said Republic of Ireland is internationally recognized and until the lapse of six months from the date of the freeing from British military control of the territory of the said Republic of Ireland.

Amount Subscribed $..................... Signed ....

Amount Paid $..................... Address ....

Amount Due $..................... City..............................

BOND-CERTIFICATE DEMONIATIONS

Den.	$10	$25	$50	$100	$250	$500	$1,000	$5,000	$10,000
No.									

Hand this Card to usher or mail to P. F. McCarthy, District Chairman, 625 Higgins Building, Los Angeles, California

SULLIVAN COMPANY

1. Republic of Ireland Bond-Certificate Subscription
(Donohue Rare Book Collection, Richard A. Gleeson Library, University of San Francisco)

2. Hanna Sheehy Skeffington (Courtesy of the Sheehy Skeffington Family)

3. Hanna and Owen Sheehy Skeffington (*Buffalo Courier*, February 22 1917)

WIDOW OF MARTYRED EDITOR IS TO SPEAK

Mrs. Francis Skeffington to Address Irish Meeting.

MRS. F. S. SKEFFINGTON.

Announcement was made by the Rochester Committee of the Irish Relief Fund yesterday that arrangements had been completed for a public meeting in Convention Hall next Monday evening at which an address will be delivered by Mrs. Sheehy Skeffington, widow of Francis Skeffington, an Irish editor and pacifist who was killed in the uprising in Dublin last year. Mrs. Skeffington eluded the British authorities last December and came to this country. Since that time she has been touring the country, lecturing on conditions as she found them to exist behind the veil of censorship in Ireland.

The Rochester Committee is affiliated with a national body which assists in caring for persons in Ireland whose distressed condition results from the unusual conditions existing there since the outbreak of the war. Cardinal Farley, of New York, is honorary president of the national body; Thomas Addis Emmet is president; John D. Moore secretary and Thomas Hughes Kelly treasurer.

Alexander B. Lamberton is honorary chairman of the Rochester organization, which came into being last fall. John D. Lynn is chairman of the committee, James P. B. Duffy is vice-chairman, Thomas E. Lannin treasurer and Rupert L. Maloney secretary.

Besides the officers mentioned members of the Rochester committee are: William A. Buckley, John Connors, Harry B. Crowley, George L. Flannery, John F. Hunt, P. P. Kelly, James O'H. Love, John F. McGraw, Thomas Mulcahy, Frank J. McGrath, James T. McGovern, Michael T. Ryan, Thomas A. Smyth, Matthew Swan, Charles E. Callihan, James C. Connolly, Daniel Crowley, P. J. Donovan, James Fee, Joseph P. Henry, J. R. McLaughlin, William B. Moynihan, W. J. Maloney, R. P. McCarthy, James M. E. O'Grady, Patrick J. Rowan, Owen P. Smith and Joseph P. McSweeney.

4. Cutting, *Rochester Democrat and Chronicle*, March 23 1917

—GRAND—

Patriotic Mass Meeting

Under the auspices of the Friends of Irish Freedom

COLUMBUS AUDITORIUM

621 South Flower Street

TO-NIGHT

APRIL 14th, 8:00 p. m.

—ADDRESS BY—

Mrs. Hanna Sheehy-Skeffington

Hear a real, genuine message to the Irish people of Los Angeles, in the big farewell address, under the auspices of the Irish Societies. She is the widow of one of the Dublin Martyrs. She stands for right and justice as outlined by President Wilson. She has interviewed the President and talked with many leading members of Congress.

* * *

The date will commemorate the 1916 Irish Rebellion.

* * *

It will be a true American Meeting. Liberty Loan will be Advocated. Come and Boost! The success of Liberty Bonds means the success of our Army. Success of our Army means the freedom of ALL Small Nations.

* * *

Hear the distinguished orators, the Gaelic and other singers.

* * *

ADMISSION IS FREE. The date is To-night, April 14

5. Hanna Sheehy Skeffington Mass Meeting handbill (Donohue, Richard A. Gleeson Library, University of San Francisco)

MRS MACSWINEY ENDS VISIT

Throng Bids Her Farewell, After Her Reception by Cardinal and Visit to State House

WIDOW OF MARTYRED LORD MAYOR OF CORK ON VISIT TO STATE HOUSE.

Left to Right—Senator George E. Curran, Mrs Muriel MacSwiney, Representative Patrick Melody, Past President of Central Council of Irish County Associations.

Sincerely grateful for the reception given her in this city, Mrs Muriel MacSwiney and her sister-in-law, Miss Mary M. MacSwiney, accompanied by Harry Boland, secretary to Pres DeValera of the Irish Republic, and John F. Harrigan, State president of the American Association for the Recognition of the Irish Republic, left Boston at 5:30 yesterday afternoon for Manchester, N H.

Mrs MacSwiney had an eventful day in Boston and had but little time for rest except in the afternoon before train time. In the morning she paid a visit to Cardinal O'Connell, received his blessing, and later visited the State House, where she was shown unusual honors, being invited to address the Massachusetts Senate.

Schoolteachers at Train

A large crowd flooded the midway of the North Station near Track 19, where the MacSwiney train was to pull out, and overflowed into the section behind the gates. About 100 school teachers, members of Carroll of Carrolltown Branch of the American Association for the Recognition of the Irish Republic, were at the station to see Mrs MacSwiney, who used to be a school teacher.

The party boarded a special car and the two women entered the drawing room. Mrs MacSwiney sat quietly, turning occasionally to wave to the crowd. As the train started to pull out Miss MacSwiney stopped writing to wave to the crowd and Mrs MacSwiney turned, smiled and waved.

John J. Hearn of Westfield, John J. Foley, Mary C. Culhane, representing the Carroll of Carrolltown Branch; women representing the League of Catholic Women, and a delegation from Manchester, were in the party that left on the special car.

Received by Cardinal O'Connell

Yesterday morning Mrs MacSwiney and Miss MacSwiney were received in audience by Cardinal O'Connell at the Cardinal's residence. The visitors were accompanied from the Copley-Plaza by a committee of women consisting of Mrs Mary C. Culhane, State director of the American Association for the Recognition of the Irish Republic; Mrs John F. Harrigan, wife of the president of the State council of this organization; Mrs Edmund J. Sheehan, vice president of the League of Catholic Women, and Mrs Frank C. Scanlon, Miss Monica Foley and Miss Lydia J. Stringer, Boston women who were invited by Pres DeValera to attend the opening session of the hearing in Washington held by the Committee of 100, investigating conditions in Ireland.

The party was greeted at the Cardinal's residence by Rev Dr Richard Haberlin, secretary to the Cardinal, heading a group of clergymen. Mrs MacSwiney was in conference with the Cardinal for a long time and he gave her his blessing, followed by words of encouragement.

Together with members of the entertainment committee, the party then motored to Arlington where personal friends were visited.

Received in Hall of Flags

On their return they went to the State House at 1:30, where they were shown unusual honors. They were received in the Hall of Flags and escorted through the Capitol by Representatives Melody and Hayes of Boston, Francis J. Coyne, Representative-elect from Ward 18, and Louis R. Sullivan of the Governor's Council. When Mrs MacSwiney saw the picture depicting the dumping of tea into Boston Harbor, she declared "Good."

The party visited the office of Speaker Joseph E. Warner and from there went to the visitors' gallery of the Senate, where the proceedings were watched for about 10 minutes, when she was invited into the Chamber and, on invitation of Edwin T. McKnight, president of the Senate, was escorted to a seat on the dais beside him.

Under a suspension of all business, Mrs MacSwiney was invited to address the Senate. She was noticeably ill and wearied. She expressed her gratitude to the assemblage for their kindly reception and the honor they had shown her. She spoke very low and her words were inaudible to most of the gathering. She was applauded when she closed.

Mrs MacSwiney's Speech

In addressing the Senate, Mrs MacSwiney said:

"It gives me great pleasure to thank you for the greeting that has been extended to me today. I never made a public speech, yet I want to tell you how grateful I am.

"I am sure my husband would be gratified also. We have always been friendly with America. We feel as you felt. You have got your freedom. We will get our freedom some day. As you have suffered, we are suffering now. Again I wish to thank you."

Mrs MacSwiney then returned to the Copley-Plaza, where she had a brief rest. She was in constant demand and, not to cause disappointment, received a few guests. Among them were Misses Nora, Mary and Violet Toomey, daughters of Pres M. J. Toomey of Terence MacSwiney Council, American Association for the Recognition of the Irish Republic. The little girls presented Mrs MacSwiney with a number of gold coins for use in relief work among the children of stricken Cork.

Framed resolutions adopted by the Charitable Irish Society on the death of Lord Mayor MacSwiney, Joseph Murphy and Michael Fitzgerald, were presented to Mrs MacSwiney.

6. *The Boston Globe*, December 21 1920

TONIGHT AT 8 O'CLOCK

At RYMAN AUDITORIUM

Free Lecture

ON CONDITIONS IN IRELAND

—*By*—

Miss Mary MacSwiney

Sister of Terrence MacSwiney, late Lord Mayor of Cork.

Miss MacSwiney is a highly cultured woman—a brilliant and interesting speaker. She is thoroughly familiar with all phases of the Irish question and qualified to present the true situation existing in Ireland today.

Rev. Maurice Murphy

A Methodist minister of Toledo, Ohio, formerly of Dublin, Ireland, will be present and will also address the meeting.

DON'T FAIL TO ATTEND

The Public Is Invited

Ladies Especially Urged to Attend

7. Cutting, *Nashville Banner*, January 31 1921

TERENCE MAC SW
SECOND ANNI

MRS. MURIEL MACSWINEY

Mrs. Muriel MacSwiney, widow of Terence MacSwiney, the late Lord Mayor of Cork, will address a meeting at the Academy of Music, Brooklyn, on Sunday October 22, under the auspices of the Brooklyn Councils of the A. A. R. I. R. This body for the past two weeks has been working with renewed vigor and energy for the purpose of increasing the membership of the various councils and thereby intensifying the campaign for the recognition of the independence of Ireland.

The last meeting of the council's board was held at Holy Family Hall, 13th street, near Fourth avenue, on Thursday evening, September 21. The veteran Nationalist, P. J. Boylan, presided, and James J. McCamphill acted as recording secretary. It was decided to hold a memorial of Terence MacSwiney and a committee was appointed which already has arranged to have a large demonstration on the evening of October 22 at the Academy of Music.

This will be in commemoration of the death of the famous Irishman, whose 84-day fast, while incarcerated in Brixton Prison, London, drew the attention of the world on Ireland's fight for freedom and made a greater impression on imperialistic England than all the armies of the ex-Kaiser. Two years ago this time the civilized world watched with unstinted admiration the brave little Irish girl (for she is as yet only 25 years of age), as she kept her lonely vigil for 84 days and nights at the bedside of her dying husband. Her sacrifice seems but to have increased her animation, intensified her enthusiasm and steeled her patriotism. Mrs. MacSwiney has as much of the freshness of youth today as when, six years ago at the age of 19, she left an Irish convent.

Miss Linda Kearns, who will also address the meeting at the Academy

MRS. MACSWINEY'S ITINERARY

Meetings have been arranged as follows for Mrs. MacSwiney and Miss Kearns in the State of Massachusetts by the State Committee in charge of her tour of that State. Padraic F. O'Hegarty og Springfield is chairman of the committee:

Oct. 1 .... Boston (Symphony Hall)
Oct. 3, 8. Boston (Municipal Bldg.)
Oct. 5 .. Dorchester (High School)
Oct. 6 ...... Lynn, Peabody, Salem
Oct. 8 .... Somerville
Oct. 10 .... New Bedford
Oct. 12 ...... Springfield, Holyoke
Oct. 13 ...... Lowell and Lawrence
Oct. 15 .... Fall River
Oct. 17 .... Worcester
Oct. 18 .... Fitchburg
Oct. 19 .... Pittsfield
Oct. 20 .... Brookline
Oct. 21 .... Cambridge

On October 22 Mrs. MacSwiney will address two meetings in Greater New York, one in the Earl Carroll Playhouse, 50th street and Seventh avenue, under the auspices of the Terence MacSwiney Council, and another in the Academy of Music, Brooklyn. The meetings will celebrate the second anniversary of the death of Terence MacSwiney. Meetings are now being arranged for Mrs. MacSwiney in the States of New York, Connecticut and Rhode Island.

8. Cutting, *The Irish World and American Industrial Liberator,* September 30 1922

Miss MacSwiney, sister of the Late Lord Mayor of Cork (Terrence MacSwiney), who died in Brixton prison after a sensation hunger strike which attracted world-wide attention, will arrive in Butte from the Pacific coast, Thursday morning at 11 o'clock over the Northern Pacific. A large delegation of Butte citizens will greet Miss MacSwiney at the station and she will be escorted to the court house, where she will deliver a short address. A squad of American Legion members will act as the guard of honor. Miss MacSwiney will address a meeting at the high school auditorium, Friday afternoon at 2 o'clock, after which she will depart over the Oregon Short Line for Salt Lake City. During her stay in Butte she will be the guest at the O'Meara home on West Granite.

9. *The Butte Miner,* March 16 1921

10. Hanna Sheehy Skeffington, Linda Kearns and Kathleen Boland, Women's Mission to America, 1922 (Donohue Rare Book Collection, Richard A. Gleeson Library, University of San Francisco)

11. Placard advertising Mass Meeting, Hibernian Hall, March 1923 (Donohue Rare Book Collection, Richard A. Gleeson Library, University of San Francisco)

The crucial hour in the whole history of Ireland is here!

Can those who are flesh of your flesh and blood of your blood count on you Today?

COUNTESS CONSTANCE GEORGINA MARKIEVICZ

who comes to San Francisco to plead for your flesh and blood in Ireland, is one of the most romantic characters in modern history and for this reason she has often been called Ireland's "Joan of Arc." Her achievements in behalf of the people of Ireland place her among the world's greatest women.

Countess Markievicz comes from the old aristicratic Gore-Booth family of Ireland. She was reared in the midst of luxury and comfort. While a young woman she studied art in Paris and there married the Polish Count Casimir Dunin Markievicz.

After her marriage she returned to Ireland and was welcomed into Dublin Castle circles. In 1907 she became interested in the Sinn Fein movement and joined a branch of Sinn Fein in Dublin.

In 1909 she founded Fianna Eireann, the Irish boy scouts. This was a campaign to enlist all the young boys in Ireland in bands such as were known in ancient Ireland when all the children of Irish warriors were trained as great fighters and athletes.

The Countess has had an especial interest in the welfare of those who work for their daily bread. In 1913 during the strike and lockout in Dublin she personally took charge of a relief kitchen where the strikers, their wives and their children, were fed. As a result of that strike the Irish Citizens' Army was established under the command of Padraig Pearse, and with this force Countess Markievicz fought for Ireland in Easter Week, 1916.

Many of the Fianna were in the Countess' army during the rising of 1916—boys 16 and 17 fighting like young heroes. The Countess was a valiant fighter but once was ordered by the commander of the Irish Republican party to surrender. Sending word to the British officer in charge that she would surrender at a certain hour the military surrounded the headquarters of the Countess. At the appointed hour the Countess, wearing the uniform of a lieutenant of the Irish Volunteers, stepped forward to the British officer and kissing her rifle handed it to the military. After this she was court-martialed and sentenced to death. This was about the time of the execution of Edith Cavell in Belgium and public opinion was much aroused. It was generally supposed that the wave of indignation might be directed against England should the death of the Countess be carried out. The sentence was then changed to penal servitude for life. During the months pending her release the Countess served as a convict among the sweepers of English streets and gutters.

She was released in the general amnesty of 1917, but was re-arrested in 1918. So dear was she to the people of Ireland that in the general election of 1918 she was victorious over her opponent, and thus was the first woman ever elected to the British Parliament. She refused to take the seat.

COUNTESS MARKIEVICZ
will speak in the Civic Auditorium
San Francisco, on Sunday, May 7th
at 8 P. M.

For one year the Countess was "on the run." Disguising herself as an old apple woman she went about Dublin, although the secret service force of the British Empire was continuously in search of her. One day on one of the principal streets of Dublin, where hundreds of people were passing by, an old beggar woman asked for alms. The Countess gave of her store. The old beggar woman, seeing the large amount which she had been given, looked up in astonishment at the disguised Countess and after studying her a few moments cried, "Och! the blessings of God on you my beautiful Countess and is it yourself I see?" And this is the woman whom certain parties who are friendly to the British Empire do not want you to hear at the Mass Meeting in the Civic Auditorium on Sunday night on May 7th. What are you going to do about it?

Do not throw this announcement away!
Help the good work by passing it on to a friend or neighbor

12. Countess Markievicz Mass Meeting handbill, May 7 1922
(Donohue Rare Book Collection, Richard A. Gleeson Library, University of San Francisco)

American newspaper coverage of the delegation during the months of November and December do not indicate that mass meetings were held. However, on November 23, Gloster Armstrong, the British Consulate-General in New York, reported to the Foreign Office in London that:

> Messrs O'Kelly and O'Doherty, Mrs Skeffington, Miss Boland, Miss Kearns, etc. continue their meetings in various part of the country and have been visiting a large number of towns in the Northeast States and in the vicinity of New York City.
>
> The Irish Republicans are joining hands with the Friends of Freedom for India and will hold a meeting at the McAlpin Hotel (New York City) tonight, as a protest against the continued imprisonment of Mary MacSwiney and other political prisoners in Ireland and India, the number of the former being given as 10,000 and the latter, 40,000. Principal speakers will be: Hanna Sheehy Skeffington; Dr Gertrude B. Kelly, New York; Rebecca Kabrisky, Friends of Freedom for India; Sailendra Nath Ghose of Calcutta, India; Revd Father John H. Dooley, presiding. The whole meeting will be under the special auspices of the Friends of Freedom for India.[12]

This appears to be the first public appearance of Irish Republicans in the United States in support of freedom for India. Dr Gertrude Kelly,[13] a long-time friend from Hanna's first tour of the United States, may have arranged her appearance as a speaker at this meeting.

During an interview at the Park Avenue Hotel in New York City, in November, Hanna told a reporter that Joseph Connolly, Consul General of the Irish Free State who had resigned on November 24, had confided to her and Peter MacSwiney, brother of Mary MacSwiney, that for some time he had been dissatisfied with some of the policies of the Free State Government. He had resigned in protest of the imprisonment of Mary MacSwiney and of the execution the previous week of four republicans by the Free State and had returned to Dublin to offer his reasons before Dáil Éireann.[14]

It is not clear whether Hanna did, in fact, travel to Ireland sometime in December and then return to the United States in January or early February 1923 to resume the tour with the other delegates. During January 1923, Linda Kearns and Kathleen Boland held a series of meetings on their own.

Kathleen and Linda spoke at a mass meeting held in the Union Labour Temple Theatre in Pittsburgh, Pennsylvania on January 10.

After Revd Father McBurney introduced Linda, *The Irish World* reported that:

> After an extended storm of applause the tall, dark-haired Irish woman bravely stepped forward dressed in an original Irish costume adorned with emblems of Ireland's ancient glory. The combined qualities in the make up of her all round culture exceeds the writer's power of description. She was shrewd, amiable, tender and war-like, could change the attitude as quickly as the keenest mind could follow her.[15]

So many members of the audience rushed to Linda after her speech to make a contribution to the Fund that she had to use the backs of the pages of her speech to record the names of the subscribers. Kathleen also received a great ovation when she rose to speak briefly. Approximately $1,000 was collected at the meeting. Kathleen and Linda then spoke in New Haven, Hartford and Waterbury, Connecticut, before they travelled on to Cincinnati, Ohio.[16]

Linda and Kathleen addressed the meeting, under the auspices of the AARIR, in Cincinnati on January 14. Linda declared: 'Ireland shall be free. This is her last stand and it is a fight to the finish'. Kathleen spoke on the death of her brother, Harry Boland, who had been shot in his bed at 2:00 a.m. by Free State troops in July.[17]

Hanna was reported to have next spoken on January 14 in Providence, Rhode Island at a meeting in Fay's Theater. She praised Eamon de Valera for his stand in refusing to accept anything less than an Irish Republic and for refusing to be bought by American politicians in New York, Massachusetts and Rhode Island. She accused them of attempting to 'control Ireland and de Valera'.[22] She also spoke on the murder of her husband, Francis Sheehy Skeffington, during the Easter Rising in 1916. At the conclusion of the meeting, many members of the audience questioned her on the conditions in Ireland. Approximately $1,000 in contributions was collected.[18]

THE MIDWEST

Hanna Sheehy Skeffington rejoined Linda Kearns and Kathleen Boland, either at the end of January or the beginning of February. When they arrived in St Paul on February 10, they were met by a delegation that accompanied them to the Hotel Dyckman in Minneapolis. In an address to the Saturday Lunch Club, Hanna described the conditions in Ireland from 1916 to the Civil War. She told of the 13,000 prisoners of war who were denied prisoner of war status. She also informed the audience that the solicitation of funds would not be permitted in Ireland. Mrs A. K. Bryant hosted a dinner and theatre party for the delegation.

The following evening, the three women spoke at a meeting in the Ryan Hotel in St Paul. Linda described the condition of republican prisoners and the clause in the Treaty requiring an oath to the King, which kept them in prison:

> There are 13,000 men in jail today and criminals have been released to make way for them. American jails are palaces compared to Irish jails. . . . There are 500 on cattle boats out in the ocean, some of them dying of fever and there are no medical facilities. These men could be released if they would swear an oath of allegiance to the King of England. So far they have refused. Many have been killed trying to escape.[19]

In reference to the dominion status of Ireland contained in the Treaty, Hanna said:

> We are not fighting hundreds of years for the love of fighting. There have been seven armed risings during the last 350 years. A gentleman told me the other day that what was good enough for Canada was good enough for Ireland. England is not the motherland to Ireland as she is to Canada. To Ireland England is not anything but a burglar and an assassin.[20]

A total of $617.63 in cash and pledges was contributed at the meeting.

Senator S. A. Stockwell invited Hanna to speak before the Minnesota State Legislature on Lincoln's Birthday, February 12. Representative Myrtle Cain introduced her. During her address, Hanna spoke of the partition of Ireland:

> No country is great enough or good enough to govern another country against its will. No nation can remain half slave and half free. You had your South in Lincoln's time, you could not allow it to secede; neither can we allow our North, as we would be obliged to do under the Treaty of 1921.[21]

Representative Cain also introduced Kathleen and Linda to the senators and representatives in attendance. The three women then answered questions presented to them on conditions in Ireland.[22]

THE WEST

Hanna Sheehy Skeffington, Kathleen Boland and Linda Kearns left Minnesota during a blizzard, which held their train up for several days along the route to Portland, Oregon. They held a mass meeting at the Hibernia Hall, 340 Russell Street, on February 25. Hanna announced during her speech that she had just received word that her home in Dublin had been burned, presumably by Free State Troops or sympathizers. (Her home had, in fact, been raided by the Free State, rather than burned.) Never at a loss for words, she gave the delegation's itinerary as: 'Portland to Sacramento, to Southern California, to Ireland, to jail'.[23]

John P. Trant, British Consulate-General in Portland, reported to his office in Washington D.C. that Linda Kearns:

> . . . denounced the perfidy of her fellow country who had associated themselves with the Irish Free State as the tools of England's cunning and declared that the Free State Government which had always been a travesty, was become more and more a direct instrument of Downing St. She also told of the 13,000 Republican prisoners, including 100 women, languishing in Irish jails, which were overcrowded and unsanitary, of the1,000 prisoners who were confined in cattle boats under intolerable conditions outside Dunleary, owing to the lack of accommodation elsewhere. . . . She announced that her party had already forwarded over $80,000 to Ireland . . . and they hope to send many further amounts before they finally return home. A collection was taken before the close of the meeting, which realized about $1,000.[24]

He reported that Hanna spoke of the murder of her late husband, 'announcing that Captain Bowen-Colthurst who was responsible for the outrage and later confined in an asylum, had now been released and was holding an important government position in England and that furthermore, he had been granted full pardon for this act'. Kathleen spoke of the assassination of her brother, Harry Boland, and the imprisonment of her other brother, Gerald Boland. She 'told of the fifty-seven executions that have already occurred under the Free State Government, without warning or without trial, including those of Liam Mellows, Rory O'Connor, Erskine Childers and many others'.[25]

Hanna was confronted with a controversy that arose during her time in Portland. Several newspapers reported that the Publicity

Department of the Free State Government published the text of a letter, allegedly written by Hanna and captured during Mary MacSwiney's arrest, complaining of the activities of Muriel MacSwiney during her tour in the United States. Hanna was accused of complaining that Muriel's 'activities had been the cause of great worry to the republican sympathizers and that she [Muriel MacSwiney] had refused a request to return to Ireland'. Hanna had allegedly also criticized Muriel for 'her tactlessness in various interviews, but the latter turned a deaf ear to the entreaties and protests and her general "wildness and irresponsibility" had worked great harm and caused dangerous comment'.[26] Muriel had been on tour with Linda in support of the Irish Republican Soldiers' and Prisoners' Dependants' Fund. Hanna completely denied writing the letter and refused to consider it as anything other than a set-up by the Free State Government:

> This [letter] is a fake. It is an old trick of the British to say they find documents and to publish fake correspondence to create divisions among workers opposed to the Free State Government. I am much too old a hand to get caught at captured correspondence. I have a code, which I use in all correspondence. Mrs MacSwiney and I have been working together, but she had to stop. She was starting on a tour when she received this news and I was obliged to make the western tour in her place.[27]

Hanna was an outspoken critic of the Free State Government and the continued presence of England in Ireland. It seems highly probably that the Free State, similar to the British during Hanna's tour of the United States in 1917–1918, attempted to sabotage the success of this tour and at the same time damage the reputation of the speakers.

The women arrived in Northern California to speak at the Red Men's Hall on March 1 1923 in Sacramento. Because of illness, Hanna did not speak at the meeting. Kathleen and Linda both described the Irishmen who signed the Anglo-Irish Treaty in London as 'traitors to their country . . . [who] should have been arrested and tried for treason by the supporters of the republican movement'. Linda reported during the address that the Free State had executed fifty-seven republicans during the previous six weeks. Kathleen said: 'The true people of Ireland are determined to carry on the struggle until real freedom has been obtained'. The collection from the meeting totalled $147.85.[28]

On March 2 1923 Linda and Kathleen spoke at the Native Sons' Hall in Stockton. They spoke 'in human terms' of the struggle in Ireland and made no attempt to discuss the political situation there. They told of the efforts being made by the republicans in Ireland to ensure Ireland's complete separation from England and the establishment of an Irish Republic. Linda spoke of Ireland's struggles during the previous seven years and then told of her jail experiences:

> I can tell you quite a lot about jail, I have been in six of them. Do any of you and I do not think you do, know what it means to be locked up in a miserable hell-hole for twenty-three out of the twenty-four? . . . In Mountjoy jail if we do anything contrary to the rules we spent three days of each week in a punishment cell. These cells drip water continually and there is absolutely nothing in those cells except a Bible and they do not even give you a candle to read it by. Each time the wardress came to the cell, I would throw the Bible at her and being a true English woman she threw up her hands in total despair.[29]

Kathleen described how her brother, Harry Boland, the first Irish envoy of the Irish Republic to the United States and secretary of the mission during de Valera's visit, was executed. He had been an active organizer of the Irish Volunteers and received a promotion to Captain during the 1916 Easter Rising. Harry had been shot by Free State troops in the Grand Hotel in Skerries. Muriel MacSwiney and Kathleen Clarke were present when he died. She also spoke of another brother, Gerald, who had fought in the 1916 Rising at Jacob's and was now being held in a Free State prison.[30]

More than 3,000 supporters met to raise funds for the Irish Women's Mission at the San Francisco Civic Auditorium on March 6 1923. Hanna, Linda and Kathleen confirmed that Irish women were dedicated to Irish liberty and would accept nothing short of the Irish Republic.[31] Hanna stated that if the British left Ireland, there would be no bloodshed. If the British would end the war and allow an election of all Irish people over twenty-one years of age, they would abide by the results of that election. Speaking of the Treaty, Linda stated that it had been 'put over on the Irish people'. She claimed the vote was taken from a 1919 register and commented that: 'many came back from their graves and voted, others, the women under thirty, the men in their early twenties and the men in the army, had no opportunity of voting'. During her address, Kathleen told the audience: 'We do not want war. We want peace, but not peace at any price'. It was reported that several thousand dollars were collected at the meeting, including a fifty-dollar gold piece from the Hindustan Club.[32]

The American Women's Independence Committee, an organization of San Francisco women, honoured Hanna Sheehy Skeffington at a banquet at the Hotel Whitcomb on March 14. The Executive Committee of the American-Irish Liberty League, as invited guests, was seated at the speaker's table. The Finoula Club arranged a table for Kathleen Boland and the Nurses' Branch of the AARIR.[33]

The *San Francisco Chronicle* reported that the three women had 'indomitable humour and courage':

> Many a light quip, albeit a sarcastic one falls from the witty lips of Mrs Skeffington, as she tells of Ireland's wrongs at the hands of the 'stepmother' country, Great Britain. There is no word of complaint for the husband who died and only an amused smile that the Black and Tans suppressed her newspaper, *The Irish Citizen*. 'They even broke up the type', she added with a little giggle of amusement.
>
> Equally humorous and equally brave are her two companions—Miss Kearns, a war nurse, whose emaciated body, pallid face and kindling black eyes tell their tale of her wasting months in the dank, dark caverns of a British dungeon. 'Quite like the horrors of old wives tale', said Kearns of the prison in England where she passed seven months in solitary. 'Rats, creeping things, dripping humid walls—nothing to make the story book dungeon complete was left out of that horrible underground cell.'
>
> [Kathleen stated:] 'Yes, my brother, Harry Boland, de Valera's secretary, was shot a year ago. A second brother is in prison in Dublin under sentence of death. His time may come any day for they kill four prisoners for every one of their own losses.' Death, that searing word, held somehow another meaning for her. She spelled it Freedom.[34]

RETURN TO THE EAST

With the California speaking engagements completed, Hanna Sheehy Skeffington returned to the East Coast to speak in Boston,

Roxbury and Watertown in Massachusetts; Brooklyn and New York City in New York; and Washington D.C. Linda Kearns and Kathleen Boland held meetings in Houston, Texas; New Orleans, Louisiana; and Chicago, Illinois.[35]

Hanna spoke at the Red Men's Hall in Hartford, Connecticut on April 12. She emphasized that 'the Free State Government is a British expedient and a puppet government, set up by the British when they realized that they could no longer maintain their dominance over Ireland'. Speaking of the problem in Northern Ireland, Hanna stated that three of the six counties recognized as the 'Government of Northern Ireland can claim to actual racial separation and that these are in reality too small to maintain a parliament of their own.' Hanna reported that, because of the response to the appeals made for the Fund, $100,000 had been collected and sent to Ireland.[36]

As during her first tour when the British wanted her out of the United States yet did not want her to return to Ireland, Hanna Sheehy Skeffington had been successful once again in provoking fear in the opposing government. Likewise, the Free State Government now evidently did not want to be faced with her return. Anticipating the conclusion of her tour, 'Sinbad' in the Saorstat Office in Washington D.C. informed Desmond Fitzgerald, Minister of External Affairs in Dublin, on April 20:

> It is announced here that Mrs Sheehy Skeffington is about to return to Ireland soon. She has been the most active of publicists in the USA for the Irregulars and has circulated everywhere the most atrocious lies about the Free State.
>
> She says when she returns to Ireland she will probably be put in Mountjoy where she will hunger strike and as she will not be allowed to die she will be released.
>
> Is it possible or feasible to prevent her entering the Free State?[37]

A farewell reception was held for Hanna on April 29 at the Academy of Music in Brooklyn, under the auspices of the AARIR. Approximately 4,000 people joined in a parade from Independence Square to the theatre. Every seat was filled and hundreds stood in the aisles and in the foyer. Hanna received an enormous ovation. During her speech she spoke of de Valera and the Treaty:

> President De Valera, who had been 'captured' several times had, during the past week offered England and her puppet Free State his terms of peace which could be summed up: 'Scrap the Treaty.'. . . It will be difficult for either England or the Free State to assign a convincing reason to the world why a free election, a free assembly, a free press and free speech should be [no] longer withheld from the people of Ireland.[38]

Hanna appeared at a mass meeting at the Ridge Avenue Theatre in Philadelphia, Pennsylvania on May 6. She told the audience that: 'I have found on my trip through America that the American people, when they hear the truth, are supporting the principles which I am defending as ones that are American in ideal if not in location'. She claimed that: 'In Ireland today two per cent of the entire population are either in prison or dependent because the breadwinner of the family is in prison'.[39] She reported that Americans had contributed $120,000 and that $3,000 had been collected at the meeting.

On May 13, Hanna spoke to a crowd of 700 people at a mass meeting in Washington D.C. at the Coliseum Arena. Her sense of humour surfaced again when she told the audience:

> The green camouflage with which the Free State was disguised by the British is already wearing off and the red of England showing through.

> We hold that the Republic was established by the vote of the Irish people twice and we claim our right to hold arms. We believe with Oliver Cromwell that we should 'trust in God but keep our powder dry'. Some say that we should be satisfied with a government similar to Canada's. What is good enough for Canada is not good enough for Ireland; what is good enough for the United States is good enough for Ireland.[40]

Before her departure from Washington D.C. to return to Ireland, Hanna attended a farewell reception and dance given by the General Richard Montgomery Council of the AARIR on May 15.[41]

CONCLUSION

The delegation raised $123,000 during their tour. The funds were used for relief of prisoners and their families—food, medical supplies and other 'necessities' of life. The declining Irish Republican support in the United States directly affected the support overall. The Treaty first and then the Irish Civil War caused a further decline in republican loyalty and support, which promoted a decrease in advance publicity of the meetings, newspaper coverage and in the attendance of the meetings throughout the United States. Most Irish-Americans believed the Treaty resolved the Irish question, the provisional Irish Republic had been replaced by the Irish Free State and the campaign for Irish independence was over.[42]

In Ireland, the Civil War ended on May 24 1923. The fighting ended; however, political resistance continued. Hanna Sheehy Skeffington returned to Ireland to continue to work wherever and whenever she was needed in support of peace and of the Irish Republican defeat of the Free State Government. She accepted a position of 'special correspondent and news reporter' offered to her by Austin Ford, editor of the *Irish World*.[43] She was sent to Paris in August 1923, as Acting Minister of Foreign Affairs of Dáil Éireann, to speak against the Free State's admission into the League of Nations.[44]

CHAPTER 10

Mrs Margaret Pearse: Most Glorious of Irish Mothers, May–October 1924

MRS MARGARET PEARSE toured America in 1924 primarily to seek funding for Patrick Pearse's nationalist school, St Enda's in Dublin, but also in support of President Eamon de Valera and the Irish Republic. As a Dáil deputy and a staunch anti-Treatyite, she remained loyal to de Valera and the ideal of republicanism. She spoke often of her commitment to the work begun by her son, Patrick and continued by de Valera.

Large crowds greeted Margaret Pearse in the United States. With a sense of respect and warmth, she was hailed as the 'most glorious of Irish mothers'. The press described her as 'a white-haired, gentle-voiced little woman with a cultured and unmistakable Irish accent . . . and eyes the blue of cornflowers'.[1] The themes of her speeches did not vary and usually began:

> Don't sympathize with me over the loss of my sons. Congratulate me. It is a grand thing to know that I have had the privilege of being the mother of two young men who died battling for our dear old land.[2]

Margaret's tour differed in several different ways from those of Hanna Sheehy Skeffington, Mary MacSwiney, Countess Markievicz and Muriel MacSwiney. The previous tours focused only on the Republic of Ireland—its fight for freedom, its recognition as an independent nation, its survival after the Anglo-Treaty was signed and for help of those Irish republicans imprisoned in Free State Government jails and their dependants. Margaret's primary purpose was to save St Enda's School, the school her son Patrick organized before his death in the Easter Rising.

Although the American press focused on Margaret's main goal of fund-raising for St Enda's, her speeches did include pleas for financial and political support of Eamon de Valera and the Irish Republic. Their reports of her speeches indicate she had grown into an active politician. She spoke adamantly against the Treaty and the Free State Government, calling it a 'farce'. She frequently spoke of carrying on the work that Patrick and William had begun. She remained ever faithful and loyal to Eamon de Valera.

BACKGROUND

Margaret Pearse was born in 1857 into a Gaelic-speaking family who moved from County Meath to Dublin in 1848 during the Great Famine.[3] She met and married James Pearse, an English monument stone-carver, in 1877.[4] Within six years, they had four children, Margaret, Patrick, Willie and Mary Bridget. James Pearse, a silent man, took up the cause of Irish nationalism and Margaret Pearse led an unusually quiet and isolated life with few friends and no visitors in her home.[5] Patrick Pearse wrote of his parents in his unfinished *Autobiography*:

> When my father and my mother married there came together two very widely remote traditions--English and Gaelic. Freedom-loving both, and neither without its strain of poetry and its experience of spiritual and other adventures. And these two traditions worked in me and prised together by a certain fire proper to myself—but nursed by that fostering of which I have spoken—made me the strange thing I am.[6]

Patrick Pearse, born on November 10 1879, founded the private bilingual school, St Enda's in Dublin, in 1908 as part of the Gaelic revival. Because he believed the English educational system in Ireland suppressed Irish nationalism, the school emphasized Irish language, history, culture and games. Five years later he became a founder member of the Irish Volunteers. In December 1913 he joined the IRB as Director of Organization and a member of their top-secret military committee and commanded the Irish Republican forces during the 1916 Easter Rising. His brother, William, a Captain in the Volunteers, participated in the take-over of the Dublin General Post Office.[7]

Desmond Ryan, secretary to Patrick, described the departure of

Patrick and Willie from St Enda's the night before the Rising: 'She [Margaret] had said: "Now, Pat, above all, do nothing rash!" and he had dutifully replied: "No, mother"'.[8]

After the Volunteer surrender on Saturday, April 29, Patrick and William were court-martialled, sentenced, shot by a firing squad in Kilmainham Jail and buried without coffins in quick lime in Arbour Hill.[9] During May, Margaret Pearse pleaded with the British authorities to release the bodies of Patrick and William for a proper burial; however, General John Maxwell refused on the grounds that it would create an unfavourable precedent. He also refused the family's request for Patrick's last writings because 'they are seditious!'[10] Such British reactions to the 1916 Rising resulted in a shift in Irish public opinion regarding the participants in the Rising. According to Lawrence J. McCaffrey, the 'back-stabbers', 'dirty bowsers' and 'hooligans' became 'martyred heroes'.[11] In addition to dealing with her grief, Margaret Pearse managed St Enda's ongoing precarious financial situation.

After the Rising, Margaret Pearse served on the committee of the National Aid and Volunteer Dependants' Fund. She was a member of Cumann na mBan and Sinn Féin. In 1921 she became a deputy of the Second Dáil, along with Kathleen Clarke, Ada English, Mary MacSwiney and Kate O'Callaghan. During the debates over the Anglo-Irish Treaty, Margaret voted to reject it. Remaining loyal to Eamon de Valera, she served in the first executive of Fianna Fáil, his newly organized party in 1926. Her daughter, Margaret Mary Pearse became a Fianna Fáil TD in 1933.

TOUR OF THE UNITED STATES

The financial difficulties of St Enda's continued through the years of the War of Independence and the Irish Civil War. With a renewed effort to save the school, seventy-year-old Margaret Pearse began a tour of the United States in 1924 to raise money.[12] Anna Smith, a friend from Brooklyn, accompanied her across the country.[13] She described her tour as non-political; however, as a very strong republican, she described conditions in Ireland during many of her speeches. She also spoke frequently against the Free State Government and against the Treaty. The American press loved Mrs Margaret Pearse. *The Irish World* praised her thus:

> It was regard for Mrs Pearse and anxiety to do honour to her who may justly be set down as the true embodiment of the patriotic Irish mother, that brought such a throng. Most of those who came never thought they would have an opportunity of seeing Mrs Pearse in person and to them the chance was one not to be lost.[14]

Margaret had gone from being a secluded housewife to committee member, politician, orator, politician and world traveller. It took tremendous courage to, at age seventy-one, stand before thousands of people and deliver an address. It is not clear who organized and sponsored her tour. The American press reported several times that she spoke under the auspices of the AARIR and Cumann na mBan. Her lectures did not receive advance publicity, the press coverage was sparse and her itineraries were not published in advance. Overall, the hectic nature of the previous lecture tours of Hanna Sheehy Skeffington, Mary MacSwiney, Countess Markievicz and Muriel MacSwiney had disappeared.

THE TOUR BEGINS

Margaret appeared first in New York City at the Brooklyn Academy of Music, on May 18 1924. In spite of heavy rain, the hall was filled to capacity long before she appeared on stage and many people could not gain admittance. In her address, she described herself as the 'proudest mother in Ireland'. Both her sons 'gave their lives to the cause of Ireland and it was their hope and wish that the school (St Enda's) should go on to perpetuate Irish culture and ideals'. She explained that she had worked extremely hard to maintain the school, but could no longer manage the mortgage. She reminded the audience that a debt of $7,250 was not a large sum to wealthy and prosperous Americans, but it was a large one to the Irish. *The Irish World* reported that $2,000 in subscriptions was collected during the meeting.[15]

Margaret also spoke to a capacity crowd at the Earl Carroll Theatre, 50th Street and Broadway, on June 1. When she walked on the stage, the crowd cheered her for several minutes. She told the audience that 'this is the most honoured night of my life—it has been the dream of my life. For over seven years, I have been looking forward to appearing here amongst you, for well I knew that you would hearken to an appeal for St Enda's. Subscriptions of $2,580 were contributed to St Enda's.[16]

A Testimonial Dinner was given for Margaret in Philadelphia on June 5 at the Banquet Hall, 1811 Spring Garden Street. Dinners were charged at $2.00 a plate to save St Enda's. Mr John J. Cabrey served as chairman for the dinner.[17]

THE WEST

Margaret travelled from New York, Massachusetts and Ohio to the West Coast during July 1924. At a meeting in Seattle, Washington, on August 11 at the A.O.U. Hall under the auspices of the AARIR, Margaret said: 'Well, Ireland is republican and nothing can save the Free State. It is built on a bad foundation and it cannot survive'. Speaking of Patrick and William, she related that: 'when my two only sons were taken and shot to death by British bullets in our own city, my daughters and I, before their dear dead bodies were cold, made up our minds that the best way to honour their memory was to carry on their work for Ireland'.[18]

Travelling next to Anaconda, Montana, Margaret gave a lecture, on July 24, at the Ancient Order of Hibernians Hall, under the auspices of the AARIR and the Cumann na mBan. During her talk, she described the Easter Rising week and gave the facts concerning the deaths of her two sons. Miss A. W. Smith, a schoolteacher from New York who accompanied Margaret, spoke briefly.[19]

On Sunday, July 27, Margaret attended a picnic in Butte at the Columbia Gardens, held jointly by the Irish Republican societies of Butte and Anaconda, to speak on 'Education in Ireland'. She also spoke of industrial and political conditions in Ireland and closed with an appeal for aid for St Enda's School.[20] *The Anaconda Standard* reported that her 'address was listened to with the closest attention and she was the recipient of hearty applause'.[21]

On August 7, Margaret spoke at the assembly room of the Portland Hotel in Portland, Oregon. *The Oregon Journal* described her as 'a sweet-faced little lady with white hair and deep blue eyes'.[22] Although she appeared in the interest of St Enda's, it was noted that she 'is not adverse to expressing her opinion that the Free State in Ireland is a farce'. She explained that in Ireland, 'it is a tradition for the women to step in and fill the gap when the men are taken from their positions'. She pointed out that she and her two daughters were carrying on the work which Patrick and William had begun.[23] The *Catholic Sentinel* reported that Margaret stated:

> I have two objects in coming—neither of them political in a sense—though I can hardly disassociate them. The one is to ask for further support for St Enda's schools, founded by my two sons, Pat and Willie. The other is to offer in person my most sincere thanks to our friends in America for their great generosity to Ireland.[24]

Margaret arrived at Port Costa, California, the railroad terminal for San Francisco, from Portland on August 9 1924. Andrew J. Gallagher, Peter J. McCormick and Mrs Thomas Fay escorted her to the San Francisco Ferry Building for a public reception. A committee headed by Peter Yorke, representatives of local Irish societies and a crowd waving American and Irish Republic flags greeted her. Yorke personally sponsored her itinerary as well as the mass meeting held at the Dreamland Rink in San Francisco.[25]

Speaking to reporters at the Whitcomb Hotel, where she was a guest of the United Irish Societies, Margaret said: 'this is a proud day for me, coming here in the winter of my years to visit this city and thank people here for their generosity to my dear land'. She was described as 'snowy haired, dressed in black, with a hammered bronze brooch at her throat framing a photograph of her two boys . . . and a locket enclosing a bit of moss from the Tara bog'.[26] From the time of her arrival, Margaret's rooms were filled with flowers from the constant stream of several thousand people who called to pay their respects.[27]

On August 15, Margaret met with California Superior Court Judge Thomas F. Graham to accept the eight thousand dollar estate of Edward F. Murphy. After working twenty-six years as an oiler for the United Railroads in San Francisco, Murphy willed his estate to the Irish cause. Margaret declared it 'a gift from heaven'. She explained that she tried to keep up the work of her son, but she was sadly in debt. Through the 'gift', Patrick's goal was given new life.[28]

On August 16, a number of local women's organizations, headed by Mrs Honor Roberts, hosted a luncheon for more than 125 guests at the Whitcomb Hotel in honour of Margaret. As a tribute to her, the tables were decorated with green, white and gold flowers.[29]

In support of her mass meeting, the only one to be held in San Francisco, Seamus Moriarty wrote in *The Leader*:

> Come and listen to Mrs Pearse. . . . California was always to the front. You sent the gallant Desmond to Australia to free the prisoners from Freemantle and California is proud to hold his ashes. You sent the

> remains of Father Eugene O'Growney, the founder of the Gaelic League, from the sand dunes of the South to his beloved Maynooth. You collected more money for Dr Douglas Hyde in 1906 than all the rest of Americans put together. And since Easter Week you have done more than any other State in the Union.[30]

On August 17 1924, 3,000 people attended a mass meeting at the Dreamland Rink to welcome Margaret as 'the greatest mother in all Ireland'.[31] The ovation given to her was reported to have 'brought tears'.[32] Seamus Moriarty welcomed her in Gaelic and W. I. O'Douglas, of the Irish Society of Sacramento, presented her with a scholarship for St Enda's. Margaret told the audience that:

> When my son, Patrick, founded St Enda's School in Dublin, he was asked: 'What are you starting that school for?' He said: 'To make Irish boys and out of Irish boys to make Irish men'. I am proud to say that it is not Irish men alone I made of my boys, but Irish volunteers, willing to give their lives for Ireland.[33]

She added she would willingly make that sacrifice again.[34]

Commenting on the situation in Ireland, Margaret declared her support for Eamon de Valera, who she believed followed in Patrick's footsteps. She declared the Free State, built on a false foundation, could not last and that Ireland stood then as it had always stood as a nation that would not surrender her birthright or give allegiance to a foreign king. Of the two parties in Ireland, she said the Free State stood for England and slavery and the Republic for Ireland and freedom.[35] Speaking on the 1921 Treaty and the men who signed it, she said that:

> they were like what we say at home, 'bold children'. They were sent on an errand and told to bring a certain thing back and they brought the wrong thing back. Well, we all know what this certain thing did and we all know that the wily Lloyd George knew what it would do. It split the country from top to toe.[36]

Every mention of Eamon de Valera's name brought applause. More than $4,000 in cash, cheques and pledges, was collected for St Enda's.[37]

Margaret spoke at the Knights of Columbus Hall in Oakland before travelling to Los Angeles, where she spoke on September 5 1924 at the Knights of Columbus Auditorium to an overflow crowd of 700 people. Joseph Scott introduced her by proclaiming:

> It has been my great pleasure to be with her the last two or three days, to read her heart and study her soul and I can safely say that she is the most extraordinary personality that ever I have come in contact with. All that she had she gave to Padraig and all that he had he obtained from his blessed mother.[38]

She told the crowd she denounced the Free State as being a 'slave state'. She said: 'it is not a Free State when women on missions of charity among the sick and poor are thrown into jail. It is not the free and independent Ireland that my boys gave their lives for'. She praised Eamon de Valera and claimed he had received harsh treatment from the Free State.[39] Contributions from the meeting amounted to $1,300.

Speaking at the meeting in the Father Meyer Hall in St Vincent's Parish the following evening to several hundred people on the 'Free State Government', Margaret stated:

> The last two years in Ireland have been the saddest in her history, but the so-called Free State Government is fast crumbling and those who love Ireland and fought for her, giving their sons and brothers for her are still fighting for her, can see the dawn of a free and independent Ireland. May God speed its coming.[40]

Margaret travelled from San Francisco to Los Angles, Salt Lake City and Chicago before returning to the east coast.[41] She was presented with a specially inscribed Medal of St Brendan in Boston in October before she returned to New York City. When a reporter from *The Monitor* asked how the United States had treated her, she replied:

> Wonderful! It was wonderful! Wonderful every step of the way, but oh! how the great West repaid our journey to them!
>
> Never, never can I forget all the friends all along the route, with California and Dr Yorke and the men and women of San Francisco at the end of it.[42]

The reporter commented that she 'seemed to hold San Francisco's welcome as the crowning joy of her whole trip'.[43]

Margaret Pearse returned to Ireland aboard the SS *Republic* on October 11 1924.

CONCLUSION

Mrs Margaret Pearse, a traditional housewife and mother prior to the Easter Rising, came to the United States eight years later as a seventy-one-year-old businesswoman and politician. She received tremendous support and affection as Patrick Pearse's mother. Both the American and Irish-American presses described her with respect and warmth. The public supported her by their great numbers, donations, subscriptions and floral gifts. Through the more than $10,000 raised during her lecture tour of the United States, Margaret saved St Enda's school.[44] In spite of the confusion caused by the 1921 Treaty and the Irish Civil War, Irish-Americans across the United States supported Mrs Margaret Pearse, the mother and the republican.

CHAPTER 11

Mary MacSwiney: The Irish Republic Still Exists, January–November 1925

When Sinn Féin members met on January 21 1919 as Dáil Éireann, Mary MacSwiney became a TD (Teachta Dála—deputy) as a representative for Cork. She delivered the longest speech—almost three hours—of the Anglo-Irish Treaty debates, December 19 to 31 1921, in the Dáil chambers. She reminded her fellow TDs:

> of the oath of allegiance that had been sworn by members of both the First and Second Dáil, each deputy swearing to 'defend the Irish Republic and the government of the Republic of Ireland, which is Dáil Éireann against all enemies foreign and domestic'.[1]

Mary joined Eamon de Valera as he walked out of the Dáil. She was astounded at the signing of the Treaty and became the most inflexible opponent of it and the Irish Free State Government. However, in spite of her unrelenting loyalty to de Valera, she did not agree with his 'external association' and believed it limited Ireland's freedoms.[2]

With de Valera imprisoned at Arbour Hill during the Civil War, she made frequent speeches throughout Ireland in support of the Republic. She condemned the Treaty, the leaders of the Free State Government and the British Government. She rejected the partition of Ireland, calling it 'England's "greatest crime in Ireland"'. She also took a stand against the Church interfering in secular matters. She was nominated to the Republican Council of State, a council of twelve members, established to ensure a functioning Republic.[3]

In November 1922, while staying in Dublin with Nancy O'Rahilly, the Free State arrested and imprisoned Mary, without charge, in Mountjoy Jail. There she went on hunger strike for twenty-four days. Cumann na mBan launched a publicity campaign against her imprisonment, with marches past government offices and nightly prayer vigils. These received international attention and support. She was arrested again while travelling to the funeral of Liam Lynch in Tipperary in April 1923, taken to Kilmainham Jail and went on hunger strike for twenty-one days. Upon her release, she set out on a speaking tour in support of the Republic in Ireland.[4]

In the August 1923 re-election of the Free State Government under President William T. Cosgrave, Mary was elected Sinn Féin representative for Cork City. However, she refused to take her place because of taking an oath of allegiance to the king.[5]

From the United States, P. J. Rutledge wrote to several Republican members of the Dáil that the situation in the US had become 'unsatisfactory'. All fund-raising had become short-term and the reorganization of the Friends of Irish Freedom (FOIF) and the American Association for the Recognition of the Irish Republic (AARIR) had not been accomplished. Clan Na Gael had become increasingly secretive and isolated.[6] Mary decided to return to the United States to describe the conditions in Ireland during the three years under the Free State Government and to ask for financial and political support for the Irish Republic.[7] It appears from newspaper reports that the meetings on her tour were organized and held under the auspices of the AARIR.

Mary realized that during her tour certain questions would be asked of her, such as why the Republic had not found the terms of the Treaty acceptable, why the majority Dáil vote on the Treaty had not been accepted by both sides and why the Republicans had not consulted American leaders regarding the Treaty and a republican constitution. She prepared herself to answer these questions prior to her arrival in the United States and her speeches focused on these points.[8]

She arrived in New York in late January 1925 alone (to reduce expenses), unannounced, incognito and allegedly without a passport from the Irish Free State Government. Unlike her first tour, on the whole there were no huge crowds or welcoming committees. The crowds attending her speeches were smaller and their responses repressed. She commented from her headquarters in the AARIR New York City office that: 'the Irish Republic is still in existence, although unrecognized. The Irish Free State is neither "Irish" nor "Free" nor a "State" and it cannot last'.[9] After two months, she wrote to de Valera that: '[the] broader-minded and better-educated people have mostly dropped out (of the AARIR)'.[10]

THE TOUR BEGINS

When Mary MacSwiney addressed a mass meeting at the Earl Carroll Theater in New York City on February 8 1925, the theatre was filled to capacity, with as many people outside as inside. While she spoke to the audience inside the theatre, her brother, Peter MacSwiney, addressed the crowd outside. Mary spoke to the 6,000 people, under the auspices of the AARIR and Clan na Gael, of her return to Ireland from the United States in August 1921 to take part in the Dáil Anglo-Irish Treaty debates and vote.[11] She told the crowd that she had returned to the United States to reach those Irish-Americans who had never wavered in their support for Ireland and to extend 'intense gratitude' for their faith in the Republic.[12]

Travelling on to Boston, Mary was welcomed by 7,000 people at Mechanics' Hall on February 20. John P. O'Sullivan of Clan na Gael, opened the meeting and Padraic O'Hagerty, state president of the AARIR, presided. She explained that 'the Treaty was accepted not by the will, but by the fear of the people, whose nerves had been for years racked by British terrorism'. She clarified the position of some who felt that the Irish could not govern themselves because of the Civil War by reminding them of the American Civil War. She said: 'We have nothing to apologize for'. She then criticized the Free State Treason and Felony Bill. She explained that under the bill, 'I can get five years of hard labour for calling Eamon de Valera President of the Irish Republic'.[13]

In support of Father Peter Yorke's revitalization of the AARIR in California, Mary returned to San Francisco to preside at the official 1925 St Patrick's Day celebration as the principal speaker at a mass meeting. Andrew J. Gallagher organized her California itinerary. Reflecting Yorke's efforts and the traditional celebration of St Patrick's Day, 100,000 people welcomed her to San Francisco on March 14. She was taken by motorcade up Market Street to the Whitcomb Hotel for an informal reception.[14] Mary spoke at several civil and social functions and was the honoured guest at several private dinners given by social and financial leaders. The delegates of the Ancient Order of Hibernians (AOH) and the Ladies' Auxiliary and organizations of the United Irish Societies made up the St

Patrick's Day convention, headed by Jeremiah V. Coffey. The celebrations began with a parade of more than 2,000 people who assembled at the Hibernian Hall, 454 Valencia Street. They proceeded down Mission Street to St Peter's Church to celebrate a high mass.[15]

More than 10,000 people crowded into the Civic Auditorium that evening. Mary began her speech in Gaelic, but continued in English. She called the Treaty by which the Irish Free State Government was established a 'sham' and gave an account of the August 1921 Dáil session, the role of the Irish delegates in the negotiations in England and the signing of the Treaty. She insisted that, 'the delegates were forbidden to sign any document until it had been submitted to the Cabinet at home, but that Lloyd George made contact again and, whatever charm he exerted in getting them to disobey the instructions of the President and Cabinet', they signed the Treaty and 'thereby not only split the country but brought on us a war more horrible than any the English had ever fought directly'.[16]

Mary was welcomed at the Central Railroad Station in Los Angeles by a delegation of supporters. The press claimed that she looked younger and appeared more optimistic about Ireland's future than she did when she was in Los Angeles in 1920. Mary told the audience that the Irish people were hopeful of winning their complete independence from England by peaceful means if they could get the people to vote for what they really wanted and believe in it.[17] Councils and divisions of the AOH presented Mary with bouquets of roses and other spring flowers and fruit.[18]

In a report to AARIR headquarters, Mary evaluated her visit to California:

> I have been on the whole disappointed at the result financially. There should have been an organiser before me on the road a full month ago. . . . The propaganda has been, I am told, excellent and it did not come before it was needed. Another thing that has injured us very much is the fact that many people went to Ireland in 1922 and 1923 Republicans and came back Free-Staters. . . . A strong membership drive is essential now . . . If we do not get a large increase in membership our resources cannot continue to meet our needs even to the extent they are doing at present. Our faithful friends are nearly drained dry. . . . The type we had in the AARIR four years ago of broader minded and better educated people have mostly dropped out and the faithful who have stuck by us and helped us don't even want the others back. . . . I have had many comments on my travelling

> alone. It is looked upon as a great indignity to me personally, but when I explain that it is my own wish for economy sake, they understand.[19]

Speaking next in Portland, Oregon, on March 29, to an audience of over 1,000 people in the Lincoln Auditorium, Mary described conditions in Ireland and made a plea for American support and financial aid. She claimed that the promises of the Treaty had not been carried out and that as long as Ireland was subject to England, there would be 'bitter hatred and enmity'. While Ireland is not free, 'Ireland is England's deadly enemy and England's difficulty will be Ireland's opportunity to strike a blow for freedom in the future as in the past'.[20]

From Portland, Mary travelled to Seattle, Washington to speak at the Knights of Columbus Hall, on March 31, on 'Present Day Conditions in Ireland'. The press reported once again that she spoke 'calmly, logically and with an intensity of conviction that deeply impressed her hearers'. She said she had returned to America to reach those who had been faithful to the 'path of honour and no compromise for Ireland'. She also wanted to 'reach those Irish-Americans who had been misled by false promises and propaganda about the Anglo-Irish Treaty'.[21]

Father Peter Yorke died at the end of March leaving Northern California without AARIR leadership. Although she had attended his funeral in an official capacity, the newspapers, including *The Leader*, did not mention her presence, creating confusion and hard feelings among many AARIR members. Andrew J. Gallagher of San Francisco wrote to Mary that he could not explain the lack of publicity, except that 'there may be some peculiar or undiscovered reason'. He expressed his concern for the future of the AARIR in Northern California, yet, he knew of no one who could replace Father Yorke. He mentioned that he could not himself take on more leadership responsibilities as he had neglected his own business.[22]

Mary held her next meetings in Butte, Montana during April. Overall, attendance at her meetings had been down, but she raised $2,000 there and another $1,000 at a meeting in Anaconda on April 21.[23] From there, she reported to Andrew Gallagher that much of her time was spent with Father Hannan. Her report provides an insight into the confusion and misunderstandings that prevailed among the Irish-Americans regarding the situation in Ireland. She said she had listened to Father Hannan 'give an unending catalogue and repeated recitation of our mistakes, beginning with the failure to shoot or at least imprison the delegates on their return from London'. She found his attitude 'most depressing'. Father Hannan believed 'those in power in Ireland were and had proved themselves a lot of babies, incapable of bringing the movement to success'.[24] When she told Father Hannan that she felt 'he did not believe in continuing the fight any longer and wanted to draw out', he replied that she 'was not far wide of the point'.[25]

On the night she spoke to the AARIR members and other Irish societies in Butte she said she felt 'almost in despair'. She spoke of the criticisms she had received and 'the fault-finding, the hopelessness expressed by some loyal friends of the Republic because of our mistakes, because we did not have the capacity of experienced statesmen, or because we erred in thinking that those who had once served Ireland well were rather mistaken than deliberate traitors'. She believed the audience had 'no idea that among our critics and fault-finders were Fr Yorke and Fr Hannan'. She believed the assurance Father Hannan gave before the end of the meeting of the 'continued and untiring support of himself and all the Republicans of Butte' was simply an 'amends' to her.[26]

Father Hannan stated at a banquet the night before Mary left Butte to travel to Chicago, that 'we are behind the Republic with our moral and financial support to the end'. However, privately he told Mary that he 'stood behind the Republic not behind any individual' and he believed there should be other ways of raising money besides mass meetings.[27]

By the time she arrived in Chicago from Butte, on April 25, a furore had developed over Mary's passport. According to newspaper reports, she not only admitted not having a passport, but had no intention of getting one and threatened to hunger strike if arrested. Local immigration officials began an inquiry on orders from the US State Department on behalf of the Irish Free State Government.[28] *The Leader* reported that the inquiry was the result 'of the mean and cowardly action of Smiddy (Timothy Smiddy, Irish Free State Minister to the United States)—the Free State "informer"'. Allegedly, immigration officials first questioned Miss MacSwiney in Chicago at Smiddy's request.[29]

Mary made a statement while in Chicago that she believed the investigation started as the result of an anonymous telephone call to the immigration authorities in Washington D.C. She stated: 'There is nothing mysterious about my presence in America. I have been here since January. I have given lectures also in Washington D.C. The newspapers there all know about my presence but no questions were asked about any passports'.[30] *The Irish World* published the following denial at the request of Mary:

> Miss Mary MacSwiney has issued a statement to the press denying that she threatened to hunger strike if arrested by the United States authorities . . . Commissioner of Immigration Husband, [from] Washington, has sent out a general order directing that Miss Mary MacSwiney be not further interfered with.[31]

Joe Begley, AARIR National Headquarters, wrote to Mary that he hoped to get generous press coverage of her denial and that the AARIR was considering a malicious libel suit against the press associations and newspapers because they had printed Mary's alleged statements as quotations. Copies of the correction of Mary's statements were sent out to the *Associated Press*, the *International News Service*, *The New York Times*, *World*, *Evening World*, *American*, *The Chicago American*, *The Irish World*, *Irish Republic*, *Monitor*, *Advocate* and the *San Francisco Leader*.[32] The correction, written by Martin Howard, State Secretary of the AARIR in New York City stated, in part:

> We are aware that the British Embassy here after consultation with the Free State authorities in Ireland instructed their Secret Service Department to keep a close watch on the activities of Miss MacSwiney and all other leading Irish Republicans in this country and to send regular reports of her meetings and lectures to the British Ambassador. The Free State people have asked, to our knowledge, that copies of these reports should be supplied to them as frequently as possible. We are aware that these Secret Service Officers of the British Government in America did attend many meetings and did follow Miss MacSwiney and other leading Irish Republicans and we are also aware that the reports requested by the Free State from the British Secret Service in this country have been furnished to the Free State government from their agent here and have been received at their Dublin headquarters.[33]

Mary's belief that her passport problems were caused by Professor Timothy Smiddy were substantiated in an extract printed in *Sinn Féin* in May 1925 which stated that:

> Due to a leak in the British Consulate, documentary evidence has fallen into republican hands showing that the British Secret Service

> have arranged with Professor Smiddy, representative of the Saorstat Government in Washington, to forward to him for transmission to Dublin the usual report of agents covering the activities and work of Irish organizations. These reports were formerly sent to the British Cabinet and had been discontinued until this newer arrangement caused a resumption.[34]

If nothing else, the passport turmoil provided Mary with an excellent source of publicity for months to come. The Free State Government apparently hoped to discredit her in an effort to sabotage her lectures while in the United States. The US Government may have reacted to this dilemma and handled it in the same manner as they had with the arrival of the Lord Mayor of Cork, Donal O'Callaghan, in the US without a passport to testify before the American Commission on Conditions in Ireland in January 1921—shifting responsibility between branches of government. (See Chapter 3.) It is not clear that it was ever determined that Mary did or did not have a passport or what ultimate decisions resolved the issue.

The exchange of correspondence between the Irish Free State Government and the British Government went on for several months beginning in July with a letter from G. G. Whiskard, Esq., Dominions Office, London, to D. O'Hegarty, Irish Free State Government, advising that their Foreign Office was afraid that Mary was in possession of a false passport. According to her, as reported in the American press, 'she had no passport to enter the United States, did not need one and had no intention of getting one'. However, she is since reported to have denied this statement as 'a pack of lies'. Whiskard advised Hegarty that Mary received a British passport in November 1920 to travel to the United States, it had been 'endorsed' at Dublin Castle in January 1922 for a trip to France, but there was no later record.[35]

The Saorstat Éireann informed the Secretary of the Executive Council on July 22 that they did not have a document from the Passport Office and that Professor Smiddy had been informed by the US State Department on February 9 that they would investigate the matter. However, 'for some reason unknown to Professor Smiddy and to the Minister of External Affairs, no apparent effort has been made to find out the nature of the document on which Miss MacSwiney travelled'.[36] The US Department of Justice informed the Secretary of the Executive Council on October 7 that 'inquiries in connection with this matter [Mary's passport] have now been completed [that] tend to show that Miss MacSwiney did not obtain any document, authentic or otherwise, in the Saorstat which would enable her to land in the United States'.[37] Finally, D. O'Hegarty wrote to G. G. Whiskard, Esq. that Mary had not asked for or received any document from the Passport Office to travel to the United States and she had not obtained any document from any other government agency in Ireland, which would enable her to land in the United States.[38]

The issue of whether Mary possessed a passport or not and the question of how she entered the United States followed her from meeting to meeting. She developed a standard answer, which stated that she would not break any US laws, she would not hunger strike over the issue of a passport and she had entered the US on the sunrays or at times on an eclipse.

While Mary was still in Chicago, Sean T. Ó Ceallaigh, TD, Irish Republican Headquarters in New York City, advised her of problems, other than her passport, between the State level of the AARIR and the Clan. For many years the Clan had held field days on July 4 and August 15. The AARIR suggested the events be held under joint auspices and the proceeds divided fifty-fifty. When the Clan refused the offer, the AARIR held their field day one week before the Clan event, on June 27 and the other a week after the Clan event in August, on August 23. Ó Ceallaigh asked Mary to try to smooth things out there and in Pittsburg, another area of conflict.[39]

The problem in Pittsburg between members of the AARIR erupted when a group within the strongest council in Pittsburg refused to recognize the local authority set up by the AARIR in Western Pennsylvania and refused to forward funds to them. Ó Ceallaigh reported that:

> Not alone do they refuse to hand in their funds to the State body, but I believe they have held for six months all the monies that they have received and have refused to send it on here unless we would give them authority to repudiate the local State executive.[40]

Here again he asked Mary to 'help to smooth things over when opportunity offers'.[41]

Mary found time amidst the passport issue and AARIR problems to address a meeting in Chicago at Orchestra Hall on April 27. Her statement that, 'England's difficulty is Ireland's opportunity' brought a round of applause. She compared her mission to the United States to that of Benjamin Franklin in Ireland in 1789. Approximately $3,600 in cash was raised at the meeting.[42]

Mary then travelled to Minneapolis, Minnesota to speak at the First Unitarian Church, on April 30, under the auspices of the AARIR. In response to the on-going passport question, she again denied she had threatened a hunger strike if jailed by the US immigration authorities. She commented that a hunger strike is used only as a 'weapon against illegal authority'. The United States was enforcing its laws and exercising its legal authority. She would do as she had always done—respect the laws of the United States. As to the question of having a passport, she answered that 'she and the United States authorities understand the situation, as she has been and is ready to give duly qualified officials all information on the subject to which they are legally entitled'.[43]

Never at a loss for words and perhaps running out of patience on this issue, she added:

> I'll never tell whether I have a passport or not. If you really want to know how I got into this country, I came in on the eclipse. Even the United States can't question my entry when I ride down on the rays of the sun. They can send me to jail—but I don't think they will. I didn't need a passport the way I came in.[44]

Mary spoke at the Knights of Columbus Hall, 169 Smith Avenue, in St Paul, Minnesota on May 1. When the chairman of the meeting mentioned the death of her brother, Terence, she broke into tears. She regained her composure and began her talk a few minutes later, first in Gaelic, but continuing in English:

> The Republic of Ireland still lives, will live forever. . . . In our hearts we have stayed loyal to the oath we took to support the Irish Republic [and] never will submit to that Treaty or to the Constitution, which gives the allegiance of Ireland to King George, nor will we submit to an authority which we hold invalid.[45]

Again the question of her passport arose. She told the audience that Mr Smiddy had denied any plot to have her deported and US immigration officials had stated that if they found evidence of a fraudulent passport, they would refer the case to the US Department of Justice.[46]

The Minneapolis Tribune reported that immigration authorities had requested officials at Ellis Island to examine the records of all ships that had entered the port during the latter part of January to determine if Mary MacSwiney's name appeared on any passenger lists or ship's employee lists.[47]

The topic of her passport issue followed Mary to Kansas City, Missouri. In an attempt to close the matter, she finally issued a statement in the *Star Report* on May 5:

> Everyone is fussing about my passport. I never said I'd go on a hunger strike over the question. I never said I hadn't obtained a passport into the United States. I've a passport into the United States. I've never said anything at all about it, but now I'm saying I came in on a sun ray during the eclipse. There is no law against that mode of entry. I've no intention of breaking the laws of your country.[48]

While speaking in Kansas City on May 5, Mary made a petition for financial aid and moral support for the Irish Republic. She was reported as saying that the true conditions in Ireland were not generally known and that there was a general misapprehension that Ireland had 'settled down'. She again stated, in answer to questions pertaining to her passport, that if called before the State Department she would be able 'to settle the matter satisfactorily'. Until then, she would keep silent because any information she gave publicly would then be known by her country's enemies.[49]

Mary then went from Kansas City to Cincinnati, Ohio where she was a guest at the home of Mr and Mrs Castellini. The Irish Literary Society gave a reception in her honour at the Castellini home at 2324 Park Avenue. She held a meeting, on May 10, at the Emery Auditorium where she told the audience that America had always recognized her debt to France for help during the Revolutionary War. She appealed for recognition of a 'like debt to Ireland'. She talked bitterly of the Treason-Felony Bill before the Free State Parliament, which would punish membership in the Irish Republican Army by death. Approximately $1,000 was raised during the meeting.[50]

A few days later, Mary spoke at a meeting in Philadelphia, Pennsylvania and then addressed a mass meeting in Newark, New Jersey, on May 17, under the joint auspices of the AARIR and the Clan na Gael, at Laurel Garden, 457 Springfield Avenue.[51]

Mary then spoke at the Opera House in Ansonia, Connecticut on

May 21, under the auspices of the AARIR. Ex-Congressman P. B. O'Sullivan refused to preside at the meeting unless he could make a statement to clarify that he was there only as a courtesy to Mary and that he was opposed to any criticism of the Free State Government. He told Mary that, 'while he would prefer, like all friends of Ireland, to see a Republic with absolute independence, the Free State was a step forward and was something that should receive the loyal support of all who believed in Ireland and its capacity for self-government'.[52] When Mary refused to honour his request, O'Sullivan took a seat in the wings and left the Opera House before AARIR State Secretary J. P. Barry gave his address. O'Sullivan said after the meeting that he accepted the invitation to speak 'under a misapprehension' and that he should have inquired more fully into the objectives of the meeting. Approximately only 100 people attended the meeting, many from out of town.[53] In her address, Mary praised the integrity of Eamon de Valera and those close to him. She said the Irish were justified in taking up arms. Once de Valera issued the 'cease fire' order, she had devoted her time to educating people on how to use the ballot and to raise funds so that the Republic could carry on its campaign. Once again she stated she would not go on hunger strike if arrested by the United States authorities over the issue of her passport. She also restated that she was bound to obey the laws and regulations of the United States while there and that she neither denied nor affirmed possession of a passport. At the conclusion of her talk, she was presented with a bouquet of American Beauty roses.[54]

After attending meetings in Waterbury, Connecticut; Toledo, Ohio; and Flint, Michigan; Mary spoke for two hours at a mass meeting held at the Fraternal Hall, 15 Elm Street, in New Haven, Connecticut, on May 31. She told the audience that, 'eventually the Crown will pack up and leave our country'. She also said the story that Irishmen love a fight for the sake of fighting is false and that, Irishmen had fought in every country in the world for freedom. She said: 'Every generation of Irishmen has fought for liberty some place or other'.[55]

Mary held meetings in Pittsfield, Massachusetts and New Bedford, Connecticut during June. During that time, she wrote a letter to Andrew Gallagher in which she expressed her disappointment that Joseph Scott had promised to write to her at the end of March and she still had not received a letter from him. She told Gallagher that what she wanted was 'to have a straight talk'.

She then brought up the controversy over her relationship with the late Father Yorke. Evidently there had been rumours in California that a rift between Father Yorke and Mary may have distressed him. The loyalties of Mary and Father Yorke had come to be at odds due to his waning support of the Irish Republic and de Valera. She informed Gallagher that on her return to New York, she had learned of a report that claimed that her visit to Father Yorke had hastened his death and, as a result there were ill feelings against her in San Francisco. She went on to say 'you can imagine how such a story hurt me. . . .*You* know that—just because he was ill—I did not show Dr Yorke how keenly I felt certain remarks he made, which gave me cause for resentment. I am glad that I said nothing to hurt or injure him'.[56]

Mary then pointedly asked Gallagher: 'Is San Francisco going to desert Ireland at this crisis—for it is desertion if you are going to do nothing *practical* to give the Republic regular financial support. If you do intend to desert us say so and we shall get along as well as we can'. She accused Gallagher of devoting most of his energies to a memorial to Father Yorke. She commented that an article in *The Leader* gave no credit to the work Father Yorke had done for the Republic of Ireland, which created an image of 'cold-shouldering Ireland'. She emphasized her understanding that the AARIR was at liberty to 'cold-shoulder Ireland' if it wanted to, but she wanted to know if the leaders in California were going to do anything to help Ireland financially until the memorial to Father Yorke was completed.[57]

Obviously tired of waiting for the promised letter from Joseph Scott, Mary wrote to him on July 11. She reproached him for failing to write to her concerning the future support in California of the Irish Republic and asked if he was going to 'desert Ireland now in the greatest crisis of her history, at a time when help such as we got four years ago would mean certain victory?' She told Scott pointedly that he was one of her biggest disappointments. She felt California had not contributed much support to Ireland since 1922.[58]

Mary evidently succeeded in gaining Scott's attention as he quickly responded to her letter. He claimed he had not written because there had been no developments in finding a new leader to replace Father Yorke. He reminded her that, 'You did not seem to grasp my thought when I told you Father Yorke's death would create at least a temporary paralysis for want of any sort of a leader to succeed him'. As to the confusion and split within the AARIR, he explained that Father Yorke may have allowed himself to become:

> 'bitter over the gap which came into his life upon the return of yourself and Harry Boland to Dublin, when it was impossible to get the slightest information from Ireland from anybody. He might as well have been in Mars. Someone could at least have written a postal card'.

He and others began to feel that as far as the future of an Irish Republic, no one in Ireland would listen to or accept advice from anyone in the United States on the adoption of the Treaty. Scott closed the letter by stating: 'I am sure you will realize that no one single sentiment of this letter is in the slightest sense personal in its criticism of your exemplary fortitude. You have gone out into the desert to pray. God help and strengthen you'.[59]

Mary replied to Scott on August 21 with point-by-point arguments that only rehashed their original positions. Not one to mince words, she wanted him to know that she had '*not* gone into the desert to pray. I regret that my prayers are the worse part of me. I may be Mary by name, but I am Martha by avocation and I can only hope that as far as the prayers go, the Lord will accept, as satisfactory, the saying of some Saint or other, "Laborare est orare" [to work is to play]'. She told him that she found it 'so frightfully hard to believe you are going to be content to do nothing. I won't believe it yet'. She candidly let him know she agreed with him that de Valera should not have resigned. She felt de Valera should have dismissed Collins and Griffith and carried on the government 'letting them attend or not as they liked'. She believed that de Valera's position had been made difficult because there was no 'machinery' for a separate election of the President—de Valera was President by national acclamation rather than by election.[60]

Publicity and newspaper coverage was waning and the number of addresses Mary gave were decreasing. She next spoke at the Moose Hall in Atlantic City, New Jersey, on July 22. She began by asking the audience to understand the position of Ireland by reading their own history 'with the gratitude to Ireland that Washington acknowledged; with the noble devotion to the ideals of the United States that Daniel Webster[61] displayed in his attitude toward Greece and Hungary; with the burning love of freedom and fair play which characterized that greatest of all your citizens—Abraham Lincoln'.[62]

The Ancient Order of Hibernians took issue with some of Mary's statements delivered at this meeting. During their 54th National

Convention at the Ambassador Hotel in Atlantic City, New Jersey, on July 25, they adopted a resolution which claimed that statements made by Miss Mary MacSwiney were 'detrimental to the best interests of Ireland [and] do not represent the sentiment of the AOH'. They claimed she had also stated during interviews that the Free State Government had failed; she had 'attacked' the British Government and had affirmed that Ireland would continue her fight for complete independence, rather than the present 'false freedom'.[63]

The AOH was in conflict during this time over the Anglo-Irish Treaty and the Free State Government. It had become very pro-Free State Government and anti-de Valera and Irish Republic though Mary McWhorter and the Ladies' Auxiliary of the AOH remained loyal to de Valera and supported the Irish Republic. Many AOH leaders bitterly denounced Mary McWhorter's position.

Once her passport conflict was settled, the remainder of Mary MacSwiney's tour received limited press coverage. She returned to Ireland in November as quietly and as unnoticed as she had arrived in the United States almost a year earlier.

CONCLUSION

The success of Mary MacSwiney's second tour of America in 1925 is questionable. At least on the East Coast, for the most part there were no large receptions or fanfare. Her mass meeting in New York City at Madison Square Garden was well attended and successful and thousands turned out to welcome her in San Francisco and to attend her mass meeting on St Patrick's Day. *The Leader* not only covered the latter meeting in detail, but also printed her speech in full. However, overall reduced newspaper coverage, both in the Irish-American and American presses, reflected the split in the Irish-American leadership and the decline of republican nationalism when many Irish-Americans accepted the Treaty, the Free State Government and the conditions in Ireland.

Mary's tour did not succeed in revitalizing Irish-American republican nationalism. The Irish-American organizations remained as they were with their same loyalties and differences. The funds she raised in 1925 were not substantial and the Irish-American organizations remained unchanged.[64]

Mary evaluated her own tour in a letter to Eamon de Valera in which she regretfully reported:

> On the whole I am very disappointed. Making all allowances for changed conditions and for the readiness with which Americans tire of things, I did not expect to find the apathy quite so bad. Much of the enthusiasm of four years ago was due to the joy and pride of the Irish here in us and in our success. For the moment we are the under dog again. They know they did not lift us out of that position before; they do not feel competent to do it again. It is a case of 'Help ourselves and America will help us'. . . . My six months in the USA are up and I am looking forward to my recall.[65]

Eamon de Valera and his supporters left Sinn Féin to form a new party, Fianna Fáil in 1926. Mary began to speak out publicly against him comparing him to others who were 'unfaithful to the men and women of 1916'. The final break with de Valera came when, in August, he and the Fianna Fáil delegates entered the Free State Parliament and took the oath—declaring it meant nothing. Sadly Mary stated: 'I have no use for Eamon de Valera or his compromise and I despise him for his conduct of recent years'.[66]

Epilogue

IRISH REPUBLICANISM DID not die with the 1921 Anglo-Irish Treaty, the Irish Civil War or the formation of the Irish Free State Government. Republicans continued their work 'on the run', in prison and in the United States. Hanna Sheehy Skeffington, Mary MacSwiney, Mrs Muriel MacSwiney, Countess Constance Markievicz and Mrs Margaret Pearse continued their support of the Irish Republic in their own ways upon their return to Ireland from their lecture tours of the United States.

In 1926, Hanna Sheehy Skeffington was appointed to the executive of Fianna Fáil, Eamon de Valera's newly organized party. A year later, when de Valera sidestepped the oath of allegiance and took his seat in the Dáil, she broke with him and Fianna Fáil. She viewed the oath as 'a lapse from republican principles and traditions'.[1] She visited the United States again in 1934–35 to publicize conditions in Ireland and in 1937–38 on the eve of World War II to speak for peace.[2] Hanna died on Easter Saturday, April 20 1946, almost exactly thirty years after the 1916 Easter Rising.[3] Hanna's son, Owen became a teacher at Trinity College Dublin and a senator during the 1950s and 1960s.[4]

Distrust between Mary MacSwiney and Eamon de Valera developed as she continued her hard-line republicanism and he took a more moderate approach. When she spoke out against his leaving Sinn Féin, feelings developed against her on both sides of the Atlantic. Irish-American groups who had previously hesitantly accepted the Irish Free State turned their support to de Valera and rejected her radicalism. She remained inflexible in her support of the Republic. She ignored feminist issues, including those of women in the workforce. When she lost a dispute within the Cumann na mBan over continued allegiance to the Republic in 1933, she resigned her membership. She became virtually politically isolated. She did, however, agree with and support Eamon de Valera's Irish neutrality stand during World War II. Mary died in her home in March 1942.[5]

Shortly after her return from the United States, Countess Constance Markievicz took an active military role in the Irish Civil War in Dublin. After the fighting moved into the country, the Countess spent her time 'on the run in Dublin'. She wrote articles in support of the Republic and worked with Maud Gonne MacBride to aid republican prisoners and their dependants. She campaigned for Fianna Fáil candidates in the June 1927 election until she became ill and died in July 1927.[6]

Mrs Muriel MacSwiney took an active front-line position during the Irish Civil War and heightened her militant political stand. Her second visit to the United States in 1922 was short, but the press took notice of the new politically astute woman she had become. Muriel and her daughter, Máire, moved to Dublin after Muriel's return to Ireland. Muriel joined the Irish Communist Party in 1922, lived in Germany and then England, where she joined the British Communist Party.[7] She also lived for a time in Paris. Life for Muriel and her daughter, Máire, was filled with sadness. Máire has since stated: 'The main problem with my mother was that she had some psychiatric illness. . . . In every other way, she was a wonderful person, . . . loving, caring, brilliantly intelligent, of great integrity and full of concern for those not well off'.[8] There are conflicting stories of her relationship with Máire. One version tells that when, at the age of fourteen, Máire asked her aunt, Mary MacSwiney, to take her home to Ireland, Mary sought and won custody of Máire. With that Muriel cut off contact with Máire. Another version alleges that Muriel signed an affidavit in Dublin in August 1944 in which she stated that Mary MacSwiney kidnapped Máire on the grounds that Muriel had joined the Irish Communist Party, was an atheist and not a fit mother. In spite of Muriel returning to Ireland and enlisting the help of Linda Kearns and Eamon de Valera, Mary MacSwiney was granted legal rights to Máire. Muriel never regained custody of her daughter.[9] She died in a London nursing home in 1982 at the age of ninety.[10]

Mrs Margaret Pearse became a senator and member of the Fianna Fail executive in 1926. She died on April 22 1939, leaving St Enda's to her daughter, Margaret Mary and then to the nation as a memorial to Patrick and William Pearse.[11] Her daughter became a Fianna Fáil TD in 1933.

APPENDIX 1

Poblacht na h-Éireann
The Provisional Government of the Irish Republic to the People of Ireland

IRISHMEN AND IRISHWOMEN in the name of God and the dead generations from which she receives her old traditions of nationhood, Ireland, through us, summons her children to her flag and strikes for her freedom. Having organized and trained her manhood through her secret revolutionary organization, the Irish Republican Brotherhood and through her open military organizations, the Irish Volunteers and the Irish Citizen Army, having patiently perfected her discipline, having resolutely waited for the right moment to reveal itself, she now seizes that moment and, supported by her exiled children in America and by gallant allies in Europe, but relying in the first on her own strength, she strikes in full confidence of victory.

We declare the right of the people of Ireland to the ownership of Ireland and the unfettered control of Irish destinies to be sovereign and indefeasible. The long usurpation of that right by a foreign people and Government has not extinguished the right, nor can it ever be extinguished except by the destruction of the Irish people. In every generation the Irish people have asserted their right to national freedom and sovereignty; six times during the past three hundred years have they asserted it in arms. Standing on that fundamental right and again asserting it in arms in the face of the world, we hereby proclaim the Irish Republic as a Sovereign Independent State and we pledge our lives and the lives of our comrades in arms to the cause of its army, of its welfare and of its exaltation among the nations.

The Irish Republic is entitled to and hereby claims, the allegiance of every Irishman and Irishwoman. The Republic guarantees religious and civil property, equal rights and equal opportunities to all its citizens and declares its resolve to pursue the happiness and prosperity of the whole nation and of all its parts, cherishing all the children of the nation equally and oblivious of the differences carefully fostered by an alien government which has divided a minority from the majority in the past.

Until our arms have brought the opportune moment for the establishment of a permanent National Government representative of the whole people of Ireland and elected by the suffrages of all her men and women the provisional Government hereby constituted will administer the civil and military affairs of the Republic in trust for the people. We place the Irish Republic under the protection of the Most High God, Whose Blessing we invoke on our arms and we pray that no one who serves that cause will dishonour it. In this supreme hour the Irish nation must by its valour and discipline, and by the readiness of its children to sacrifice themselves for the common good, prove itself worthy of the august destiny to which it is called.

Signed on behalf of the Provision Government:

Thomas J. Clarke
Seán MacDiarmada
P. H. Pearse
James Connolly
Thomas MacDonagh
Eamon Ceannt
Joseph Plunkett

APPENDIX 2

Some Women in Easter Week[1] *(Account of Countess Markievicz of Easter Week as given to members of Cumann na mBan)*

YOU ASK ME to write you an account of my experiences and of the activities of the women of Easter Week. I am afraid that I can only give you a little account of those who were enrolled like me in the Irish Citizen Army and those who were with me or whom I met during the Week. Some were members of Cumann na mBan, and others, just women who were ready to die for Ireland.

My activities were confined to a very limited area. I was mobilized for Liberty Hall and was sent from there via the City Hall to St Stephen's Green, where I remained.

On Easter Monday morning there was a great hosting of disciplined and armed men at Liberty Hall.

Padraic Pearse and James Connolly addressed us and told us that from now on the Volunteers and the ICA were not two forces, but the wings of the Irish Republican Army.

There were a considerable number of ICA women. These were absolutely on the same footing as the men. They took part in all marches and even in the manoeuvres that lasted all night. Moreover, Connolly made it quite clear to us that unless we took our share of the drudgery of training and preparing, we should not be allowed to take any share at all in the fight. You may judge how fit we were when I tell you that sixteen miles was the length of our last route march.

Connolly had appointed two staff officers—Commandant Mallin and myself. I held a commission, giving me the rank of Staff Lieutenant. I was accepted by Tom Clarke and the members of the provisional Government as the second of Connolly's 'ghosts'. 'Ghosts' was the name we gave to those who stood secretly behind the leaders and were entrusted with enough of the plans of the Rising to enable them to carry on that leader's work should anything happen to himself. Commandant Mallin was over me and next in command to Connolly. Dr Kathleen Lynn was our medical officer, holding the rank of Captain.

We watched the little bodies of men and women march off, Pearse and Connolly to the GPO, Sean Connolly to the City Hall. I went off then with the doctor in her car. We carried a large store of First Aid necessities and drove off through quiet dusty streets and across the river, reaching the City Hall just at the very moment that Commandant Sean Connolly and his little troop of men and women swung round the corner, and he raised his gun and shot the policeman who barred the way. A wild excitement ensued, people running from every side to see what was up. The doctor got out and I remember Mrs Barrett—sister of Sean Connolly—and others helping to carry in the doctor's bundles. I did not meet Dr Lynn again until my release, when her car met me and she welcomed me to her house, where she cared for me and fed me up and looked after me 'till I had recovered from the evil effects of the English prison system.

When I reported with the car to Commandant Mallin in Stephen's Green, he told me that he must keep me. He said that owing to MacNeill's calling off the Volunteers, a lot of the men who should have been under him had to be distributed round other posts and that few of those left him were trained to shoot, so I must stay and be ready to take up the work of a sniper. He took me round the Green and showed me how the barricading of the gates and digging trenches had begun and he left me in charge of this work while he went to superintend the erection of barricades in the streets and arrange other work. About two hours later he definitely promoted me to be his second in command. This work was very exciting when the fighting began. I continued round and round the Green, reporting back if anything was wanted, or tackling any sniper who was particularly objectionable.

Madeleine ffrench Mullen was in charge of the Red Cross and the commissariat in the Green. Some of the girls had revolvers and with these they sallied forth and held up bread vans.

This was necessary because the first prisoner we took was a British officer and Commandant Mallin treated him as such. He took his parole 'as an officer and a gentleman' not to escape and he left him at large in the Green before the gates were shut. This English gentleman walked around and found out all he could and then 'bunked'.

We had a couple of sick men and prisoners in the bandstand, the Red Cross flag flying to protect them. The English in the Shelbourne turned a machine-gun on to them. A big group of our girls were attending to the sick, making tea for the prisoners or resting themselves. I never saw anything like their courage. Madeleine ffrench Mullen brought them, with the sick and the prisoners, out and into a safer place.

It was all done slowly and in perfect order. More than one young girl said to me, 'What is there to be afraid of? Won't I go straight to heaven if I die for Ireland?' However it was, they came out unscathed from a shower of shrapnel. On Tuesday we began to be short of food. There were no bread carts on the streets. We retired into the College of Surgeons that evening and were joined by some of our men who had been in other places and by quite a large squad of Volunteers and with this increase in our numbers the problem of food became very serious.

Nellie Gifford was put in charge of one large classroom with a big grate, but alas, there was nothing to cook. When we were all starving she produced a quantity of oatmeal from somewhere and made pot after pot of the most delicious porridge, which kept us going. But all the same, on Tuesday and Wednesday we absolutely starved. There seemed to be no bread in the town.

Later on Mary Hyland was given charge of a little kitchen, somewhere down through the houses, near where the Eithne workroom now is.

We had only one woman casualty—Margaret Skinnader. She, like myself, was in uniform and carried an army rifle. She had enlisted as a private in the ICA. She was one of the party who went out to set fire to a house just behind Russell's Hotel. The English opened fire on them from the ground floor of a house just opposite. Poor Freddy Ryan was killed and Margaret was very badly wounded. She owes her life to William Partridge. He carried her away under fire and back to the College. God rest his noble soul. Brilliant orator and Labour leader, comrade and friend of Connolly's, he was content to serve as a private in the ICA. He was never strong and the privations he suffered in an English jail left him a dying man.

Margaret's only regret was her bad luck in being disabled so early in the day (Wednesday of Easter Week) though she must have suffered terribly, but the end was nearer than we thought, for it was only a few days later that we carried her over to Vincent's Hospital, so that she would not fall wounded into the hands of the English.

The memory of Easter Week with its heroic dead is sacred to us who survived. Many of us could almost wish that we had died in the moment of ecstasy when, with the tricolour over our heads we went out and proclaimed the Irish Republic and with guns in our hands tried to establish it.

We failed, but not until we had seen regiment after regiment run from our few guns. Our effort will inspire the people who come after us and will give them hope and courage. If we failed to win, so did the English. They slaughtered and imprisoned, only to arouse the nation to a passion of love and loyalty, loyalty to Ireland and hatred of foreign rule. Once they see clearly that the English rule us still, only with a new personnel of traitors and new uniforms, they will finish the work begun by the men and women of Easter Week. CONSTANCE DE MARKIEVICZ.

APPENDIX 3

To the President and Houses of Congress of the United States of America

WE, THE UNDERSIGNED, representing a large body of Irish Women whose President was condemned to death for her share in a struggle for the freedom of our country, make an appeal to you and we base our appeal, first, on the generosity of the American Administration in all things affecting Women's lives and welfare, and secondly, on your recognition, many times extended, of the justice of Ireland's demand for political freedom.

For many lamentable generations the Women of Ireland have had to bring up their Children in a country in a perpetual state of economic and political disarray consequent on its being governed in the interest of another country. Your Declaration concerning a war settlement which has called into being and endowed with hope the spirit of Democracy in every country, has made us feel that a new era is opening for us. Our appeal now is to remind you of a cause which should not be overlooked when so many European Nationalities are to be reconstructed in accordance with your Declaration. Our country, having behind it twenty generations of repression has, we believe, a profound claim upon those who have declared their will to make the world safe for Democracy. We appeal to you to recognize the political independence of Ireland in the form of an Irish Republic.

And encouraged by the knowledge that the States of Wyoming, Colorado, Utah, Idaho, Washington, California, Arizona, Kansas, Nevada, Montana, Oregon and New York have granted full suffrage to their women, we feel that your generous sympathy will be extended to the women of our country in our demand before the world for the recognition of an Irish Republic virtually in existence since April 1916—the only Republic which from its inauguration was prepared to give women their full place in the Councils of their Nation.

Signed on behalf of Cumann na mBan *(The Irishwomen's Council)*

Constance de Markievicz
Nannie O'Rahilly
Mary Ryan
Elizabeth Bloxham
Kathlin Clarke
Annie Kent
Louise Gavan Duffy
Niamh Plunkett
Jennie Wyse Power
Mary S. Walsh

APPENDIX 4

Speech delivered by Mrs Hanna Sheehy Skeffington At Madison Square Garden on the evening of May 4 1918[1]

MR CHAIRMAN, LADIES and gentlemen, at this late hour I am not going to keep you by making a speech. I feel that I have spoken so often already in this country that I would now prefer to leave it and go home to help to keep Ireland free from conscription and safe for democracy (applause). This was to have been my last meeting in New York but the British Government has decided otherwise. I learned last week in California that my passport to Ireland has been withdrawn. I think I know the reason for that, as you know, Mr Preston, the Federal Attorney in San Francisco, was very anxious to lock me up in Angel Island (hisses). Mr Preston, however, did not succeed and it seemed to me that England would like Uncle Sam to lock me up and therefore she has refused a passport, but I have confidence that Uncle Sam will not lock me up. (applause) And it seems to me that if it is to be decided in this country that it is treason to the United States to talk against conscription in Ireland, then I think the best place for any self-respecting man or woman is prison. (wild applause) And my friends, if enough of you, as apparently you do, agree with that sentiment, there will not be prisons big enough to hold us Irish in this country. (applause) The ground has been amply and ably covered by the other speakers. I am not going to weary you now by going over reasons against conscription. People have said to me 'But the British Empire may depend upon Irish conscription'. Now, I say deliberately this,—and I hope the Secret Service men are listening to me and have their pencils sharp. (wild applause) I say, if the continuance of the British Empire depends upon the life of a single Irish conscript, then I say, let the British Empire be wiped out. (wild applause) And I for one and there are a good many others who think like me; they may be aliens, but they are friendly aliens. I for one will lose no sleep at any time over the extinction of the British Empire. (wild applause)

I read in the *New York Tribune* yesterday (hisses)—oh, I don't think these papers are worth any demonstration—I read that Ireland was greatly placated and why do you think? Because Mr S. was sent to us as a Chief Secretary instead of Mr Duke. You wouldn't be surprised, would you, if Belgium refused to be placated if they sent Ludendorff instead of Hindenberg? One rotten liberal instead of another rotten liberal makes no difference in Ireland. And the people who write that kind of stuff for Americans to read well deserve all they get. And I can say that if you read these kind of papers, you are also criminals after the act. (applause) We are told in Ireland again by the omniscient American press,—we are told that Ireland ought to accept conscription in return for home rule. (cries of 'Never') We say, my friends, as you say, 'Never, Never, NEVER!' (loud applause); not for any kind of home rule that Great Britain, in her hour of crisis, was prepared to cough up! What would be said if Belgium was offered home rule in return for conscription by Germany? Belgium would very probably reject that offer with scorn; and so will Ireland. There will be no bargaining with Great Britain; she has broken her words too often; she is nothing but a discredited bankrupt today (enthusiastic applause). Who knows whether any cheque that she is prepared, in her hour of extremity, to write, will ever be honoured internationally?

I am interested particularly in the anti-conscription movement in Ireland because it was my husband Francis Sheehy Skeffington who first advised that pledge which has since been administered generally throughout Ireland. I heard him at many meetings in Dublin administering that pledge to thousands of Irish men and it was on account [of] administering that pledge that he was done to death at the bidding of the Liberal Government (hisses). And I heard these men swear with uplifted hands in the P., as he administered the oath, 'If England should conscript us, we swear we will not go'. (applause) and that is the spirit that is winning today. We Irish were never more attacked and maligned than we are at present; but, for my part, I am proud of Ireland today (applause). She is standing practically alone in her fight and she is the only country in the world today that says that she will choose her quarrel and know what she is dying for if she is to die.

You need not worry about the psychology of the Irish people. Everybody knows that the Irish love a fight; but everybody who respects the Irish race know that we like to choose our fight (applause). We are not going at this hour. Who will dare to blame us or to deride us? We are not going to be driven to that slaughter-pen in Flanders at the bidding of a government that is dripping red with the blood of our best countrymen (applause).

And now a word about American responsibility. America has not yet definitely and officially pronounced on this question. It is time that the American Government do so. You are told my friends that secret messages have been sent over telling Mr Lloyd George (hisses) that this is not the opportune time to conscript the Irish. I thought we had enough of secret treaties and secret diplomacy. You ought not to be satisfied unless there is an unmistakable official pronouncement from your government on this important question, which concerns the very life of our nation. President Wilson has stretched out a hand to Russia: He has said to Russia in her hour of crisis,—and has said it finally,—that America is not going to desert Russia,—that America will help Russia all she can. All we ask him is that he say just the same on behalf of Ireland to the British Government. And we think,—and we shall dare to say us 'Nay' we think that Ireland has fully as big a claim on the Government of the United States as Russia or any one of the other nations. That is for you to demand and if you do not immediately take steps and this Government does not take steps on the question of conscription for Ireland, then I say deliberately that this Government is an accomplice in one of the foulest crimes in the foul history of Great Britain. (applause) There is one remarkable thing that that charlatan from Wales, Premier Lloyd George (hisses) who said apropos of conscription and home rule 'conscription is going to be held out like a club with one hand'. Lloyd George said, in order that you may realize, in the House of Commons, that it was necessary that England placate America on the question of Ireland; he said it was necessary that the Irish Government be settled. And why do you think he said it? Do you think he said it for the sake of justice or humanity, or freedom? He said it was necessary for England to settle the question of Ireland. Why? Because, he said, we must have the good will of America. As you say here, 'Here is the nigger in the wood pile' of America. Do you think that Mr Lloyd George would waste his time talking about securing the goodwill of America if he felt that he had really got that commodity? This is exactly the spot on which to meet Mr Lloyd George.—Otherwise it should be forever silent,—forever silent on the question of liberty. (Commotion caused by interruption of speech by two loyal American women, Dr Eleanor Keller, 55 East 76th Street, New York City and Mrs John Oakman of 3 West Sixteenth Street, New York City having members of the family fighting for the United States).

I remember a story of a woman in Ireland which reminds me of the Irish question today. The Irish question has now become, as Mr Lloyd George confesses, an international one and we thank God for that, because there is not a nation in the world, with the exception of Great Britain, that would not willingly see Ireland free. This old woman in Ireland had an important lawsuit on and she engaged no lawyer; and after a time when her friends came to her and said 'You are very foolish; why do you not engage counsel?' And she said 'No, I will not engage counsel; I do not need them'. And her friend said 'Why?' And she smiled knowingly and she said 'I have got a few friends on the jury'. No, we feel exactly like that in Ireland today. We feel, if our case comes up before an international tribunal of nations, we are all right; we need no one to plead for us; we have got a few good friends on the jury.

And I for one am convinced that the United States is one of these friends. And I am convinced that the plot of Mr Preston in San Francisco,—Mrs Preston, by the way, is of English descent and this is significant,—the plot set on foot by him to interfere with the Irish meetings has been badly defeated in San Francisco. And quite an interesting thing happened there a week ago that you in New York will also be interested in. I was arrested for an interrupted meeting on Wednesday and told that I was not, by orders of Mr Preston, to discuss any question in California,—conscription or anything else. I was arrested; I was taken away; I was not detained. Mr Preston worked himself up into a fury of indignation in the papers the next morning so grinding that it wiped out the Western Offensive for the time being (laughter and derision). And Mr Preston said he was going to stamp out sedition, as he called it,—in other words, Irish meetings. Then he added, by way of after-thought,—because he is not yet a czar,—that he had asked for instructions from Washington as to how he was to proceed in this question. I waited for a week in San Francisco in order that those instructions would have plenty of time to reach Mr Preston. The following week after my interrupted meeting on last Wednesday, we held a magnificent protest meeting in San Francisco and I delivered every word of the interrupted speech at the meeting (howling applause).

I do not mention it for any personal bearing, but I think the result of this is instructive everywhere. It means that if you stand out and know that you are right,—stand out for a principle, whether it is that of free speech or any other such principle,—that you will be able to drive the Prestons and the politicians under cover pretty quickly. (applause)

I congratulate the Irish Progressive League in the face of many obstacles,—untold obstacles,—for having held this magnificent gathering. I think they are doing wonderful work for Irish freedom just now and I hope that American public opinion will be so aroused on this question of Irish conscription that the British will shortly get into a second line trench, as you call it, on the matter. (applause)

We are told that this Conscription Act which was rushed through Parliament,—rushed through both houses in a few days,—that this Conscription Act is going to be held up for the time being. We may find that it will be held up, as the saying is, for the duration of the war. However that may be, if conscription is defeated in Ireland, it will be defeated by the spirit of Sinn Féin (wild applause, waving of rebel flags and hats, stamping of feet, etc.) I want every one of you men and women to do your part now to see that the question of conscription will never be mentioned by a British statesman again.

APPENDIX 5

Miss Mary MacSwiney's Testimony[1] *American Commission on Conditions in Ireland December 8 1920*

Before the Commission sitting in Oddfellows Hall, Washington D.C., Wednesday, December 8 1920.

Session called to order by Chairman Howe at 10:23 a.m.

The first witness this morning is Miss Mary MacSwiney. Miss MacSwiney is on the witness stand.

Mr F. P. Walsh: Your name is Miss Mary MacSwiney? A: Yes sir.

Q: Where do you reside, Miss MacSwiney? A: In Cork, Cork City.

Q: I believe you stated that there was something you wanted to say to the Commission. A: I felt that I wanted, before I started my evidence this morning to thank the Commission and the American people first, for the kindly reception we got and to thank the Commission in its endeavour to help Ireland by getting at the truth.

III. EXPLAINING SINN FÉIN

. . . I have seen in American papers, for instance, 'the Sinn Féin', as if Sinn Féin were a noun. Now, Sinn Féin is a policy, as you have the Democratic policy and the Republican policy.

COMMISSIONER MAURER: We do not have it now. We used to have it. THE WITNESS: Like we used to have West Britons in Ireland? Well, I do not know enough about your policies to know if they are a good thing or a bad thing, but if you Americans want it that is your business. Now, Sinn Féin is a policy, but the Irish Republic is a country. Suppose, for instance, I asked you what nationality you were and you told me you were Democratic. I am quite sure that your countrymen, your fellow citizens, would resent that very much. A Democrat is a member of a particular organization or a particular policy. Sinn Féin is a policy, but the Irish Republican Government is the authorized recognized government of the Irish people, their chosen government. As so we do not call ourselves Sinn Féiners. We call ourselves Irish Republicans, just as you call yourselves Americans. We may have a Sinn Féin policy or some other kind of policy within our own country.

I will tell you where the confusion comes. When Parnell and Redmond had failed to secure even a measure of freedom for Ireland, Arthur Griffith, who was founder of the Sinn Féin policy and vice-president of our Republic today, took a wide policy. He wanted a reversion to the Grattan Parliament of 1782, with proper Republican franchise and an executive which would be subject to Parliament. Grattan's Parliament, while it did a great deal of good, had none of these. It had a strictly confined franchise and the executive was under the control of England. He said, 'We are to reach this goal by a policy of self-development'. And he took the name Sinn Féin, which simply is the Irish word for 'ourselves'. And he took it as a policy of self-reliance. Up to that time we had been working at Westminster for a very long time to see what we could get out of Westminster. We also had our eyes on America to see if there would be anything good coming from that quarter. But Griffith said, 'There is no good casting your eyes to the ends of the earth. Only the fool's eyes are there. We can do a good deal more at home. We can develop our industries. We can study the Irish language'. The Gaelic Club had started shortly before that. He made the main plank in his policy abstention from Westminster.

That was the policy of Sinn Féin. The reversion to Grattan's Parliament meant a separate parliament for Ireland. He took Parnell's view that you cannot put bounds to the onward march of a nation. But although he wanted a different parliament, there would be the same king over both countries. That was the original policy of Sinn Féin. The name has stuck to what has become the policy of the Irish people all along—utter and entire independence. Certain of us in Ireland have never joined Sinn Féin. My brother was never a member of any Sinn Féin club, simply because it was not expressly Republican. It was implied. But he took the attitude that the mere expression of the statement that we are aiming at a Republic is a compromise. And we stand where Wolfe Tone stood. So he said, 'We will not join Sinn Féin'. But he helped it, especially the policy of development of Irish industry. He worked for the policy of Sinn Féin without ever declaring himself a Sinn Féiner.

Q: How old was your brother when he died? A: Forty.

Early Days of Terence MacSwiney

My brother went to school to the Christian Brothers, but he was not satisfied with it. It was not national, as has been stated; but it was so far ahead of the others that we gave them credit for having the only Irish schools in Ireland. He went into the exhibitions and got a money prize in each class. He left school when he was about sixteen and went into business. In normal times and in less strenuous conditions, as far as money went, he would have remained at school and entered a college course and would have become a writer or a poet. But he had to leave school because the family was not well off. And he did not like business. And he educated himself and was able to take a university degree and he became a bachelor of arts. Not only that, but he did a great deal of writing besides. He wrote poems. In looking through his papers after his death I came across the letter that I wrote him congratulating him on the first poem that was published under his name. He became very interested in national things. There is a society in Cork called the Gaelic Literary Society. I think he must have been about seventeen when he was one of the founders of that. It was a body of young men animated by the Republican ideal. They used to meet together after business hours and they would read and write essays and bring out a little magazine that would circulate among a certain crowd. And that Gaelic Literary Society did develop other national activities. The thing that stands most to its credit is the Irish Industrial Development Association, which is one of the things they started. I told you that he never joined Arthur Griffith's Sinn Féin Society because it was not primarily for Republican independence, but he worked along that line and with one or two others was responsible for the founding of the Irish Industrial Development Association.

Mr F. P. WALSH: You might sketch that. THE WITNESS: It was really a society that was non-political. They did not talk any division of politics and it was absolutely non-secretarian and formed for the special purpose of developing Irish industries—to make the people of Ireland who had been avoiding Irish goods without any thought to buy Irish goods wherever they could get them. They started industries. It spread from Cork to Dublin and naturally Dublin, being the capital, became the centre. But Cork had the honour of starting it. Mr Fawsitt, who is now the consul general of the Irish Republic here, was secretary in Cork for many years. He was considered the best man to send over here for that reason. The fact that we have a consul here today and have a consul in almost every European country, against the wishes of Great Britain, is entirely due to my brother and his comrades, who started this society in Cork in 1901, I think. It might be a year one way or another. That was one of his activities. Another was the Gaelic League. This was a society, also non-secretarian and non-political, for the purpose of developing the Irish language and making the people Irish-speaking again. The soul of a people is expressed in its language. And if you go and speak a foreign language continuously, you will naturally develop the soul of that language within you. And the great Anglicizing power that England had over Ireland was in that she had almost killed the Irish language. She was very clever in her propaganda. It is a great mistake to think that England is not a clever nation. She is very clever and very insidious in her propaganda. She never said to the people outright, 'You shall not speak Irish'. But she took the children and educated it out of them. There is a little verse about the truth coming out in spite of oneself, like the story I told you of Archbishop Whately and the verse of Sir Walter Scott. When Lloyd George said the other day, when Irish atrocities were mentioned in the House of Commons, that those things will happen in a state of war, he thereby admitted that there was a state of war in Ireland. And so you get the truth out like that occasionally in a moment of high pressure.

IV. THE VOLUNTEERS

Mr F. P. WALSH: Where were we? A: I am coming to the Volunteer movement. You remember that there was a Home Rule bill introduced in Parliament in 1912, one of many. It was in the hope of stopping all this activity and getting the people to accept definitely Home Rule in the British Empire,—which would, of course, leave England's hands in our pockets all the time. It was absolutely no use, that Home Rule Bill of 1912, except that it would be centring Irish interest in Dublin instead of London. I said that Mr Arthur Griffith's policy in the old days was abstention from Westminster. Westminster, of course, means the House of Parliament. The only good that a Home Rule Bill would have done would be the centre of gravity would have been shifted from London to Ireland. That would have had a very great effect. The people would have said then, Why should we have so little when we might have had more? Sir Edward Carson said he did not want Home Rule. He started in 1913 the idea of forcible resistance to Home Rule. He got guns and ammunition and he got them from Germany. He also said, 'We will not come under a Catholic government and if the English people throw us over, we will enrol ourselves under the greatest Protestant nation in the world, under the German nation'. He said he would invite the German Emperor over himself if the English forced Home Rule upon them.

SENATOR WALSH: Are those things matters of public record? A: They are in all the English papers and Irish papers of the time. You will find them in book form, Sir Edward Carson's statement. They have been put into book form and called, 'The Grammar of Anarchy'. When Sir Edward Carson made those statements, he got something like two million pounds from England for propaganda and also the promise that the English Tories would fight with them. He also stirred up a revolt at the Curragh camp and the British officers in the Curragh camp said they would not, if they were ordered, go and put down a revolution in the Covenanters' camp. They were called Covenanters because they covenanted together that they would not have Home Rule.

We were very happy when we knew what Sir Edward Carson was doing. His statements have been collected in book form, as I said. One Sinn Féiner got something like six months' imprisonment for having in his possession seditious literature and the only seditious literature he had in his possession, besides a few newspapers, was Sir Edward Carson's statements.

Sir Edward Carson started the Ulster Volunteers. There was always an Act in Ireland that you must not have arms in your possession. It was not enforced, however. Sir Edward Carson succeeded in getting a large quantity of arms. We looked on and said nothing. If we could have patted him on the back, we would have told him to go ahead. He went ahead a good while. And then our people in the south began to say publicly, 'Well, of course, if Sir Edward Carson is getting arms for a march on Cork, we will have to arm also'. And they started the Irish Volunteers. England was in a fix. She had patted Sir Edward Carson on the back when he formed the Ulster Volunteers. English societies had been organized to subscribe money for drums for these Ulster Volunteers. The English Government had looked on with a more or less benevolent eye. And then if she had said, There must be no Irish Volunteers, the world would have said, That is not impartial.

But within one week of our starting the Irish Volunteers, the Arms Act was enforced and the Government said, No arms in Ireland. Within one week! Sir Edward Carson had been getting arms for several months.

SENATOR WALSH: What date was this? A: This was in the early days of 1914, in May, before the war.

Q: Had the Home Rule Bill passed Parliament? A: Oh, it had passed in 1912, but on account of the House of Lords it had been thrown out for two years.

Q: It passed the House of Commons in 1912? A: Yes and it went to the House of Lords and the House of Lords threw it out.

Q: What date was it passed? A: In 1914. In the spring of 1914 a ship loaded with arms set out from Germany for Sir Edward Carson. The English government knew perfectly well what was being done and that those arms were going to Sir Edward Carson. There was a little camouflage done. The boat started with one name from Hamburg and was stopped in mid-ocean and repainted and renamed and came into Larne. The boat came into Larne because it is one of the Orange ports up there. The policemen are all Orangemen. They were all sympathetic with Sir Edward Carson. It was absolutely contrary to law, of course, but that made no matter. The guns were safely landed in Larne and safely stored. And the next morning it was all over the English and Irish press. The English Parliament held up their hands in horror. It was a very illegal act, said Mr Asquith, but he made no motion to punish that act. Well, we will take a good example from people when we get it; and as we followed the Irish Volunteers after the Ulster Volunteers, we were not too proud to follow Sir Edward Carson in gun-running. And in July 1914, the Howth gun-running started. I was in England at the time on a little holiday. The Howth gun-running,—now notice the difference. The Ulster gun-running was in support of what England wanted. So she allowed those guns into Ulster, but when we started gun-running she knew that what we said we meant and therefore our gun-running had to be stopped. Well, it was not. Our people got in quite a number of guns that day. In spite of a regiment of soldiers and all the Royal Irish Constabulary that were available, the guns were not captured. But several men, women and children were shot down on the streets of Dublin by the soldiers returning empty-handed from Howth. That was the massacre of Bachelors' Walk, which took place one week before the celebration of war on the continent and two weeks before England declared it.

That shows you whether England wants to be impartial. She tries to say that she wants to treat the north and south alike. I could give you a hundred, a thousand examples if time permitted to show you that she never does,—instances of this kind. Then came the war.

SENATOR WALSH: These Volunteers meanwhile had organized all over Ireland? A: All over Ireland. But there was this against them. Mr Redmond set his face against any volunteers whatever. He wanted to keep to the constitutional movement. At the time the Volunteers were started, it was said that they only wanted to take measures against Sir Edward Carson's rebellion. He felt that it was dangerous to let the young men take things into their own hands.

Q: And this organization was called the Irish Volunteers? A: The Irish Volunteers.

Q: And they included the people of all classes? A: Oh, no, only the men were armed. But the women formed the Cumann na mBan, a society something like your Red Cross, a patriotic society to help carry on the work.

SENATOR WALSH: Up to this time, Miss MacSwiney, was there a Sinn Féin movement, or was this simply a movement among the people? A movement among the Irish Volunteers to arm and protect themselves against attacks from the north? A: Well, this was a movement among the young men to arm to defend themselves for Irish rights.

Q: Exactly. But up to this time there was no movement for independence? A: No. Of course, that was the idea back of every movement in Ireland. But it was not precisely stated until the first Volunteer convention, which was held in 1914. They definitely stated their policy as a Republic. The policy of the Irish Volunteers was the policy of the Irish Republic, a continuation of the fight for freedom that had been always going on. They armed themselves in defence of the rights and liberties of the Irish nation. The women joined Cumann na mBan.

SENATOR WALSH: You answer my question. Now, going back to Redmond's position before the outbreak of the war? A: Before the war, Mr Redmond disapproved of the Irish Volunteers. He sent messages and letters to all the A.O.H. branches all over the country forbidding them to join the Irish Volunteers. But that is where I would like to point out to you, as I said a while ago, that the policy of Ireland was always Republican and when they found that a leader set himself against Irish independence, then the leader fell and not the movement. Mr Redmond sent orders that no member of his organization was to join the Irish Volunteers, but they joined in hundreds and thousands all over the country. So that by June, 1914, they were coming in in very large numbers and Mr Redmond began to see that he could not possibly forbid the movement. And therefore the next step was to control it. A great number of people, though they did not refrain from joining the Irish Volunteers at the bidding of Mr Redmond, believed in his sincerity and in his desire for ultimate separation from England. And when he wanted to come and control the movement, they didn't see any reason why he should not, when he was going to improve it, you see. So he demanded that he have a voice in the counsels of the Irish Volunteers and he demanded twenty-five members nominated by him to sit on the council. A great many were against giving him that,—a great man, the majority, in their hearts. But as a matter of policy they felt this: If we refuse to allow Mr Redmond's nominees on the council of the Irish Volunteers, we will immediately have a split, which of all things should be avoided at the present moment. And so the majority of the council gave in and allowed Mr Redmond to nominate members for the Irish Volunteers' council. There were nine who opposed it. Of those nine there were many who lost their lives in Easter Week, 1916. What would have happened if they had gone on? The whole policy of Mr Redmond was to weaken the Volunteers. He got a number of guns, they were useless. He did not want war. He didn't want any physical force in Ireland. We knew that he didn't want it and that his action was weakening our movement. But it would have been worse to start out against him and say, 'You will not get a single nominee on our council'. When the war came Mr Redmond started as recruiter-in-chief for England.

The Cork Volunteers

My brother was one of the very first Volunteers in Cork. In regard to the founding of the Volunteers in Cork, there is a very interesting story. It was founded in November 1913. Eoin MacNeill and other people came down to speak at the inaugural meeting. I have told you that we Republicans were very much pleased when we saw what Sir Edward Carson was doing, because it gave us our chance. But we rather forgot that the mind of the country was not educated up to that point of view and to them Sir Edward Carson was anathema because he was opposing Home Rule. Eoin MacNeill forgot that and in the course of his speech said Sir Edward Carson deserved three cheers from us for forming his Ulster Volunteers. That night there was a little body of men at the hall that were sent there for the purpose of making a row. That little remark of MacNeill gave them a chance and they broke up the meeting. The Redmondite papers the next day spoke of the awful iniquity of calling for cheers for Sir Edward Carson, who was marching on Cork to put us to death. It was a foolish remark to make, because psychologically the people were not up to it at the time. They simply looked upon Sir Edward Carson as the opponent of independence and Home Rule. That retarded the work of the Volunteers in Cork for some time and they never got the start they did in Dublin.

In the spring of 1914 we started this women's side movement, Cumann na mBan, as I have said, like Red Cross work and we trained the minds of the people to know what the Republican movement meant. But our chief work was to support the Irish Volunteers by every means possible in their fight for the independence of Ireland. We wanted to get a big inaugural meeting and we succeeded in getting a big inaugural meeting, which really gave the Volunteers a big chance to have a meeting also. Our meeting was a real help to them. You know how meetings are sometimes delayed. We began in March and it was April when we got going. We invited Sir Roger Casement to come, but he could not. One of my dearest possessions today is an autographed letter from him explaining that he could not come down to the meeting. That was in May; and in the beginning of June Mr Redmond's call for Volunteers came. Then came the war.

In 1914 we had a meeting in Dublin when the women had to decide whether they would remain neutral or side with the Irish Volunteers, or with Mr Redmond's Volunteers, or split. Thank God we did not split, but remained on the side of the Irish Volunteers. Cumann na mBan has never deviated from that day and they are still fighting on that position.

Easter Week in Dublin

In 1916 we began our first open battle. The first battle in this phase of the war that has been going on for so long was in Easter Week, 1916. That battle failed. We lost it. But Padraig Pearse said on the night before we were forced to evacuate the general post-office, 'We have lost the first battle, but we have saved the soul of Ireland and now the people can go ahead'. Easter Week saved the soul of Ireland. From that day on there was no more possibility of the Irish people mistaking where their duty lay. From that day on there was no such thing as recruiting for any army except the Irish Volunteers.

The essential point for you to understand is that this insurrection was confined mainly to Dublin. Galway rose also, but most of the fighting was in Dublin. You have often heard that Ireland was divided over this insurrection. I should like to explain about that. We expected help in this insurrection. We expected arms. We had very few arms at that time. We were expecting Roger Casement to come from Germany with arms. I have no hesitation about acknowledging that. We were at war with England and we were at liberty to get guns where we could to carry on that war. England said she was fighting for the rights of small nations. We had absolutely as much right to our liberty as Belgium had, about whose rights England was so solicitous. If we wanted to take Germany as an ally we had a right to take her as an ally. England had a great deal of talk about us being pro-German. She did turn France against us. Only my brother's death has softened France. She said we weakened her ally at a critical moment. But what right had France to expect that we should not weaken the cause of her ally when her ally was oppressing us.

Q: We were told you took German gold. A: We did not take German gold. We took the pennies and sixpence of our people. But did not we have a right to take it if we had wanted it? Did not France take English gold and did not England take American gold when she could get it? Surely no one had a right to speak if we had taken it. But we did not. Surely not England, who was borrowing from America. Any nation has a right to make alliances when she is fighting against an enemy. It is said that we wanted to invite the Germans into Ireland. We did not. The only man who ever tried to invite Germans into Ireland was Sir Edward Carson. If Germany tried to take Ireland we would fight her just as long and just as effectively as we are fighting England. Of course, it was a lie that we took German money, but if we had taken it, what difference would it make? England says she wants people to have fair play, but she does not give us fair play. If it is right for France to borrow money from England, it would be just as right for us to borrow money from Germany, if we had gotten it, but we didn't. Germany would have been glad for us to create a revolution in her favour, of course. But we were not doing it to please Germany. England's difficulty has always been Ireland's opportunity and we are absolutely right in taking advantage of that opportunity. The sooner you can get that in a common sense way, the better. It was no crime for us to take help where we could get it. To make an alliance with anybody we wanted to.

In 1778 France happened to be at war with England and she wanted to hurt England in any way she could and she acknowledged you as a republic to hurt England and it did. You also wanted, in 1774 and 1775 to appeal to the sympathy of the Irish people and you got it. And I do not think America needs to be told of the many Irishmen she has had then and since to fight for the freedom of her country.

And therefore I protest against the statement that I or my fellow citizens would choose to ally ourselves with the Central Empires. We did not because they would be no good to us. But if we had, it would have been no worse than England taking your help and she was very glad to get it, because if she had not gotten it, she would not be where she is today.

I ask you American people, do you think you have helped democracy by entering the war? President Wilson said: 'The reasons for this war have been so clearly avowed that no man can make a mistake by entering it'. He said—I do not know whether I am stating it exactly, 'America has gone to war for the rights and liberties of all peoples everywhere under the sun, for the right of self-determination for small nations and for their release from an autocratic power'. Are we not a people and are we not under the sun somewhere? If you say 'all people, you must count us'. If you say 'the release of small nations from autocratic power', you must not leave out Ireland. As America went out for the right and liberties of all peoples everywhere, for liberty and self-determination and for the 'undictated policies of all peoples'. (I think that was another phrase of President Wilson), I ask you, have we got rights and liberties and an undictated policy of our own? We have got it, but we have got it in spite of England's oppression.

You people in America have not carried out the policies for which you went into the war. You sheathed the sword when England got what she wanted. I do not want to hurt you. You have been very good to us and you have given us a chance by this Commission to tell the truth about Ireland. But you have not made the world safe for democracy. You have only made the world safe for a time for the British Empire. But I know this. When England begins to collar all the coal fields and all the oil fields and when she begins to hamper your navy and your shipping by collaring the coal and oil fields of the world, she will not find it as easy to conquer America as she has to conquer Ireland.

It was a point made very much of by England that the Easter Week insurrection was not an insurrection of the Irish nation. That it was only a few extremists. And they pointed to the fact that the fighting took place in Dublin only. I had begun to tell you that we had expected help in the shape of arms. We had hoped to get some arms to enable us to carry on the fight, because the arms and ammunition of the country did not amount to much. And those arms failed us. They did not come. An insurrection had been arranged for Easter Sunday 1916. The leaders had counted on getting the arms the last of the week, on Good Friday. The ship bringing the arms was sunk by the British. They were perfectly justified from their point of view in sinking that ship, just as we were justified in bringing it in if we could. However, it was sunk. The result of that was that some of the leaders, notably Mr MacNeill, thought that the time was not opportune to begin. And though the orders had gone out for the whole country for the insurrection on Sunday, the orders were cancelled at the last moment by Mr

MacNeill. Many of the leaders did not agree with the cancelling of those orders and I think that some of them thought that Mr MacNeill had exceeded his powers and his rights in sending these cancellation orders. One section, the Irish Citizens' Army, was not under the control of the Volunteers. That was a labour organization only. You have heard of Jim Larkin here and he and James Connolly were concerned with the organization of that Citizens' Army. They had threatened to go out in any case. The secret history of those few days has not been fully published and the documentary evidence in connection with it was largely burned during Easter Week. And some of us, even though we were on the inside of Republican affairs, are not exactly certain of all the orders and counter orders of that week. It ended by only a portion of the Volunteers rising in Dublin. They began on Monday morning. Mr MacNeill had sent the order all over Ireland that the Volunteers were not to rise. An order followed signed by Padraig Pearse and John McDermott that they were to rise, that the orders were to be kept to. By the time these orders reached the outlying districts it was too late.

THE FIRST ARRESTS

The birds had flown. They did not take the women back, but they began arresting the men in twos and threes all over Ireland until they had about 2,000 of them arrested and put in jail in England. My brother was arrested in the country and taken. We did not know for a long time where he was. To show you how they can tell lies. We were very uneasy because for over a week we did not have a single word from my brother. We knew he had been arrested. Someone had seen him brought into Cork at half past four in the morning and they were taking him up to Cork jail. A few days afterwards we learned that someone had seen him about five o'clock in the morning removed from Cork jail. We applied to the Governor, but got no information where he was. After a question asked in the House of Commons as to why those men were not allowed to see their relatives, Mr Asquith, the Prime Minister at the time, replied that all the Cork prisoners were allowed to see their friends and had fresh air and food and visitors and all other nice things. It was utterly false. That appeared on Thursday morning, about the thirteenth of May, I think. He had been missing since the third. Some of us whose relatives had been taken away and did not know their whereabouts went to the general post-office and sent a series of telegrams to Mr Asquith and sent him each one his own particular story and told him that our relatives had been taken away and we had been denied all information as to where they were. We also sent copies of these telegrams to William O'Brien, because it was he who asked for information from Mr Asquith and to Laurence Ginnell, because he was the only one in the House of Commons on whom we could depend to bring out the truth. We sent them in great hurry because there was to be a debate in the House of Commons that day on the Irish question. Mr Ginnell told me that these telegrams created a great sensation when read in the House. That was on Thursday. On Saturday morning we all got letters from our friends. That is the way. And then when you catch them at it, they correct it and say, It is a lie, you are not telling the truth.

That was my brother's second term of imprisonment. They were all in prison most of the time until Christmas. There was a general amnesty at Christmas. But the men who were concerned actually in the rising, the men who were in Dublin, were sent most of them to penal servitude, those who were not shot. And they were not released from prison by the amnesty.

Mr Walsh asked me this morning to tell you something about education in Ireland. There is a little addition I would like to make here. I was teaching in a large secondary school, in one of the intermediate schools of which I spoke, in the city at that time. The nuns were personally very fond of me, I know that, but they highly disapproved of my political opinions and they were very nervous at having them in that exceedingly respectable school. In January preceding the Easter Rising my brother had been arrested for making a speech and a district inspector of police who had a child in the school went up to the Reverend Mother and told her I was not a proper person to be teaching in a school like that and I ought to be dismissed. Now, I do not want to say an unnecessarily harsh word about that school. It was my alma mater and I am very attached to it. And the only crime I convict the nuns of was cowardice. It is a pretty bad one in my category of crimes. But it was absolutely unavoidable in the condition of mind engendered by the education of the country. It was so fearfully unrespectable to be a Sinn Féiner. We are all called Sinn Féiners. And Sinn Féin by that time had become Republican. However, some time before Easter the Reverend Mother complained of my tendency to make Sinn Féiners of the pupils. I said, 'I have never mentioned the name Sinn Féin in the class. I am not a Sinn Féiner at all. I am a Republican. But I have never told the children what I am'. And she said, 'But at the same time there is something there'. And she finally brought it out with great burst that I was too Irish. And I asked her if she ever heard of an Englishwoman being too English, or a Frenchwoman being too French and it was not a crime for me to be too Irish. Then she said, 'You must keep to the textbook in teaching history'. I said, 'If I keep to the textbook, the senior girls will fail in the examination, because there is not enough of it'. That was not exactly what she meant and I told her what she meant. 'You want me to teach Irish history from the English point of view. I would no more do that than as a Catholic I would teach the history of the Reformation from the Protestant point of view'. 'And whether you are Catholic or Protestant or nothing at all, you can perfectly understand that I would not teach the Protestant point of view against my own than you would, if you were a Protestant, teach the Catholic point of view against your own. Naturally, the teaching of all history must be coloured by the point of view of the country in which it is taught. I think before this war there was an idea that history should be wholly colourless, that it should be taken from state documents. If there is anything that this past war has taught the world it is that of all the lies that it is possible to tell, official documents are the biggest lies. I have friends who were in the war who told me exactly how these official documents were compiled'.

CHAIRMAN HOWE: Please keep to the recital of the Irish situation, Miss MacSwiney.

The Dawn of the Republic

The first chance they had to give expression to that [being consciously Republican] was in the General Election of 1918. In that election the Republican movement swept the country. There were very few constituencies in which there was a fight. But where there was a fight in the whole of Ireland, outside of Ulster, there was only one man got in who was a Redmondite and that was John Redmond's son, who because of sympathy for his father and because of his hold on the people of Waterford, was returned.

In Ulster, the case was rather peculiar. You have at present four men representing the Constitutional Home Rule Party in Ulster,—five men. Four of them got in this way. There were eight seats in Ulster in which the proportion of, we will say Nationalists, using the word Nationalists in its broad sense—Ireland versus England, there were eight of them, they had a majority. But if Sinn Féin and Redmondites and Unionists went up, the three cornered division would probably let the Unionists in. On these seats, upon the advice of Cardinal Logue, there was a compromise suggested that they should have them. Our people wanted a much fairer thing than that. Our people wanted an election of the Nationalist population held, a kind of a plebiscite of the National population held on the preceding week, everyone to vote and the seats to be given to either the Republican or the Redmondite according to the votes cast. If that had been so, we would have had seven or eight seats. Consequently the Redmondites did not agree to it.

This does not deal with the contests with the Unionists, but only with the contests between the Republicans and the Redmondites. They would not agree to this plebiscite, so it was either let them have the seats or give them to the Unionists. I mean the risk would be letting the Unionists slip in. So the people agreed to have them and that is why you have a few representatives still of Redmond's party.

With regard to the General Election of 1918, it was eighty per cent Republican. It was an anti-Redmond election rather than a pro-Republican election. And they said that ever so many people had got tired of a parliamentary policy and were willing to give Sinn Féin a chance. We knew it was not so, but of course they had a certain amount of plausibility behind their argument; and so it was not until 1919 and 1920 that we were able to counter that and prove that they were false by the municipal and county elections. Then every candidate who went up had to take the Republican oath.

Mr F. P. WALSH: What was that oath? A: 'I pledge my allegiance to Dáil Éireann' (the congress of Ireland). I do not know the exact words, but it was pledging allegiance to the Irish Republican Congress and renouncing everything English.

Q: CHAIRMAN HOWE: Every candidate? A: Every candidate, yes, who received Republican support. Some had said, after the Republican victory in 1918: 'Even so, the candidates were Republican, but we have people voting for the Republican candidates not because they were Republicans but because they were anti-parliamentarian'. They were sick of parliamentarianism. When the municipal and county elections came and were overwhelmingly Republican, even more so than the general elections had been, that argument was killed.

MISS ADDAMS: That was the general election of 1920? A: Yes. In spite of the fact that proportional representation laws had been passed by the House of Commons for Ireland for the purpose of destroying Republicans and getting in candidates who would not otherwise have got in. Our people had from 1906 advocated proportional representation and so when it was passed by the House of Commons it was opposed, not by us, because we welcomed it, but by the Carsonites. And the result showed that they had good reason to be afraid of it. For the first time we have Irish members in the Belfast corporation. We have Irish Republican members in county councils that before were wholly Unionists. We have won all over the country and have lost nothing. Probably in the south and west there are Unionist members on the councils who might not have been there otherwise; but we have no fear whatever of Unionists getting on, providing they get on fairly and in proper proportion. We do not dread proportional representation, but proportional representation was passed to ruin the Irish Republicans in the elections and the only people who opposed it were the Carsonites.

The Republican Courts

COMMISSIONER THOMAS: Does the authority of the Irish courts rest upon the consent of the people or upon some other force? A: Upon the consent of the population entirely. And I do not think anything could show the truth about the false contention put out by England that we are not a law-abiding people better than the success of these courts, with only moral force, in many cases, to enforce their decrees. We are a law-abiding people absolutely if we are given a chance to have our own laws.

I would like to stress the good the courts did in bringing together the people. Unionists brought their cases to the Irish courts. Protestants brought their cases to the Irish courts. And although they may not have ceased to be Unionists, they have come to the conclusion that if they want their claims settled they must bring them to the Republican courts. There was one case where a Protestant landlord had a case which he felt he must have settled and so he took it to the Irish courts. And his friends were shocked and remonstrated. And he said, 'I do not care. If I take it into the English courts I might get a just judgment, but it will not be obeyed. And if I take it into the Irish courts I will get a just judgment and it will be obeyed'. And he did get a just judgment and it was obeyed.

There is a rather interesting incident in connection with those courts. Three men were arrested for breaking down a wall. They were convicted in a Republican court. One consented to repair the damage and the other two refused. We have no jails. However, it happened to be on the coast of Galway. So these gentlemen were taken to one of these islands off the coast of Galway. They were given food and everything, for we believe in treating our prisoners humanely. After a couple of days the British police heard where they were and went out in a boat to rescue them. But when the British police came out these prisoners stoned the police and said to go away; that they were prisoners of the Irish Republic and would not be molested.

SENATOR WALSH: Is nearly all the civil litigation and criminal litigation carried on in these Irish courts—in the Republican courts of Ireland? A: The civil litigation altogether. The criminal litigation would be a burden if there were much of it. But it is not an excessive exaggeration to say that there is no crime in Ireland. That would be true before the trouble started rather than now. In Ireland there is a rule that when a judge goes on circuit and has no cases to try he is presented with a pair of white kid gloves. And there were sessions after sessions where the judges going around their circuit got white gloves. There was a joke about it, that the judges should set up a glove factory. And that is an absolute fact. There may be little petty larceny cases and breach of promises and the like and I think that is about the most serious thing. We occasionally have a murder case, but very, very rarely. And with a view to the English support of law and order in Ireland, I would like to tell of the last murder case before I left Ireland. A man named Quaid in County Clare in Ireland, a man without a good reputation, a blustering sort of a bully, who took England's part in the war and advocated recruiting and did his very best to get recruits for her. He was a man with a very hot temper. And some time, about a year and a half ago—he was a publican—he kicked one of his bar attendants to death. She was a woman. Kicked her to death absolutely. She was found dead in the yard the next morning. That man deserved to be hanged in any civilized country. His counsel made a very long speech on his behalf, showing that he was a very loyal subject, that he had done a great deal of recruiting for the army and had got a great many recruits and that he asked for a light sentence.

SENATOR WALSH: This was in the British courts? A: Yes, in the British courts. He got a sentence of twelve months as a first-class misdeameanant, which meant that he could have his friends visit him and his own clothes and all the other privileges except that of walking out when he liked.

The Truth about the Police

The second thing I was asked is about what is called often the murdering of policemen. Here it is called the shooting of policemen. I will simply take the murders of policemen by denying that there ever has been a policeman murdered in Ireland. Now, I will deal with the shooting of policemen. Will you please start out the premise that Ireland and England are at war. One of the instances about the shooting of policemen was the ambush of seventeen Black and Tans last week at a place not far from Mallow, when the whole seventeen of them were captured, sixteen of them killed and the seventeenth very severely wounded. That was put down as a very horrible murder. Suppose that in the recent war an American scouting party went out on a Belgian road and got information that three or four lorries of German soldiers carrying ammunition were coming along the road. If they felt strong enough and if they were very plucky—perhaps even if they did not feel strong enough—they would get into a nice little ambush and they would give the best account of that German party that they possibly could. I think you will agree with me that that is a statement of what would happen. Would you do anything but laugh at any man that would call that ambush party murder? Of course it is not a murder. It is an act of war. The Black and Tans were armed to the teeth. I should like to tell you how the Black and Tans go around the streets of our cities and country places. Four or five days ago there was an ambush at Bandon and in that ambush our men got the worst of it—four or five of our men were killed. You will not find any Irish citizen coming before this Commission and claiming that these men were murdered. Why? Because it was an act of war. It was the shooting of one set of soldiers by another set of soldiers.

I have also been told that individual policemen who were unarmed have been shot. That is also true. Now, I will tell you who those individual policemen are. I was asked a little while ago about the police in Ireland. The police in any civilized country are a civil force under the control of the civil authorities and that civil force deals with offences against the civil law only. The police in Ireland have always been under the authority of the British government. They have not always carried arms, because there have been times when we were not in a state of war. But they carry arms at present and therefore they are among the armed forces of the Crown. Among the Royal Irish Constabulary was a division known as the G Division. Their work was purely detective work. The people they were sent to spy upon were our fellow citizens. And that went on during every political agitation in Ireland. During the present war, since 1916—since 1914, in fact—the police in that G Division were very active. I am sorry to have to acknowledge that they were Irishmen. That only makes them greater sinners. No one is held in greater horror and contempt than Judas and every one of these men was a Judas because he betrayed his own. In that G Division were men who were expert spies, because they were people that mixed freely with the Irish people and picked up information from girls whom they met and other people and they gave that information to the British government and that information led very often to the arrest and imprisonment of their fellow countrymen. Therefore they were spies. In the recent times in Ireland, when the times got very hot, these spies have done very good work for the English government in Ireland. One of our leaders who was executed in 1916 was executed through one of these spies, who has himself been shot since. During Easter week some of the Volunteers were anxious to shoot down every policeman, every police spy, that is, every policeman of the G Division and the leaders, Pearse and MacDermott, said, 'No, this is a clean fight and we will deal with them afterwards'. There was one detective who was very active in tracking down our men. His life was saved by John MacDermott, one of the signatories of the Irish Declaration of Independence. John MacDermott was a very young man and he was very lame. As a solider he would be considered as among the unfit in any army in the world. But he was one of the greatest workers we had. Because of his lameness the military officers who captured the people after Easter week came to the conclusion that he could not be one of the leaders and so he was thrown into the barracks along with the rank and file and he was put in the batch to be sent to the Wakefield prison in England. They were paraded in the Richmond barrack yards before leaving Dublin and this particular detective was sent up and down the ranks to see if there was any man there who ought to get penal servitude rather than deportation. And in going up and down the ranks he saw John MacDermott and he pointed him out to the British authorities as one of the seven signatories of the Irish Declaration of Independence. And John MacDermott was taken out and shot a few days afterward.

Mr F. P. WALSH: Was this the man whose life he had saved? A: This was the very man whose life he saved. And that man has subsequently been shot and shooting was too gentle a death for such a wretch.

APPENDIX 6

The Testimony of Mrs Muriel MacSwiney[1] *American Commission on Conditions in Ireland December 9 1920*

Before the Commission sitting in Odd Fellows Hall, Washington D.C., Thursday, December 9 1920. Session called to order by Chairman Howe at 9:50 a.m. Present: Commissioners Addams, Howe, Maurer, Newman, Norris, Thomas, Walsh, Wood.

Q: Mr F. P. Walsh: Will you please state your name, Mrs MacSwiney. A: Muriel MacSwiney.

Q: And where do you reside? A: In Cork.

Q: You are the widow of Terence MacSwiney? A: Yes, I am.

Q: And he died on what day? A: I am not sure—I am not sure of the exact date.

Q: And where? A: In Brixton prison, in London.

Q: And at the time of your husband's arrest, what was your husband's business or profession. A: He was the Lord Mayor of the city of Cork.

Q: And did he have any other official connection? A: Yes, he was an officer in the Irish Republican Army.

Q: You were born where? A: I was born in Cork.

Q: And what was the name of your parent? A: My father's name was Nicholas Murphy.

Q: Of Cork? A: Yes, of Cork. And Mary Purcell was my mother's name.

Q: And your father is dead? A: Yes, he died when I was sixteen.

Q: And you have brothers and sisters? A: Yes, I have.

Q: How many? A: Three sisters and two brothers.

Q: What was the date of your marriage with Mr MacSwiney? A: June 9 1917.

Q: You can go ahead now and state your own position in this matter.

When, if at any time, did you become interested in the cause of Irish independence and what actuated you? A: Well, I think what actuated me was that all my life, even when still quite a baby, I never understood why there should be poor people and rich people. You know there is a great deal of poverty in Ireland, especially in Cork. You cannot help noticing the many poor children with no shoes and stockings and the like. I noticed that when a baby. I could not understand why it should be. However, I do not think it is right to give people things only in charity. There should be no need of that. There's plenty in Ireland for everybody to have enough. As I grew older I saw that things could not be set right except by government.

Q: Was this prior to your marriage? A: Oh yes, that was when I was quite a child. And I saw that while England was there we could do nothing, because she destroyed our business and kept us poor.

Q: What was the business of your father? A: He had a big distillery.

Q: Briefly stated, he was a man in comfortable circumstances? A: Oh yes, very.

Q: You say as a child you were moved by the poverty that existed in your country and the reasons for it and why it should be so? A: Yes, I was.

Q: Please proceed. A: As I got older, as I have told you, I saw that England was responsible for all that and if we had our own government we could do something; and until we had our own government we could do nothing. I saw that and I picked up other things and I learned that England was only there as a thief and had no right to be there at all.

Q: Where were you educated, Mrs MacSwiney? A: I was educated at home until I was fifteen and then I was sent to England for two years.

Q: To what school? A: To the Convent of the Holy Child Saint Leonard's, Hastings. They have a great many convents in America, by the way; and many in England.

Q: And where was your education finished? A: There, at Hastings, in the South of England.

Q: Did you have any personal interest in the Irish republican movement after your graduation? A: Yes, I did. You see, my parents are not quite like myself. I think I am rather characteristic of a certain section in Ireland. The younger people of Ireland have been thinking in a way that some of the older ones have not. Some years ago the Unionists did not wish an Irish Republic. They wished to belong to England. They were well off and quite comfortable and thought only of themselves. That is dying out now. The younger members of such families are Republican. On that account I did not get the opportunity to meet Republicans when I was a child. That was why I was sent to England to school. I am only characteristic of a great many who were brought up shut up at home. And still the Irish spirit comes out of them in spite of everything. So until I was about twenty-two I did not get the opportunity to do very much.

Q: What is your age now? A: I am twenty-eight.

THEIR FIRST MEETING

Q: When did you first meet Terence MacSwiney? A: I met him in 1915, about Christmas.

Q: Were you interested in the republican movement before then? A: Oh yes, I was, sometime before then.

Q: You might state what your activities had been prior to that time? A: My thought had long been that we should have an Irish Republic and that England should go from Ireland.

Q: Did you belong to any organization up to that time? A: I did not, up to that time. I had spoken to people, of course.

Q: I wish you would proceed and tell about your husband and your marriage and tell the whole story down to the present. A: Well, I met my husband at the house of mutual friends about Christmas 1915. And, well, I did not really get to know him very intimately at that time. Some time after that I met him a few times. At that time he was a commandant of the Irish Republican Army.

Q: He was a commandant? A: Yes, in the South of Ireland. Of course, my husband has been in all the movements ever since he was a boy; because, of course, as his sister has told you, theirs is a very old family around Cork. She can tell you about that better than I can, because she knew him before I did. I met him, as I said, about Christmas. And he was arrested about a month after Christmas.

Q: Upon what charge, if any? A: There was no charge. He was kept without trial for a whole month. He was never tried at all. He had to be released in the end.

Q: Where was he confined? A: In Cork prison. And he was quite ill then.

Q: What was the date? A: February 1916.

Q: Was it after the insurrection or before? A: Oh, before. Well, when we got the news in Cork of the insurrection in 1916, we heard there was something up in Dublin. And I went into town to try to find out what had happened. I heard that Terence MacSwiney was up at the Volunteer Hall, the headquarters of the republican army in Cork. There was danger in Cork then. He and Thomas MacCurtain had been sleeping there for several weeks with an armed guard because they thought it was safer for him. It was not well for him to be alone. He might be shot or arrested. He was up at the hall all that week. I had a chance to see him and get the news of what was happening in Dublin and Cork. He was arrested after that.

Q: What date was that? A: I cannot give the date exactly. It was during Easter Week.

Q: What was the date of your marriage? A: The ninth of June 1917.

Q: And I believe you have one child? A: Yes.

Q: And the name of your child? A: Maura.

Q: And when was Maura born? A: She was born on the twenty-third of

June 1918.

Q: How long was he confined after his arrest? A: He was confined until after Christmas.

Q: And where was he sent? A: First of all, he was sent to Richmond barracks, in Dublin and he was then deported to Wakefield prison in England.

Q: And he got out under the general amnesty? A: Yes, with the other prisoners at Christmas.

Q: During all that time there was no formal charge lodged against him? A: No, none of those were charged.

Q: They just kept him in jail until Christmas time? A: They did, for nearly a year.

Q: From that time what was the course of your husband? A: I visited him in Richmond barracks, I should say. And then I was sent over by our own people to England to do something for the men who were in prisons there. Our men were in a terrible condition at that time. In the beginning none of their folks were allowed to see them. When I went over first, I went to Wandsworth Prison in London and then I went to Wakefield, where Terence MacSwiney and most of the men from Cork were, because I was supposed to look after the Cork men.

Q: How many were confined? A: Hundreds, if not thousands. The whole of Ireland was in jail at that time and people who had never handled arms also. When I went there our men were in a terrible condition. They were literally starving. I know one friend of mine—he had never handled arms. He was from Bandon in County Cork. I was godmother to one of his children. He was sent to Wakefield before my husband was. He was not allowed anything, not a book, not even a prayerbook. All of his wife's letters were stopped and he thought that something had happened to her, because she was not very strong at that time. But his wife was one of the first to get into the jails to see their people. Well, I went over just to help those men. It was June when I went over. They were in a frightful state. They had literally no food except what we brought them. Of course, there were many Dublin men there, too, but I was looking after the Cork men.

Q: After they were released in 1916, tell what happened. A: I was ill after they were released in 1916.

Q: Were you in Cork? A: Yes, I was in Cork and then in Dublin for a month and then I went over to England for a visit. And while I was there I got the news that my husband had been arrested again. He had been out a very short time, about a month, I think.

Q: What was the date of that? A: In February 1917.

A MARRIAGE IN JAIL

Q: On what charge? A: There was no charge whatever. He was deported to

England with several others from different parts of the country. I heard just that they were arrested and deported to England. I did not know where they were of course. At that time we were not engaged, but only friends; but I think I felt how things were and that he felt the same as myself. I was staying in Cambridge with an Irish friend. She was at the university there. I found out from Mr Laurence Ginnell, the Irish MP, that he had seen some of the men and he thought that Terence MacSwiney was in Shrewsbury. I went there immediately. I met a policeman at the station and asked him where the men were and he said that the military had charge of them and told me to ask a soldier. I asked a soldier and he said they had gone and that nobody would ever know where they had gone. I felt very badly. I did not know what to do. I went back to Cambridge and that night I heard from him. They had been sent up to Bromyard in Herefordshire. And I went up to see him. And we really became engaged that night.

Q: He was in jail then? A: Yes, he was the same as in jail. He was confined to a certain area and could not go out of it.

Q: What date was that? A: That would be—Oh, we were engaged on the third of March.

Q: And how long was he interned after that time? A: He was there until after we were married.

Q: When were you married? A: About a fortnight in June.

Q: And how long did you remain in England? A: We had to remain in England for a time after that. But although we were in England, we were married by an Irish priest, Father Augustine. You have had him over here. And we were married in our own language, the Irish language.

Q: And that was on what date? A: The ninth of June 1917.

Q: And you went back to Ireland when? A: About a fortnight after that. The men were released, those who were interned and we all went back to Ireland at that time. I went back to Ireland with him and then we went off in the country together. And that time was about the only one that we had together.

Q: How long did you remain there? A: For some time.

Q: Where were you? A: At Ballingeary, in County Cork, a very, very beautiful place out in the country where they still do things in the old Irish way. Some of the old people do not know English there yet, I am glad to say and they are very much better off for it.

Q: Where did you go from Ballingeary? A: We returned to Cork.

Q: How long then, did you remain at Cork? A: About three months. And then my husband had to go up to Dublin to look after his affairs, but he did not stay there.

Q: He came back to Cork then? A: Yes, he came back to Cork and tried to settle down and it was while we were there, in the house that we had just got, that he was arrested.

Q: He was arrested? A: Yes, he was arrested in November at 2:30 in the morning by seven policemen.

Q: Were you there then? A: Yes, I was.

Q: How was he arrested? A: They came to the house for him and took him and although it was but so very early in the morning, they were afraid to take him through the streets of the city where someone might see them. And although my husband had lived in Cork all his life and knew the city well, they went in such a roundabout way that he said he did not know some of the streets through which they took him.

Q: What was the charge on which they arrested him? A: Wearing a uniform of the Irish Republican Army.

Q: Your husband was taken to prison and went on a hunger strike? A: Yes sir.

Q: How long did your husband go without food? A: He went without food for three days.

Q: That was at what time? A: Just before Christmas.

Q: 1917? A: Yes, 1917. He was at home for Christmas.

Commissioner Walsh: Was that the hunger strike that the Irish prisoners all demanded that a hearing be given them and charges produced or that they be freed? A: No sir.

Mr F. P. Walsh: That was not the Mountjoy hunger strike? A: Oh no. This was in Cork.

Q: There was a large hunger strike later in Mountjoy? A: Yes, there was.

Q: About how many went on this strike? A: About twenty, I think.

Q: They all went without food for several days? A: Yes. After six weeks' imprisonment they went on hunger strike, to protest against not being treated as prisoners of war and were released after a few days.

Q: And how long after this was he again arrested? A: I want to say that this was the only Christmas I ever had my husband for. It was the only Christmas that we were together. He was arrested again in the beginning of March.

Q: 1917? A: 1918. I had to go up to Dublin and he went up with me to keep me company. We arrived in Dublin about two, and three of those G Division men came and arrested him about six. I never speak to these people at all, because I think it is better not to. But this time I had to. I asked them where they were taking my husband and they would not tell me. They twisted and twisted and said, 'It's uncertain'. I know very well that they knew, because they were men high up. I kept after them and two of the men said they would come back the next morning and tell me where my husband was taken to.

Q: Where was he taken? A: He was taken to the Bridewell in Dublin. It was a terrible place.

Q: Where is the Bridewell located? A: There are several Bridewells in Dublin. This Bridewell was near the Four Courts.

Q: Describe this place. A: The men were not treated like human beings there. They had no mattresses, no bed-clothing, no anything. And what struck me as most terrible was that they had sort of round holes in the doors and the prisoners could just stick their heads through. And some of them were mere boys there in that frightful place.

Q: How long was your husband there? A: He was taken away the next morning to Belfast. And those men came back the next morning and would give me no information whatever. And there I was, not knowing where to look or what to do. And then I learned he was at Belfast. He was in jail there for about three weeks and then he was removed to Dundalk.

Q: Mr F. P. Walsh: How long was he in Dundalk? A: He was there until the beginning of September.

Q: From what date? A: From about the middle of March.

Q: What time was Maura born? A: In June. He was up in Dundalk. Of course, I was with him in Belfast first and then in Dundalk until I had to go home—until the baby was about to be born. My husband wished that she should be born in Cork, his native city. He said that most of her work for Ireland would probably have to be done in Cork and he wanted her to be born there. I went home the end of May and she was born the twenty-third of June.

A SOLDIER'S DAUGHTER

Q: When did your husband first see her? A: He was in Dundalk when she was born, but he was moved to Belfast soon afterwards and we had to take her up there to see her father, because, although his sentence would be completed soon, they had at that time taken to arresting people at the door of the jail just as they were walking out on finishing their sentence and then deporting them to England without any charge at all.

Q: What was your husband's sentence on the original charge against him? A: That was the sentence against him just after we were married. He got six months for wearing a uniform of the Irish Republican Army.

Q: Did your husband have any official position in it then? A: Yes, he was a commandant in the Irish Army at that time.

Q: You say you went up to be there at the time of his release? A: Yes, I went up there, for we knew that probably he would be deported to England like the others and that was the reason that I took the baby up; because if he was deported to England I would not be allowed to see him at all and he might never see his little daughter. I was staying a good distance from the prison, because I thought it would be better to be where I was when I stayed in Belfast before, because the lady there liked children.

Q: How old was the baby? A: She was six weeks old. We left Cork at three and we did not get to Belfast until half past ten at night. My sister-in-law went with me—not this one, but the other sister-in-law. Of course, a long trip like that was not very good for the baby, as your wife can tell you.

Q: How long did you stay there? A: About a fortnight. She used to be taken into the prison every day. I don't suppose anyone so young had ever been taken into that prison before. She was so young. Her father, of course, was delighted to see her. If he could have acted according to his interests and desires, he would have stayed at home with the baby and me. He liked his home. That is, he would have liked to do that if Ireland had been free.

Q: When did you return home? A: Oh, you see he was arrested just as he was walking out of jail, as we expected.

Q: Were you there? A: He did not wish me to be present, because the police might pull me back and hurt me, as they often do in Ireland.

Q: Where did you go? A: I went back to Cork and I was there when he was deported.

Q: What was that date? A: About the beginning of September. About the fourth of September, I think.

Q: Where was he taken? A: He was taken to Lincoln. President de Valera was there at that time. He was sent there earlier than my husband.

Q: Did you visit him there? A: I was not allowed to see him. I had practically no communication with him at that time because the letters I sent had to go through the prison authorities and through the English authorities at London also.

Q: How long did that endure? A: From September to the beginning of March.

Q: When did you again see your husband? A: In March.

Q: He returned to Cork? A: Yes, to Cork. He was released before the others a little bit on parole, because I had the influenza. He got a week on parole and by the time that was up he was released. He expected that they intended to release him or they would not have let him be with me then. Because, you see, at the time the baby was born he was in Ireland.

Q: Did he attempt to be paroled at the time of the birth of the baby? A: He would have liked to, of course.

Q: Was any effort made that you know of? A: Not that I know of. Of course, I was ill at the time.

Q: What was the date of his release from prison that you spoke of? A: In March 1919.

Q: Who was Lord Mayor of Cork at that time? Was it before the election of Mr MacCurtain? A: It was Mr Butterfield who was Lord Mayor then.

Q: Was he arrested from that time down to the time he was elected Lord Mayor of Cork? A: No, he was not.

Q: I wish you would detail what took place from that time to the time he was elected Lord Mayor of Cork. The elections intervened? A: Yes, they did; while my husband was still in Lincoln Prison.

Q: He was a candidate from where? A: He was a candidate from Mid Cork.

Q: Is that a part of the county of Cork? A: Yes. That is the place where my husband's family came from. That was the place where we spent our honeymoon. Because what time we spent in England when we were married we did not count as a honeymoon. When my husband was released in March we went to live in Ballingeary. The little girl was about nine months old. She was beginning to understand what we said to her and we wanted her to speak her own language first. I did not know very much Irish at that time. My husband knew it very very well, but I did not know much. I had not made much headway with it. So we all went to live in this Irish-speaking district.

Q: For how long? A: For seven months, I think it was. Of course, in the country almost everybody knows Irish. In the towns the Irish language had died out a bit and only the old folks knew it. But most of us nowadays have learnt it. Do you see this? This is called the Faínne (indicating small gold circle on dress). You can get this ring when you sign a paper and say that you will not speak any English to anybody else who has this ring. And after I was back in Ballingeary a while I got this ring. And after I got it, I never spoke a word of English to my husband or to the baby.

Q: The baby is how old? A: About two and one-half years.

Q: And she speaks Irish? A: Yes, Irish. In this district where I was, there are a lot of tourists and they speak English, of course. But for the last three months I was there I never spoke a word of English to anybody. Of course, my husband was there then and he never spoke a word of English either. We gave one of these rings to the baby when she was born, so that she would always speak her own language. We had to take it away from her because she put it in her mouth, but I think it is time to give it to her again.

Q: When did you return to Cork? A: November 1919. I should like to say that while we were in Ballingeary the English soldiers and police twice raided the house we were living in at 4 o'clock in the morning. Luckily my husband was not there either time. He used to go back and forth from Cork.

Q: Did you vote at the election? A: No, I did not.

Q: They held a general election, however, at which all the men and women of Cork were entitled to vote? A: Yes.

Q: And did they vote? A: Oh, yes.

Q: Where were you at the time? A: I was in Cork, but I was ill.

Q: What is the age of the franchise for women? A: I do not know. My sister-in-law can tell you that better than I can.

Q: It is thirty, I understand? A: Yes, I think so.

Q: You are still an infant so far as the franchise is concerned. A: Yes sir.

Q: In this general election there was a full and free vote for members of the Council? A: Yes.

Q: Do you recall the number of candidates voted on at that time? A: About thirty, I think.

Miss Mary MacSwiney: There were more than that, about sixty-six.

Mr F. P. Walsh: Miss MacSwiney says thirty-six.

The Witness: Yes, I don't know much about it.

Q: Following that election who was elected Mayor of Cork? A: Mayor MacCurtain.

Q: And he was a friend of your husband? A: Yes, indeed, a lifelong friend. Mrs MacCurtain used to tell me that if my husband was a girl, she would be jealous of him, because they were together for so long a time and planned and worked for Ireland together.

Q: Were you in Cork at the time of the death of Lord Mayor MacCurtain? A: Yes.

Q: Were you there at the inquest? A: I was in Cork, but I was very ill at the time.

ELECTED LORD MAYOR

Q: Just describe the events leading up to the death of your husband. After the death of Lord Mayor MacCurtain your husband was elected Lord Mayor of Cork? A: Yes, he was.

Q: And you were not present when he was invested with office. A: No.

Q: How long was he Lord Mayor of Cork until his arrest? A: About six months.

Q: And you were in Cork all that time? A: We came back to Cork before the election and we got another house. We gave up the other. But my husband could not stay there nights.

Q: Why? A: Because he would be arrested. The English police and soldiers would arrest him. For years he has had to do that. He really could not be with me at all. He could not be where they might find him nights. The house was likely to be raided at any moment even if I was there alone, so we left it. I stayed with friends, cousins of my husband. The house was a little bit out of Cork and we were not known to be living there, so he could come there occasionally, but always at a very great risk of being arrested. The baby was nearly two years old then, but she did not see much of her father. And she was awfully fond of him. He had a telephone in his office when he was made Lord Mayor in his office at the City Hall. And I used to speak to him on the telephone. Sometime I was speaking to other people, but whoever I was speaking to on the telephone, the baby would shout and snatch the receiver out of my hand and think it was her father and she would whisper, just whisper to him. She loved him and he loved her and wanted to be with her more than anything else.

Q: Your husband was a literary man, I believe? A: Yes, he was. He wrote a lot. He wrote some very excellent poems and plays.

Q: You might describe him, his inclinations, age, appearance and so forth. A: I think the chief characteristic of my husband—apart from his love of Ireland, which was above everything else—was his love of people, his charity. He never said a word against anybody. I never heard him say a word against his very worst enemies. I remember that when he was in Wakefield, a few of our men were put into solitary confinement and they thought that surely they would be shot, because some others had been shot who were in solitary confinement. And even then when he expected death, he would not say anything harsh against the English.

Q: He tall was he? A: Fairly tall.

Q: Dark complexion? A: Yes, very dark, with black hair—a lot of it, with one big lock that was always getting over his face. We used to tease him about that lock of hair. He was very good looking, I think.

Q: Of course, you were familiar with what he wrote? A: Yes.

Q: What was it, in a general way? Did he write verse? A: Oh, yes he was always more of a poet than anything else, I think.

Q: And did that go back to his young manhood? A: Oh, yes. When he was about thirteen or fourteen he wrote some beautiful things, some of his most beautiful things. He wrote plays, too.

Q: What was his education? A: He was educated at the North Monastery in Cork, the Christian Brothers in Cork. But, of course, he educated himself as most Irish people do. My husband's father died when he was fifteen and he had to be taken away from school and go into business. And so he studied at night, although he was working hard from eight-thirty in the morning until six.

Q: What was his business? A: He was an accountant in Cork. At first he used to stay up most of the night and study, but he found that was very bad for him and he got headaches and the like. And then he used to come home and have tea and go to bed and then get up about two in the morning and study. And when I heard that, I thought that a man like that could do anything. At first he would have a fire, but he found that that would make him sleepy, so that even in cold weather, in the winter, he would be without a fire. And he studied like that until he got his degree.

Q: What degree did he get? A: A degree from the Royal University of Ireland.

Q: Just describe his election as Lord Mayor of Cork. He expected to be elected Lord Mayor? A: Of course, he thought he would be. He knew it was a very dangerous post, after what had happened to his predecessor. Mayor MacCurtain was his greatest friend, I might say and it was his duty to fill his place.

Q: Did you have any conversation with him about it? A: Not very much because I was ill at the time.

Q: Briefly, for the record, tell what did happen to his predecessor. A: He was just at home one night asleep in his own house

THE MURDER OF MAYOR MACCURTAIN

Q: What was his name. A: Thomas MacCurtain. He was a very quiet sort of man and just like my husband, he would have liked to be at home with his wife and children all the time. He had five children, very sweet little children. One was only a year old. He was at home one night sleeping with his wife and children and his sisters-in-law were also there. And there was a knock at the door and his wife went to the door—the men do not answer the door at night in Ireland, for they might be shot. The men broke into the house and pinioned her arms and went upstairs and shot the Lord Mayor.

Q: In the presence of his wife? A: Yes.

Q: Chairman Howe: At what hour? A: In the middle of the night. At a time when there would be nobody about.

Q: Mr F. P. Walsh: Was it developed afterwards in the coroner's inquest who did the shooting of the Lord Mayor? A: Yes, it was. The police.

Q: The British police? A: Yes, of course, the British police in Ireland, but at the orders of their Government.

Q: The coroner's jury found that Mayor MacCurtain was killed by the Irish Police under orders from the British Government? A: Yes, the Irish police, being part of the English forces.

Q: How long after the killing of Lord Mayor MacCurtain was your husband elected? A: Almost immediately afterwards, when the funeral and all that was over.

Q: And during the time that he was Lord Mayor of Cork did he live at home? A: No, he could not.

Q: He was still pursued and had to live in the homes of other people? A: Yes. It was very much worse after he was Lord Mayor of Cork than it was ever before.

Q: Did the corporation meet from time to time? A: Yes.

Q: And did he preside at the meetings? A: Certainly.

Chairman Howe: Did they meet in the town hall? A: Yes, in the city hall. It was not secret. Anybody could go in.

Q: Mr F. P. Walsh: It might be interesting to know why they did not arrest the Lord Mayor when they were meeting? A: I do not know. Perhaps they were afraid of public opinion.

Q: As a matter of fact the police do not work in the daytime? Do they not expect to surprise these men in their homes and in their beds? A: Oh, yes. I think that they are afraid of doing it in a public place.

Commissioner Norris: He thought he would be arrested or murdered if he stayed in his own home? A: Oh, yes. He never even went about alone. He could not. Someone went with him, not so much to guard him as to identify anyone who might attack him. A volunteer went with him or I often went.

Chairman Howe: And that was the reason they did not do it in public. A: Yes. Of course, they did not want to be identified.

Q: Mr F. P. Walsh: And furthermore it would create a hostile popular demonstration to shoot him in public? A: Oh, yes, certainly it would. They would not shoot him where they might be identified. I could identify an assailant as well as anybody else, so I was often with him.

Q: Just give us your own general description of his life after that. A: As I told you, since the Christmas before, after I came back from the country, I lived with distant relations and friends, because we could not stay in a house of our own when he could never be there at all and I could not very well be there on account of the raids and that sort of thing going on. And so I saw my husband sometimes because I was in the house of friends, but indeed very very seldom and always at a very great risk. Sometimes he would come up after dark, because it was a little out of the way place, outside of the city. And then he would come after dark and go away the first thing in the morning. The only meal I could have him for was breakfast and that on rare occasions. I hardly ever saw my husband at all, to tell the truth.

Q: And that continued for six months, after he was elected Lord Mayor? A: Yes, of course, ever since we were married. But it was very very much worse after he was elected Lord Mayor.

THE FINAL ARREST

Q: When was your husband arrested the last time? A: August 12.

Q: Where were you at that time? A: I was in Cork on the twelfth of August and at two o'clock on that day I and my little girl went to the seaside, to Youghal, an out of the way place not very far from Cork. I did not know about my husband's arrest until the next morning, when a friend came over with the paper and told me that he was arrested the night before about seven o'clock.

Q: What did you do then? A: What could I do? There was nobody to mind the baby except myself. I had nobody to take her except strangers and she would not go to them. My sister-in-law here came down to take care of the baby. She came down the next day, Saturday. They had tried to see my husband—both of my sisters-in-law tried to see him. He had been arrested and taken to the military barracks and they were not allowed to see him. They could not see him until Saturday morning. He had been on hunger strike since the moment of his arrest the previous Thursday.

Q: When did you go to Cork? A: I did not go to Cork until Monday. I went up to my sister-in-law's house. This sister-in-law (indicating Miss Mary MacSwiney) was down at the seashore taking care of the baby. That was the day of the trial.

Q: Did you see him before the trial? A: My sister-in-law and myself went up to the barracks. That was where he was to be tried. A big military lorry came up, a very large one. I never saw so many soldiers in a military lorry in my life before. My husband was sitting in the centre of them on a chair. That was Monday morning. He had been on a hunger strike since his arrest on Thursday.

Q: Had you been advised of that? A: Yes. I need not tell you that he was very weak. It seemed such a cruel thing to have so many armed men guarding so weak a one.

Q: Was he all alone in the lorry? A: Yes, there were no other prisoners. He was in very great pain. He looked it. I think that was one of the worse times for me. From the morning that I heard my husband was on a hunger strike, I believed that he would die. I felt terrible on that day when I saw him, because I knew he was in pain and it was an awful thing that I could not give him anything to eat. They took him up very high stairs to a place where they were going to try him; and then they changed and took him down again. I saw by his face that he was suffering and I said to one of the soldiers, could they not give him a chair, because he had been without food for so long. That is one of the worst times in a hunger strike—the first few days, because it is so painful. I was speaking to him in Irish and they did not interfere. He told me that he felt himself that he would be sentenced and that he would be deported to England and that the others arrested with him would get out. But, of course, he was pleased with that. He wanted to suffer for everybody else's wrongs.

Q: Had he stated his intentions at any time to you? A: Oh yes, he did. He felt that what might happen to him was very unimportant to whatever he could do to help Ireland.

Q: Anything that you think would be of interest just tell the Commission. A: I think I would like to describe the trial. Of course, I always knew what my husband's motives and intentions were. He had no other idea in his mind but to die for his country if need be.

Q: Describe the trial, then. A: Might I read my husband's speech at this trial? It is quite short.

Q: Yes, certainly. Did he make it in the beginning of the trial? A: No. We went upstairs then. There were several soldiers standing around him armed to the teeth. The room was full of soldiers.

Q: Before what sort of a court was he tried? A: A court martial—soldiers.

Q: In uniform. A: Oh yes. One of them was presiding.

Q: How many judges? A: Three judges—three soldiers.

Q: How long a time did the trial last? A: Three hours.

Q: Did he make a statement? A: Yes, he did. I will read you this. First of all, when they brought the charges against him, they asked him if he had anything to say. He said that if he were an ordinary individual as he had been before he was elected, he would not say anything at all. He would disregard the charges because he never recognized England's courts, which have no right to function in Ireland. But he said that because he was Lord Mayor of the city, he represented more than himself and that was why he spoke. He said this more or less at the end of the charges.

Q: What was the charge against him? A: There were three charges, one of which was that when they arrested him and raided the city hall, they found in his desk the text of a speech he had made when he was made Lord Mayor. Of course, this was made six months before and it had been published in all the papers and so if there was anything objectionable in it, they could have mentioned it sooner. As a matter of fact, he had a right to make any speech in Ireland that he liked.

Q: What were the other charges? A: He was charged with having a code used by the police.

Q: And yet he was the chief magistrate of the city? A: Yes. What he said was that as chief magistrate of the city, no one else had the right to have anything like that without his permission and that it was illegal for any person in Ireland to have any such code for the purpose of using it against the Irish Republic.

Q: In the City of Cork? A: In the City of Cork, yes.

Q: There was a third charge? A: Yes, there was. It was a resolution that was passed by the corporation recognizing Dáil Éireann and renouncing allegiance to England. It was passed by every public body all over Ireland and if they wanted to arrest everybody who had passed that, they simply could not do it, because the jails could not hold them.

Q: There was no other charge? A: That was all. Shall I read this (indicating paper)?

The Commission: Yes, please.

MAYOR MACSWINEY'S SPEECH AT THE TRIAL

The Witness (reading): 'We see in the manner in which the late Lord Mayor was murdered an attempt to terrify us all. Our first duty is to answer that threat in the only fitting manner: to show ourselves unterrified, cool and inflexible for the fulfillment of our chief purpose—the establishment of the independence and integrity of our country and the peace and happiness of the Irish Republic. To that end I am here. This contest on our side is not one of rivalry or vengeance, but of endurance.'

I would like to say something about that. My husband, as I said before, was essentially charitable—a very charitable man. It was his chief characteristic. He hadn't anything like vengeance in him. And certainly he wished for nothing more than that the English army of occupation be gone out of our country and that we could have peace and be friends with all people.

'It is not those who can inflict the most, but those who can suffer the most, who will conquer, though we do not abrogate our function to demand that murderers and evil-doers be punished for their crimes. It is conceivable that the army of occupation could stop our functioning for a time. Then it becomes simply a question of endurance. Those whose faith is strong will endure to the end in triumph.'

Well, of course, my husband was one of the first in Ireland who started this movement and a great many people were against it then—they did not believe that we could be free from England. In Dublin those who started the movement for independence had an easier time than in Cork. In Cork they had a very hard time in the beginning. So only for my husband's great faith in our country and his faith that they would win out, I don't suppose that we would be very far along today.

'God is over us and in His divine intervention we must have perfect trust. Anyone surveying the events in Ireland in the past five years must see that it is approaching a miracle how our country has been preserved during a persecution unexampled in history, culminating in the murder of the head of our great city. You among us who have no vision have been led astray by false prophets. I will give a recent example. Only last week in our city a judge, acting for English usurpation in Ireland and speaking in the presumptuous manner of such people, ventured to lecture us and uttered this pagan sentiment: "There is no beauty in liberty that comes to us in innocent blood". At one stroke this judge would shatter the foundations of Christianity by denying beauty to that spiritual liberty that comes to us dripping in the blood of Christ crucified. He, by His voluntary sacrifice on Calvary, delivered us from the domination of the devil when the pall of evil was closing down and darkening the world. The liberty for which we strive today is a sacred thing, inseparably entwined with that spiritual liberty for which the Saviour of man died and which is the foundation of all just government. Because it is sacred and death for it akin to the sacrifice on Calvary, following far off and but constant to the divine example, in every generation our best and bravest have died. Sometimes in our grief we cry out the foolish and unthinking words, "The sacrifice is too great". It is not we who take innocent blood, but we offer it, sustained by the example of our immortal dead and that divine example which inspires us all for the redemption of our country. Facing our enemy, we must declare our attitude simply. We see in their regime a thing of evil incarnate. With it there can be no parley any more than there can be truce with the powers of Hell. We ask no mercy and we will accept no compromise. The civilized world dare not look on indifferent while new tortures are being prepared for our country, or they will see undermined the pillars of their own Government and the world involved in unimaginable anarchy. But if the rulers of earth fail us, we still have refuge in the Ruler of Heaven and though to some the judgments of God seem slow, they never fail and when they fall they are overwhelming.'

Mr F. P. Walsh: Now that was the speech which your husband delivered as his inaugural speech on being made Lord Mayor of Cork? A: No. But I have that one here also.

Commissioner Norris: This is the speech that he delivered at his trial?

Mr F. P. Walsh: This is the speech is it not—if it is not, correct me—that your husband made at his inauguration as Lord Mayor of Cork and the document which he was charged with having in his possession which they claimed to be seditious? A: That was practically the same. This was the speech that he made at his trial.

Q: Have you another one there? A: Yes. This was the speech he made when he was made Lord Mayor (indicating another paper).

Q: He delivered this speech at the trial? A: Yes, practically the same thing. I wish to say something else. You know this speech was one of the charges against him. Of course, one of the soldiers, the president of the court, read the speech and even coming from him, it made a very great impression on everybody there. And even on the soldiers—no matter who they were—it impressed everybody. As I told you, I think I felt that day more myself than at any other time. Because now I felt that my husband was going to die. After that I was accustomed to it. The shock was more in the beginning for me. Of course, I was upset, although I did not mean to be. But when he spoke himself, he made me feel all right. You have heard, I suppose, of the message that he sent to the men of Cork, that when we are doing work for Ireland, it should be not in tears but in joy. And so I think that it is Ireland that has kept me up all through. That is the only thing. There has been nothing else.

Q: When was he removed from Cork? A: He was removed that night, or at four o'clock the next morning, I believe.

Commissioner Norris: What was the result of the trial? A: He was found guilty by the court martial.

Mr F. P. Walsh: And sentenced to what? A: To two years. Of course, he told them then that it meant nothing what his sentence was, because in a month's time he would be free, either alive or dead. None of us dreamed that it would be a month. I certainly did not think it would be more than a fortnight at the outside and I did not think it would be that much.

Q: You say that after you heard his speech you were reconciled? A: Of course, I was always reconciled, but after that I felt quite happy about his work.

Q: You say you went to London? A: Yes, but I was able to speak to him after the trial. I asked one of the officers going out where they were going to take him. Of course, he knew. He did not deny that he knew, but you know they are very petty. He would not tell me anything. My husband was taken off that night in the state he was in on a British gunboat or destroyer. They were afraid to take him from Cork during the day. He was taken to Pembroke in the destroyer and arrived there about two o'clock in the afternoon and he was kept waiting until about six o'clock. Of course, his sufferings were terrible coming over in such a manner. In an ordinary boat it would have been very different. He arrived in London about half past two in the morning. They were afraid to take him there during the day. It was put in the London papers at first that he did arrive during the day. But that was a lie. And then he was taken to Brixton prison. My sister-in-law who is here went over first. My mother was not in Cork so she could not take the baby for me. Some people with whom I had been staying since Christmas, who were very kind to me, took her. I arrived in London on Saturday morning and went straightway to see my husband.

Q: Where was he then? A: In Brixton prison. Before I saw him one of the doctors of the prison, Dr Higson, spoke to me. He was not the head doctor. Of course, he was an Englishman. He said to me, 'You will see your husband in a few minutes and will you not try to get him to take food?' He said he hoped I would see the foolishness of what he was doing. The greatest danger was not if he lost his life, but if he was injured for life. And he said, of course, that any injury which he would receive from the hunger strike might harm our children. I told him that I understood the harm of going without food and from a health point of view quite agreed with him, but that I did not interfere with my husband in anything, especially in a matter of conscience and that each one was his own best judge in matters of conscience. He could not say very much to that.

THE HUNGER STRIKE

I saw my husband then. He was greatly changed. He looked very very badly indeed. Then we used to see him every day. And after a bit, I think it was about a fortnight, the head doctor came back. He had been away. And, of course, he often asked me to ask my husband to take food. We never had anything like scenes, because I do not give people opportunity to do that, to have a fight or anything like scenes. We were always very civil to each other. But he thought it was utter foolishness for a man to refuse to eat when he always had food before him. Being an Englishman, he could not understand why a man should die for a principle. But the subordinate doctor, I must say, was more sympathetic. He never urged me to get my husband to take food after that one time.

My husband was very charitable and he never said a word against anyone. The only thing he did say—he did not like the head doctor—and he said once, 'I am fed up with him'.

Q: Did you see your husband every day? A: I saw him every day. After a bit he did not like to be there without some one of us. My brother-in-law came over and his other sister afterwards. For, of course, we were afraid that he would die any moment. Nothing but his faith kept him alive. There is no doubt about that. So one of us would go in the morning and another at noon and another in the evening. This went on for some time. My husband was perfectly peaceful and happy. I do not think I could have gone on like that if I had not seen him every day, because he absolutely radiated peace. He told me in the beginning that one reason that he was glad to be doing what he was doing was that he had not taken a part in any of the dangerous things in Ireland, except the rebellion, and of course, they did not fight in Cork; and he hated their being in danger when he was not in any. But what could he do? So he told me that he felt what he was doing was as dangerous as anything and on account of that he was glad to do it. He always wished to die for his country. He never had any other thought. Things went on very much the same. We always saw him. After a bit they got two nurses for him, one for the day and the other for the night.

Then it came to the Wednesday before he died. There isn't very much to tell up to that. Well, the Wednesday before he died, the news had already come that one of the hunger strikers in Cork was dead. Of course, the doctors had promised us that they would not feed my husband and would not put any food in his medicine or anything of that kind, but they said that if he became unconscious then they would feed him. Of course, if a person becomes unconscious, he is unconscious and he has no will of his own and they could do anything they liked with him. And so feeding him when he was unconscious was like feeding him when he was dead. Of course, they did promise not to feed him at all, or to make any attempt to forcibly feed him—it would have been forcible, as long as he was conscious. It was on Tuesday, the Tuesday before my husband died, the news came from Cork to London of the death of one of the hunger strikers there. Of course, he had gone a bit longer than my husband. This frightened the doctors in the prison. One of them went to my husband on his usual visit and he turned everybody out of the room, including the nurse, which was not usual, for she always remained there. One of my sisters was there at the time. When she went back into the room my husband was frightfully upset and he said that this doctor told him that he would make him eat. When I got there in the evening the other doctor, the second doctor, whom I do not think would have done a thing like that, was on duty. My sister-in-law said to him that Dr Griffiths, the head doctor had threatened to make my husband eat and had made him awfully uneasy that morning. When I went in my husband was quiet as usual, but looking very badly—worse than usual.

The next morning I was in the office of the Self-Determination League in London. The papers wished to get bulletins and your American paper, too, wished to get bulletins on my husband's condition every two hours. We were allowed to use the prison telephone—they did not make any difficulty at all whatever about it. All the news was sent out from the office of the Self-Determination League; and, of course, if there was any news about my husband for us, we would get it there. I happened to be in there in the morning. My two brothers-in-law were in there too. I was told that a telephone message had come and that they were afraid the news was bad. So I and my brothers-in-law went out to the prison with Mr O'Brien, who is the president of the Self-Determination League.

Mr F. P. Walsh: Mr Art O'Brien? A: Mr Art O'Brien; yes. Do you know him?

Mr F. P. Walsh: I know him very well.

The Witness: So we went out and when we got there we heard that my husband had become quite delirious. My sister-in-law, Annie, was with him. There was hammering going on outside and my husband said to her, 'That is Dr Griffiths' new treatment'. She said, 'Shall I stop it?' And he said, 'no', and then went out of his head completely. She asked the warden to telephone to the office so that we would know and he was very reluctant to do it. It was half past twelve when we got there. Both my brothers-in-law and my sister-in-law were there then. They said my husband was normal again. But when I went in I saw that he was not. He was fairly himself, but not completely. The others all went away then, but myself and my elder sister-in-law. We remained there. And he said to me, 'I want the nurse'. The nurse was at her dinner. My husband always had a most extraordinary consideration for everybody and when he asked for the nurse when she was at her dinner, I knew he was not himself. Then they asked us to go outside the door. We always went outside the door when they asked us; we never made any difficulties about that. We heard my husband shouting out and we went in then and he was sitting up in bed and shouting. It was the delirium, because before this he could hardly move a finger and he spoke only in a whisper. And he was sitting up in bed and crying quite strong and saying, 'This nurse will not let me have my wife and sister'. And we said, 'Here we are', and he knew us perfectly well. That was the worst of it. And in other things he was as mad as could be. But one thing he said to me then when I came into the room I liked. He said, 'Muriel, you have always stuck by me'. And he was very bad then and talked rubbish. He could not have been more mad than he was. I have seen mad people and they were not worse. And then Dr Higson came up, stroked him and got him to lie down, but he went on throwing his arms about and talking. Finally the doctor gave him morphia and then he got quieter and in about an hour he was asleep.

I must tell you this occurrence. I wanted to do the best I could and wanted to try to make him better and did not know what to do. I used to speak to him a little and then the nurse said, 'I think it is better not to speak to him because it disturbs him'. And so from that time on I did not speak to him, thinking it might disturb him. In fact, I never spoke to him first because it was hard for him to respond. But if he spoke, I answered him back, because we did not want to cross him and offend him when he was ill. He would say to me, 'this is awful for you because you have to stay here'. And I said, 'It is a better time than we have had since we were married or since you have been Lord Mayor, because I can be with you all the time'. And then we laughed. Anyway, he got bad during the night. Of course, I was not there. Up to that time, although my husband had got terribly emaciated, his mind was perfectly clear and anybody could recognize him, because the face is the last thing that the hunger strike affects. But the next morning when I went in, I would not have known him at all. He was very quiet and only moved his hands a little bit. That was Wednesday. Of course, they started feeding him when he was unconscious. The nurse used to do that. I know very well that as long as the nurse was there at all, she had to do what the doctor told her and I never interfered with her in any way. I would not have spoken to her while she was doing it, because I was on one side of the bed and she was on the other and I might have disturbed my husband. He did not understand what was going on about him I know, but there was a chance that it might have disturbed him.

On Friday I was there in the evening, with my brother-in-law, Peter, the one who was in New York. And the doctor came in the evening, the head one, Dr Griffiths. I went out of the room as usual. We always did that when the doctor was there, naturally. When he came out he told the warden to tell me that we were not to go into the room any more, any of us. I must say that after he got very bad the nurse used to turn us out very often. So they now said also that we were not even to stay outside the door as we used to when we could not go in. And they also stopped up every little hole or window we could see through. The warden said we could not stay outside the door and I said I wanted to speak to the doctor and he went down and found him. I asked him if he was dying if he would not want his wife to be near him. And he said he would. And he said it was bad for us to be in the room, so many of us. And I said, 'We will go out and only one stay'. And then he laid the blame for the new order on the nurse. He said the nurse said it was bad for so many of us to be in the room. And I said, 'What harm have I done since I have been here with my husband?' And he said nothing. He could not tell me a single thing that I had done to harm my husband. After a bit—he was a very weak man, you see—he gave in. Then I went upstairs. They were feeding him. They were giving him two teaspoonfuls of liquid food.

MAYOR MACSWINEY'S DEATH

Q: When did they begin that? A: Five days before his death. That was on Wednesday and he died the following Monday.

Commissioner Walsh: Did the newspapers of Great Britain announce that he was being fed? A: Yes, they did.

Q: There were announcements in the American press that his relatives were feeding him? A: Yes, that was British propaganda.

Mr F. P. Walsh: As a matter of fact, did his relatives at any time put food before him? A: Never. His relatives never did that.

Q: Did the prison officials offer him food? A: Yes, always; it was always beside him.

Q: Did they bring him fresh food? A: Oh, yes, it was milk and broth and things like that. Food was always put before him. The next day was Saturday. My brother-in-law had been there with him through the night and my sister-in-law was there to relieve him. I found her in the waiting room just inside the gate and then she told me they had refused to let her into the prison at all. I went upstairs immediately and it was about ten-thirty and the nurse would not let me in. At about half past twelve she let me in for half an hour and then I was asked to go out. She made some excuse that she had to take his temperature. I expect she was feeding my husband. And then I was in again a half hour later. Then the head doctor, Dr Griffiths, came in and asked the nurse to go out and I went out too. So I had only about a half hour with my husband that day. As a matter of fact, it was the last day I saw him; but I think he may have half known me that day, because he smiled a little bit when I kissed him. I do not know, but I think he did.

There was another thing about my husband that I want to mention. I think the hardest thing on him was being separated from his little daughter. And I asked him if he would like to have her over and he said, 'Oh no, it would only be cruelty to have her over', and she would not recognize him if she saw him because he was so changed.

On Saturday afternoon Mr O'Brien came up and took me to the Home Office and we spoke to the officials there about the treatment of my sister-in-law and myself, requesting them to let my husband's relatives be near him. Of course they refused; and they refused about the telephone, point blank. There was no humanity in them whatever.

The next morning was the first time that I collapsed at all. I had kept up until then and really felt very well. But the next morning I felt ill and could not go and went to bed again. And in the afternoon, since I was about the only person that was allowed in the room, Mr O'Brien took me down in a taxi. I opened the door and the nurse was there and she said, 'Would you wait outside a few minutes'. I had not been there at all that day and my brother-in-law had not been there. I must tell you that the day before I had not been allowed in to see him until half past twelve, although I had come about ten. This day the nurse said, 'Would you wait just a little while?' They had a habit then of having a warden just inside the door. And I opened the door again in about five minutes and asked if I could go in, and he said he would ask the nurse and she said no, she was taking his temperature. And in about five minutes more, about twenty minutes from the time I came, I sent in word again if I could see him and she said no, I could not. And so I did not see my husband again until after his death. He died on Monday, October 15, at 4:40 a.m. My brother-in-law, Sean was there and his chaplain, Father Dominick—they were with him when he died. When dead, he looked like a perfect martyr.

The inquest was on Wednesday. I was in bed after he died. But they thought it was important for me to be at the inquest and I went. I was addressed by the coroner who asked me my address. I was puzzled, because we had no address. We could not have a home. And I said, 'Cork'. And he said, 'Cork is a big place'. But that was the best I could do. He asked me my husband's profession and I said, 'An officer of the Irish Republican Army'. And he said that was no profession. Being English, he could not understand why a man should have a profession when he was not working for money. And I said, 'You have an army and you have officers'. And then I think he understood, quite. Of course, I told him that my husband did not wish to die. And the specialist who had seen him, Sir Norman Moore, had told me so himself. I was glad that we had called him in to see my husband. I told him that as soon as my husband got out of jail that he would take food and get better. My husband was only on hunger strike, as you know, as a protest for being arrested illegally, arrested by the forces of England in Ireland. It was illegal for them to arrest the Lord Mayor, the chief magistrate of the city of Cork. It was entirely against the laws of the Irish Republic that they should do such a thing.

When the inquest was over our solicitor asked the Crown solicitor for my husband's body. And he said, 'Where is the funeral to take place?' And my brother-in-law said, 'In Cork, of course'. Then the chief solicitor said, 'You cannot do that. You must get a permit to take his body out of England'. And he said we should ask the governor. We asked the governor and he referred us to the Home Office. And so Mr O'Brien and Mr MacDonald and I all went to the Home Office. We saw Mr Shortt and he hemmed and hawed and all that but tried to evade telling us anything definite. I never met a man who was a greater brute. He was not a gentleman in any sense. He was just jesting and laughing all the time. I said, 'I understand that there is a technical difficulty about my husband's body coming with us, but I supposed there would be no difficulty'. He said, 'I know nothing at all about it'. They all say that over there. And I said, 'I suppose I can go and take my husband's body'. And he then got afraid and he said, 'Oh, you cannot do that. There may be some law against it'. And I said, 'Will you find out what the law is?' 'How long will it take you to do it?' He said, 'I cannot tell you how long it will take—an hour or more. I don't know'. I said, 'Do you refuse to give me my husband's body?' And he said, 'Oh, no; I cannot say that'.

One of Mr Shortt's secretaries came out with us. I must say that he was a contrast to Mr Shortt. He gave me a chair and asked me if I wanted to sit down. He said that if we would come back in an hour, he would see about it. He said they would make arrangements and perhaps give us a special boat back to Dublin. Of course our arrangements had been made. When Mr MacDonald saw him a little later, Mr Shortt said it would be all right and he was sorry there had been any delay and of course it had absolutely nothing to do with him and that we could take the body. My sister-in-law will tell you what happened afterwards and how they broke their word.

Mr F. P. Walsh: Senator Walsh would like to ask you a few questions.

Q: Commissioner Walsh: I would like to ask you what the spirit of the Irish women in Ireland is about the establishment of the Irish Republic. A: Just what mine is and what my husband's was. Of course, we all want our republic and we want England to leave the country and there will not be peace in the world until we get it.

Q: To what extent have the women organized and taken action? A: They have a society called the Cumann na mBan. That is a society of women like the Red Cross

Q: Do you know anything about the present sufferings of the people, especially among the women and children in Ireland? A: Yes, indeed I do. One of the things the Black and Tans did was to prevent the people going into the shops and buying food. Also they are destroying creameries and that means no milk distributed in the towns for the children. And, of course, there has always been great deal of poverty in Ireland, as I told you; and they are making things a hundred times worse.

Q: Is it your opinion that relief is needed in Ireland? A: It is absolutely essential or all the people will die.

Q: To what extent was the policy of starvation being carried out when you left Ireland? A: Well, I left Ireland three months ago, you see and it is since then that all that has come in force. I was ill, of course and did not go back for my husband's funeral, but my sister-in-law did and she can tell you.

Q: You did not go to your husband's funeral? A: No, I was ill. My sister-in-law was there. I was only in Ireland for a few days before I came here. The day I was there they shot into a football match and killed several people.

Q: Were you there at the game? A: No. But then in Cork it was very much the same. They threw a bomb into a crowd and killed four people. One young man whom I knew, they took both his legs off and he did not die until the next day. And, if course, ever so many people were injured. But even before I left for England there were motor lorries and armoured cars going through the streets so close that often one could scarcely pass between them. One day while I was on the tram they fired. Nobody in the tram was hurt, but we all saw them fire. And these lorries full of soldiers have terrorized the countryside. There was a Mrs Quinn, a younger woman than I am. She was on a lonely country road, as I often did when I was in the country with the baby. She was sitting by the road with one baby and was going to have another soon. And the Black and Tans came along the road in a lorry and shot her.

Q: Had she committed any offence? A: Oh, no, none whatever. To prove that there was no one with her, it was some time before a priest came. It was a very out of the way place. I felt that that case might have been mine.

Q: Some one has related that the women of Ireland have steeled themselves to such an extent that weeping is unknown among them. A: Well, I never cry.

Q: Is that the general feeling—that they must steel themselves for any emergency? A: Yes, it is. Weeping is almost unknown. But there is just one thing; you know I did not go back to my own country except for two or three days, but I never cried all through, not even at the end. But since I have been here I feel that there is so much sympathy—I am not speaking of sympathy in letters and what people say to me, but it is what I feel from everyone. But that sympathy has almost made me cry here and it did yesterday and I felt that I might not be able to go through this hearing today.

Q: Did your husband ever say what he felt his sacrifice would do for Ireland? A: He hoped that it would strengthen them still further in their struggle for independence.

Q: That was one of his considerations? A: That was, of course, the main consideration of his life. He never thought of anything else.

Q: Where is your baby now? A: In Cork.

Q: Is she well? A: Very well. Would you like to see her photo? I've just got it from home.

The Commission: Very very much.

Q: Commissioner Thomas: Your husband's hunger strike lasted seventy-four days? A: Yes.

Q: You saw your husband the last time how many days, before his death? A: I saw him on Saturday. I was not allowed in at all on Sunday. And he died on Monday.

Q: On Monday? A: I was not called at all when he died. He died at six and I did not hear about it until eight o'clock.

Q: Did the doctor persist in feeding him when he was unconscious until the very end? A: Oh, yes and I think that they really killed him. It was terrible to see him when he was more helpless than our baby was when she was born.

Q: That feeding continued from Wednesday, then, until Monday? A: Oh, yes. And I know that he was in pain, because I could see it on his face. Another time when I saw him in great pain was on the tenth day. He said to me that it was not so that people never desired food after the tenth day. He suffered right to the end.

Q: He wanted food right to the end? A: Yes, indeed. I hope you will all help us win our republic, because that was what my husband lived and died for. And we look on you in America very much as our own people, because you have been all so very kind to us. I looked upon this hearing as an ordeal, but it has not been at all. So I hope you will all do what you can for us. Also in the relief which I think has been started for Ireland. But, of course, the chief thing is for Ireland to get her freedom.

Q: Commissioner Walsh: Do you think the relief work is the greatest thing that can be done for the Irish people? A: Yes, I do; but I think recognizing our Republic is the more immediate. The people who have suffered and are suffering most from hunger would choose that too. It is the most immediate.

APPENDIX 7

Mary MacSwiney's Address at the Civic Auditorium, San Francisco, Thursday, March 10 1921[1]

I have already tried to tell the people of San Francisco how grateful I am to you all for the wonderful welcome you have given me to your great city. It has surpassed anything that I thought possible. And I thank you sincerely, in Ireland's name, for the promise it gives to me of your practical help. You know, as well as I do that the day of sympathy alone is past. Ireland must have help—practical help—and that speedily. And the practical help that she asks of you people now—you people of America today, is the recognition of her Republic by this great Sister Republic of the West.

ONE-HUNDRED-PER-CENT AMERICAN

I know that this city of San Francisco contains perhaps as large a percentage of Irish-American people as any other city of America, but I have not come to speak to you as Irish-Americans, I do not appeal to you as Irish-Americans, but as One-Hundred-Per-Cent Americans.

In so far as you are all white people, and not part of the Indian race, you must all be hyphenated Americans, and you are only One-Hundred-Per-Cent Americans if you are true to this land, whether it is the land of your birth or of your adoption, if you are true to the spirit, to the traditions, and to the ideals of this great Republic, and if you are loyal citizens of this United States. It is in that sense that I wish to speak to you, for I have not come here to ask you to do or to think or to say any single thing which would be subversive of or inconsistent with your duty as American citizens. When our President asked me to stay in this country (as he was obliged to go back to Ireland) and to take the message of the people of Ireland throughout this country, I realized that I was an alien here, that I was unused to political trickery, and that I might very easily make mistakes in a strange land; and so I fortified myself with some excellent advice and some good textbooks before I set out on my mission. The good advice I got from some of the most eminent jurists of the United States, judges and senators and congressmen, who knew the laws of the United States; and the books that I carry around with me are the Declaration of Independence of the United States, the Constitution of the United States, and the War Speeches of Woodrow Wilson. With such good advice and such excellent textbooks, I am not likely to say anything un-American. I want those of you who are of Irish blood to realize that it is not as Irish-Americans that you can best help Ireland today, but by being American citizens. I want those of you who are not of Irish blood—and I hope there are many such among you, my audience—to realize that if you are going to be true One-Hundred-Per-Cent Americans, you must be true to the ideals and the traditions of this great country, and that the better Americans you are, the more you love freedom, the closer you are to following the precepts of Washington and Jefferson and Patrick Henry and Daniel Webster and Abraham Lincoln, the closer you will be to realizing the justice of the Irish cause, and its claim on your recognition.

AMERICA 1776—IRELAND 1921

I should like to draw for you for a short time the parallel between your trial and ours. Less than 150 years ago, your land was the scene of a struggle very similar to ours today. You were suffering from oppression such as Ireland suffers today. You were suffering from the tyranny, the very self-same tyranny, that is oppressing our land. Your struggle differed from ours, for the fathers of this great Republic were the inhabitants of an English colony. They had accepted the laws and the constitution of what they called their mother country, and therefore when the tyranny and oppression of that mother country drove them into rebellion, they rose in revolt and rightly so; but still it was a rebellion, and they who fought were rebels—except those of them that were Irish. We in Ireland are not rebels. We call ourselves rebels sometimes, but in reality we are not rebels, and never have been. Because one cannot be a rebel except against lawfully constituted authority. And the authority in Ireland of England was never lawful, and has never been constituted by the Irish people. Our struggle differed from yours in yet another way. Ours is much harder, for you were 3,000 miles away from your enemy's base, and we are but sixty, and all the weapons of warfare, the powerful engines of destruction in which the science of the centuries seems to have concentrated, are turned on our small nation by a mighty empire. And so our struggle is harder than yours; but it is not less brave, not less gallant, and still more just and with the help of a just and almighty God, we shall take it to the same successful conclusion.

In 1776, you declared your independence, and in 1916 we declared ours.

You did not by the mere act of declaring your independence, rid yourself of your enemy. We have not yet rid ourselves of our enemy, but five years after your declaration of independence you had your Yorktown. This is the fifth year of our declaration of independence—on the 24th of next April we shall celebrate the fifth anniversary of our declaration of independence. It asks the people of America to give us our Yorktown this year by recognizing the government of the Irish Republic by that date.

FOREIGN PROPAGANDISTS

When you were a young nation, a struggling, weak Republic, you, too, had to set out looking for recognition. I have been told that I am a foreign propagandist, come here to stir up mischief between you and your friends. I have been told that we are trying to drive this nation into war. After 1776, you sent embassadors to every court in Europe to ask for recognition. They were foreign propagandists, too. They were not turned out of any country! And even before that, in 1769, when you sent Benjamin Franklin to our country, not for recognition, because we had it not in our power to give it to you, but for help and sympathy, Benjamin Franklin was not called a foreign propagandist, except by the English Tory papers. And it is exactly the same type of papers today that are writing editorials against those of the Irish people who have come to plead Ireland's cause to you, as your envoys pleaded the cause of the United States in every country of Europe. Only the other day I read an extract from a Tory paper of Massachusetts in the year 1776—and that paper was one of the Tory organs that from beginning to end denounced your great Revolution—and this sentence occurred in it: 'Never have the annals of the world been so deformed by such a wicked, wanton, unnatural and causeless rebellion'. Now that paper was not speaking of the Irish struggle today, but of the American struggle of '76, and it was published by the Lord Northcliffe of his day in Massachusetts. Lord Northcliffe has boasted that he has spent $150,000,000, and that he has left in this country 10,000 British agents for the spreading of British propaganda. It is as well for you to know that, before spending that $150,000,000 teaching the people of America what to think and how to think it, that he borrowed the money from you first. But there are papers in America today making the same remarks about Ireland as that Massachusetts Tory paper from which I have quoted made about the struggle which you so glory in today. And those papers are not American, they are British. They tell you that this is not an American question, that it is a domestic question of England, and that it is not for the American people to interfere. But the Revolution of '76 was much more of a domestic question of England than is the Irish cause today, and if America has no right to give Ireland recognition, what right had France or Spain or

Italy, or any other country in Europe, to give your people recognition in the days of your revolution?

When it seemed as if France were going to listen to the plea of the United States and recognize your republic, England came to your forefathers with open hands. She promised to do everything for which you had begun the war—for when you began that war you did not mean to set up an independent republic. She promised you complete control of your own taxation. She promised you the right of free trade. She promised you the right to import machinery and manufacture your own raw materials—all of which rights she had refused to you before, and all of which rights you had gone to fight for. When she realized that you were asking now for more than Home Rule, she came to you with outstretched arms and offered you Home Rule. She told the people of the world that you Americans did not want a republic, she told the world that it was only a wicked band of extremists that wanted a republic, and that the real American people wanted to remain a loyal daughter of the English Crown. So she made you promises that you might remain a loyal daughter of the English Crown. But—your forefathers had set up their republic. They had declared allegiance to their republic, and they refused to commit treason to their own government.

IRISH REPUBLICAN MAJORITY, 91 PER CENT—AMERICAN REPUBLICAN MAJORITY, 75 PER CENT

Our cause today is the very same as yours; we have set up our republic, and we have declared allegiance to that republic; and remember that 91 per cent of the people of Ireland are behind the Irish Republic today. When your forefathers fought, their Tory minority was not 9 per cent, but it was at least 25 per cent, and I am told by some excellent American authorities that it was as big as 40 per cent of the American colonists. And yet you refused—for, though you had a large Tory minority, you had a majority for the republic—you refused all the offers made to you by England, and declared your allegiance again to your republic.

And today, today England tells you that there is only a handful of Irish extremists who wish for an Irish Republic, and that the moderate Sinn Féiners would be satisfied to accept Home Rule, and King George the Fifth tells us that he is much distressed at the criminal violence of a certain section of the Irish people.

And he also tells us that we can hope for no union and no self-government as long as we ask for a republic. And it is not so very long ago since King George the Third at the opening of Parliament declared that he was very much distressed at the criminal violence of a certain section of his rebellious American subjects, and that they would never get self government or anything that they were asking for, until they gave up their desire for a republic; and the answer that your forefathers gave to George the Third, we have given to George the Fifth. And that is this: 'Our Republic is there, and there it will remain'.

FIRST RELIEF CAME FROM IRELAND

Still another point of similarity between your revolutionary struggle and ours. You have all read of the bitter winter that Washington's army spent in the Valley Forge. You have heard how his heart was broken with sorrow at the sufferings of his soldiers. When I stood in Washington's headquarters at the Valley Forge two months ago, I thought that though Washington was sick at heart when he watched the bleeding footprints of his soldiers in the snow, that Washington's sorrow was less than ours, for he had only to see the sufferings of his soldiers—and soldiers must always be prepared to suffer—but we this winter have had to watch the sufferings, not of our soldiers only, but of the mothers and of the little children of Ireland. When Washington sent forth the cry from the Valley Forge that he must have help at once, that he must have food and clothing for his soldiers, he must have money to carry on the struggle, the first food ship that sailed up to the shores of Philadelphia came from Ireland. And twelve men met in the city of Philadelphia and subscribed $517,000, a mighty sum in those days, to Washington's army, and every one of the twelve had been born in Ireland. This year America is paying back some of the material debts that she owes to Ireland, for the Relief Committee in New York and its branches throughout this great country are striving to ensure that the women and children of Ireland shall not starve to death, as England wishes them to do. For the policy of England today is a deliberate policy of extermination; it is a policy which aims at the death or submission of the Irish people. We have risen, and said with Patrick Henry, 'Give us liberty or give us death'. England with her mighty empire has decided that it is to be death. We with our four and a quarter millions have decided that it is to be victory. For we do not believe it possible that it is consistent with the justice of Almighty God that a people like ours that have fought for 700 years and have kept alive and unsullied its traditions of freedom, could be exterminated now.

And we thank the people of this great country who are coming to the assistance of the Irish people in this hour of the Valley Forge in Ireland. And take care, take care, that your work is not made ineffective, for I warned the American Relief Committee before they began their work in New York that what they did should be done by American citizens and through American channels. I told them that they should take care that the money that you subscribe to help the Irish people was not confiscated by England under the plea that it was to be used for seditious purposes. For today in

Ireland it is sedition to feed the hungry, and the warning that I gave them is proving true, for I have heard that the committee of American citizens sent to help the people of Ireland have been informed by the English government that they may not help any one who is not a loyal citizen of Great Britain. Moreover, England has made it today criminal for one district to help another. People who are over there investigating conditions have sent me word that not since the days of the early Christian Church was there such community of goods, such unselfish help of one group by another, of one citizen by another, of those who have to those who have not, as is being shown in Ireland today. And I am confident that the American people will see to it somehow that the relief which the people of America send will reach the people for whom it is intended.

Now, I want to remind you again that you went looking for recognition of your country, that you realized that your republic could not continue unless you did get recognition from the civilized people of the world, and so you sent envoys to all the countries of Europe. You wanted the recognition of France first, because France was the greatest country in Europe at that time. We want the recognition of the United States today, because the United States is the greatest country in the world at this time. We know that if you give us the recognition which we crave, and which we are entitled to, every country in Europe will follow your example, most of them within a month. We know that England cannot hold out against the moral force of the world, and moreover there are in England today two forces that will eventually help us, and will help us to establish ourselves if the United States grants us recognition. The first of those forces is that group of honourable, upright English people who love their land, and who up to now have believed in its sincerity, believed in it as a great civilizing power, and who are shamed to their very soul at the doings of their government in Ireland today. They are sorry that the people of Ireland want to break away from the Empire, but they realize our right to break away, and they realize that the land which could behave as their land is behaving in Ireland is unfit to govern anybody. The other source in England that will help us, but that source I am not quite so sure about yet, is the English Labour Party. They will not help us because they believe it is right, for they have said—at least the majority of them through their spokesman, Arthur Henderson—that they would like Ireland to have Dominion Home Rule, but that we will never, never, never get a republic. But that was said a year and a half ago, and since that time the English government has done much to convert the English Labour Party to Irish Republicanism, because the English Labour Party has grown sore afraid. They are afraid that this undisciplined fiendish force of Black and Tans which England has trained to commit murder unlimited in Ireland, and to which she has promised perfect immunity for every murder they commit, that that English force will be used as a sort of White Guard against the English labour people, if ever they have been able to overcome the Irish people. And so through self-interest, if for nothing else, the English Labour Party will support the recognition of the Irish Republic by the civilized governments of the world.

I do not want to make it appear that all the English Labour Party is purely selfish, but I have reason to know that most of it is. There is a minority in the English Labour Party whom I will include in the first body that I have mentioned, of upright, honourable English people who are ashamed of the deeds of their own government in Ireland. And so we know that if the United States will give us recognition, our troubles will be at an end within a year.

RECOGNITION DOES NOT MEAN WAR

Some of those Tory elements among you say that the recognition of the United States, the recognition of the Irish Republic by the United States, will be the cause of war between England and America, and that we have no right to come here to stir up war between you and a friendly power.

In the year 1793, France threw off the yoke of the Bourbon king, and set up a republic. I am not going to discuss the question of the rights or wrongs of the French Republic of that date. I know, and those of you who know your European history will agree with me, that that Republic had not the moral force of the French people behind it. Moreover, the Republic which you were asked to recognize was a Republic that had cut off the head of the king, Louis, who in the year 1778 had recognized your Republic. And yet Jefferson said, 'Why should we not recognize a people who desire to set up the same form of government as our own?'

YOU RECOGNIZED THE FRENCH REPUBLIC WHILE YOU WERE STILL A STRUGGLING NATION

Still, anxious as Jefferson was to recognize the Republic, it was a matter of serious consideration for your Continental Congress, because France and England were at war then, as Ireland and England are at war today. And your fathers feared that recognition of the French Republic by the people of the United States would involve you in war with Great Britain. Then, as now, it was the duty of the American people to consider America's interest first. You had, only ten short years before, driven the English out of your country. You were a weak power, a poor, struggling Republic—an infant among the nations of the earth—and it was a serious thing for you to risk involving yourselves in war with England again. But, weighing the pros and cons of the question, the fathers of this Republic came to the conclusion that they might safely risk it—for England had her hands full in Ireland, she had her hands full in India, and she had a depleted exchequer. My friends, if England had her hands full in Ireland in 1793, I promise you she has them much fuller today. If she had her hands full in India in 1793, she has them much fuller there today, and if she had a depleted exchequer in 1793, what has she today? She owes you already five thousand million dollars. She cannot even pay you the interest on that five thousand million dollars, and before she could go to war with you she would have to borrow five thousand million dollars more, and she has no one to borrow it from but the United States.

Now, you are a very altruistic people, but you are not quite so altruistic as to hand England another five billion dollars and invite her to come and fight you. Moreover, she could not afford to fight you. She could not get the money; no one could lend it to her except yourselves. France has not got it, could not lend it to her if she wanted to; and you might be quite sure that Germany would not, if she could. So much for England declaring war on you.

RECOGNITION WITHOUT MILITARY INTERVENTION

And now, what about you declaring war on England? From that very self-same year, 1793, when you first recognized the Republic of France, you laid down what has always been the settled policy of the United States since—'recognition without military intervention is not an unfriendly act'. Therefore, in your own settled policy, you have it in your power to recognize Ireland, and the Republic which she set up, and not to fire a shot on our behalf. You have exercised that right of recognition without military intervention in the case of the Argentine Republic, in 1819; in the case of Greece, in 1821; for Belgium, in 1832; and for more than a score of South American republics, between 1822 and 1852—and you have never gone to war on behalf of one of them. Why cannot you recognize the Republic of Ireland when it is the settled policy of the United States to recognize small nations rightly struggling to be free? What can be the reason? If the young, weak, struggling infant Republic of 1793 were not afraid to do what was right, and to take the risk, is it possible that this mighty Republic of 110,000,000 of people—the greatest, the most powerful, the most wealthy people in the whole wide world—is afraid to do right today? Are we, in Ireland—four and one quarter millions of people against a mighty Empire—are we the only people in the whole wide world that are not afraid of England? My friends, I know that you are not afraid, but, frankly, I do believe that a large proportion of these people, these great people of the United States are hypnotized by England. It is perhaps the result of that $150,000,000, but there is no doubt, from whatever cause it has arisen, that the people of this country have in many places extraordinary and utterly unjust prejudices against the people of our country, and that those prejudices are the result of British propaganda. I cannot wait to talk to you about all those prejudices. I shall only deal with one of them tonight, and that is the one that has done most harm to Ireland in America: the falsehood told by England that this is a religious war.

THE RELIGIOUS BOGEY

Last June there was a Labour Congress in Cork, and I was invited to some function there, and in the course of our conversation a gentleman whom I have known for six years, with whom I have sat on committee after committee on social work and labour work and national work, spoke of that prejudice that exists in the United States, because of that slander of England. It was agreed among us that no lie that England has ever told has done more mischief to the Irish people than that one. And he said: 'In the parts of Ireland that are Catholic and Irish, you are never asked your religion, but you are not half an hour in Belfast when it is the first thing that they find out; and when they learn that you are a Catholic, you are damned forever'. He had been a labour organizer, and he said: 'I was not half an hour in Belfast, when they found out my religion; I had no more chance'—and in surprise I looked at him, because he had a strong northern accent, he came from Belfast himself, and I should have concluded that he was a Protestant, if I had thought about it at all, and I said, 'And are you a Catholic?' 'There', he said, 'I have known Miss MacSwiney six years, and she doesn't yet know my religion'—and that was literally true. I had to come to America to learn the religion of two of my own fellow countrymen, members of our Irish Republican Parliament, whose names I had known and had honoured for years, whose religion I never knew until I reached America. One of them was a Northerner, and he turns out to be a Catholic; the other is from Limerick, and he turns out to be a Protestant. My friends, if this were a religious question, as England tries to tell you it is, how is that in the southern and eastern and western parts of Ireland, where the population is predominately Catholic, you never hear of a religious riot, but in Belfast, the home of the Orangemen—where England holds her stronghold, where she carries out the principle of divide and conquer, where she tells a foolish, ignorant, stupid handful of people that if Ireland got her independence, the Pope would come over and live in Dublin and have a high old orgy of persecution—that this is the only corner in Ireland where you hear of religious riots, and that they are never riots begun by the Catholics or the Irish Republicans, but by the Orange, British, foolish dupes of England and Sir Edward Carson?

We have carried on this struggle against England for 750 years—for since the day that she set foot first on our shores there has never been a generation when the Irish people were not in arms against England—and if this is a religious war today, what was it 400 years ago, before Martin Luther was born? If this is a religious war today, what was it in the day of the Catholic Queen Mary, who was about as bitter an enemy as the Irish had? Let me tell you about Catholic Queen Mary. She very wickedly—for persecution is always wicked—persecuted her Protestant subjects; she burned them at the stake; she confiscated their property, and she persecuted them by prison and by torture, and many of her Protestant subjects fled to Catholic Ireland for protection, and got it. And there, their Protestant descendants are living in Ireland today, as free and as unmolested as the day they first sought shelter there. Queen Mary persecuted her Protestant subjects, but she was honest about it. Queen Elizabeth persecuted her Catholic subjects. But just look at the peculiarity of the English mentality! Queen Mary is called 'Bloody Mary', and Queen Elizabeth is called 'Good Queen Bess'; and the English histories tell you that Mary wickedly persecuted her subjects, for their faith; but Queen Elizabeth never did anything so wicked—no, she only made it high treason to be a Catholic, and then she persecuted them for high treason. Now, that is just a type of the English mentality—yesterday, today, and for all time. I am not going into any discussions on English history. I only mention Queen Mary to prove to you that this is not a religious question, but I will come down to later history. If this is a religious question; if, as England tells you, we are a priest ridden people, how is it that you find the English government intriguing at the Vatican to destroy the Irish Republic? The late Duke of Norfolk was the first nobleman in England, and he was a Catholic; and like all English Catholics of his class, he was one of the worst enemies that Ireland ever had. If it was a religious war, he should be standing in with us against his own government, but he spent many a day and many a week and month at Rome, trying to persuade the Pope to condemn one Irish movement after another. England wanted the Pope to condemn the Irish movement, in the hope that the Irish people would get frightened and give it up.

When my brother was dying in prison last August, an eminent English ecclesiastic visited the Bishop of Cork, who had gone over to London to see my brother, and he told that Bishop that if the bishops of Ireland would ask the Pope to condemn Sinn Féin, my brother would be released within a week. Of course, if the Bishop had written to the newspapers about that, the English government would have come out and said, 'Oh, nonsense! He had no official authority for saying such a thing'. May I remind you of a little recent history of your own? A few weeks ago, the American press correspondents in London were called to the office of an important English official—so high up, so important, that his name could not be divulged—and there they were lectured like a lot of school boys. They were told that the United States has been drifting into war with England, and that it would be a terrible thing for the United States, and for the world, if such a terrible catastrophe came to pass as war between the United States and England; and they were told that the United States had better keep its meddling fingers out of England's domestic questions. And the press correspondents sent their message home, and the congressmen and senators at Washington pooh-poohed the idea and said it was ridiculous, and laughed at it, and the American people scoffed at the implied threat—and the English official government comes out and says, 'Oh, that was not official at all!' Of course it was not official at all; it was just a nice little kite which they sent up to see how the American people would take it; and when the American public laughed, then it was not official.

BRITISH INTRIGUE AT THE VATICAN

I have told you what happened a few weeks ago to press home the point of what happened a few months ago, when Bishop Bidwell tried to bribe the bishops of Ireland with a life that they valued, to get a condemnation of the Irish people's fight. And today in Rome, the English government is using every possible intrigue that it knows how to use, it is calling to its help all the influence—the great, undoubted influence that it has—to try and get the Pope to condemn the Irish people. Yesterday and today you have seen notices in the papers that the Pope has made a general remark condemning crime—crime everywhere. He has especially mentioned the crimes of the British government in the doings of the Black and Tans. He has also said that if there are crimes on the Irish side, he condemns them too. We commit none. The fight that is being carried on in Ireland today is as clean and brave and gallant a fight as any small nation ever put up before against a might empire. We in Ireland today are proud of our soldiers, and justly so. You are told that they are 'assassins'. Your Minute Men were 'assassins' not so very long ago. The men that fought at Bunker Hill and at Lexington were 'assassins', too. Our men are not assassins. You are told that they fight in ambush. You are told that they have shot down unarmed men. They have shot spies—and every nation in the whole wide world shoots spies. They have laid ambushes; but try to remember that our country is at war, that the English government has declared that there is a state of war in Ireland. Remember that the judges of the Supreme Court have declared that there is a state of war in Ireland and therefore they have no power to interfere with the military tribunals, and remember too, an ambush is a recognized act of war.

AMBUSHES AND AMBUSHES

Try to imagine yourself five years ago listening to the tale of a handful of Belgian soldiers, who hear that a large German force is on its way to raid and destroy the homes of Belgian women, and they know that they have not the tanks and the armoured cars that accompany the German soldiers. Moreover, they are but a handful and they plan an ambush to catch the German soldiers before they attack the Belgian women and children. So they lay that ambush. They watch behind the hedges and they call on the German force to surrender, and the German force fights if it can, and surrenders if it cannot. Would you call those Belgians assassins? No. You would laud them up to the skies; they would receive every honour ever known. They would probably receive a Croix de Guerre from France, and probably the Victoria Cross from King George. They would be told what gallant little fellows they were, and the story of their heroism, and the way they saved their homes from the enemy, would be spread abroad to the world. But when the Irish soldiers set an ambush, and when they, as terrible odds hold back the enemy that is devastating their homes, they are 'assassins'. That is an English point of view. I ask you, freedom-loving people of America, no matter what your ancestry or what your religion is, why the Irish people should be assassins and the Belgians heroes? You were told of a case recently where seventeen Black and Tans were ambushed near Macroon, and nearly every one of them killed. You heard that much; I give you the real story.

Seventeen Black and Tans were ambushed. They were called upon to lay down their arms, and they did so. One moment. They held up a flag of truce; they held up the white flag of surrender; they were asked by the captain of the handful of Irish boys that were there whether they surrendered, and they said 'yes', and three of the Irish soldiers crossed the road to take that surrender—and the British officer ordered his men to fire, and they shot dead the three that went to take the surrender that had been given, and the Irishmen naturally set to the rest of them and fought, and when they fought they won.

Go back to Belgium, and imagine those Germans surrendering to the Belgian soldiers, holding up a white flag; and imagine the Belgians coming to take the surrender which was offered, and being shot down. Oh! What a German atrocity! I can tell you of another ambush which took place, on the Ballingeary road, to my own knowledge. To my own knowledge, on the 29th of last July, a military lorry half full of ammunition, and an escort lorry with fifteen soldiers, were going along that country road, and the lorries stuck in the road. The fifteen soldiers (an officer and fourteen under him) gathered around the cart with the ammunition, and a few—not more than ten at the outside—of the Irish Volunteers of the neighbourhood got word that they were there, and they came along, very badly equipped. They had not more than four rifles between them, and the whole fifteen of the English were armed with trench helmets, guns, bandoliers and all sorts of war kit, but they were in no mood to put up a fight—they rarely are—the English—unless they can do it at big odds. They were called on to surrender, and they did so. They were told to lay down their arms, and they did so. And then the handful of Irish soldiers took possession of the arms, also took the trench helmets and the bandoliers, and they marched their prisoners back through the village of Ballingeary, on the road to Inchigheela, and they did not shoot them, for our Irish soldiers never shoot unarmed men, except spies. They respect the laws of warfare, and they never shoot men who have surrendered or who are prisoners. They gave them instead cigarettes to comfort them on their six mile march—and sent them back to their barracks. They then returned, took the ammunition, put it in a place of safety, and burned the lorries. And those men were called, by the English papers, robbers!

Now, so much for ambushes. In the early days of the recent war, England shot spy after spy, in the Tower of London, after secret trial; and one day in the House of Commons a question was asked as to why these men did not get an open trial, and the answer given was this: 'They could not be tried openly, because it would be giving information to the enemy'. The very same reason applies in Ireland today. We cannot give spies an open trial, because it would not only be giving information to the enemy, but be giving valuable lives to the enemy; but we are as much entitled to shoot spies as any country in the world. And when the nations of the world make it against international warfare to shoot spies, and when the nations of the world succeed in making England obey the laws of civilized warfare, then we shall cease to shoot spies. Understand, you citizens of America, that we will not allow you to look upon our country as the Cinderella among the nations. We will not allow you to have one law for us and another for yourselves. We will not allow you to consider that if your duty is to America first, if England's duty is to England first, if France's duty is to France first, that Ireland's duty must be to England first. We are a race older than any in Europe except Greece. We are a race civilized before any race in Europe, except Greece. We are a race more cultured, more noble, more gallant, than the race that is trying to oppress us. And if Abraham Lincoln declared that God had made no man worthy to enslave his fellow man, then I declare that God never made a nation worthy to enslave another nation. And that of all nations of the earth who may, from time to time, have had smaller nations in their power, the one least worthy to govern another is England.

BRITISH ATROCITIES

I do not like to talk about the atrocities that are being committed in Ireland today, but I am told that the people of America do not believe that there are atrocities. In a recent letter which I got from home, I was asked these questions: 'What is America doing? What are the people there thinking of? Have they any feeling? Have they any civilization, or is it that they do not know the truth, and that English propaganda is so powerful still? For we here cannot imagine any civilized nation looking on at such vileness, and letting it go unchecked'. Those are the questions that Ireland is asking today. And it is the truth that English propaganda is so powerful among you. England controls your press, England controls the cables, England seems to control your very news centres, for looking at your papers day after day, I find that when I want news of Russia or China or Japan, or the continent of Europe, I must see it under the heading, 'London'. The idea of this great people taking their news of what happens abroad through the world through London! If you are not very careful, if you do not watch the English propaganda, if you do not watch the tendency that is abroad to make you think that it was not England that fought you in '76, but a wicked Prussian king, if you do not take care you will have your children being taught that George Washington was a fool, and the revolution a mistake, and before you know where you are you will wake up some fine morning to find London again the capital of the United States. Before that day comes, and while you are still a free and a mighty people, let Ireland have recognition and save America for itself.

WHAT ENGLAND DOES WITH AMERICAN MONEY

I have reminded you that England owes you five thousand million dollars. She cannot even pay you the interest on the money, but the $125,000,000 which represents about the interest that England owes you, and cannot pay you, is being spent to pay her army of occupation in Ireland, it is being spent to pay the most fiendish and wicked human beings that ever walked the earth, for atrocities such as the world has never heard of. England is using your money to exterminate the people of Ireland. I am told that you cannot even afford to pay your soldiers a decent war bonus. I am told that your income tax is so high that you are, many of you, very heavily burdened by it. I am told there is a large amount of unemployment in your country. Call back your five thousand million dollars. Call back the money that England is using to exterminate our people, and she will have to call back her armies of occupation, not only from Ireland, but from India and Egypt, and every other corner of the world that she is oppressing. You remember how four short years ago you went into the war—the World War—on behalf of the small nations of the earth. You went into that war with a programme so beautiful, so ideal, so magnificent, that if you had carried it out it would have made the world a beautiful place to live in. You laid down fourteen points which were to be the basis of the world's freedom. We in Ireland analyzed all your statements, all your promises. We heard that you were fighting for 'freedom for all peoples everywhere', for 'liberty and self-determination and the undicated development of every small nation'. You were fighting 'to make the world safe for democracy', to 'insure that no small nation would henceforth have to live under a sovereignty under which it did not wish to live'. You promised that as a result of your entry into the war, no great nation would henceforth be allowed to exploit a weaker nation for its own benefit. You declared that the great nations of the earth should have the same standard of morals and conduct as individuals had—and we in Ireland listened, and we said, 'America is going into the war as England's ally' and we knew that England was not sincere in her declaration that she was fighting for freedom and civilization and small nationalities; but we said, 'America is honest, America is powerful, and although America is England's ally she is an ally that England cannot ignore, an ally powerful enough to carry out the programme that she has laid down, an ally that has nothing to fear from England, and that will never bow the knee to England, and so the day that America wins the war Ireland will be free'.

MAKING THE WORLD SAFE FOR BRITAIN

England says you did not win the war. She has told you that you came late, and did a little, and made a profit out of the miseries of Europe. That is her gratitude to you for saving her when her back was to the wall. We know, to our cost, that America saved England; we believed that America would win the war and would keep her word. But—you have come out of the war, you have left 70,000 of your best and bravest dead on the fields of France and Flanders, and you have left your beautiful ideals shattered on the diplomatic tables at Versailles. You have not made the world safe for democracy, you have made it safe for the British Empire a little while longer. You have not freed the small nations of the earth, for you have left in chains the biggest of the small nations, the oldest of the small nations, and the small nation to which Christianity and civilization owes most. We today in Ireland ask the people of America to remember their promises. We believed you were sincere. We believe it still. We know that the programme which was laid won for you was endorsed by the American people, and we know that the failure to carry out that programme was not endorsed by the American people. And today we plead to you in the name of liberty for which your forefathers fought, for which they sent leaders to every country in Europe, in the name of the policy of the United States—recognition of small nations rightly struggling to be free—in the name of the pledges which you made to humanity when you entered the war four years ago, we ask you to extend that recognized policy of yours to Ireland, and to give us recognition. You cannot shake off responsibility, because your money is paying England's army of occupation to commit atrocities such as Belgium never knew.

ENGLAND'S POLICY OF EXTERMINATION

Today in Ireland, England has set out on a determined policy of exterminating the people of Ireland. She is burning down factories and workshops, the centres of production and distribution, to disorganize our country, to starve our people into submission. She is shooting down men wholesale. She is breaking every law of international warfare, for she is taking men prisoners and shooting them while in her power. She is breaking every law of civilization, for she is taking men prisoners and then supplying the evidence before she convicts them on it. Do you think that I am exaggerating?

What I will tell you of my own family is true of nearly every family in Ireland today. On the 12th of last August my brother was arrested. He was arrested at seven o'clock, but the five o'clock post brought to our house a letter addressed to 'The Lord Mayor MacSwiney, or Miss Mary MacSwiney', and I opened it, to find an anonymous letter written by someone professing to be a friend of the Irish Republic and calling on my brother to get a certain policeman, named Quinn of Kilkenny, killed; his name and address were given in full, and the names of the Volunteers, the Irish Volunteers, whom he was said to have got imprisoned. He was denounced as a spy, and my brother was called upon to have him shot. I knew where that letter came from—I had seen similar communications; it had come from an English agent in our country, from the English authorities themselves. When our people go to condemn spies, they do not go that way about it. I put the letter in the fire. My brother was arrested at seven o'clock; they searched the City Hall for incriminating documents until ten; they came to my house at half past eleven, and they spent three hours looking for that letter. My friends, it is no laughing matter. If they had found that letter, my brother would have been tried on charge of shooting that policeman, and that policeman would have been shot by British agents in time. I am not inventing for you, I am telling you things that I know personally. I have known of documents like that coming to house after house. I know a young friend of my own, a young man of the city of Cork, whose house was visited by the military last September. He was taken down, by an officer and three soldiers, to his bathroom to be searched, and while he was gone others of the party of military placed ammunition in the drawer of his bedroom, and when the officers brought him back into the bedroom another of the soldiers opened the drawer and found the ammunition, and on that find that boy is serving three years' penal servitude.

JOHN MACSWINEY

Three weeks ago I got a cablegram from home telling me that my youngest brother had been arrested, with ten of his comrades; that they were charged with having arms and ammunition, and that the charge was absolutely false, because they had no arms and ammunition when they were arrested, and that the death penalty was involved. For England has made it a crime, punishable by death, to carry a revolver in defence of freedom. A fortnight before that she had sentenced to death a young Corkman, named Cornelius Murphy. She had tried him on the charge of having a revolver. The death penalty was involved, but no one believed that England would be so barbarous, so false, would so break all the laws of civilized warfare as to shoot a Republican soldier for carrying a revolver. They expected him to get a certain term of imprisonment. And a fortnight later his mother and his sisters, taking up the morning paper read this: 'Cornelius Murphy was tried by court martial on February 8th, was charged with having a revolver, was sentenced to death, and the sentence was carried out this morning at eight o'clock'. And his mother and his sisters read it from the paper for the first time. I knew that, and I knew that the death penalty was involved, and I spoke of it from every platform where I lectured. I sent it to the papers of America, and I waited for the result. There were eleven arrested—six of the eleven have been shot. My brother and his comrades have been sentenced to fifteen years' penal servitude—and if I were not in America today they would probably have been shot too. Now, it is against all laws of warfare to shoot soldiers for carrying arms, but they were not carrying arms. I do not say they did not carry them, for my youngest brother left this country last June to go and join the Irish Republican army. He is a soldier of the Irish Republic, and I should be very much ashamed of him if he were not. But the point is this: those men had no arms on them when they were arrested; the arms were taken and placed on them after their arrest, and they were taken from their beds in the house where they were hiding, without being allowed to put on any clothes, and they were taken, bound hand and foot, in open lorries through the worst downpour of rain that fell for the whole winter. This is the sort of warfare that England is carrying on in our country, and that you are paying for.

SHOOTING UNBORN CHILDREN

England is not satisfied with murdering men. She has murdered many women, too. Two of the women she has murdered, that she has shot down at their own doorsteps—Mrs Quinn, of County Galway, and Mrs Ryan, of Tipperary—carried with them into eternity the young lives that they were going to bring into the world within a few weeks. They have shot down children too. One little girl walking down the street was shot as the result of a bet between the Black and Tans as to which of them could shoot straightest; and two little children standing at their own door in Cork, on the first Saturday that the English government declared the curfew for five oíclock in the afternoon—standing at their own door, as the clock struck five—were shot dead. That has not reached the American papers. Nor has it reached the American papers that young girls in Ireland are asking if it is a sin to carry poison with them to take it to save themselves from worse than death. You will not get particulars of the stories that make the Irish girls ask such questions, for they will not give their names or give their details—but crimes are being committed in Ireland today, by your friend and ally, and with the help of your money, such as you never heard of Germany committing in Belgium. I do not want to stir up hatred between you and any nation with which you wish to make friends. Stretch your hands across the sea in friendship, but see to it that the clean, freedom-loving hand of the American nation is not held out to any hand which is dripping with the blood of Irish women and children. And if the Anglo-Saxon nations are to make friends—though if we came to make an analysis I doubt if the Anglo-Saxon portion of you would be fifty per cent—but if the Anglo-Saxon, English-speaking peoples are to clasp hands across the sea, one of two things must happen: Either the American people must be false to their own traditions of freedom and democracy, or they must say to England, 'We shall join hands with you on the day that you do justice, and let Ireland free'.

PRACTICAL HELP

I want to give you a practical programme before I leave. I have told you I do not want you to go to war. How, then, are you to help in the recognition? You have a government here which is the government of the people, for the people, by the people. Let that government of yours hear your voice. Write and wire to your senators and congressmen. Write a letter or a telegram every day of the week; send it on Monday to your President, on Tuesday to one of your senators, on Wednesday to another of your senators, on Thursday to your congressman, on Friday to your Secretary of State, on Saturday to your Foreign Relations Committee. Tell them all that you believe in the principles of the American Constitution, that you believe in the freedom of small nations for which America went to war, and that you demand of your government the recognition of the Irish Republic in fulfilment of the pledges which you made four years ago. Write that letter every day. Take a rest on Sunday, and begin all over again on Monday morning, and keep on writing it, keep on making your voice heard until we get recognition. We shall get it if you wish us to get it. If the people of America will make their voice heard at Congress, the government of this country will realize that they are there to do your will and not their own. Make your voice heard then; let them hear you loudly proclaiming that the people of America demand with united voices the freedom of the Irish Republic, its recognition by the United States—and they will realize that the voice of the people is the voice of God.

Notes

CHAPTER 1

1 Alan J. Ward, *The Easter Rising, Revolution and Irish Nationalism* (Illinois: Harlan Davidson, Inc., 1980), p. 5; Lawrence J. McCaffrey, *Ireland from Colony to Nation State* (New Jersey: Prentice-Hall, Inc., 1979), p. 140.
2 McCaffrey, *Ireland*, pp. 5, 140; *The New York Times*, April 29 1916, p. 1; May 15 1916, p. 2; *San Francisco Chronicle*, April 30 1916, p. 1.
3 Dorothy Macardle, *The Irish Republic*, (Dublin: Wolfhound Press, Ltd, 1999), p. 200.
4 McCaffrey, *Ireland*, p. 141.
5 John O'Beirne Ranelagh, *A Short History of Ireland* (Cambridge: Cambridge University Press, 1983), p. 182; The Earl of Longford and Thomas P. O'Neill, *Eamon de Valera* (London: Hutchinson of London, 1970), p. 50; Jacqueline Van Voris, *Constance de Markievicz: In the Cause of Ireland* (Amherst: The University of Massachusetts Press, 1967), pp. 197, 210.
6 Van Voris, p. 201; McCaffrey, *Ireland*, p. 147.
7 Louise Ryan,'"Furies" and "Die-hards": Women and Irish Republicanism in the Early Twentieth Century', *Gender & History* 11 (No. 2, July 1999), pp. 260–61.
8 Margaret MacCurtain, 'Women, The Vote and Revolution', in *Women in Irish Society* ed. Margaret MacCurtain and Donncha O'Corrain (Connecticut: Greenwood Press, 1979), p. 52.
9 Brian Farrell, 'Markievicz and the Women of the Revolution', in *Leaders and Men of the Easter Rising: Dublin 1916*, ed. F. X. Martin (New York: Cornell University Press, 1967), p. 229.
10 Margaret Ward, *Unmanageable Revolutionaries, Women and Irish Nationalism* (London: Pluto Press, 1983), p. 69.
11 Ibid., p. 77.
12 Ibid., p. 51.
13 Ibid., p. 86.
14 Van Voris, p. 64; Leah Levenson and Jerry H. Natterstad, *Hanna Sheehy Skeffington: Irish Feminist* (New York: Syracuse University Press, 1986), p. 24.
15 Maria Luddy, *Women in Ireland, 1800–1918* (Cork: Cork University Press, 1995), pp. 273–74, 301, 320; Cliona Murphy, *The Women's Suffrage Movement and Irish Society in the Early Twentieth Century* (Philadelphia: Temple University Press, 1989), p. 7.
16 Margaret Ward, *Unmanageable Revolutionaries*, pp. 72–3.
17 Van Voris, pp. 59, 67, 70.
18 Ibid., p. 71.
19 Ibid., p. 145; Anne Marreco, *The Rebel Countess: The Life and Times of Constance Markievicz* (Philadelphia and New York: Chilton Books, 1967), pp. 114–15.
20 Marreco, p. 113.
21 Van Voris, p. 66; MacCurtain, p. 53.

22 Alan J. Ward, *The Easter Rising*, p. 100; Robert Kee, *The Green Flag, Volume Two: The Bold Fenian Men* (London: Penguin Books, 1972), p. 199; Margaret Ward, *Unmanageable Revolutionaries*, p. 99.
23 M. O. O'Dubhghaill, comp., *Insurrection Fires at Eastertide: A Golden Jubilee Anthology of the Easter Rising* (Cork: The Mercier Press, 1966), pp. 101–2.
24 Anne Haverty, *Constance Markievicz: An Independent Life* (London: Pandora Press, 1988), p. 121.
25 Ruth Taillon, *When History Was Made: The Women of 1916* (Belfast: Beyond the Pale Publications, 1996), pp. 18, 23.
26 Elizabeth Coxhead, *Daughters of Erin* (Gerrards Cross: Colin Smythe Limited, 1979), p. 93.
27 Ruth Taillon, p. 5.
28 Van Voris, p. 148.
29 Ibid., pp. 148–49.
30 Ibid., p. 149; Henry Boylan, *A Dictionary of Irish Biography* (New York: St Martin's Press, 1988), p. 65.
31 Marreco, p. 182; Van Voris, p. 149.
32 Margaret Ward, *Unmanageable Revolutionaries*, p. 113.
33 Coxhead, p. 92; Farrell, p. 234.
34 Margaret Ward, *Unmanageable Revolutionaries*, p. 113.
35 Lil Conlon, *Cumann na mBan and the Women of Ireland, 1913–25* (Kilkenny: Kilkenny People Ltd, 1969), p. 8.
36 Margaret Ward, *Unmanageable Revolutionaries*, p. 93.
37 Ibid., pp. 92–5; Charlotte H. Fallon, *Soul of Fire: A Biography of Mary MacSwiney* (Cork and Dublin: The Mercier Press, 1986), p. 22.
38 Quoted in Amanda Sebestyen, 'Introduction', in *Prison Letters of Countess Markievicz* (London: Virago Press Limited, 1987), p. xviii.
39 Van Voris, p. 157.
40 MacCurtain, p. 52; Margaret Ward, *Unmanageable Revolutionaries*, p. 103; Fallon, *Soul of Fire*, p. 25; Luddy, *Women in Ireland*, p. 307.
41 MacCurtain, pp. 54–5.
42 Ibid., pp. 52–3.
43 Ryan, p. 257.
44 MacCurtain, p. 111; Luddy, *Women in Ireland*, p. 309.
45 Ryan, p. 257.
46 Luddy, p. 110.
47 Sinead McCoole, *Women Revolutionaries and Kilmainham Gaol: Guns & Chiffon, 1916–1923* (Dublin: Published by the Stationery Office, 1997), p. 18.
48 Van Voris, p. 173.
49 Constance Markievicz, 'Some Women in Easter Week', in *Prison Letters of Countess Markievicz* (London: Virago Press Limited, 1987), pp. 37–9.
50 O'Dubhghaill, pp. 253–54.
51 *The New York Times*, April 29 1916, p. 1.
52 Markievicz, p. 38.
53 Charles Duff, *Six Days to Shake an Empire* (New York: A. S. Barnes and Co., Inc., 1966), p. 130.
54 Haverty, p. 149, Taillon, p. 67; Marreco, pp. 203–4.
55 Marreco, pp. 203–4; Haverty, p. 149.
56 Max Caulfield, *The Easter Rebellion* (New York: Holt, Rinehart and Winston, 1963), pp. 87–8.
57 Ibid., p. 358; Marreco, p. 207.
58 Marreco, p. 162.
59 Ibid., p. 205; Haverty, p. 154.

60 Margaret Ward, *Unmanageable Revolutionaries*, p. 112; Van Voris, p. 184.
61 Conlon, p. 25.
62 Markievicz, p. 39; Conlon, p. 22–5; Margaret Ward, Unmanageable Revolutionaries, pp. 114–15; Caulfield, pp. 158–59.
63 Duff, pp. 173–76; Conlon, p. 25.
64 Leah Levenson and Natterstad, pp. 77–80.
65 Margaret Ward, *Hanna Sheehy Skeffington: A Life* (Cork: Attic Press, 1997), p. 155.
66 Ibid., pp. 154–55; Taillan, p. 68.
67 Coxhead, pp. 58–9.
68 Samuel Levenson, *Maud Gonne* (New York: Reader's Digest Press, 1976), p. 296.
69 Coxhead, pp. 64–5.
70 Fallon, *Soul of Fire*, pp. 30–1; Taillon, p. 30.
71 Ryan, p. 260.
72 Farrell, p. 235.
73 Margaret Ward, *Unmanageable Revolutionaries*, pp. 119–20; Kathleen Clarke, ed. Helen Litton, *Revolutionary Woman, Kathleen Clarke, 1878–1972: An Autobiography* (Dublin: The O'Brien Press, Ltd, 1991), p. 121.
74 Ibid., pp. 126, 136.
75 Kathleen Clark, p. 126.
76 Ibid., pp. 136–37.
77 Margaret Ward, *Unmanageable Revolutionaries*, pp. 119–22.
78 Ibid., p. 120.
79 Oswald Garrison Villard, editor of *The Nation*, formed the Committee of One Hundred to investigate charges of atrocities in Ireland. The committee then led to the formation of the American Commission on Conditions in Ireland, made up of eight members and referred to as the Villard Commission.
80 John A. Murphy, *Ireland in the Twentieth Century* (Dublin: Gill and Macmillan, 1975), p. 7; MacCurtain, p. 55.
81 Farrell, p. 236.
82 McCoole, p. 15.
83 Margaret Ward, *In Their Own Voice: Women and Irish Nationalism* (Dublin: Attic Press, 1995), p. 68.
84 Beth McKillen, 'Irish Feminism and Nationalist Separatism, 1914–23', *Éire-Ireland* 17 (No. 4, 1982), p. 72; Luddy, *Women in Ireland*, pp. 239–44.
85 Macardle, p. 265.
86 Ibid., p. 256.
87 Ibid., p. 290.
88 John A. Murphy, pp. 13–15.
89 Robert Kee, *The Green Flag, Volume III: Ourselves Alone* (London: Penguin Books, 1972), pp. 86–7.
90 Ibid., 18.
91 J. J. Lee, *Ireland, 1912–1985, Politics and Society* (Cambridge: Cambridge University Press, 1989), p. 43.
92 Ryan, pp. 262–63.
93 Ibid.
94 Ibid.; Margaret Ward, *Unmanageable Revolutionaries*, p. 144.
95 Margaret Ward, *Unmanageable Revolutionaries*, p. 158; Ryan, p. 263.
96 Margaret Ward, *Unmanageable Revolutionaries*, p. 148.
97 Ibid., pp. 171–73.
98 Ibid., pp. 183, 189–90
99 Ryan, pp. 263, 267–68.

100 Margaret Ward, *Unmanageable Revolutionaries*, p. 190.
101 Quoted in Ryan, p. 267.
102 Ibid., pp. 265, 267–70.
103 Ibid., p. 270.

CHAPTER 2

1 Lawrence J. McCaffrey, *The Irish Diaspora in America* (Bloomington: Indiana University Press, 1976), pp. 107, 109.
2 Alan J. Ward, *Easter Rising, Revolution and Irish Nationalism* (Illinois: Harlan Davidson, Inc., 1980), pp. 64, 66.
3 Donald Harman Akenson, *The United States and Ireland* (Cambridge, Massachusetts: Harvard University Press, 1973), pp. 39–40.
4 Ibid., p. 41.
5 Ibid., pp. 54, 72; Charles Callan Tansill, *America and the Fight for Irish Freedom: 1866–1922* (New York: The Devin-Adair Co., 1957), pp. 120–21; Lawrence J. McCaffrey, *Ireland from Colony to Nation State* (New Jersey: Prentice-Hall, Inc., 1979), p. 124; Lawrence J. McCaffrey, *The Irish Diaspora in America* (Bloomington: Indiana University Press, 1976), p. 130; Henry Boylan, *A Dictionary of Irish Biography* (New York: St Martin's Press, 1988), p. 93.
6 Carl Wittke, *The Irish in America* (Baton Rouge: Louisiana State University Press, 1956), p. 164.
7 Sean Cronin, *The McGarrity Papers: Revelations of the Irish Revolutionary Movement in Ireland and America, 1900–1940* (Tralee: Anvil Books, Ltd, 1971), p. 28.
8 Boylan, p. 60; Alan J. Ward, *Easter Rising*, p. 54; Sean Cronin, *The McGarrity Papers*, p. 30.
9 Alan J. Ward, *Easter Rising*, p. 54; McCaffrey, *Ireland*, p. 124.
10 Tansill, p. 189.
11 Alan J. Ward, *Easter Rising*, p. 128.
12 Tansill, p. 220.
13 Ibid.; McCaffrey, *Irish Diaspora*, p. 135.
14 McCaffrey, *Irish Diaspora*, p. 135.
15 Ibid., p. 136.
16 Francis M. Carroll, 'Irish Progressive League', in *Irish American Voluntary Organizations*, ed. Michael F. Funchion (Westport, Connecticut: Greenwood Press, 1983), pp. 206–8.
17 Terry Golway, *Irish Rebel: John Devoy and America's Fight for Ireland's Freedom* (New York: St Martin's Press, 1998), p. 249.
18 McCaffrey, *Ireland*, p. 144; Jacqueline Van Voris, *Constance de Markievicz in the Cause of Ireland* (Amherst: The University of Massachusetts Press, 1967), p. 256.
19 Timothy J. Sarbaugh, 'Culture, Militancy and de Valera: Irish-American Republican Nationalism in California, 1900–1936', (San Jose State University: MA thesis, 1980), p. 168.
20 Alan J. Ward, *Easter Rising*, pp. 125–6; McCaffrey, Ireland, p. 146.
21 Ibid., p. 340; John A. Murphy, *Ireland in the Twentieth Century* (Dublin: Gill and Macmillan, 1975), pp. 15–16.
22 McCaffrey, *Irish Diaspora*, p. 137.
23 Sean Cronin, *The McGarrity Papers*, pp. 17, 74.

24 Tansill, p. 345.
25 Ibid., p. 346–7.
26 Alan J. Ward, *Easter Rising*, p. 128.
27 Terry Golway, p. 263.
28 Tim Pat Coogan, *Michael Collins: the Man Who Made Ireland* (Boulder, Colorado: Roberts Rinehart Publishers, 1992), p. 106.
29 'Blue Sky' laws in this case are intended to prevent fraud in the sale of stocks and bonds.
30 Tansill, pp. 348–9, 352.
31 Eamon de Valera to Frank P. Walsh, September 28 1919, Cohalan Collection, Box 4, File 2, AIHS, New York.
32 Eamon de Valera to Trustees, FOIF, September 12 1919, Cohalan Collection, Box 4, File 1, AIHS, New York.
33 Tansill, pp. 350–2.
34 Memorandum to FOIF, n/d, Dáil Éireann Papers, DE 2/265, National Archives, Dublin.
35 Unsigned letter from Dáil Éireann Department of Foreign Affairs to Michael Collins, 19/5/22, Dáil Éireann Papers, DE 2/265, National Archives, Dublin.
36 G. Mac anBhaird to S. M. O'Mara, 6-1-22, Dáil Éireann Papers, DE 2/265, National Archives, Dublin.
37 Quoted in Jim Maher, *Harry Boland: A Biography* (Boulder, Colorado: Mercier Press, 1998), pp. 83, 166.
38 Dorothy Macardle, *The Irish Republic* (Dublin: Wolfhound Press Ltd, 1999), pp. 986–7.
39 De Valera's Speech, Worcester, MA, 6-2-20, 'The Moral Basis of the Claim of the Elected Government of the Republic of Ireland for Official Recognition', Dáil Éireann Papers, DE 2/239, National Archives, Dublin.
40 De Valera to American Commission on Irish Independence, New York, 6-2-20, Dáil Éireann Papers, DE 2/239, National Archives, Dublin.
41 'De Valera Corrects Summary of Interview', Dáil Éireann Papers, DE 2/239, National Archives, Dublin.
42 The Platt Amendment to the Army Appropriations Bill of 1901 specified conditions under which the US government could intervene in the internal affairs of Cuba.
43 'An Unwise Proposition by John Devoy', Dáil Éireann Papers, DE 2/239, National Archives, Dublin.
44 Arthur Mitchell and Padraig Ó Snodaigh, *Irish Political Documents, 1916–1949* (Dublin: Irish Academic Press, 1985), pp. 69–70.
45 Eamon de Valera, Washington, DC, to Hon. Daniel F. Cohalan, New York City, February 20 1920, Cohalan Collection, Box 4, File 1, AIHS, New York.
46 Daniel F. Cohalan, New York City, to Hon. Eamon de Valera, Washington DC, Cohalan Collection, Box 4: File 1, AIHS, New York.
47 Tansill, pp. 373–4.
48 Quoted in Tansill, pp. 374–5.
49 Ibid., pp. 377–8.
50 Ibid., pp. 381–2.
51 Sarbaugh, 'Culture, Militancy and de Valera', p. 87; Tansill, p. 112.
52 Sean Cronin, *Washington's Irish Policy, 1916–1986: Independence, Partition, Neutrality* (Dublin: Anvil Books, 1986) p. 26.
53 *The New York Times*, December 1 1920, p. 10.
54 Michael Kazin, *Barons of Labour: The San Francisco Building Trades and Union Power in the Progressive Era* (Urbana and Chicago: University of Illinois Press, 1989), Centre Section. Walton Bean, *Boss Ruef's San Francisco:*

The Story of The Union Labor Party, Big Business and The Graft Prosecution (Berkeley, Los Angeles, London: University of California Press, 1952), pp. 15, 17. During the 'great' teamsters' and waterfront strike in San Francisco in 1901, Father Peter Yorke became a 'spiritual leader' of the strikers. He urged them to be 'peaceable and temperate', while he charged city authorities with aiding employers.

55 Sarbaugh, 'Culture, Militancy and de Valera', pp. 4, 14.

56 Ibid.

57 Ibid., p. 4; Timothy Sarbaugh, 'Exiles of Confidence: The Irish-American Community of San Francisco, 1880 to 1920', in *From Paddy to Studs: Irish-American Communities in the Turn of the Century Era, 1880 to 1920*, ed. Timothy J. Meagher (New York: Greenwood Press, 1986), p. 168.

58 *The Gaelic American*, April 21 1917, p. 1.

59 Ibid.

60 Sarbaugh, 'Culture, Militancy and de Valera', pp. 4–5.

61 Ibid., pp. 5, 89, 91.

62 Ibid., p. 105; *The Monitor*, January 2 1922, p. 7; January 22 1922, p. 7.

63 Non-catalogued Miscellaneous Irish Box, Donohue Rare Book Collection, Richard A. Gleeson Library, University of San Francisco, San Francisco.

64 R. A. Burchell, *The San Francisco Irish, 1848–1880* (Berkeley and Los Angeles: University of California Press, 1980), p. 102.

65 *The Monitor*, July 12 1919, p. 1; July 19 1919, p. 1.

66 *The Leader*, May 31 1919, p. 5.

67 Ibid.; Burchell, p. 101.

68 *The Leader*, January 6 1917, p. 6.

69 Ibid., February 21 1920, p. 1; Sarbaugh, 'Culture, Militancy and de Valera', pp. 54, 68–9.

70 *The Leader*, March 20 1920, p. 7.

71 Ibid., February 21 1920, p. 1.

72 Ibid., February 28 1920, p. 1.

73 Michael Kazin, p. 247. 'Unlike previous San Francisco ventures in radical journalism, this weekly newspaper which proclaimed itself "100 per cent for the working class" was actually sponsored and financed by local unions. . . . During its first year, the paper added sponsoring groups with almost every issue until the editorial page listed, among the owners, over sixty locals and a score of single-issue, leftist clubs such as the Union of Russian Toilers and the Women's Irish Educational League'.

74 *The Monitor*, September 13 1919, p. 7; October 24 1919, p. 3; November 1 1919, p. 7.

75 *The Monitor*, August 9 1919, p. 7; November 5 1921, p. 7; *The Irish World*, June 3 1922, p. 10.

76 Lisa Rubens, 'The Patrician Radical, Charlotte Anita Whitney', *California History*, September 1986, pp. 158, 163. Charlotte Anita Whitney does not appear to have an Irish background. She was a socialist, organizer of the I.W.W. and a communist who believed in 'freedom of opinion and freedom of speech'. She was convicted and imprisoned in 1920 under the 1919 California criminal syndicalist law.

77 Ibid. May 31 1919, 7; July 12 1919, 3; *San Francisco Chronicle*, May 23 1919, p. 2.

78 *The Monitor*, June 14 1919, p. 7.

79 *San Francisco Chronicle*, June 10 1919, p. 7.

80 *The Monitor*, June 14 1919, p. 7; July 12 1919, p. 1; July 19 1919, p. 5.

81 Ibid. September 13 1919, p. 7.

82 Ibid. September 11 1920, p. 5.
83 Non-catalogued Miscellaneous Irish Box, Donohue Rare Book Collection.
84 *The Monitor*, January 21 1922, p. 7.
85 *The Irish World*, February 5 1921, p. 3.
86 John A. Murphy, p. 17.
87 John A. Murphy, pp. 35, 39, 41–2, 47; The Earl of Longford and Thomas P. O'Neill, *Eamon de Valera, a Biography* (Boston: Houghton Mifflin Company, 1971), p. 171; Tony Gray, *The Irish Answer* (Boston: Little, Brown and Company, 1966), pp. 86–7.
88 John A. Murphy, p. 39; McCaffrey, *Ireland*, p. 149; J. J. Lee, *Ireland, 1912–1985 Politics and Society* (Cambridge: Cambridge University Press, 1989), p. 51.
89 John A. Murphy, p. 39.
90 Ibid. pp. 54, 58–9.
91 Edward F. Gray to HMS Principal Secretary of State for Foreign Affairs, July 20 1923, Taoiseach Papers, S1976, File 463, National Archives, Dublin.
92 Michael F. Funchion, ed. *Irish American Voluntary Organizations* (Westport, Connecticut: Greenwood Press, 1983), pp. 59–60.
93 Edward F. Gray to HMS Principal Secretary of State for Foreign Affairs, July 26 1923, Taoiseach Papers, S1976, file 489, National Archives, Dublin.
94 P. T. O'Sullivan to Judge Daniel F. Cohalan, January 15 1923, Cohalan Collection, Box 1, File 17, AIHS, New York.
95 *The Irish World*, February 4 1922, p. 4.
96 Ibid., February 11 1922, p. 4.
97 Sarbaugh, 'Culture, Militancy and de Valera', pp. 113, 116–18.
98 *The Monitor*, July 28 1923, p. 5; *The Leader*, September 22 1923, p. 1; October 6 1923, p. 1.
99 Alan J. Ward, *Ireland and Anglo-American Relations, 1899–1921* (Toronto: University of Toronto Press, 1969), p. 267.
100 Sarbaugh, 'Culture, Militancy and de Valera', p. 6.
101 Ibid., p. 133.

CHAPTER 3

1 Sean Cronin, *The McGarrity Paper: Revelations of the Irish Revolutionary Movement in Ireland and America, 1900–1940* (Tralee: Anvil Books, Ltd, 1972), p. 63.
2 Michael F. Funchion, ed., *Irish American Voluntary Organizations* (Westport, Connecticut: Greenwood Press, 1983), pp. 121, 187.
3 Charles Callan Tansill, *America and the Fight for Irish Freedom: 1866–1922* (New York: The Devin-Adair Co., 1957), p. 251.
4 Sean Cronin, p. 64; Tansill, p. 193.
5 Tansill, pp. 173–5; 181; 187–8; 204.
6 Sean Cronin, p. 64; Michael F. Doyle to Tumulty, April 29 1916; Tumulty to President Wilson, May 1 1916; President Wilson to Tumulty, May 1 1916, Casement File, Wilson Papers, Library of Congress in Tansill pp. 205, 211.
7 Tansill, p. 213.
8 Robert A. Divine, T. H. Breen, George M. Fredrickson, R. Hall Williams, eds, *America, Past and Present* (United States of America: Scott, Foresman and Company, 1984), pp. 663-65, 731.
9 Investigative FBI Case Files, 1908–1922, Reel 936, A65, M-1085, National

Archives, Washington D.C.

10 Margaret Ward, *Hanna Sheehy Skeffington, A Life* (Cork: Attic Press, 1997), p. 197.

11 Hanna Sheehy Skeffington, *Impressions of Sinn Féin in America* (Dublin: O'Laughlin, Murphy and Boland, Ltd, n/d), p. 23.

12 Ibid., p. 29.

13 *The Washington Post*, January 23 1918, p. 5.

14 Ibid.; As defined in Barbara A. Barnes, Mack C. Shelley, II, Steffen W. Schmidt, *American Government and Politics Today*, (St Paul: West Publishing Company, 1986), p. 100: The Espionage Act, passed in June 1917, prohibited all activities that obstructed the war effort. Two provisions limited free speech. One made it a crime to send through the mail any material violating the act by 'advocating or urging treason, insurrection, or forcible resistance to any law of the United States'. The second made it a crime to utter false statements with the intent to interfere with American military forces or to cause insubordination, disloyalty, mutiny, or refusal of duty 'among American military personnel'.

15 Tansill, p. 300.

16 F. M. Carroll, ed., *The American Commission on Irish Independence, 1919: the Diary, Correspondence and Report*, (Dublin: Mount Salus Press Ltd, 1985) p. 5.

17 Ibid.

18 Tansill, p. 301.

19 Tim Pat Coogan, *Michael Collins: The Man Who Made Ireland*, (Boulder, Colorado: Roberts Rinehart; T Publishers, 1992), pp. 109–10; Tansill, p. 303.

20 Tim Pat Coogan, pp. 109–10.

21 F. M. Carroll, *American Commission*, p. 6.

22 Tim Pat Coogan, pp. 109–10.

23 F. M. Carroll, *American Commission*, pp. vi, 3–4, 8–9.

24 Ibid., pp. 11–20; *The Monitor*, May 31 1919, p. 7.

25 Tansill, p. 306.

26 Tim Pat Coogan, p. 110.

27 Ibid.

28 F. M. Carroll, *American Commission*, p. 12.

29 Ibid.

30 Ambassador John W. Davis to the Secretary of State, May 28 1919, 841d.00/57. MS, National Archives, in Tansill, p. 314.

31 Tansill, p. 319.

32 Ibid., p. 320.

33 *Illinois State Journal*, January 5 1921, p. 1.

34 Tansill, p. 410.

35 Ibid.

36 Norman H. Davis to Secretary W. B. Wilson, January 11 1921, Wilson MS, Library of Congress, in Tansill, p. 411.

37 *Buffalo Courier*, January 12 1921, p. 1; *Illinois State Journal*, January 13 1921, p. 1.

38 *Illinois State Journal*, January 16 1921, p. 1.

39 Secretary W. B. Wilson to Norman H. Davis, Acting Secretary of State, January 17 1921, Wilson MS, Library of Congress, in Tansill, pp. 411–12.

40 *The Pittsburg Press*, January 19 1921, p. 1.

41 *The Lexington Herald*, January 20 1921, p. 1.

42 *The Commercial Appeal*, January 30 1921, p. 2.

43 Ibid., January 11 1921, p. 1; Tansill, p. 411.

CHAPTER 4

1 Margaret Ward, *Unmanageable Revolutionaries: Women and Irish Nationalism* (London: Pluto Press, 1983), p. 120.
2 Leah Levenson, *With Wooden Sword: A Portrait of Francis Sheehy-Skeffington, Militant Pacifist* (Boston: Northeastern University Press, 1983), Title Page.
3 *The Gaelic American*, December 8, 1917, p. 8.
4 Cliona Murphy, *The Women's Suffrage Movement and Irish Society in the Early Twentieth Century* (Philadelphia: Temple University Press, 1989), p. 80.
5 Hanna Sheehy Skeffington, *Impressions of Sinn Féin in America* (Dublin: O'Loughlin, Murphy and Boland, Ltd, n/d), p. 13.
6 Margaret Ward, *Hanna Sheehy Skeffington: A Life* (Cork: Attic Press, 1997), p. 191.
7 Ibid.
8 Ibid.
9 Ibid., 91; Leah Levenson and Jerry H. Natterstad, *Hanna Sheehy-Skeffington: Irish Feminist* (New York: Syracuse University Press, 1986), pp. 2–3.
10 Leah Levenson and Natterstad, pp. 6–9.
11 Ibid., pp. 7, 24.
12 Leah Levenson, p. 79.
13 Leah Levenson and Natterstad, pp. 37–8, 45; Margaret MacCurtain, 'Women, The Vote and Revolution'. In *Women in Irish Society*, ed. Margaret MacCurtain and Donncha Ó'Corráin, 46–57 (Connecticut: Greenwood Press, 1979), p. 50.
14 Leah Levenson and Natterstad, p. 57.
15 Margaret Ward, 'Nationalism, Pacifism, Internationalism: Louie Bennett, Hanna Sheehy-Skeffington, and the Problems of "Defining Feminism"'. In *Gender and Sexuality in Modern Ireland*, ed. Anthony Bradley and Maryann Gialanella Valiulis (Amherst: University of Massachusetts Press, 1997, pp. 71–2.
16 Ibid., pp. 77–9.
17 Ibid., pp. 79–80.
18 Leah Levenson and Natterstad, pp. 231, 235.
19 Ibid., pp. 92, 94, 96.
20 Hanna Sheehy Skeffington, *Impressions*, p. 1.
21 Leah Levenson and Natterstad, pp. 101–2; Margaret Ward, *Hanna Sheehy Skeffington*, p. 187.
22 *The Gaelic American*, January 6 1917, p. 4.
23 Quoted in *The Gaelic American*, December 23 1916, p. 5.
24 Quoted in Margaret Ward, *Hanna Sheehy Skeffington*, p. 187.
25 Leah Levenson and Natterstad, p. 112.
26 *The Gaelic American*, July 28 1917, p. 3.
27 *The New York Evening Post*, November 17 1917, p. 3.
28 Maria Luddy, *Hanna Sheehy Skeffington* (Dundalk: Dundalgan Press, 1995), p. 27.
29 Margaret Ward, *Hanna Sheehy Skeffington*, pp. 147–8.
30 Ibid., p. 101; Margaret Ward, *Hanna Sheehy Skeffington*, p. 185.
31 *The Gaelic American*, December 23 1916, p. 5.
32 *The Monitor*, March 3 1917, p. 7.
33 Ibid., p. 9.
34 Hanna Sheehy Skeffington, *Impressions*, pp. 10–11.
35 Ibid., p. 10.

36 *The New York Times*, January 7 1917, p. 7; Margaret Ward, *Hanna Sheehy Skeffington*, p. 186.
37 *The New York Times*, January 7 1917, p. 4; *The Monitor*, January 20 1917, p. 1.
38 *The Monitor*, January 20 1917, p. 1.
39 *The Gaelic American*, December 23 1916, p. 5.
40 Margaret Ward, *Hanna Sheehy Skeffington*, pp. 189–90; Andrée Sheehy Skeffington, *Skeff: A Life of Owen Sheehy Skeffington, 1909–1970*, (Dublin: the Lilliput Press, 1991), p. 23.
41 Hanna Sheehy Skeffington, March 3 1917, p. 5; *The Monitor*, March 3 1917, p. 7.
42 *The Gaelic American*, January 20 1917, p. 8.
43 Ibid.
44 Ibid., February 3 1917, p. 2.
45 *The New Haven Evening Union*, January 29 1917, p. 3; *New Haven Evening Register*, January 29 1917, p. 10.
46 *The Torrington Register*, February 5 1917, p. 8.
47 *Waterbury Register*, February 5 1917, p. 1.
48 Ibid., February 17 1917, p. 3.
49 Ibid., February 5 1917, p. 1.
50 *Meridian Morning Record*, February 12 1917, p. 10.
51 *Fitchburg Daily Sentinel*, February 13 1917, pp. 1, 5.
52 Ibid.
53 *The New York Times*, February 14 1915, p. 5.
54 *The New Bedford Evening Standard*, February 16 1921, p. 7.
55 *Worcester Telegram*, February 17 1917, p. 16.
56 Hanna Sheehy Skeffington, *Impressions*, pp. 11, 12.
57 *The Lowell Sun*, February 19 1917, p. 1.
58 *Holyoke Telegram*, February 23 1917, p. 1.
59 *The Gaelic American*, March 3 1917, p. 3.
60 Hanna Sheehy Skeffington, *Impressions*, p. 12.
61 *The Gaelic American*, March 3 1917, p. 3.
62 Ibid.
63 *The Chicago Tribune*, February 27 1917, p. 5.
64 *The Gaelic American*, March 31 1917, p. 3.
65 *The Indianapolis News*, February 26 1917, p. 8.
66 *Buffalo Courier*, March 2 1917, p. 5; *Buffalo Evening News*, March 5 1917, p. 12.
67 *The Gaelic American*, March 31 1917, p. 2.
68 *Rochester Democrat and Chronicle*, March 27 1917, p. 19.
69 John Moore to Hanna Sheehy Skeffington, 28-3-17, Sheehy Skeffington Papers, Box C, File 15, National Library, Dublin.
70 *The Gaelic American*, April 14 1917, p. 8.
71 Hanna Sheehy Skeffington, *Impressions*, p. 19.
72 Leah Levenson and Natterstad, p. 104.
73 Elizabeth Gurley Flynn, *The Rebel Girl: An Autobiography, My First Life (1908–1926)*, (New York: International Publishers, 1994), p. 270.
74 *The Gaelic American*, April 28 1917, p. 7.
75 *The Milwaukee Journal*, April 13 1917, p. 13.
76 Ibid., March 3 1917, p. 3; *St Louis Globe Democrat*, April 16 1917, Part Two-Editorial, p. l.
77 *The Gaelic American*, March 3 1917, p. 3.
78 Ibid.
79 *The Monitor*, May 5 1917, p. 6.
80 *The Leader*, May 5 1917, p. 7

81 *Los Angeles Times*, April 30 1917, Part I, p. 4; *The Gaelic American*, June 23 1917, p. 2.
82 *The Seattle Times*, May 27 1917, p. 18; May 28 1917, p. 12; *Gaelic American*, June 9 1917, p. 8.
83 *The Oregon Daily Journal*, May 21 1917, p. 14.
84 Ibid., June 1 1917, p. 1; David M. Emmons, *The Butte Irish: Class and Ethnicity in an American Mining Town, 1875–1925* (Urbana and Chicago: University of Illinois Press, 1990), p. 363.
85 *The Butte Miner*, June 2 1917, p. 10.
86 Emmons, pp. 363–4.
87 Emmons, p. 363.
88 *The Butte Miner*, June 4 1917, p. 8.
89 Ibid., June 4 1917, p. 8.
90 Ibid., June 6 1917, Emmons, p. 364.
91 *The Butte Miner*, June 1 1917, p. 1; Emmons, pp. 363–4.
92 *The Gaelic American*, June 23 1917, p. 2.
93 Margaret Ward, *Hanna Sheehy Skeffington*, p. 195.
94 Andrée Sheehy Skeffington, p. 22.
95 *The Monitor*, June 23 1917, p. 1; *The Leader*, June 23 1917, p. 1.
96 *The Monitor*, January 20 1917, p. 1; June 23 1917, p. 1.
97 *San Francisco Chronicle*, June 15 1917, p. 4.
98 *The San Francisco Examiner*, June 13 1917, p. 8.
99 *The Gaelic American*, June 30 1917, p. 2.
100 Ibid.
101 Ibid.
102 *The Leader*, June 9 1917, p. 1.
103 *The Monitor*, June 30 1917, p. 7.
104 *San Francisco Chronicle*, June 26 1917, p. 3.
105 *The Monitor*, July 14 1917, p. 3.
106 *The Gaelic American*, March 31 1917, p. 2.
107 Cited in Margaret Ward, *Hanna Sheehy Skeffington*, p. 190.
108 *The Sacramento Bee*, July 20 1917, p. 2.
109 *Stockton Daily Evening Record*, July 24 1917, p. 4.
110 *The Monitor*, July 28 1917, p. 5.
111 *San Francisco Chronicle*, August 3 1917, p. 8.
112 Hanna Sheehy Skeffington, *Impressions*, p. 19.
113 Walter B. Dillon to Hanna Sheehy Skeffington, 13-8-17, Sheehy Skeffington Papers, Box C, File 10, National Library, Dublin.
114 William J. Moroney to Hanna Sheehy Skeffington, 10-9-17, Sheehy Skeffington Papers, Box C, File 10, National Library, Dublin.
115 Leah Levenson and Natterstad, pp. 104–5.
116 Margaret Ward, *Hanna Sheehy Skeffington*, p. 195.
117 John Neland to Hanna Sheehy Skeffington, 15/10/17, Sheehy Skeffington Papers, Box C, File 12, National Library, Dublin; Rev Bernard Lee to Mr Greene, 17/10/17, Sheehy Skeffington Papers, Box C, File 12, National Library, Dublin.
118 Michael Hogan to Hanna Sheehy Skeffington, 26-9-17, Sheehy Skeffington Papers, Box C, File 11, National Library, Dublin.
119 Redmond Brennan to Hanna Sheehy Skeffington, 27-9-17, Sheehy Skeffington Papers, Box C, File 11, National Library, Dublin.
120 Catherine O'Gallagher to Hanna Sheehy Skeffington, 9/17, Sheehy Skeffington Papers, Box C, File 11, National Library, Dublin.
121 Mrs Robert Griger to Hanna Sheehy Skeffington, 9/17, Sheehy Skeffington

Papers, Box C, File 10, National Library, Dublin.
122 Edgar Steinem to Hanna Sheehy Skeffington, 30-9-17, Sheehy Skeffington Papers, Box C, File 11, National Library, Dublin.
123 Joseph McGarrity to Hanna Sheehy Skeffington, 14/12/17, Sheehy Skeffington Papers, Box C, File 14, National Library, Dublin.
124 Michael F. Funchion, ed., *Irish-American Voluntary Organizations* (Westport, Connecticut: Greenwood Press, 1983), pp. 206–7.
125 Ibid.
126 Margaret Ward, Hanna Sheehy Skeffington, p. 199.
127 Ibid., p. 198.
128 Ibid., pp. 198–200.
129 Report of Seamus O'Sheel on Visit of Hanna Sheehy Skeffington to Washington, D.C., John Devoy Papers, MS 18107, National Library, Dublin.
130 Report of Seamus O'Sheel on Visit of Hanna Sheehy Skeffington, John Devoy Papers, MS 18107, National Archives, Dublin.
131 Margaret Ward, *Hanna Sheehy Skeffington*, p. 199.
132 Margaret Ward, *In Their Own Voice: Women and Irish Nationalism* (Dublin: Attic Press, 1995), p. 87.
133 Ibid., p. 201; Leah Levenson and Natterstad, p. 106; *Margaret Ward: In Their Own Voice*, p. 87.
134 Leah Levenson and Natterstad, p. 106; Lil Conlon, *Cumann na mBan and the Women of Ireland, 1913–25* (Kilkenny: Kilkenny People Ltd, 1969), p. 58.
135 Margaret Ward, *Unmanageable Revolutionaries*, p. 121.
136 Margaret Ward, *In Their Own Words*, pp. 87–8.
137 *The Monitor*, February 16 1918, p. 7.
138 Ibid., January 26 1918, p. 7.
139 Charles Callan Tansill, *America and the Fight for Irish Freedom: 1866–1922* (New York: The Devin-Adair Co., 1957), p. 241.
140 Margaret Ward, *In Their Own Voice*, p. 88.
141 *The Springfield Daily Republican*, January 27 1918, p. 4.
142 Quoted in Margaret Ward, *Hanna Sheehy Skeffington*, p. 202.
143 *The Gaelic American*, February 16 1918, p. 1.
144 *The Minneapolis Tribune*, May 3 1918, p. 4.
145 *The Capitol Times*, March 5 1918, p. 3.
146 Ibid.
147 Estolv Ethan Ward, *The Gentle Dynamiter: A Biography of Tom Mooney* (Palo Alto, California: Ramparts Press, 1983, pp. 14–19.
148 Hanna Sheehy Skeffington, 'Nineteen Years Fight For Justice, Will They Free Mooney'?, written for *The Distributive Worker*, April 1936, Tom Mooney Papers, Manuscripts Division, C-B 410, Carton 17, University of California, Berkeley Bancroft Library.
149 Telegram from Declan Hurton to Hanna Sheehy Skeffington, April 4, 1918, Sheehy Skeffington Papers, Box C, File 17, National Library, Dublin.
150 Poster, Alice Park Papers, Hoover Institution, Stanford, California.
151 Letter from E. D. Nolan to Hanna Sheehy Skeffington, April 17 1918, Sheehy Skeffington Papers, Box C, File 17, National Library, Dublin.
152 *The Leader*, April 20, 1918, p. 5.
153 Ibid.
154 *The Sacramento Bee*, April 23 1918, p. 1; April 24 1918, p. 11.
155 Ibid., April 24 1918, p. 11.
156 *The Gaelic American*, May 4 1918, p. 1.
157 *San Francisco Chronicle*, April 26 1918, p. 1; *The Monitor*, April 27 1918, p. 8.
158 *The Sacramento Bee*, April 25 1918, p. 6.

159 According to Charlotte Fallon, 'Civil War Hungerstrikes: Women and Men', *Éire-Ireland* 22 (No. 3, 1987): pp. 75–6, the hunger strike in ancient Ireland goes back to the Brehon Laws which allowed creditors to hunger strike at their debtors doors until repayment could be worked out. English and Irish suffragists renewed the tradition between 1911 and 1913 to acquire release from prison after arrest for militant activities. The hunger strike became a sanctioned tool by republican leadership during the Irish Civil War.
160 *San Francisco Chronicle*, April 25 1918, p. 1; April 26 1918, p. 1.
161 *The Sacramento Bee*, April 25 1918, p. 6.
162 *The Monitor*, April 27 1918, p. 8.
163 *San Francisco Chronicle*, April 25 1918, p. 1; April 26 1918, p. 1; *The Monitor*, April 27 1918, p. 8.
164 *The Sacramento Bee*, April 25 1918, p. 6.
165 *San Francisco Chronicle*, April 26 1918, p. 1
166 Margaret Ward, *Hanna Sheehy Skeffington*, p. 206.
167 *San Francisco Chronicle*, April 19 1918, Second Section, p. 9; April 26 1918, p. 1.
168 *The Gaelic American*, May 4 1918, p. 1.
169 *San Francisco Chronicle*, April 29 1918, p. 9; *The Monitor*, May 4 1918, p. 7.
170 *The Monitor*, May 4 1918, p. 7.
171 *The New York Times*, May 5 1918, p. 12.
172 Ibid.
173 Ibid.
174 *The Gaelic American*, May 11 1918, p. 8.
175 *The New York Times*, May 27 1918, p. 12.
176 A. G. Burleson to Secretary of State, June 1, 1918, Department of Justice File No. 50107, National Archives, Washington D.C.
177 Dr Keller to President Wilson, n/d, Department of Justice File No. 191319, National Archives, Washington, D.C.
178 Chief Bielaski to Attorney General, May 11 1918, Department of Justice File No. 191962, National Archives, Washington D.C.
179 *The New York Times*, May 21 1918, p. 4.
180 Ibid., May 20 1918, p. 3.
181 Ibid., May 27 1918, p. 14.
182 Francis G. Caffey to Mr Frederick M. Rogers, May 9, 1918, Department of Justice Files, 191962, National Archives, Washington D.C.
183 A. B. Bielaski, Memorandum For The Attorney General, May 11, 1918, Department of Justice Files, 191962, National Archives, Washington D.C.
184 *The Gaelic American*, July 13 1918, p. 1.
185 *The New York Times*, August 6 1918, p. 24; Leah Levenson and Natterstad, pp. 112–14.
186 Leah Levenson and Natterstad, pp. 36–8, 42.
187 *The Monitor*, September 21 1918, p. 7.
188 Leah Levenson and Natterstad, p. 112.
189 *The Gaelic American*, March 3 1917, p. 5.
190 *The Leader*, September 7 1923, p. 4.
191 Quoted in Margaret Ward, *Hanna Sheehy Skeffington*, p. 212.
192 Leah Levenson and Natterstad, p. 121.
193 Ibid., p. 122.
194 *San Francisco Chronicle*, June 29 1921, p. 1.
195 Leah Levenson and Natterstad, p. 138.
196 Ibid., pp. 139–41.

CHAPTER 5

1 Donal O'Callaghan, 'The Devastation of Cork', in *The Need for Relief in Ireland* (New York City: American Committee for Relief in Ireland), Donohue Rare Book Collection, Richard A. Gleeson Library, University of San Francisco, San Francisco, California, Miscellaneous Irish Box.
2 *The Monitor*, October 9 1920, p. 1.
3 *The Leader*, November 20 1920, p. 2.
4 Ibid.
5 Charles Callan Tansill, *America and the fight for Irish Freedom: 1866–1922* (New York: the Devin-Adair Co., 1957), pp. 409–10.
6 *The Irish World*, February 19 1921, p. 6.
7 Ibid., February 26 1921, p. 6.
8 Quoted in Charlotte H. Fallon, *Soul of Fire* (Cork and Dublin: The Mercier Press, 1986), pp. 20, 30–3.
9 *The New York Times*, December 6 1920, p. 2.
10 John A. Murphy, *Ireland in the Twentieth Century* (Dublin: Gill and Macmillan, 1975), p. 17.
11 *The New York Times*, December 2 1920, p. 3; December 5 1920, p. 1.
12 Jacqueline Van Voris, *Constance de Markievicz: In the Cause of Ireland* (Amherst: The University of Massachusetts Press, 1967), p. 287; Tansill, pp. 406–10.
13 C. J. France to M. Collins TD, 23-3-22, Dáil Éireann Papers, DE 2/229, National Archives, Dublin; Tansill, pp. 409–10.
14 Carroll, F. M. 'All Standards of Human Conduct: The American Commission on Conditions in Ireland, 1920-21', *Éire-Ireland* 16 (No. 4, 1981): pp. 59–74.
15 *The Monitor*, October 9 1920, p. 1.
16 Propaganda Department Memorandum, n/d, Dáil Éireann Papers, DE 2/118, National Archives, Dublin.
17 Tansill, p. 409; Alan J. Ward, *The Easter Rising, Revolution and Irish Nationalism* (Illinois: Harlan Davidson, Inc., 1980), p. 131.
18 *The Gaelic American*, December 11 1920, p. 1; *The New York Times*, December 2 1920, p. 3; December 5 1920, p. 1; *The Boston Globe*, December 4, 1920, p. 1.
19 *The Gaelic American*, December 11 1920, p. 1.
20 *The Monitor*, December 4 1920, p. 7.
21 *The Leader*, December 11 1920, p. 1.
22 *The Irish World*, December 11 1920, p. 3.
23 *New York Tribune*, December 7 1920, p. 4.
24 *The Irish World*, December 11 1920, p. 6.
25 *The Gaelic American*, December 11 1920, p. 1; *New York Tribune*, December 6 1920, p. 4; *The Washington Post*, December 6 1920, p. 3.
26 *The Monitor*, December 11 1920, p. 7.
27 *The Washington Post*, December 12 1920, p. 3.
28 *The Leader*, November 20 1920, p. 2.
29 Ibid.
30 Carroll, 'All Standards of Human Conduct', p. 67.
31 *The Gaelic American*, December 18 1920, p. 1.
32 'The Background of the Irish Republic, Testimony given by Mary MacSwiney before the American Commission on Conditions in Ireland' (Chicago: Benjamin Franklin Bureau), Donohue Collection, University of San Francisco, Miscellaneous Irish Box.
33 Ibid.

34 Fallon, *Soul of Fire*, p. 59.
35 'The Background of The Irish Republic', Donohue Collection, University of San Francisco, Miscellaneous Irish Box.
36 Ibid., p. 89.
37 Ibid., p. 53.
38 *The Boston Globe*, December 8 1920, p. 10.
39 *The Irish Times*, December 10 1920, p. 5, National Archives, Dublin.
40 *The Gaelic American*, December 18 1920, p. 2.
41 'Mrs MacSwiney's Story' (Chicago: Benjamin Franklin Bureau), Mary MacSwiney Papers, P 48a/179, University College, Dublin Archives.
42 Ibid.
43 Ibid.
44 *The New York Times*, December 8 1920, p. 3; December 10 1920, p. 2.
45 In a letter to Florence O'Donoghue, 19/5/59, Muriel stated that after Terence got out of Lincoln Prison he told her that 'if he was arrested again he would try to escape (as De Valera had just done), and would not go on hunger strike'. He told her in Brixton after his last arrest, that 'he would not have started a hunger strike, but that when he was taken to the prison in Cork the prisoners were already a few days on hunger strike, he could have called it off but would not do that'. She added: 'However things being as they are I think he died at the right time, one could still be happy then on the whole about Éire. . . . You know I would not have married Terry if he had not had the principles we all know about Éire, and even then although I should have loved him I would not have married him either if he had had money. I am the same today'. Florence O'Donoghue Papers, Ms 31295, National Archives, Dublin.
46 Ibid., December 10 1920, p. 2.
47 Ibid.
48 *The Irish World*, December 25 1920, p. 6.
49 *The Irish Times*, December 11 1920, p. 5, National Archives, Dublin.
50 *The San Francisco Examiner*, December 14 1920, p. 1.
51 Quoted in Fallon, *Soul of Fire*, p. 61.
52 *The San Francisco Examiner*, December 14 1920, p. 1.
53 Ibid., p. 3.
54 Ibid.
55 Francis J. Costello, *Enduring the Most: The Life and Death of Terence MacSwiney* (Co. Kerry, Ireland: Brandon Book Publishers Ltd., 1995), p. 153.
56 Fallon, *Soul of Fire*, p. 63.
57 Ibid.
58 Ibid., p. 6.
59 *The Boston Globe*, December 20 1920, pp. 1, 8.
60 Ibid., December 20 1920, p. 8.
61 Ibid., December 21 1920, p. 10.
62 Ibid., p. 1.
63 Ibid., p. 1, 6.
64 Ibid., December 20 1920, p. 6.
65 Ibid., December 21 1921, p. 10.
66 Ibid.
67 *Irish World*, January 1, 1921, p. 3.
68 Ibid.
69 Ibid.
70 *The Gaelic American*, January 8 1921, p. 4.
71 *The Irish World*, January 8 1921, p. 1.
72 *The Gaelic American*, January 8 1921, p. 4.

73 *The Monitor*, January 8 1921, p. 7.
74 *The Gaelic American*, January 8 1921, p. 4.
75 *The American Commission on Conditions in Ireland: Interim Report* (London: Harding & Mare Ltd, 1921), Ir94109 P69, National Library, Dublin.
76 Michael F. Funchion, ed., *Irish American Voluntary Organizations* (Westport, Connecticut: Greenwood Press, 1983), pp. 14, 16–17.
77 Michael Wreszin, *Oswald Garrison Villard: Pacifist at War*, (Bloomington: Indiana University Press, 1965), p. 143.
78 Ibid.
79 Maria Luddy, *Hanna Sheehy Skeffington*, (Dundalk: Dundalgan Press, 1995), p. 32; Margaret Ward, *In Their Own Voice: Women and Irish Nationalism* (Dublin: Attic Press, 1995), p. 96.
80 Michael F. Funchion, ed., p. 17.
81 Muriel MacSwiney to Oswald Garrison Villard, 27-20-21, Oswald Garrison Villard Collection, bMsAm1323, Houghton Library, Harvard University, Cambridge, Massachusetts.

CHAPTER 6

1 *The Monitor*, January 1 1921, p. 6; February 23 1921, p. 2.
2 *The New York Times*, February 11 1921, p. 15.
3 *The Dallas Morning News*, February 12 1921, p. 2.
4 Mary's secretary and companion, Catherine Flanagan of Hartford, Connecticut, had been appointed by the AARIR.
5 *Akron Beacon Journal*, June 25 1921, p. 8.
6 Fallon, *Soul of Fire: A Biography of Mary MacSwiney* (Cork and Dublin: The Mercier Press, 1986), pp. 11–12, 14–15; *The Leader*, February 18 1921, p. 1; *The New York Times*, January 7 1921, p. 2.
7 Fallon, *Soul of Fire*, p. 15.
8 Quoted in Margaret Ward, *Unmanageable Revolutionaries: Women and Irish Nationalism* (London: Pluto Press, 1983), p. 71.
9 Quoted in Fallon, *Soul of Fire*, p. 17.
10 Ibid., pp. 17–18.
11 Ibid., pp. 17, 19.
12 Mary MacSwiney, 'The Background of the Irish Republic', Donohue Rare Book Collection, Miscellaneous Irish Box, University of San Francisco.
13 Margaret Ward, *Unmanageable Revolutionaries*, p. 67.
14 Monsignor Florence D. Cohalan, son of Judge Daniel F. Cohalan, Interview by author, July 15, 1989, New York City, tape recording, San Jose State University Special Collections, San Jose.
15 Quoted in Fallon, *Soul of Fire*, p. 22.
16 Ibid., pp. 20, 30–33.
17 Ibid., pp. 33–35.
18 Ibid., p. 64; Terry Golway, *Irish Rebel: John Devoy and America's Fight for Ireland's Freedom* (New York: St Martin's Press, 1998), p. 283.
19 S. Magleari, Accountant General, to Mary MacSwiney, 18-1-22, Mary MacSwiney Papers, P48a/32(2), University College, Dublin Archives.
20 *Philadelphia Public Ledger*, January 7 1921, p. 10.
21 *The Irish World*, January 29 1921, p. 3.
22 Charles Callan Tansill, *America and the Fight for Irish Freedom: 1866–1922* (New York: The Devin-Adair Co., 1957), p. 348.

23 *The Gaelic American*, January 1 1921, p. 1.
24 Ibid., pp. 1, 4.
25 Fallon, *Soul of Fire*, p. 60.
26 Ibid., p. 70.
27 Investigative FBI Case Files, 1908–1922, Case 202600, File 1177, National Archives, Washington D.C.
28 Ibid., p. 64
29 *The Irish World*, January 22 1921, p. 3.
30 *The New York Times*, January 7 1921, p. 2.
31 *The Albany Journal*, January 11 1921, p. 2.
32 Ibid.
33 Ibid., pp. 2, 10.
34 Ibid., p. 10.
35 *The Irish World*, January 22 1921, p. 3.
36 Catherine Flanagan to Mr O'Mara, 3-2-21, Mary MacSwiney Papers, P48a/115(3), UCDA.
37 *Buffalo Courier*, January 20 1921, p. 9.
38 Ibid.
39 Ibid., January 21 1921, p. 12.
40 Ibid., *The Pittsburg Press*, January 21 1921, p. 1.
41 *The Cleveland Plain Dealer*, January 25 1921, p. 8.
42 Catherine Flanagan to Mr O'Mara, 3-2-21, Mary MacSwiney Papers, P48a/115(3), UCDA; *The Cleveland Plain Dealer*, January 25 1921, p. 8.
43 *The Irish World*, February 12 1921, p. 6; Catherine Flanagan to Mr O'Mara, 3-2-21, Mary MacSwiney Papers, P48a/115(3), UCDA.
44 *The Irish World*, February 12 1921, p. 6.
45 Ibid.
46 Catherine Flanagan to Mr O'Mara, 3-2-21, Mary MacSwiney Papers, P48a/115(3), UCDA.
47 *The Ohio State Journal*, January 25 1921, p. 1.
48 *The Irish World*, February 19 1921, p. 6.
49 *The Lexington Herald*, January 29 1921, p. 8; Catherine Flanagan to Mr O'Mara, 3-2-21, Mary MacSwiney Papers, P48a/115(3), UCDA.
50 *The Journal and Tribune*, February 1 1921, p. 1; Catherine Flanagan to Mr O'Mara, 3-2-21, Mary MacSwiney Papers, P48a/115(3), UCDA.
51 *Nashville Banner*, February 2 1921, p. 2; Catherine Flanagan to Mr O'Mara, 3-2-21, Mary MacSwiney Papers, P48a/115(3), UCDA.
52 *The Commercial Appeal*, February 3 1921, p. 1.
53 Catherine Flanagan to Mr O'Mara, 3-2-21, Mary MacSwiney Papers, P48a/115(3), UCDA.
54 Ibid.
55 *St Louis Globe Democrat*, February 4 1921, p. 6; February 5 1921, p. 3; Catherine Flanagan to Mr O'Mara, 3-2-21, Mary MacSwiney Papers, P48a/115(3), UCDA.
56 *The Irish World*, February 19 1921, p. 6.
57 *Chicago Herald and Examiner*, February 6 1921, p. 4.
58 *Chicago Daily Tribune*, February 7 1921, p. 2.
59 *The Irish World*, February 19 1921, p. 6.
60 *Chicago Daily Tribune*, February 4 1921, p. 2.
61 Ibid., February 8 1921, p. 5.
62 *The Irish World*, February 19 1921, p. 6.
63 *The Fort Wayne Journal Gazette*, February 12 1921, p. 2.
64 Ibid., February 13 1921, p. 2.

65 *Des Moines Register*, February 12 1921, p. 1.
66 Ibid., *The Irish World*, February 25 1921, p. 6.
67 *Des Moines Register*, February 13 1921, p. 2.
68 Mary to Harry Boland, 12-2-21, Mary MacSwiney Papers, P48a/115(6), UCDA.
69 Ibid.
70 *Omaha Daily News*, February 10 1921, p. 2.
71 *The Nebraska House Journal*, Twenty-Ninth Day, House of Representatives, Lincoln, Nebraska, February 10 1921, Senate File No. 52, 495, Love Memorial Library, University of Nebraska, Lincoln, Nebraska.
72 *Omaha Bee*, February 11 1921, p. 2.
73 *The Nebraska State Journal*, February 15 1921, p. 3.
74 *The Omaha Bee*, February 14 1921, p. 1.
75 *The Omaha Daily News*, February 14 1921, pp. 4, 5; Catherine Flanagan to Mr O'Mara, 3-2-21, Mary MacSwiney Papers, P48a/115(3), UCDA.
76 *The Omaha Bee*, February 14 1921, p. 1.
77 *The Lincoln Daily Star*, February 12 1921, p. 4.
78 *The Topeka State Journal*, February 16 1921, p. 1.
79 *The Topeka Daily Capital*, February 17 1921, p. 1.
80 *The Topeka State Journal*, February 17 1921, p. 2.
81 *The Kansas City Kansan*, February 17 1921, p. 1.
82 *The Irish World*, March 5 1921, p. 6.
83 *The Oklahoman*, February 18 1921, pp. 1, 8.
84 Ibid.
85 Ibid.
86 *The Irish World*, March 5, 1921, p. 6.
87 Ibid.
88 *The Oklahoman*, February 20 1921, p. 1.
89 *The Dallas Morning News*, February 12 1921, p. 2.
90 *The Irish World*, March 12 1921, p. 8.
91 Ibid., March 26 1921, p. 6.
92 Ibid., March 12 1921, p. 8.
93 Ibid.
94 Ibid.
95 Ibid.
96 Ibid.
97 *The Times Picayune*, February 26 1921, p. 2.
98 Mary to Mr O'Mara, 25-2-21, Mary MacSwiney Papers, P48a/115(12), UCDA.
99 *Los Angeles Times*, March 6 1921 [Part I.], p. 11.
100 Ibid.
101 Joseph Scott to Peter Yorke, 5-3-21, Mary MacSwiney Papers, P48a/115(14), UCDA.
102 *San Francisco Chronicle*, March 1 1921, p. 2; *The Sacramento Bee*, March 2 1921, p. 1; March 3 1921, p. 3; March 5 1921, Second Sec., p. 15.
103 *The Sacramento Bee*, March 3 1921, p. 11; *The San Francisco Examiner*, March 5 1921, p. 4.
104 *The San Francisco Examiner*, March 8 1921, p. l.
105 Ibid., March 7 1921, p. 12; *The Leader*, January 15 1921, p. 5.
106 *The Leader*, March 12 1921, p. 1.
107 Ibid., March 7 1921, p. 12.
108 Ibid., March 9 1921, p. 13; *San Francisco Chronicle*, March 9 1921, p. 6.
109 *San Francisco Chronicle*, March 9 1921, p. 6.

110 Ibid.
111 *The Sacramento Bee*, March 8 1921, p. 1.
112 Ibid., March 9 1921, p. 6.
113 *The Leader*, February 26 1921, p. 1; March 5 1921, p. 1; *The Irish World*, March 26 1921, p. 6.
114 *San Francisco Chronicle*, March 7 1921, p. 3; *The Leader*, March 12 1921, p. 1.
115 *The Sacramento Bee*, March 8 1921, p. 1.
116 *The San Francisco Examiner*, March 7 1921, p. 1; March 10 1921, p. 1.
117 *The Sacramento Bee*, March 8 1921, p. 1.
118 Ibid.
119 Mary MacSwiney's Address, March 10 1921, pp. 11–12, John Byrne Collection, File: G453, San Jose State University Library.
120 Ibid., p. 15.
121 Ibid., pp. 17–18.
122 Ibid., p. 25.
123 Ibid., p. 26.
124 *The Monitor*, April 3 1921, p. 7.
125 *The Oregon Journal*, March 12 1921, p. 2.
126 *The Oregonian*, March 14 1921, p. 5.
127 Ibid.
128 *The Irish World*, April 9 1921, p. 3.
129 *The Spokesman-Review*, March 16 1921, p. 6.
130 Ibid., March 16 1921, p. 6.
131 *The Butte Miner*, March 9 1921, p. 6; March 14 1921, p. 8.
132 Ibid., March 17 1921, p. 1.
133 Ibid., March 18 1921, p. 4.
134 Ibid., March 19 1921, p. 7.
135 *The Salt Lake City Tribune*, March 20 1921, p. 24.
136 Ibid., March 23 1921, p. 11.
137 *The Rocky Mountain News*, March 27 1921, Section One, p. 3.
138 Ibid.
139 Ibid., March 28 1921, p. 1.
140 Ibid., March 13 1921, Section Two, p. 11.
141 *The Kansas City Kansan*, March 30 1921, p. 9.
142 Ibid., March 31 1921, p. 8.
143 Ibid.
144 Ibid.
145 Ibid., March 30 1921, p. 9.
146 *The Illinois State Journal*, April 1 1921, p. 3.
147 Ibid., March 31 1921, 1; April 2 1921, p. 1.
148 Ibid., April 2 1921, p. 1.
149 *The Milwaukee Journal*, April 2 1921, p. 1.
150 Ibid.
151 *Chicago Tribune*, April 19 1921, pp. 1, 2.
152 *The New York Times*, June 17 1921, p. 4.
153 *Columbus Dispatch*, June 25 1921, p. 3.
154 *Akron Beacon Journal*, July 4 1921, p. 12.
155 *Philadelphia Public Ledger*, July 18 1921, p. 2.
156 Mary MacSwiney to Mr President [Eamon de Valera] 20-7-21, Mary MacSwiney Papers, P 48a/115(47), UCDA.
157 Ibid.
158 Fallon, *Soul of Fire*, pp. 75–6; *The Leader*, August 25 1921, p. 1, August 27 1921, p. 1.

159 *The Irish World*, April 9 1921, p. 3.
160 Fallon, *Soul of Fire*, p. 73.
161 Quoted in Fallon, *Soul of Fire*, pp. 72–3.
162 Investigative FBI Case Files, 1908–1922, Reel 936, A65, M-1085, National Archives, Washington D.C.
163 *The San Francisco Examiner*, December 22 1921, p. 1.
164 Fallon, *Soul of Fire*, pp. 89–90.

CHAPTER 7

1 *The Irish World*, April 15 1922, p. 1.
2 Jacqueline Van Voris, *Constance de Markievicz: In the Cause of Ireland* (Amherst: The University of Massachusetts Press, 1967), pp. 42–3, 63.
3 Ibid., pp. 15, 20; Esther Roper, 'Biographical Sketch', in *Prison Letters of Countess Markievicz* (London: Virago Press Ltd, 1987), p. 55.
4 Van Voris, p. 15.
5 Lil Conlon, *Cumann na mBan and the Women of Ireland, 1913–25* (Kilkenny: Kilkenny People Ltd, 1969), pp. 12–13; Elizabeth Coxhead, *Daughters of Erin* (Gerrards Cross: Colin Smythe Ltd, 1979), p. 89; Van Voris, p. 100.
6 Countess Constance Markievicz, 'Some Women in Easter Week', in *Prison Letters of Countess Markievicz* (London: Virago Press Ltd, 1987), p. 174; Anne Haverty, *Constance Markievicz: An Independent Life* (London: Pandora Press, 1988), p. 177; Van Voris, p. 245.
7 Coxhead, pp. 104, 107; Van Voris, p. 217.
8 Margaret Ward, *Unmanageable Revolutionaries: Women and Irish Nationalism* (Dublin: Attic Press, 1995), p. 145.
9 Quoted in Dorothy Macardle, *The Irish Republic* (Dublin: Wolfhound Press Ltd, 1999), p. 630.
10 Quoted in Margaret Ward, *Unmanageable Revolutionaries*, pp. 137, 163, 168; Coxhead, pp. 108–9.
11 Macardle., pp. 597–9, 611–13.
12 Ibid., p. 637.
13 Jim Maher, *Harry Boland: A Biography* (Boulder, Colorado: Mercier Press, 1998), p. 148.
14 Quoted in Jim Maher, p. 163.
15 Van Voris, p. 304–5.
16 De Valera to Collins, 16-20-21, Dáil Éireann Papers, DE 2/450, National Archives, Dublin.
17 List of Decisions at Meeting on 23 September 1921, Dáil Éireann Papers, DE 2/450, National Archives, Dublin.
18 Eighteen-year-old Kevin Barry, a medical student at UCD, was captured, court-martialled and hanged in Mountjoy jail for taking part in a raid for arms.
19 Coxhead, pp. 113-14; Anne Marreco, *The Rebel Countess, The Life and Times of Constance Markievicz* (Philadelphia and New York: Chilton Books, 1967), pp. 273–4; Van Voris, p. 310; Haverty, p. 212; Letter from AARIR, Congress District Council, No. 3, LA, April 29 1922, Byrne Collection, File: B123a, San Jose State University Library; *The New York Times*, April 5 1922, p. 4.
20 *The Irish World*, April 15 1922, p. 6.

21 Ibid.
22 Marreco, p. 274; Van Voris, p. 310; *The Irish World*, May 27 1922, p. 1
23 Van Voris, pp. 10–11.
24 *The New York Times*, April 8 1922, p. 6.
25 Emmet Larkin, *James Larkin: Irish Labour Leader, 1876–1947* (London: The New English Library, 1965), pp. 214–20; Henry Boylan, *A Dictionary of Irish Biography* (New York: St Martin's Press, 1988), pp. 192–3.
26 Van Voris, pp. 310–11; Marreco, p. 275.
27 *The Irish World*, April 15 1922, p.1.
28 *The New York Times*, April 10 1922, p. 5.
29 Marreco, pp. 275–6.
30 *The Irish World*, April 22 1922, p. 1, 3; *Philadelphia Inquirer*, April 17 1922, p. 2.
31 *Akron Beacon Journal*, April 12 1922, p. 1.
32 *The Detroit Free Press*, April 19 1922, Part Two, p. 1; Marreco, p. 277.
33 Van Voris, p. 303.
34 *The Irish World*, April 29 1922, p. 3.
35 Ibid. April 22 1922, p. 9.
36 *Markievicz*, p. 287.
37 Ibid.; Haverty, p. 213; Van Voris, p. 312.
38 Countess Markievicz to Staskou Markievicz, May 1922, Joseph McGarrity Collection, MS 13,778(1), National Library, Dublin.
39 *St Paul Daily News*, April 24 1921, p. 1.
40 Ibid., p. 21; April 24 1922, p. 6.
41 Ibid., April 25 1922, p. 7.
42 *Markievicz*, p. 287, David M. Emmons, *The Butte Irish: Class and Ethnicity in an American Mining Town, 1875–1925* (Urbana and Chicago: University of Illinois Press, 1990), p. 404; Van Voris, p. 311.
43 Countess Markievicz to Staskou Markievicz, May 1922, Joseph McGarrity Collection, MS 13,778(1), NLI, Dublin.
44 *The Butte Miner*, April 28 1922, p. 1.
45 Ibid., p. 3.
46 Ibid., April 28 1922, p. 1.
47 Marreco, p. 279.
48 *The Butte Miner*, April 29 1922, p. 11
49 *Markievicz*, p. 289; Van Voris, p. 311.
50 *The Butte Miner*, May 1 1922, p. 2.
51 Ibid., May 3 1922, p. 5.
52 *The Seattle Daily Times*, May 3 1922, p. 5.
53 Ibid.
54 *The Oregon Journal*, May 4 1922, p. 1.
55 Ibid., May 5 1922, p. 6.
56 *The Monitor*, April 29 1922, p. 7; *San Francisco Chronicle*, May 6 1922, p. 12; May 7 1922, p. 3.
57 *San Francisco Chronicle*, May 5 1922, p. 5; May 6 1922, p. 12; May 8 1922, p. 15.
58 Ibid., May 8 1922, p. 15.
59 Ibid.
60 Ibid.
61 Ibid., May 9 1922, p. 15.
62 John A. Murphy, *Ireland in the Twentieth Century* (Dublin: Gill and Macmillan, 1975), p. 52.
63 Van Voris, p. 312; Coxhead, p. 115; Van Voris, p. 311.

64 *Los Angeles Times*, May 10 1922, Part II, p. 9; Marreco, p. 280.
65 *Chicago Tribune*, May 14 1922, Part I, p. 5.
66 *Markievicz*, p. 290; Van Voris, p. 312.
67 *The Irish World*, June 3 1922, p. 3.
68 Marreco, pp. 280–1.
69 Ibid., p. 281; *The New York Times*, May 25 1922, p. 2.
70 Ibid., May 22 1922, p. 3; May 30 1922, p. 3; *The Irish World*, May 6 1922, p. 3.
71 *The New York Times*, May 22 1922, p. 3.
72 Ibid., May 30 1922, p. 3.
73 Ibid., June 10 1922, p. 3.
74 Van Voris, pp. 312, 314; Haverty, p. 215.
75 *Markievicz*, pp. 290–1.

CHAPTER 8

1 *The Irish World*, September 30 1922, p. 3.
2 Ibid., July 15 1922, p. 1.
3 Ibid., September 30 1922, p. 3.
4 Ibid.
5 Ibid., September 23 1922, p. 3.
6 Ibid.
7 Ibid.
8 Ibid.
9 Ibid., September 30 1922, p. 3.
10 Ibid.
11 *The Gaelic American*, September 30 1922, p. 1.
12 Ibid.
13 Ibid.
14 Ibid.
15 Ibid.
16 Ibid., October 7 1922, p. 2.
17 Ibid.
18 Ibid., September 30 1922, p. 2.
19 Ibid., p. 1.
20 Ibid.
21 *The Irish World*, September 23 1922, p. 3.
22 Ibid., October 28 1922, p. 12.
23 Ibid.
24 Ibid.
25 Ibid.
26 Ibid.
27 Ibid.
28 Ibid.
29 Ibid.
30 Ibid.
31 Ibid.
32 Ibid., October 28 1922, p. 3.
33 Ibid.
34 Ibid.
35 Ibid.

36 Ibid.
37 Ibid.
38 Ibid.
39 *The Irish World*, November 25 1922, p. 3.
40 Ibid.
41 Ibid.
42 Ibid.
43 Ibid.
44 Ibid., December 9 1922, p. 10.
45 Ibid., March 3 1923, p. 1; *The New York Times*, February 25 1923, p. 5.
46 British Consulate-General, New York, to HMS Principal Secretary of State for Foreign Affairs, Foreign Office, London, England, July 13 1923, Taoiseach Papers, S1976, File 452, National Archives, Dublin, Ireland.
47 *The Irish World*, August 18 1923, p. 8.
48 Ibid., January 6 1923. p. 3

CHAPTER 9

1 *San Francisco Chronicle*, June 29 1921, p. 1.
2 Leah Levenson and Jerry H. Natterstad, *Hanna Sheehy-Skeffington: Irish Feminist* (New York: Syracuse University Press, 1986), pp. 138–41.
3 Dorothy Macardle, *The Irish Republic* (Dublin: Wolfhound Press Ltd., 1965), p. 435; Margaret Ward, *Hanna Sheehy Skeffington*, p. 239.
4 Ibid., pp. 254–5. The Women's Prisoners' Defence League (WPDL), had been organized in Ireland by Maud Gonne MacBride and Sarah Mellows. All that was required for membership was a relative in jail and a paid subscription of one halfpenny a week.
5 *The Irish World*, October 21 1922, p. 12.
6 External Affairs File: 'The American Press on Ireland, October 14–November 14', Taoiseach Papers, S1904, National Archives, Dublin, Ireland.
7 *The Irish World*, October 28327 327 1922, p. 3.
8 Ibid.
9 Ibid., p. 10.
10 Kathryn Heaney to George Staunton, n/d (captured 20-5-23, censored 24-5-23), George Staunton Papers, Lot No. 91(1)(a), A/1081, Military Archives, Rathmines, Ireland.
11 Linda Kearns to Annie Smithson, Annie Smithson, MP Papers, Lot No. 46, File A/1035, Military Archives, Rathmines, Ireland.
12 Ibid.
13 Gloster Armstrong to HMS Principal Secretary of State for Foreign Affairs, Foreign Office, London, England, November 23 1922, Taoiseach Papers S1967, National Archives, Dublin, Ireland.
14 *New York Times*, November 24 1922, p. 19.
15 *The Irish World*, January 27 1923, p. 6.
16 Ibid.
17 Ibid.
18 Ibid.
19 *The Irish World*, February 24 1923, p. 3. The number of republican prisoners, including women, reported by Linda Kearns does not agree with those quoted by Hanna Sheehy Skeffington. Linda was consistent in her estimate of 13,000 male prisoners, while Hanna estimated 14,000. The press and members of the

British Government reporting on their activities may have misquoted them. It is also possible that the women used estimates from different sources.

20 Ibid.
21 Ibid.
22 Ibid.
23 Ibid., *The Oregonian*, February 25 1923, p. 12.
24 John P. Trant to HM Ambassador Extraordinary and Plenipotentiary, British Embassy, Washington D.C., February 26 1923, Taoiseach Papers S1976, File 184, National Archives, Dublin, Ireland.
25 Ibid.
26 *The Oregonian*, February 25 1923, p. 12.
27 *New York Times*, February 25 1923, p. 5.
28 *The Sacramento Bee*, March 2 1923, p. 2.
29 *Stockton Daily Evening Record*, March 3 1923, p. 6.
30 Ibid.
31 *San Francisco Chronicle*, March 7 1923, p. 7.
32 *San Francisco Examiner*, March 7 1923, p. 6.
33 Ibid., May 12 1923, p. 3.
34 Ibid.
35 *The Irish World*, April 21 1923, p. 12.
36 Ibid.
37 Sinbad to The Honorable Desmond Fitzgerald, April 20 1923, Taoiseach Papers, S1976, National Archives, Dublin, Ireland.
38 *The Irish World*, May 15 1923, p. 3.
39 Ibid.
40 *The Washington Post*, May 14 1923, p. 2.
41 *The Irish World*, May 12 1923, p. 3.
42 Timothy J. Sarbaugh, 'Culture, Militancy and de Valera: Irish-American Republican Nationalism in California, 1900–1936', MA thesis, San Jose State University, 1980, p. 5.
43 Margaret Ward, *Hanna Sheehy Skeffington*, p. 258.
44 Ibid., p. 260.

CHAPTER 10

1 *The Irish World*, August 23 1924, p. 11; *The Leader*, August 2 1924, p. 1.
2 *The Leader*, August 2 1924, p. 1.
3 Ruth Dudley Edwards, *Patrick Pearse: The Triumph of Failure* (London: Victor Gollancz Ltd, 1977), p. 5; Seamas Ó'Buachalla, *The Letters of P. H. Pearse* (New Jersey: Humanities Press, 1980), pp. 460–1.
4 Edwards, p. 5.
5 Ibid., pp. 6–7; John O'Beirne Ranelagh, *A Short History of Ireland* (Cambridge: Cambridge University Press, 1983), p. 174.
6 Padraig Pearse, *The Home Life of Padraig Pearse, as Told by Himself, His Family and Friends*, ed. Mary Brigid Pearse (Dublin and Cork: The Mercier Press, 1979), p. 11.
7 Padraig Pearse, p. 11; Xavier Carty, *In Bloody Protest—The Tragedy of Patrick Pearse* (Dublin: Able Press, 1978), p. 15; Lawrence J. McCaffrey, *Ireland from Colony to Nation State* (Englewood Cliffs: Prentice-Hall, Inc., 1979), p. 137; Alan J. Ward, *The Easter Rising, Revolution and Irish Nationalism* (Illinois: Harlan Davidson, Inc., 1980), pp. 3–4, 8, 61; Brian O'Higgins, *The Soldier's*

Story of Easter Week (Dublin: Elo Press, Ltd, 1966), p. 65; Henry Boylan, *A Dictionary of Irish Biography* (New York: St Martin's Press, 1998), p. 326.
8 Edwards, p. 273.
9 Ibid., p. 323.
10 Ibid., pp. 327–8; Xavier Carty, *In Bloody Protest—The Tragedy of Patrick Pearse* (Dublin: Able Press, 1978), p. 12.
11 McCaffrey, *Ireland*, p. 141.
12 Carty, p. 12; Edwards, pp. 330, 334, 327–8.
13 *The Monitor*, October 4 1924, p. 7, Pearse Museum, File N. 112–26, Rathfarnham, Ireland.
14 *The Irish World*, May 24 1924, p. 12.
15 Ibid.; *The New York Times*, May 19 1924, p. 4; June 2 1924, p. 5.
16 *The Irish World*, June 7 1924, p. 12.
17 Pamphlet, n/d, J. McGarrity Collection, MS 17633, National Library, Dublin.
18 Ibid., August 23 1924, p. 11.
19 *The Butte Miner*, July 25 1924, p. 8; *The Anaconda Standard*, July 23 1924, p. 8.
20 *The Butte Miner*, July 28 1924, p. 5.
21 *The Anaconda Standard*, July 28 1924, p. 5.
22 *The Oregon Journal*, August 6 1924, p. 14.
23 Ibid.
24 *Catholic Sentinel*, August 14 1924, Pearse Museum, File N 112–26, Rathfarnham, Ireland.
25 *The San Francisco Examiner*, August 8 1924, p. 8; *San Francisco Chronicle*, August 9 1924 p. 5; August 10 1924, p. 9; *The Monitor*, August 16 1924, p. 1.
26 *The San Francisco Examiner*, August 11 1924, p. 5.
27 *San Francisco Chronicle*, August 11 1924, p. 11.
28 Ibid., August 16 1924, Second Sec., p. 17.
29 *The Leader*, August 16 1924, p. 1; September 6 1924, p. 5.
30 Ibid., August 16 1924, p. 1.
31 Ibid.
32 *San Francisco Chronicle*, August 14 1924, Second Section, p. 13; August 16 1924, p. 9; August 18 1924, p. 4.
33 Ibid., August 18 1924, p. 4.
34 Ibid.
35 Ibid.
36 *The Leader*, August 23 1924, p. 1.
37 *The Monitor*, August 23 1924, p. 4.
38 *The Leader*, September 6 1924, p. 5.
39 Ibid., August 30 1924, p. 5.
40 Ibid.
41 *The Monitor*, August 18 1924, p. 4; *The Leader*, September 6 1924, p. 5.
42 *The Monitor*, October 4 1924, p. 7, Pearse Museum, File N 112–26, Rathfarnham, Ireland.
43 Ibid.
44 Edwards, p. 330.

CHAPTER 11

1 Charlotte H. Fallon, *Soul of Fire: A Biography of Mary MacSwiney* (Cork and Dublin: The Mercier Press, 1986), p. 81.
2 Ibid., pp. 76–7.

3 Ibid., pp. 79, 82, 87–8.
4 Ibid., p. 89.
5 Ibid., p. 105; *The Leader*, March 14 1925, p. 4.
6 Fallon, *Soul of Fire*, p. 117.
7 Publicity, John Byrne Collection, File B195, San Jose State University Library.
8 Fallon, *Soul of Fire*, pp. 118–20.
9 *The Irish World*, February 7 1925, p. 1.
10 Mary MacSwiney to Eamon de Valera, 30-3-25, Mary MacSwiney Papers, P48a/119(47), UCDA.
11 Ibid., February 14 1925, pp. 1, 10.
12 Ibid., p. 1.
13 Ibid., February 21 1925, p. 1.
14 *The Monitor*, March 7 1925, p. 1; *San Francisco Chronicle*, March 15 1925, p. 6; *The Leader*, March 14 1925, p. 1.
15 *The Leader*, March 14 1925, p. 1; *The Irish World*, April 4 1925, p. 2; *The Leader*, March 14 1925, p. 1; *San Francisco Chronicle*, March 18 1925, p. 3.
16 *The Leader*, March 21 1925, pp. 1, 5.
17 *The Irish World*, April 18 1921, p. 2.
18 Ibid.
19 Report from Mary MacSwiney, 30-3-25, Mary MacSwiney Papers, P48a/119(47), UCDA.
20 Ibid.; *The Oregon Journal*, March 30 1925, p. 3; *The Oregonian*, March 30 1925, p. 4.
21 *The Oregonian*, March 30 1925, p. 4.
22 Andrew Gallagher to Mary MacSwiney, 11-3-25, Mary MacSwiney Papers, P48/120(28), UCDA.
23 Ibid.
24 Ibid.
25 Ibid.
26 Ibid.
27 Report of Mary MacSwiney, 25-4-25; Mary MacSwiney Papers, P48a/120(2), UDCA.
28 *The Irish World*, April 18 1925, p. 2; *The New York Times*, April 30 1925, p. 1; *San Francisco Chronicle*, May 1 1925, p. 11.
29 *The Leader*, June 6 1925, p. 1; AARIR Bulletin No. 13, National Headquarters, New York City, May 20 1925, John Byrne Collection, File B219, San Jose State University Library.
30 *The Irish World*, May 9 1925, p. 12.
31 Ibid., May 16 1925, p. 1.
32 Joe Begley to Mary MacSwiney, 7-5-25, Mary MacSwiney Papers, P48a/120(30), UCDA.
33 Extract from *Irish World*, May 9 1925, Taoiseach Papers, S1976, National Archives, Dublin.
34 Extract from 'Our American Letter', Sinn Féin, May 1925, Taoiseach Papers, S1976, National Archives, Dublin.
35 G. G. Whiskard to D. O'Hegarty, Taoiseach Papers, July 16 1925, File S 4532, National Archives, Dublin.
36 Runaí, Saorstat Éireann to Secretary, Executive Council, July 22 1925, Taoiseach Papers, File S 4532, National Archives, Dublin.
37 Runaidhe, Department of Justice to Secretary, Executive Council, October 7 1925, Taoiseach Papers, File S 4532, National Archives, Dublin.
38 D. O'Hegarty to G. G. Whiskard, Esq., October 14 1925, Taoiseach Papers, File S 4532, National Archives, Dublin.

39 Sean T. Ó Ceallaigh to Mary MacSwiney, 22-4-25, Mary MacSwiney Papers, P48a/120(17)/1, UCDA.
40 Ibid.
41 Ibid.
42 *The Irish World*, May 16 1925, p. 1.
43 *Minneapolis Tribune*, May 1925, p. 1.
44 *Minneapolis Journal*, April 30 1925, p. 12.
45 *St Paul Pioneer Press*, May 1 1925, p. 1; May 2 1925, p. 1.
46 Ibid.
47 *Minneapolis Tribune*, May 1 1925, p. 1.
48 *The Irish World*, May 18 1925, p. 1.
49 Ibid., May 16 1925, p. 12.
50 Ibid. May 30 1925, p. 2.
51 Ibid. May 16 1925, p. 12.
52 *The Evening Sentinel*, May 22, 1925, p. 3.
53 Ibid.
54 *The Irish World*, June 6 1925, p. 2.
55 *New Haven Register*, May 31 1925, p. 4; June 1 1925, p. 2; *The Irish World*, June 20 1925, p. 2.
56 Mary MacSwiney to Andrew Gallagher, 9-7-25, Mary MacSwiney Papers, P48a/121(1), UCDA.
57 Ibid.
58 Mary MacSwiney to Joseph Scott, 11-7-25, Mary MacSwiney Papers, P48a/121(2), UCDA.
59 Joseph Scott to Mary MacSwiney, 16-7-25, Mary MacSwiney Papers, P48a/121(4), UCDA.
60 Mary MacSwiney to Joseph Scott, 21-8-25, Mary MacSwiney Papers, P48a/121(15), UCDA.
61 Daniel Webster was one of the leading lawyers and orators of his time (1782–1852) in the United States. He served in the US Congress and as Secretary of State to President Millard Fillmore.
62 Ibid., August 1 1925, p. 12.
63 *New York Times*, July 25 1925, p. 6.
64 Fallon, *Soul of Fire*, p. 124.
65 Mary MacSwiney to Eamon de Valera, 27-6-25, Mary MacSwiney Papers, P48a/120(42), UCDA.
66 Quoted in Charlotte Fallon, *Soul of Fire*, p. 128.

EPILOGUE

1 Leah Levenson and Jerry H. Natterstad, *Hanna Sheehy-Skeffington: Irish Feminist* (New York: Syracuse University Press, 1986), p. 152.
2 Ibid., pp. 160–6, 176.
3 Margaret Ward, *Hanna Sheehy Skeffington: A Life* (Cork: Attic Press, 1997), p. 344.
4 Andree Sheehy Skeffington, *Skeff: A Life of Owen Sheehy Skeffington, 1909–1970* (Dublin: The Lilliput Press, 1991), pp. 118–40, 163–80.
5 Charlotte H. Fallon, *Soul of Fire: A Biography of Mary MacSwiney* (Cork and Dublin: The Mercier Press, 1986), pp. 126–8, 131–2, 180.
6 Jacqueline Van Voris, *Constance de Markievicz: In the Cause of Ireland* (Amherst: The University of Massachusetts Press, 1967), pp. 324–7, 346–8.

7 Margaret Ward, *Unmanageable Revolutionaries: Women and Irish Nationalism* (London: Pluto Press, 1983), pp. 282–3.
8 Frank Costello, *Enduring the Most: The Life and Death of Terence MacSwiney* (Kerry, Ireland: Brandon Book Publishers Ltd., 1995), p. 239, 242–4.
9 Margaret Ward, *Unmanageable Revolutionaries*, p. 282, n38.
10 Frank Costello, p. 244.
11 Mourning Card and Last Will and Testament, Pearse Museum, File 100–119, Rathfarnham, Ireland.

APPENDIX 1

1 Countess Constance Markievicz, *Prison Letters of Countess Markievicz* (London: Virago Press, 1987), pp. 37–41.

APPENDIX 4

1 Hanna Sheehy Skeffington Speech, May 4 1918, Department of Justice File No. 191 962, National Archives, Washington D.C.

APPENDIX 5

1 'Miss Mary MacSwiney's Testimony, Hearings on Conditions in Ireland Before the American Commission of Inquiry on Conditions in Ireland', Donohue Rare Book Collection, Richard A. Gleeson Library, University of San Francisco, San Francisco, California. Excerpts only of Mary MacSwiney's testimony are contained in this appendix. Omitted are the sections pertaining to early Irish history. Included testimony pertains to the period of the Easter Rising and family history. Also excluded is her testimony referring to Terence MacSwiney's last days and his funeral.

APPENDIX 6

1 Mrs MacSwiney's Story, Complete Report of the testimony given before the American Commission on Conditions in Ireland, by Mrs Muriel MacSwiney, widow of Terence MacSwiney, Lord Mayor of Cork, Mary MacSwiney Papers, UCDA, P48a/179.

APPENDIX 7

1 'Mary MacSwiney's Address at the Civic Auditorium, San Francisco, Thursday, March 10 1921', John Byrne Collection, San Jose State University, G453.

Bibliography

PRIMARY SOURCES

American Irish Historical Society, New York, New York
Daniel F. Cohalan Collection

Hoover Institution Library and Archives, Stanford, California
Alice Park Collection

Houghton Library, Harvard University, Cambridge, Massachusetts
Oswald Garrison Villard Collection

Love Memorial Library, University of Nebraska, Lincoln Nebraska
The Nebraska House Journal, House of Representatives, Senate File No. 52,495

Military Archives, Cathal Brugha Barracks, Rathmines, Ireland

National Archives, Dublin, Ireland
Dáil Éireann Papers
Department of Foreign Affairs Papers

National Archives, Washington D.C.
Department of Justice File No. 191319
Department of Justice File No. 191962
Department of Justice File No. 50107
Investigative FBI Case Files, 1908–22, Reel 936

National Library, Dublin, Ireland
Florence O'Donoghue Papers
Hanna Sheehy Skeffington Papers
John Devoy Papers
Joseph McGarrity Collection

Pearse Museum, Rathfarnham, Ireland

Richard A. Gleeson Library, University of San Francisco, San Francisco, California
Donohue Rare Book Collection

San Jose State University Archives, San Jose, California
John Byrne Collection

University College Dublin Archives, Belfield, Ireland
Mary MacSwiney Papers

Interviews
Cohalan, Florence D., Monsignor, son of Judge Daniel J. Cohalan. Interview by author, July 15 1989, New York City. Tape recording. San Jose State University, San Jose, California.

Newspapers
Akron Beacon Journal
Albany Journal
Buffalo Courier
Buffalo Evening News
Chicago Herald and Examiner
Chicago Tribune
Cleveland Plain Dealer
Columbus Dispatch
Des Moines Register
Fitchburg Daily Sentinel
Holyoke Telegram
Illinois State Journal
Los Angeles Times
Meridan Morning Record
Nashville Banner
New Haven Register
New York Tribune
Omaha Daily News
Philadelphia Public Ledger
Rochester Democrat and Chronicle
San Francisco Chronicle
St Louis Globe Democrat
St Paul Daily News

Stockton Daily Evening Record
Waterbury Register
Worcester Telegram
The Anaconda Standard
The Boston Globe
The Butte Miner
The Capital Times
The Commercial Appeal
The Dallas Morning News
The Detroit Free Press
The Fort Wayne Journal Gazette
The Gaelic American
The Hartford Daily
The Indianapolis News
The Irish World and American Industrial Liberator
The Journal and Tribune
The Kansas City Kansan
The Leader
The Lexington Herald
The Lincoln Daily Star
The Lowell Sun
The Milwaukee Journal
The Minneapolis Journal
The Minneapolis Tribune
The Monitor
The Nebraska State Journal
The New Bedford Evening Standard
The New Haven Union
The New York Times
The Ohio State Journal
The Oklahoman
The Omaha Bee
The Oregonian
The Oregon Journal
The Philadelphia Inquirer
The Pilot
The Pittsburg Press
The Rocky Mountain News
The Sacramento Bee
The Salt Lake City Tribune
The San Francisco Examiner

The Seattle Times
The Spokesman-Review
The Springfield Daily Republican
The Times-Picayune
The Topeka Daily Capital
The Topeka State Journal
The Torrington Register
The Washington Post

Journals
Éire-Ireland
Gender & History
The Distributive Worker

Works by Countess Constance Markievicz

_______. 'Some Women in Easter Week'. In *Prison Letters of Countess Markievicz*. London: Virago Press Ltd, 1987.

Works by Hanna Sheehy Skeffington

_______. *Impressions of Sinn Féin in America*. Dublin: O'Laughlin, Murphy and Boland, Ltd, nd.

_______. 'Nineteen Years' Fight for Justice, Will They Free Mooney?', *The Distributive Worker,* April 1936, Tom Mooney Papers, University of California, Berkeley, Bancroft Library.

SECONDARY SOURCES

Akenson, Donald Harman. *The United States and Ireland*. Cambridge, Massachusetts: Harvard University Press, 1973.

Barnes, Barbara; Mack C. Shelley, II; Steffen W. Schmidt, eds *American Government and Politics Today*. St Paul: West Publishing Company, 1986.

Bean, Walton. *Boss Ruef's San Francisco: The Story of the Union Labour Party, Big Business and the Graft Prosecution*. Berkeley, Los Angeles, London: University of California Press, 1952.

Boylan, Henry. *A Dictionary of Irish Biography*. New York: St Martin's Press, 1988.

Burchell, R. A. *The San Francisco Irish, 1848–1880*. Berkeley and Los Angeles: University of California Press, 1980.

Carroll, F. M. 'All Standards of Human Conduct: The American Commission on Conditions in Ireland, 1920–21'. *Éire-Ireland* 16 (No. 4, 1981): 59–74.

_______. *The American Commission on Irish Independence, 1919: The Diary, Correspondence and Report.* Dublin: Mount Salus Press Ltd, 1985.

_______. 'Irish Progressive League', In *Irish-American Voluntary Organizations,* ed. Michael F. Funchion, 206–10. Westport, Connecticut: Greenwood Press, 1983.

Carty, Xavier. *In Bloody Protest—The Tragedy of Patrick Pearse.* Dublin: Able Press, 1978.

Caulfield, Max. *The Easter Rebellion.* New York: Holt, Rinehart and Winston, 1963.

Clancy, Mary. 'Aspects of Women's Contribution to the Oireachtas Debate in the Irish Free State, 1922–37'. In *Women Surviving: Studies in Irish Women's History in the 19th and 20th Centuries,* ed. Maria Luddy and Cliona Murphy, 206–32. Dublin: Poolbeg, 1990.

Clarke, Kathleen, ed. Helen Litton. *Revolutionary Woman, Kathleen Clarke, 1878–1972: An Autobiography.* Dublin: The O'Brien Press Ltd, 1991.

Conlon, Lil. *Cumann na mBan and the Women of Ireland, 1913–25.* Kilkenny: Kilkenny People Ltd, 1969.

Coogan, Tim Pat. *Michael Collins: The Man Who Made Ireland.* Boulder, Colorado: Roberts Rinehart Publishers, 1992.

Costello, Frank. *Enduring the Most: The Life and Death of Terence MacSwiney*. Kerry, Ireland: Brandon Book Publishers Ltd, 1995.

Coxhead, Elizabeth. *Daughters of Erin.* Gerrards Cross: Colin Smythe Ltd, 1979.

Cronin, Sean. *The McGarrity Papers: Revelations of the Irish Revolutionary Movement in Ireland and America, 1900–1940.* Tralee: Anvil Books, Ltd, 1972.

_______. *Washington's Irish Policy, 1916–1986: Independence, Partition, Neutrality*. Dublin: Anvil Books, 1987.

Divine, Robert A., T. H. Breer, George M. Fredrickson, R. Hall Williams, eds, *America, Past and Present.* United States of America: Scott, Foresman and Company, 1984.

Duff, Charles. *Six Days to Shake an Empire*. New York: A. S. Barnes and Co., Inc., 1966.

Edwards, Ruth Dudley. *Patrick Pearse: The Triumph of Failure.* London: Victor Gollancz Ltd, 1977.

Emmons, David M. *The Butte Irish: Class and Ethnicity in an American Mining Town, 1875–1925*. Urbana and Chicago: University of Illinois Press, 1990.

Fallon, Charlotte H. *Soul of Fire: A Biography of Mary MacSwiney*. Cork and Dublin: The Mercier Press, 1986.

_______. 'Civil War Hungerstrikes: Women and Men'. *Éire-Ireland* 22 (No. 3, 1987), 75–91.

Farrell, Brian. 'Markievicz and the Women of the Revolution'. In *Leaders and Men of the Easter Rising: Dublin 1916*, ed. F. X. Martin, 227–38. New York: Cornell University Press, 1967.

Flynn, Elizabeth Gurley. *The Rebel Girl: An Autobiography*. New York: International Publishers, 1994.

Funchion, Michael F., ed. *Irish American Voluntary Organizations*. Westport, Connecticut: Greenwood Press, 1983.

Golway, Terry. *Irish Rebel: John Devoy and America's Fight for Ireland's Freedom*. New York: St Martin's Press, 1998.

Gray, Tony. *The Irish Answer*. Boston: Little, Brown and Company, 1966.

Haverty, Anne. *Constance Markievicz: An Independent Life*. London: Pandora Press, 1988.

Hopkinson, Michael. *Green Against Green: The Irish Civil War*. New York: St Martin's Press, 1988.

Kazin, Michael. *Barons of Labour: The San Francisco Building Trades and Union Power in the Progressive Era*. Urbana and Chicago: University of Illinois Press, 1989.

Kee, Robert. *The Green Flag, Volume II: The Bold Fenian Men*. London: Penguin Books, 1972.

_______. *The Green Flag, Volume III: Ourselves Alone*. London: Penguin Books, 1972.

Larkin, Emmet. *James Larkin, Irish Labour Leader, 1876–1947*. London: The New English Library, 1965.

Lee, J. J. *Ireland, 1912–1985, Politics and Society*. Cambridge: Cambridge University Press, 1989.

Levenson, Leah. *With Wooden Sword: A Portrait of Francis Sheehy-Skeffington, Militant Pacifist*. Boston: Northeastern University Press, 1983.

Levenson, Leah and Jerry H. Natterstad. *Hanna Sheehy-Skeffington: Irish Feminist*. New York: Syracuse University Press, 1986.

Levenson, Samuel. *Maud Gonne*. New York: Reader's Digest Press, 1976.

Longford, The Earl of, and Thomas P. O'Neill. *Eamon de Valera*.

London: Hutchinson of London, 1970.

Luddy, Maria. *Hanna Sheehy Skeffington*, Dundalk: Dundalgan Press, 1995.

_______. *Women in Ireland, 1800–1918*. Cork: Cork University Press, 1995.

Macardle, Dorothy. *The Irish Republic*. Dublin: Wolfhound Press, Ltd, 1999.

MacCurtain, Margaret. 'Women, the Vote and Revolution'. In *Women in Irish Society*, ed. Margaret MacCurtain and Donncha Ó'Corráin, 46–57. Connecticut: Greenwood Press, 1979.

Maher, Jim. *Harry Boland: A Biography*. Boulder, Colorado: Mercier Press, 1998.

Marreco, Anne. *The Rebel Countess: The Life and Times of Constance Markievicz*. Philadelphia and New York: Chilton Books, 1967.

McCaffrey, Lawrence J. *Ireland from Colony to Nation State*. Englewood Cliffs: Prentice-Hall, Inc. 1979.

_______. *The Irish Diaspora in America*. Bloomington: Indiana University Press, 1976.

McCoole, Sinead. *Women Revolutionaries and Kilmainham Gaol: Guns and Chiffon, 1916–1923*. Dublin: Published by the Stationery Office, 1997.

_______. *Ireland From Colony to Nation State*. New Jersey: Prentice-Hall, Inc., 1979.

McKillen, Beth. 'Irish Feminism and Nationalist Separatism, 1914–23'. *Éire-Ireland* 17 (No. 4, 1982): 72–90.

Mitchell, Arthur and Padraig Ó'Snodaigh, ed. *Irish Political Documents, 1916–1949*. Dublin: Irish Academic Press, 1985.

Murphy, Cliona. *The Women's Suffrage Movement and Irish Society in the Early Twentieth Century*. Philadelphia: Temple University Press, 1989.

Murphy, John A: *Ireland in the Twentieth Century*. Dublin: Gill and Macmillan, 1975.

Ó Buachalla, Seamas, ed. *The Letters of P. H. Pearse*. New Jersey: Humanities Press, 1980.

Ó Dubhghaill, M., comp. *Insurrection Fires at Eastertide: A Golden Jubilee Anthology of the Easter Rising*. Cork: The Mercier Press, 1966.

O'Higgins, Brian O. *The Soldier's Story of Easter Week*. Dublin: Elo Press Ltd, 1966.

Pearse, Mary Brigid, ed. *The Home Life of Padraig Pearse, as Told by Himself, His Family and Friends*. Dublin and Cork: The Mercier Press, 1979.

Ranelagh, John O'Beirne. *A Short History of Ireland*. Cambridge: Cambridge University Press, 1983.

Roper, Esther. 'Biographical Sketch'. In *Prison Letters of Countess Markievicz*, 1–123. London: Virago Press Ltd, 1987.

Ryan, Louise. '"Furies" and "Die-hards": Women and Irish Republicanism in the Early Twentieth Century'. *Gender & History* 11 (No. 2, July 1999), 256–75.

Sarbaugh, Timothy J. 'Culture, Militancy and de Valera: Irish-American Republican Nationalism in California, 1900–1936'. MA thesis, San Jose State University, 1980.

_______. 'Exiles of Confidence: The Irish-American Community of San Francisco, 1880 to 1920'. In *From Paddy to Studs: Irish-American Communities in the Turn of the Century Era, 1880 to 1920*, ed. Timothy J. Meagher, 161–79. New York: Greenwood Press, 1986.

Sebestyen, Amanda. 'Introduction'. In *Prison Letters of Countess Markievicz*, ix–xxxv. London: Virago Press Limited, 1987.

Sheehy Skeffington, Andrée. *Skeff: A Life of Owen Sheehy Skeffington, 1909–1970*. Dublin: The Lilliput Press, 1991.

Taillon, Ruth. *When History Was Made: The Women of 1916*. Belfast: Beyond the Pale Publications, 1996.

Tansill, Charles Callan. *America and the Fight for Irish Freedom: 1866–1922*. New York: The Devin-Adair Co., 1957.

Van Voris, Jacqueline. *Constance de Markievicz: In the Cause of Ireland*. Amherst: The University of Massachusetts Press, 1967.

Ward, Alan J. *Ireland and Anglo-American Relations, 1899–1921*. Toronto: University of Toronto Press, 1969.

_______. *The Easter Rising, Revolution and Irish Nationalism*. Illinois: Harlan Davidson, Inc., 1980.

Ward, Estolv Ethan. *The Gentle Dynamiter: A Biography of Tom Mooney*. Palo Alto, California: Ramparts Press, 1983.

Ward, Margaret. *Unmanageable Revolutionaries: Women and Irish Nationalism*. London: Pluto Press, 1983.

_______. *In Their Own Voice: Women and Irish Nationalism*. Dublin: Attic Press, 1995.

_______. *Hanna Sheehy Skeffington: A Life*. Cork: Attic Press, 1997.

_______. 'Nationalism, Pacifism, Internationalism: Louie Bennett, Hanna Sheehy-Skeffington and the Problems of "Defining

Feminism". In *Gender and Sexuality in Modern Ireland,* 60–84, ed. Anthony Bradley and Maryann Gialanella Valiulis. Amherst: University of Massachusetts Press, 1997.

Wittke, Carl. *The Irish in America.* Baton Rouge: Louisiana State University Press, 1956.

Wreszin, Michael. *Oswald Garrison Villard: Pacifist at War.* Bloomington: Indiana University Press, 1965.

Index

Page numbers in bold indicate major entry